BISMARCK
ANDRÁSSY
AND THEIR
SUCCESSORS

Count Julius Andrássy

Bismarck, Andrássy and their Successors

Simon Publications

2001

Library of Congress Card Number: 27017430

ISBN: 1-931313-55-5

Distributed by Ingram Book Company

Printed by Lightning Source Inc., La Vergne, TN

Published by Simon Publications, Safety Harbor, FL

CONTENTS

BOOK I

BISMARCK AND ANDRÁSSY

CHAPTER   PAGE

I. 1. Bismarck's changed attitude after the Franco-Prussian War. 2. The Iron Chancellor's Peace Policy. 3. Bismarck and Andrássy. 4. Characters of Bismarck and Andrássy contrasted 3

II. 1. Gladstone's estrangement from Germany. 2. Improvement in the strained relations between Germany and France. 3. Extension of Germany's Colonial Empire. 4. Renewal of the Three Emperors' Alliance. 5. The Triple Alliance. 6. Serbia and Rumania join the Triple Alliance. 7. The Weakness of Bismarck's System of Alliances 54

III. 1. The Growth of *Revanche* in France. 2. Salisbury's letter to Bismarck. 3. The Bulgarian Crisis and the Great Powers. 4. The agreement between England, Italy, and Austria-Hungary. 5. Renewal of the Triple Alliance. 6. The Russo-German Secret Treaty. 7. Bismarck's Explanation of the Secret Treaty. 8. Scheme for an Anglo-German Alliance. 9. The fall of Bismarck 99

 Contents

BOOK II

FROM BISMARCK TO BÜLOW
I. CAPRIVI (1890–1894)

CHAPTER   PAGE

I. Renewal of the Alliance 171

II. The Russo-French Treaty . . . 179

III. Relations with England (Heligoland, Egypt, Tunis, the Dardanelles) . . . 192

IV. England and the Congo Dispute . . 212

V. Summary 220

BOOK II

FROM BISMARCK TO BÜLOW
II. HOHENLOHE (1894–1897)

I. The Triple Alliance of Asia . . . 223

II. Strained Relations between England and Germany 230

III. The Boers 247

IV. Weakening of the Triple Alliance . . 258

V. England, Egypt, the Armenian Question, Crete 262

VI. William II and Nicholas II . . . 279

Contents

vii

BOOK III

WELTPOLITIK

CHAPTER	PAGE
I. William II and Bülow 287
II. Opening of Alliances. Italy, Austria-Hungary, Rumania 307
III. Germany's favourable situation . . 318
IV. The " Free Hand " Policy. First Overtures from England 324
V. *Weltpolitik* Successes. The German Navy 340
VI. The Boer War and the Chinese Question . 360
VII. England's Last Overtures to Germany . 372
VIII. The Anglo-French Entente . . . 394
IX. Russian Friendship 407
X. The Russo-Japanese War. The Björkö Alliance 415
XI. Conclusion 440

BOOK I
BISMARCK AND ANDRÁSSY

CHAPTER I

FROM THE PEACE OF FRANKFORT TO THE GERMAN-AUSTRO-HUNGARIAN ALLIANCE (1871–1879)

1. Bismarck's Changed Attitude after the Franco-Prussian War

IN publishing its foreign correspondence from 1870 to 1914 the German Government has rendered an immense service to the cause of historical truth.[1] It is on the basis of that publication that I now propose to write on the recent past, in the firm conviction that in the past alone can be found the clue to the right understanding of both the present and the future.

The central figure and chief hero of the six volumes (1870–1890) that have already appeared is Bismarck, the Iron Chancellor, one of the greatest geniuses in foreign politics that ever directed the destinies of any nation. The chief contents of the books are the record of the struggles of the famous German statesman for a peace such as would secure to Germany her unity and the frontiers she had sealed with so much of her blood.

These documents conjure up before my mental vision the illustrious German patriot whom in the eighties it was my privilege frequently to meet; with his tall, commanding stature, the piercing gaze of his wise, expressive grey eyes, his interesting bushy eyebrows, reminiscent to a Hungarian of Francis Deák, his prominent forehead, and his square jaw indicative of an inflexible will. Add to these features the air of power and quiet

[1] *Die Grosse Politik der europäischen Kabinette*, 1871–1914. Sammlung der diplomatischen Akten des auswärtigen Amtes, Berlin.

dignity enveloping him, the effect of which was enhanced by his legendary renown, his dramatic life, his peculiar mode of speech, his distinguished manners, and you have a picture of Bismarck as I knew him. Anyone after a few moments' conversation with him involuntarily realised that he was in the presence of one of those born geniuses that shape the history of the world.

The publications referred to permit a glimpse into the innermost recesses of Bismarck's brain, revealing his hidden thoughts. Much of their contents was not intended for the public eye, to win the good opinion of his contemporaries and of posterity, not intended to turn on his acts the light in which he was anxious for the outside world to see them. Their sole purpose was to expound in a lucid manner his views and convictions partly to his royal master and sovereign and partly to his colleagues and fellow-servants of the State.

It is important for our times that these volumes finally and fully dispose of the legend propagated partly through misunderstanding and partly with malicious intent, and believed by millions until it became one of the psychological causes of the Great War—the legend, namely, that the German Empire had pursued a policy of aggression from its very inception, and that the only thing that had prevented war from breaking out before was the pacific temper and foresight of the opposition. Bismarck's correspondence has documents which prove with remarkable lucidity the very contrary of the assertion.

The German Empire, though owing its foundation to aggression, nevertheless owed its consolidation to a policy of peace.

Bismarck's career consists of two entirely different parts. One of the most remarkable and rarest characteristics of his titanic personality was his ability completely to change his habits, his political mentality, and to adapt his powerful intellect to the interests of his country.

Clemenceau made the peace in the same manner as he prosecuted his home policy and led the war—with dominating will-power, passion, and hate. In every aspect of his life we see how he ravaged and destroyed. On that account he was useful for France during the war, when destruction was deemed necessary; but he injured her interests in his manner of making the peace, when reconciliation and reconstruction were essential to lasting harmony and good-fellowship.

Bismarck acted quite otherwise. Not led astray by his choleric temperament, but guided by his insight, he —the hardened, uncompromising statesman—could be obsequious and pacific if the interests of the Fatherland demanded it. He understood equally well the sanguinary art of winning martial victories and the peaceful cultivation of the fruits thereof.

As Prime Minister of Prussia (1862–1870) in seven years he waged three bloody and hazardous wars, the first against Denmark to secure the northern frontier, in alliance with an antagonistic Austria, and exposed to the ill-will of the entire public opinion of Germany, as well as of England, France, and Sweden. Later he desired to exclude the Habsburgs from Germany, and therefore deliberately provoked a quarrel with Austria— a country itself larger than Prussia—notwithstanding that nearly the whole population of Germany was Austrophil; that thus Prussia got between two fires, while the leading factor in Europe—Napoleon III—was merely biding his time for the striking of the hour when he could undertake armed intervention; and while, moreover, the fratricidal contest was unpopular in the country itself. At length, in his ambition to unite the German people, he desired to overcome the final obstacle to the realisation of that unity—namely, the French Emperor—though the shadow of revenge for Königgrätz hung over him like the sword of Damocles. At this point of Bismarck's career the looker-on is overwhelmed by the same feeling of awe as were the spectators of Blondin crossing the Niagara Falls on a frail tight-rope, when had he but slipped or got in the least dizzy he would have been precipitated into the yawning abyss below. But in his bold adventure Bismarck's iron nerve never for a moment failed him, his indomitable courage carried him unflinchingly along the path he had marked out. He reasoned and acted coldly and with a stern logic amidst circumstances which would have appalled an ordinary man.

When, however, he had attained his positive aim— the unity of Germany under Prussian hegemony—he changed as by magic, and with consummate skill and caution avoided the possibility of an open rupture, holding peace as the pearl of great price. He exchanged the tactics of a Napoleon for those of a Montecucculi. The man who had so often dared to sever the Gordian knot of coalitions, who had never been known to quail before the strongest, now suffered a very nightmare on their account and feared to offend the weak.

This dual aspect of Bismarck, this change of front, was, strictly speaking, only the result of his consistency. His altered attitude was not due to his having got tired of taking risks, or because he needed rest, or because his views as to the morality of war had undergone any modification ; he had by no means become a pacifist, nor was he disposed to condemn his former actions.

The change in him was due to the fact that the world-situation had become different, and he always did what the interests of the Fatherland demanded in given circumstances.

As in winter we need different clothing from that which we wear in summer, as children lead a different life from that of the grown-ups and invalids from that of the robust, as in a blustering north wind we hoist other sails than when the soft southern breezes blow : so a nation sometimes finds it necessary to change her policy. But it requires a truly great statesman to adapt himself to such contrary needs, and Bismarck was *par excellence* such an one.

The works of Goethe or of Shakespeare can be recognised by their style ; the paintings of Raphael or of Dürer are characterised by the brush-strokes, colouring, and style of beauty of the masters ; Széchényi, Kossuth, Napoleon, and Metternich are in all their actions classic examples of the same type and qualities of statesmanship. Bismarck, however, could display the most opposite qualities, he could satisfy the most contrary requirements of the life of his nation.

In the former part of his career we see him as a Prussian, regretting and pronouncing impossible the situation of his country. Prussia, geographically hardly coherent—wedged in amidst hostile Austria, Hanover, Denmark, Saxony, and South Germany—was not an independent State in any true sense. The days of Olmütz might return at any time—those days of shame when Radowitz, Prime Minister of Prussia, had to knuckle under to Schwartzenberg, the Austrian Minister for Foreign Affairs.

Neither could Bismarck, as a German, feel any sense of satisfaction. His German self-consciousness must perforce revolt against the disunion and supineness of his race, and he consequently desired to transform the cultural unity into a political unity. That race which had bestowed on humanity a Kant, a Goethe, a Schiller, had a right to assert itself politically.

The towering genius of Bismarck also realised that if Prussia abandoned utopian dreams and accepted the Pan-German idea, she might hope thereby to reap constant brilliant successes corresponding to actual conditions, to the immense benefit of herself and her race.

Bismarck's ambitions were so lofty, so splendid, and at the same time so practical, that he was prepared to risk all for them—his own life and the lives of thousands, his reputation as a statesman, and, what is more important and even more sacred than everything else, the very existence of the Fatherland! Convinced that without the means to assert themselves politically his country and people could not live a life worthy of themselves, that they would be debarred from fulfilling their high destiny in which he unswervingly believed, but would wither and decay amidst futile squabbling under pressure of the petty conditions of existence ; seeing clearly that inertia would sooner or later only end in ruin, while a bold dash—though through the very gates of hell—would lead to Olympus, Bismarck was urged by the fervour of his patriotism to the policy of the " forlorn hope."

The classic saying of Deák, the great Hungarian statesman, that " Anything may be risked for the Fatherland, but the Fatherland may not be risked for anything," is not contrary to Bismarck's policy ; for the policy of audacity was also that of far-sightedness. To refuse to take risks would have meant cowardly resignation—a resignation the nation could not have tolerated for long without a final moral collapse.

When, however, after his triumph, Bismarck could call Germany (to use Metternich's expression) " satisfied," he regarded every risk as criminal, and he led the policy of the conservative (or " satisfied ") State with just the same zeal and efficiency as previously, when in an unnatural situation, he had led the policy of aggression. Thenceforth his sole object was to retain and, if possible, strengthen by peaceful means what he had won in war. Waiting, passivity was no longer a risk, but wise calculation, while war was but an unnecessary adventure, a species of gamble not to be entertained.

Politicians lacking his foresight frequently advised Bismarck in these days to attack France or Russia—to settle the scores of those hostile neighbours—on the argument that sooner or later war would be inevitable and would probably break out at a time when conditions were less favourable than those now enjoyed by Bismarck and Moltke. But he rejected these temptations at the outset. He considered it criminal frivolity to start a war on the ground of such predictions, for even a wise man is not necessarily a prophet, and the best are liable to err. How many war-dangers have been averted without war actually occurring ! Would any responsible statesman dare to say to a dying or wounded soldier : " You must suffer, since I believe that this war, which I have made, would in any case have broken out later on ; but at the same time I must tell you that no advantage to the Fatherland may be expected from victory, while the war might certainly have been avoided for the present without sacrifice of our vital interests or loss of prestige "? For to Bismarck's strong mind any war, to be justified, must stand the test of criticism by the most interested party—the common soldier who had to shed his blood for it.

Bismarck considered war justifiable only if it promised advantages proportionate to the risks incurred, or if it were to solve a problem of vital importance to the Fatherland which could not be solved by less drastic measures.

Before 1870 there were many such cases, but there have been none since. This explains the fact that, as Prime Minister of Prussia, Bismarck wrought with " blood and iron," and as German Chancellor he employed the milder weapons of diplomacy, patience, moderation, and compromise.

Napoleon I, that great military genius, fell because he was unable to govern and restrain his impetuous nature, because he could not adapt himself to changed conditions, because after the Peaces of Amiens and Lunéville—which secured for France her independence, power, and even European supremacy—he could not transform himself into a peaceful defensive statesman, like Bismarck after the Peace of Frankfort. But it was scarcely the ulterior motive of Napoleon, the Corsican fortuitously placed at the head of France, to safeguard the real and permanent interests of France: it was rather his own glory, his unquenchable thirst for *éclat,* and the exercise of his brilliant talents, to parade his striking personality before the admiring gaze of an awestruck world. In this respect Bismarck was immeasurably superior to Bonaparte. The greatness of the Iron Chancellor was rooted deep in a moral foundation, in his profound patriotic sense. We might call him rude and ruthless, pronounce his methods wrong, but his motives could never be impugned: they were honourable, majestic, splendid examples of German thoroughness in the sphere of politics.

2. The Iron Chancellor's Peace Policy

Now let us take a glance at the instruments of Bismarck's peace policy. What was his system after the Peace of Frankfort ? To what methods did he resort in order to accomplish his aims ?

First of all, he armed. For he was well aware that the only absolutely reliable help is always and everywhere that of the power of the nation itself. He was guided by the fundamental conception of German policy which Moltke, the famous strategist, expressed with crystal clarity of vision when defending the treaty concluded with us, that *" the existence of Germany would become problematical if ever she should become too weak to fight France single-handed."*

It was Bismarck's firm conviction that his Gallic neighbours would attack the moment they felt strong enough to defeat Germany. He detested France from the bottom of his heart ; he saw in her history nothing save an offensive, aggressive spirit ; and he held that in the many struggles between French and Germans since the break-up of the empire of the Carlovingians, the Germans had always been wantonly and unjustly attacked. He could not believe that the French would ever forgive the Germans for defeating them, and was convinced that France would begin a new war if ever the time came when she had no longer to fear another German victory. And though his reasonings were exaggerations rooted in his German chauvinism, his conclusions were unquestionably right, for the policy of France could be relied on to be peaceful only so long as her defeat was more probable than her victory.

An implicit will to peace was rendered impossible by the fact that the Germans had conquered territory in Alsace-Lorraine, which resisted germanisation, whose French patriotism stood rock-firm to all the onslaughts of Berlin. As soon as ever France might reasonably expect a favourable issue, she would have to risk war. As soon as she was fairly in a position to liberate her children, she could not leave them longer under alien yoke ; it would be a suicidal act for her to turn a deaf ear to their yearning cry to return to "*la Patrie.*"

And indeed the French nation through fifty weary years never forgot this duty. France, in spite of the loss of Alsace-Lorraine, was able to exist and progress, and thus she could afford to wait in patience for the day of realisation of her resolve : to redeem (as soon as a cold political calculation permitted) her children under German rule. This attitude of the French perpetuated the strained state of European politics, rendering it impossible—greatly to the detriment of humanity— for these two neighbours sincerely and without mental reservation to co-operate. It cost untold millions of money and constituted one of the psychological causes of the awful World War. Nevertheless we too, who particularly suffered from the policy of France, recognise that it was to her honour and furnishes a glorious example of the way in which other nations in a similar situation should behave. Only we must profoundly regret that it was France who, forgetting her own sorrowful experiences, allowed herself to create so many other Alsace-Lorraines, to the constant peril of the peace and progress of herself and the world.

Bismarck felt that the annexation of the purely French portion of Alsace-Lorraine was a blunder, and he only deferred to the representations of Moltke that the possession by Germany of Metz and Strasburg would enable them to dispense with a hundred thousand troops. In that respect the great soldier may have been right, but it was no just argument for annexation ; for owing to the spirit of revenge that it engendered in the French, the Germans were obliged for many long years to keep far more men under arms than the more favourable strategic frontier would have rendered necessary ; and the armed peace made permanent by the annexation seriously impaired economic development. It fostered the constant enmity of France, which at length became one of the constituent elements in the recent cataclysm. And this mistake influences the second part of Bismarck's career to a remarkable degree. All his energies were required in the ceaseless struggle against the dangers created by the annexation.

In spite of this, however, Bismarck never thought of the one radical solution—the rectification of the error, i.e. by returning Alsace-Lorraine to the French on the basis of suitable agreements. But we have no right to judge him ; the overwhelming majority of the German people would have rejected such a proposal with scorn ; and even we, their allies, would never have thought of any such solution. Even I myself failed to perceive it until the Great War was approaching its final stage. But to-day, in the light of subsequently acquired wisdom, we have to confess that the chief cause of our undoing was that the thorn of annexation could not be plucked from the world's flesh.

If only the statesmen of our time would learn this lesson, if only they would try to understand that a bad, tyrannical peace, with unnatural frontiers, with a régime that the subdued nation is unwilling to submit to, with impossible economic conditions, will always rob a victorious war of all its fruits, for it obliges the conqueror to defend situations unnatural and therefore impossible to maintain, and bears within itself the germs of future wars of revenge. If only the present victors would see that the only effectual remedy is to make amends for the wrongs done—which can also be demanded from those who stood for the right of nations to self-determination and severely censured the annexation of Bismarck !

But armaments alone were no satisfactory safeguard for Bismarck. They merely prevented an isolated France from attacking, but not a coalition grouped around France which considered itself stronger than Germany. The possibility of such a coalition arising obsessed Bismarck to the end of his days. Herein we discern the real clue to his foreign policy. Against this, the far-seeing, cautious Chancellor was constantly on the look-out for allies with whose aid he could isolate France, or at least ensure that she with her allies should be kept unquestionably weaker than Germany with her allies, and consequently she (France) could never contemplate aggressive movements against Germany.

For this purpose the ideal solution was an alliance with Russia and Austria-Hungary—the so-called Alliance of the Three Emperors. This combination kept Bismarck from the beginning strong enough to exclude any other counter-coalition. At first he considered this also the safest. The chief pillar and corner-stone of this alliance he considered the intimacy of the Hohenzollern and the Romanoff, the personal friendship of these two Emperors, the common monarchical principle, the anti-Polish policy in vogue in St. Petersburg and Berlin alike—that is to say, the common Russo-German traditions which had stood the test of history, which had enabled Russia to quell the Polish insurrection (1863), and cancel the humiliating Black Sea Agreements (1871), and given Bismarck Königgrätz and Sedan. Bismarck sought to round off this old, tried friendship by the inclusion of Austria-Hungary, lest France should bind us to her car; though the basis of the combination would have remained the Russo-Prussian sympathy.

In 1873 Bismarck attained his object. The impulse was furnished by us. The Chancellor's wisdom in not demanding annexation, against the will of his sovereign and public opinion, bore good fruit on the fall of Beust, the representative of the *revanche* policy. Andrássy, the Germanophil and friend of reconciliation, now became Foreign Minister: exemplifying that a reasonable and just peace is as wise and useful as an unreasonable and severe one is dangerous.

The first step, the *rapprochement* of those erstwhile adversaries, Germany and Austria-Hungary, was naturally followed by another. For as the Russians perceived that the rivalry of the two Danubian neighbours (which contributed so largely to the Czar's power) had ceased, they began to fear that, if they failed to secure a closer connection with Germany than hitherto, a German-Austro-Hungarian alliance might be concluded. Thus the Czar offered a written treaty of alliance to the Germans.

Bismarck hastened to seize the opportunity. He concluded with Russia a military convention which bound both contracting parties to assist each other in arms against an attack from any quarter (24th April 1873).

This treaty was offered to Andrássy too. As Bismarck forced the hand of Russia by approaching Austria-Hungary, so he now stimulated us by the Russian agreement. Andrássy, however, though aware of the fact that if he did not want to be left in the lurch he

must join the alliance of the two Emperors, was unwilling
to accept it in the form offered. For this treaty would
have bound us to side with Russia even if, on account
of their conflicting ambitions in the East, the Czar
should be attacked by England or Turkey; also to
defend Alsace-Lorraine against the French: in short,
to jeopardise our existence in the interests of others.
Andrássy was too careful of the blood and treasure of his
country to sign such a bond. In case of dire necessity,
he was not averse to war, but only for the most immediate
and highest interests of his own nation.

His first great achievement in foreign politics was his
success in carrying through his own policy against the
agreement of his two mighty neighbours. He took
shelter behind constitutional scruples, and so manœuvred
that the negotiations had to be put on a new basis.

Agreement was reached by the three Emperors at
Schönbrunn (May 1873), though no one of them would
accept the obligation to defend the other two; they
were in accord only so far that the three conservative
monarchs, united for peaceful aims, were willing to
endeavour to adjust their eventual conflicting interests,
and in case of danger from without would strive to come
to an agreement with each other before seeking alliances
elsewhere.

Thus we escaped being isolated without having
undertaken any disagreeable or risky obligations, and by
the same means Bismarck realised his chief aim—the
isolation of France.

But by the conclusion of this Alliance of the Three
Emperors, Bismarck had accomplished only the easier
part of his task. It was a more difficult matter to maintain the Alliance and to supply it with real vital force.
The new work suffered from the initial mistake of the

leading statesmen wanting to use it for realising their conflicting ambitions.

Russia needed no defence. Her immense size, her good fortune to be vulnerable only on her comparatively narrow western border, secured her from any surprise attack, and therefore her Government sought the alliance of her western neighbours merely in order to enable her to prosecute her Oriental policy under their ægis. On one occasion Gortchakoff stated that " he did not wish to take leave of public life like a snuffed-out candle, but like the sun, whose last rays shed dazzling radiance over the landscape." The vain old diplomat yearned to finish his career in a blaze of glory equal to that of Bismarck, and hoped to exploit the Alliance of the Three Emperors to that end. With Bismarck's assistance during the Franco-Prussian War he succeeded in eliminating the most oppressive measures of the Peace of Paris, and now—also with Bismarck's assistance—he sought to put an end to all the baneful consequences of the Crimean War and thus make Russia once more the prime factor in the East. He was anxious to revive the old Russian traditions, the aims of Peter the Great and Catherine, to become absolute lord of the Bosphorus and the Dardanelles, and to rally the Balkan Christians and Slavs around himself.

Contrary to this, Andrássy accepted the Alliance of the Three Emperors in order to get nearer to Germany, to win her confidence, and with her assistance to repel Russian encroachments. He desired to carry out reforms in the Balkans which would ensure the existence of the Ottoman Empire and at the same time render conditions more tolerable for the Christian nations, and thus gain a halo of popularity for Austria-Hungary in the East. Or, in case all these reforms proved futile, if it were impossible to save the Ottoman Empire, then he would endeavour to have Mohammedan rule superseded by formations of Christian States which should be independent of the Czar and which would rely on us to safeguard their economic and cultural development and progress.

While both Gortchakoff and Andrássy were anxious to make use of the Alliance for the promotion of their differing Eastern policies, Bismarck had formed it for the very purpose of eliminating the Eastern Question and isolating France. For Gortchakoff and Andrássy the Alliance was an organ of Eastern policy, for Bismarck an instrument for pushing it into the background.

It would have been the most favourable opportunity for Bismarck if the Eastern Question had not become acute. However, it was child's-play for Russia to have prevented this. The parlous Turkish administration, the perpetual clash between Mussulman rule and the ever-increasing Christian self-consciousness, piled up a mass of inflammable material in the Balkans. The national ideal, strengthened by the Italian and the German unity, facilitated conflagrations—or fed them if already existing—in the realm of the Padishah, and rendered it difficult to avoid or extinguish them by peaceful means. Historical development aggravated and complicated the Eastern Question (Bosnian revolt 1875) and prevented the formation suitable for Bismarck's conception. Consequently the future would thenceforth depend on his ability to so direct the Eastern Question (which could not be burked) as to avoid collision between Russian and Austro-Hungarian interests in the Orient; or failing that, on whether the conception of the Russian or that of the Austro-Hungarian statesman should prevail.

3. BISMARCK AND ANDRÁSSY

Andrássy's position in the Three Emperors' Alliance was a most difficult one. He was at the head of the weakest Power, regarded from the military standpoint, while success and brute force are commonly associated with each other. Besides this, the Dual Monarchy had received a *damnosa hæreditas* from Austria : she was everywhere mistrusted and regarded askance. In Berlin, Austria had long been considered the chief foe, and Bismarck could not rid himself of the idea that the Ultramontanes might come into their own again and revive the old Habsburg German policy. Russia, too, had neither forgotten nor forgiven us for the Crimea, and the antagonism between her and us was shown at the London Conference on the Pontus Question. Moreover, the Polish Question constituted another barrier between Austro-Hungary and Russia.

Again, Andrássy's *personal* position was difficult. His political past and his fundamental principles kept him aloof from the two Chancellors. They both considered Andrássy a rebel because he had borne arms against his sovereign, who had even sentenced him to death ; they ignored the fact that the said sovereign had ridden roughshod over the Hungarian laws and unconstitutionally abolished the independence of the Magyars. Such trifling matters were beneath their notice. Andrássy had served from 1848 to 1899, as soldier and diplomat, that cause which Bismarck desired, with the aid of Prussian bayonets, to crush, and which was ultimately defeated by the Russians at Világos. Nor was Andrássy's stupendous task by any means facilitated by his present rôle. He was an advocate of parliamentarism, while Gortchakoff was a courtier—a servant of absolutism—and Bismarck entertained a strong antipathy to parliamentarism and cast on its adherents the suspicion of putting party interests before those of their country.   Both Chancellors were diplomats, proud of their craft.   Andrássy was an outsider, whose diplomatic career had, as it were, commenced in the chair of the Minister for Foreign Affairs.   Would there not be a better understanding between the two old autocrats, experienced diplomats and old friends, than with the tyro-diplomat, the dilettante, the man who stood for liberty and constitutionalism ?   Yet in spite of all this, Andrássy's policy was carried through !   How was it possible ?

It soon came about that Andrássy got nearer to both of his colleagues than did either of them to each other. The Iron Chancellor came to appreciate him as the straightforward man, the downright statesman, in contrast with the senile, petty, gossiping Russian, notwithstanding all the externals separating him from Andrássy and attaching him to Gortchakoff.   With every passing day Bismarck trusted Andrássy more and more, and Gortchakoff less and less.

On the other hand, the Russian Chancellor found his dealings with Andrássy easier than with Bismarck.   He had no need to be jealous of the Hungarian, as he was of the German, whose glory he envied.   On their first meeting Gortchakoff paid Andrássy the highest compliment that an inordinately conceited person can pay to another : he compared Andrássy to himself.   A little later (in 1878) Bismarck began to betray anxiety lest his two colleagues should become too intimate, and considered whether he should look to England for a counterpoise or negotiate for a separate alliance with Austria-Hungary.

A serious rupture was caused between Germany and Russia in 1875 through Gortchakoff, the avowed friend and ally, claiming all the credit for preventing another war that, it was alleged, Germany had intended to spring upon France. There was not a word of truth in the allegation. Both Kaiser William and Bismarck abhorred the idea of attacking France.

In the Eastern Question, too, Gortchakoff neglected no single opportunity of driving Bismarck—actually against his will—into Andrássy's arms. His deplorable tactlessness not infrequently brought the Iron Chancellor into the disagreeable situation of having to decline a proposition, though every such case of refusal erected a new barrier separating the two old friends, provoked each against the other, and created in Bismarck a consciousness that their long-standing friendship had waned, while it aroused in the Russian the dangerous feeling of wounded vanity.

Such a rebuff was Gortchakoff's fate when, at the period of the Serbo-Turkish conflict, he proposed to call a congress, though Bismarck feared it, knowing that he could not observe in it that neutrality he would have liked to secure for himself, and that a *rapprochement* would have been brought about at such a congress between Austria-Hungary and England, a *rapprochement* which might upset his political schemes. Bismarck put the matter down to personal vanity and lack of conscientiousness on the part of Gortchakoff (14th August 1876).

A further rebuff was administered to the Russian Chancellor when the Czar vaguely and in general terms invited the co-operation of the German Emperor in his Oriental action (26th August 1876). Bismarck was indignant, and declared that " he was not going to sign a blank cheque for anyone ; Russia must at least acquaint

him with the policy in which she desired his assistance."
An even more serious blunder was committed when
Gortchakoff based the application on alleged services
rendered by Russia to Germany in former years. He
asked for gratitude from one who knew of nothing he
had to be grateful for, from one who would have given
his utmost assistance for a suitable equivalent, but not
in return for alleged obligations which he declined to
acknowledge !

It shook Bismarck's confidence in Russian friendship,
especially when the Czar, ostensibly on the best terms
with Austria-Hungary, enquired of Berlin through the
German Military Attaché in St. Petersburg : " What
would be the attitude of William I in the event of Russia
becoming entangled in a war with the Dual Monarchy ? "
This clumsy and tactless question was characterised by
Bismarck as a piece of pure perfidy ! It excited his
righteous wrath, and, dreading to be driven into a
corner, he gave expression to his suspicion that if he
answered favourably, Gortchakoff would at once inform
Vienna accordingly ; and if unfavourably, he would egg
on the Czar against Germany. The suspicion was most
probably unfounded, but there is no doubt that when
Bismarck could think so ill of Gortchakoff he could
no longer have any confidence in his profession of friendship ; and his very caution and foresight obliged him
to approach those whom he considered incapable of
treachery. At length Bismarck was embittered by the
Czar assuming the rôle of the injured party before the
German Minister at St. Petersburg and his unjustifiable
complaint against the conduct of the Germans at the
Ambassadors' Conference at Constantinople. Bismarck
then failed not to rub it into the Czar's representative
that Gortchakoff and Ignatieff were nearer at heart to

France than to Germany, that they desired to encompass the fall of Andrássy and to make terms with his successor against Germany, and that in those circumstances it would be a gross dereliction of his duty to neglect his friendship with the States on which he might have to rely owing to the policy of Gortchakoff (24th January 1877).

While the Russian Chancellor had thus weakened his position at Berlin, Andrássy had correspondingly strengthened his own.

In 1875 the latter did not claim any glory for having preserved the peace which was not imperilled, and for this correct conduct he received the gratitude of his friend, while Gortchakoff earned nothing but contempt and anger.

Andrássy was perfectly informed on the Eastern Question and Bismarck's interest therein, and he attempted to do justice to the latter as far as possible. His task was facilitated by the fact that in not a few instances he regarded as profitable for the Dual Monarchy what was also compatible with the interests of Germany. Like Bismarck, he considered as useless the conference proposed by Gortchakoff ; more, he considered it even dangerous.   Like Bismarck, he was willing to agree with Russia, but would not veto the Czar's Oriental action lest Russian public opinion should turn against us, and we should be subjected to the fate of Turkey and have to face a very grave Russian war.

Andrássy did not threaten Bismarck or worry him with interminable diplomatic notes, but played his cards in suchwise that it should be to the interest of Germany to stand by us at the critical moment. Thereby he improved his position in the Alliance of the Three Emperors. All the same, however, he had many a bitter and painful experience before he reached his goal. The bitterest of all was when he had to agree with Gortchakoff before Russia would determine her Oriental policy and engage her army in the Balkans. Then he found himself on the horns of a dilemma : If the conditions of the agreement should promise no advantage for the Russians, there would arise the danger of the Czar seeking the road to Constantinople (according to the taste and advice of the Pan-Slavs) through Vienna. If, on the other hand, Andrássy should concede too much, it would either mean a surrender of the interests of the Monarchy or a violation of his pledged word.

A heavy burden was lifted from Andrássy's mind when at Reichstadt (1875) the first agreement was signed, Russia accepting his standpoint, i.e. that the object of the Oriental operations was to maintain and improve the *status quo*, or if that were impossible, then the erection of Christian States (none of which, however, should be a great Slav State), and that the eventual territorial changes should be limited to Russia receiving Bessarabia and Austria-Hungary Bosnia-Herzegovina, without any promise on our part of active assistance to Russia. I well recall the exciting days somewhat later when the Czar, through Suwarow, urged that common military action should be taken against Turkey, and Andrássy succeeded in turning down this proposal, the object of which was the dismemberment of Turkey, without however deterring Gortchakoff from his original purpose and inducing him to attack us instead of the Ottomans. I well remember the strenuous labour, and the resulting satisfaction of Andrássy, of the final negotiations before the beginning of the Russo-Turkish War, when once more everything hung by a single hair, and when, moreover, there was reason to fear that

Russia would rather turn against us than commence operations in the Balkans with tied hands, and when Andrássy again succeeded in averting this disaster (Convention of 15th January 1877). Thus Russia entered on a war burdened with obligations, in the fulfilment of which we knew our own interests to be safeguarded.

Bismarck did not regard Andrássy's policy with unmixed pleasure or satisfaction, since they did not represent identity of interests. Whereas the former would strengthen the Alliance by the co-operation of Austria-Hungary and Russia in a positive form, concluding with her an agreement as like that on the division of Poland as is one egg to another, the latter declined to listen to anything of the sort. The ultimate aim of Bismarck at this time, as he explained in an interesting note, was that Austria-Hungary, Russia, and England should agree for each of them to occupy in the East— at Turkey's expense—a position satisfying them for the time being, and preventing them turning against each other as well as preventing any one of them seeking the assistance of France; but later setting those Powers at loggerheads, so that they all should become dependent on the good-will of Germany. With this object in view he reserved for Russia (on the basis of a mutual agreement) the east of the Balkan Peninsula, for us Bosnia-Herzegovina, and for England Egypt.

However, so long as Turkey held out, Andrássy would not occupy Bosnia-Herzegovina. As Bismarck said : " Bosnia-Herzegovina is no desirable acquisition for Andrássy, but merely a *pis aller*, which he would take only if he had to choose between the annexation and a Pan-Slav formation which would endanger the other dominions of the Dual Monarchy (i.e. Dalmatia, etc.)."

Andrássy would not with Russia attack Turkey in order to acquire spoils there. He condemned such a policy, saying he was ashamed of it.

On one occasion in the special ministerial saloon-car between Tiszadob (the ancestral home of the Andrássy family) and Budapest, Andrássy, who always took his family into his confidence, addressed to me and my brother, his sons, the following query: " Would we approve the annexation of Bosnia-Herzegovina in co-operation with the Russians against the Turks, as many advocated ? " (He did this partly with the object of training his sons to think, and partly also to formulate his own thoughts so lucidly that even young and inexperienced boys like ourselves might be able to understand.) And then he proceeded to explain with noonday clearness that to do so would be a grave mistake ; for we were no aggressive State, and we ought to extend the sphere of our power only if there were no other means of defending our present possessions. To that we were compelled as much out of respect for the rights of others as for our own interests.

This difference of view, however, did not disturb the harmony between the two statesmen. Bismarck had no desire to impose his views on us, for he was on the whole satisfied with Andrássy and was aware that the latter did not want a Russian war. He knew that Andrássy would not deceive him, and he had found by experience that the Hungarian did not, like Gortchakoff, constantly importune him to take sides with one or the other ally. Moreover, he knew Andrássy's strong convictions too well to attempt to influence him and play the rôle of mentor as against his successor. Thus until the outbreak of the Russo-Turkish War (24th April 1877) the internal situation of the Three Emperors

Alliance was as follows : Austria-Hungary was on far better and more intimate terms with Germany than with Russia, and than those two Powers with each other. Andrássy communicated more easily with both his allies than they did with each other. Austria-Hungary had separate agreements with Russia which determined in advance what the consequences of the war should be. If Russia kept her word, all three statesmen might expect to a certain extent to realise their aims. Bismarck would be able to continue the Alliance of the Three Emperors and isolate France ; Andrássy could come into more confidential and friendly relations with Germany and be able to protect our interests in the East ; Gortchakoff, though he would not become master of the Balkans, as he hoped, nor be able to accomplish the ancient Russian ambitions, yet need not be discomfited, as he could swap the Peace of Paris—representing the defeat of Russia—for international agreements securing certain advantages for his country.

All these things, however, would have been possible only if Russia had faithfully discharged the obligations she had undertaken towards us—and this she failed to do. The Czar's Government, counting on the effect of the *fait accompli*—in view of the excited Slav public opinion—contemplated exploiting the results achieved at such tremendous cost and upsetting the agreement concluded with us. At San Stefano (March 1878) Russia dictated to Turkey conditions which signified the formation of a great Slav State, the occupation for a long period of the east of the Balkans by Russian troops, and while Bessarabia was annexed, no mention was made of Bosnia ! In short she laid the foundation of Russian hegemony and coolly repudiated her obligations to us.

This meant the miscarriage of Bismarck's carefully conceived scheme ; whose weakness had been that whenever it became necessary to act, to exercise pressure on one of its parts, the whole became paralysed, and the part against which the pressure was directed sooner or later succumbed—that is to say, the State in question was driven into the arms of France. Friendship is a thing that cannot be enforced, yet Bismarck attempted in that manner to secure two friends.

The future now depended on one fact alone, there was but a single question : Which conception would prevail, Andrássy's or Gortchakoff's ? Would Andrássy's calculations prove correct ?

In agreeing with Russia with regard to the peace terms, Andrássy relied on the Czar's honour, but to a greater extent on our own power, on our ability to compel Russia to keep her pledges. He was convinced that the farther the Russian armies advanced in the Balkans, the nearer they got to Constantinople, the more effective would be our word, the more critical would become their position as represented by the Transylvanian mountains and Bukovina behind their line of retreat ; and he was fully convinced that Bismarck would place no obstacle in the way of his exploiting this strategical advantage.

Events proved him quite right. The drama of real life unfolded like a play, in a well-thought-out, methodically arranged order: the plot, the counterplot, the climax, the happy *dénouement*.

The Russian forces, exhausted by the prolonged campaign, could not contend against us ; their situation had become desperate. They would have found themselves opposed by England, who had committed herself in the negotiations with Andrássy to stand by the interests we were defending in the Balkans; with the Turkish Army, still in fighting trim; with Rumania, smarting under unmerited perfidy and wanton ingratitude in that after she had saved the Russians at Plevna, they now proposed to rob her of Bessarabia! Neither could they count on aid from Italy, for she was restrained by England. This situation could only have been altered by Bismarck turning against us and identifying himself with Russia; but in that also Andrássy's calculations proved sound. Bismarck had now less confidence in Russia than he had before, and declined to risk himself in her behalf.

He showed his opinion of Gortchakoff's policy when he declared that that statesman had " during the past three years perpetrated all the blunders he possibly could." He had alienated all his old friends without acquiring new ones; aroused his enemies against him without providing himself with the means to oppose them. In April 1877 Bismarck stigmatised Gortchakoff's attitude as " impertinent," and desired the latter to know that he could have succeeded far better with him (Bismarck) by confidence and good manners than by reproaches, objections, and captious criticism. He declared that Gortchakoff's lack of sincerity compelled him to look to his good relations with the rest of his friends.

In Andrássy, on the other hand, Bismarck placed implicit confidence. He emphasised that he would always avoid doing anything that might render Andrássy's position untenable, for it was in the best interests of Germany that there should be a reliable man at the head of affairs in Vienna. How could he (Bismarck) know whether Andrássy, if obliged to resign, might not be succeeded by some minister who would deviate from his foreign policy ?   Therefore Bismarck felt a serious responsibility not to allow Andrássy to be tripped up. The friendship and confidence that Andrássy had thus won for himself became a source of strength for the Austro-Hungarian Monarchy.

And in the actual circumstances Bismarck considered us more powerful even than Russia. On 30th January 1878 Bismarck wrote : " If Austria-Hungary is given a free hand against Russia (which she has merited if Russia fails to keep her promise), and if Austria-Hungary comes to an agreement with England (which has in fact taken place), Czar Alexander must perforce realise that the work of his valiant soldiers has been discounted by the exacting rather than skilful behaviour of his statesmen." Again, on 2nd February of the same year : " He could exercise pressure on Austria-Hungary with impunity only if France were non-existent. In the present circumstances, however, by leaning to Russia he might find himself up against an Austro-Hungarian-English-French alliance, which, if not a desperate, would be a dangerous situation."

Bismarck's mind was manifested by his thus regarding us as the more powerful and safer State. When Andrássy threatened to resign if a Congress were not convened to revise the peace forced on Turkey, Bismarck decided to refrain from doing anything that might tend to weaken Andrássy's position. He wrote that " though he had no interests in Turkey that he would not be willing to sacrifice for Russia, yet in Austria he certainly had such. It was in Germany's interest to be on good terms with Austria-Hungary and to have in Vienna a friendly and reliable minister." This was his starting-point in accepting the proposed Congress because Andrássy desired it and in the form that Andrássy desired it.

The Czar was brought to his knees, and the Congress met (13th June—13th July 1878). Russia—partly at the Congress itself and partly during the preliminary negotiations with us and England—surrendered most of her acquisitions and proved herself less powerful in the Balkans than ourselves. We were appointed by the consent of Europe to the administration of the region whence Russia had been expelled.

Bismarck would rather that Andrássy had sent an ultimatum to Russia and armed (30th January and 2nd February 1878) than that a conference should have been called " to argue and reply on the honour of the Czar," as he wrote. From his point of view the Chancellor's attitude was perfectly comprehensible ; as by our sabre-rattling he would have escaped the necessity of publicly declaring for either side and the odium would have descended entirely on us. On the other hand, Andrássy was equally right from the point of view of the Dual Monarchy.

It was useful for our prestige that our occupation of Bosnia-Herzegovina should not be an ordinary act of conquest—the fruit of the war—or of an agreement with Russia, but the result of a mandate originating in the confidence and consensus of opinion of Europe, entrusted to us in the interests of civilisation and humanity. It signified an immense moral distinction and positive increase of our power and prestige in the East that Europe—in that very document by which it abased the pretensions of Russia, ordered her troops to evacuate the Balkans, and curtailed the privileges she had unilaterally acquired—should put us, the heirs of that Austria which it was customary to style as a rotten, reactionary, oppressive oligarchy, into the foreground " in the name of civilisation and humanity." Thus we were able to defend our interests without resort to brute force, by keeping in the path of progress towards world peace and solidarity. But, alas! this " narrow way " was ere long abandoned, and the annexation of Bosnia-Herzegovina followed. Greatly to our discredit, we sought to have this act (which had begun by occupation on the basis of the mandate of Europe) ratified by a violation of international law.

It was lucky for us that a great part of the odium for what happened at the Congress fell upon Bismarck's shoulders.

Thus the great conception of the Iron Chancellor—the Triple Alliance of Emperors based on Russian friendship—became impossible to maintain, not only because relations between Vienna and St. Petersburg had become strained, but further because the Russo-German friendship had collapsed.

For the failure at Berlin the Russians, fortunately for us, cast the chief blame on Bismarck—the greatest statesman of them all, the illustrious host, and president of the Congress. And it added fuel to the fire of their rage that they considered Bismarck under obligation to them, and affected to see ingratitude in his behaviour.

Bismarck protested against such injustice ; his indignation was aroused thereby. It was rather for him —he contended—to complain of ingratitude on the part of the Russians, for the alliance between them had in the past been equally useful for both nations. By it Russia was enabled to suppress the Polish insurrection and regain her freedom of movement on the Black Sea. In the last Turkish War Bismarck had kept Austria-Hungary from intervening, and thus made it possible for the Czar to defeat Turkey ; while at the Berlin Congress he had supported all the Russian claims : so why should he be blamed for the pusillanimity of the Russians in not having the pluck to insist on demands more satisfactory to themselves ? How could he be more Russian than the Russians ?

This was not correct, however ; Bismarck's arguments were mere sophisms. Although it is a debatable point whether the Alliance could ever have been equally useful to both Prussia and Russia, it cannot be denied that Bismarck employed his great genius to exploit the opportunities presented by this Alliance far more radically than did Gortchakoff, and that in this very difference lies the superiority of Bismarck over his Russian colleague. It is likewise beyond dispute that it was not German pressure which had kept Austria-Hungary out of the fray at the time of the Oriental crisis. Our Government had no intention of entering it. It is also quite certain that the political situation to which Gortchakoff had to bow, and on account of which, at the Berlin Congress, he could not put forward demands satisfactory to himself, could easily have been upset by Bismarck had he stood by the Czar to the same extent as the Czar had stood by Emperor William in 1870. But on the point that Russia had no right to demand more from him, Bismarck was absolutely justified in his contention, as he had never promised active assistance ; but this was no solace to the Czar, for " he had always expected more of the Iron Chancellor, and had on more than one occasion pointed out to Berlin that the decision lay in his [Bismarck's] hands, and Austria-Hungary would yield if only Bismarck seriously wished it."

Therefore we cannot share Bismarck's indignation, nor be surprised at the Czar seeing in the Berlin Congress, as he expressed it, " Europe led by Bismarck opposing Russia in the interests of Austria-Hungary." But it

3

was unimporant who was right, the salient fact affecting the future being, fortunately for Andrássy, that the people at St. Petersburg held Bismarck responsible even for their own errors, and thus the original moral conditions of the Three Emperors' Alliance disappeared.

Bismarck would not have been himself—the man of finely tempered steel, the many-sided statesman we know him to have been—if in the newly arisen situation he had not immediately laid his plans for the defence of his old aims, when he saw the Russian press (notwithstanding the Czar's influence over it) bitterly attacking the German Government, Russian troops being despatched to the German frontier, Alexander II writing to William I hinting at Bismarck that "it is unworthy of a true statesman to pursue a policy animated by personal sympathies and antipathies." When he heard of the Czar's declaration, tantamount to a veiled threat, that "the policy of Germany might come to be deeply regretted by both countries," Bismarck decided that the time had arrived for breaking with his past and making his choice between Austria-Hungary and Russia, and substituting the Dual Alliance for the Alliance of the Three Emperors.

Bismarck envisaged two dangers. Firstly, he feared an immediate attack on the part of Russia. A precautionary measure against this was to establish a strong defensive front with the aid of Austria-Hungary and England. He enquired of England how far he might rely on British support in the event of an attack on account of a policy he had pursued, not for selfish interests, but for those of England and Austria-Hungary. Both Beaconsfield and Salisbury replied favourably : they would back Germany. But as, in the meantime, the danger had removed, Bismarck quietly dropped negotiations with the British Government, and contented himself with making up to Austria-Hungary.

The more remote, but more lasting and I think more serious, danger was that France, by availing herself of the dissolution of the Three Emperors' Alliance, might gain an ally in Russia or Austria-Hungary, or possibly in both. The only effective safeguard against such a contingency was a permanent alliance with Austria-Hungary. If Bismarck, in the altered circumstances, should adhere to his former idea and attempt to attack both the Emperors, he might only succeed in losing them both. If he continued to seek the good-will of the Czar, Austria-Hungary might turn away from him ; and for the time being there was no hope of Russia, as she was already in spirit alienated from him. After the Berlin Congress, in the Germanophobe humour of the Muscovites, a French orientation by Russia could only be prevented by giving her to understand that she would in that case find herself opposed by superior forces. Bismarck was occupied by these problems when he received information that Andrássy contemplated resigning his post. He realised that he must act promptly. If he could not induce Andrássy (in whom, he says, he " has perfect confidence and easily gets on with ") to reconsider his decision, even a successor following the same policy might look to England for help against Russia—which would bring him nearer to France, so that Germany would remain in a boresome *tête-à-tête* with a perfidious, excited, antagonistic Russia, and it would thus be in the power of the Czar to conciliate Austria-Hungary and completely isolate Germany.

But the German Chancellor, alert to every possibility, foresaw the probable eventuality of the Russian standpoint carrying the day in Vienna, on which a counterpart of Kaunitz's coalition, which even Frederick the Great could scarcely contend against, would be immediately formed : an Austro-Russo-French Alliance—a veritable nightmare to Bismarck ! Such a culmination would place him in an even worse plight than the great King, for it was doubtful whether he could rely on England.

The experiences of Bismarck, moreover, convinced him that an alliance with us would be safer and more durable than with Russia. Formerly he had considered the friendship of the Muscovites to be more valuable, trusting more the asseverations of the autocratic sovereign than the pledged word of the constitutional Dual Monarchy, which latter was liable to be swayed by the whims and vacillating will of the people. But now, in his anxiety for the welfare of his Fatherland, he feared the awakening of " a Slav Napoleonism," he saw the Czar under the influence of demagogy, and concluded that our Monarchy was a surer guarantee, in spite of its constitutionalism. He was the more inclined to this view by Germany's great need of peace, the sympathy of the Austro-Germans, and the Slavophobia of the Hungarians. All these considerations convinced him that a defensive alliance with us would be alone able to restrain the revolutionary movement attendant on Pan-Slavism, and to lead back the Czar's policy into the path in which Germany had agreed with it in the past, as it desired to do also in the future.

Andrássy received Bismarck's overtures with sincere pleasure ; they afforded him peculiar satisfaction. His final object appeared to be accomplished at the moment of his resignation, and even on account of it. Nevertheless he did not grasp the offer too eagerly.

Bismarck offered him a defensive alliance against attack from any quarter. Andrássy, however, showed himself as little inclined to accept this in 1879 as he had been in 1873 ; since such a fact would force the Monarchy to shed the blood of its subjects for foreign interests, to fight against France, when there was no cause of quarrel between them, when the *débâcle* of France would overthrow the balance of power in Europe. In Andrássy's view this would drive France into the arms of Russia and result in a Franco-Russian alliance, which later would be joined by Italy too. Consequently he accepted the *casus fœderis* only in the event of war with Russia, or with some coalition of which Russia was a member.

Andrássy preferred to abandon the idea of concluding the treaty to accepting it in the form offered. He paid homage to the great mind of Bismarck, but preferred to remain independent of him. Andrássy was no victim of that intellectual snobbery, then in fashion, which was manifested in people being ashamed to differ from Bismarck, the popular idol, the universally recognised political genius—not daring to believe in themselves if the Iron Chancellor condemned them. Andrássy did not credit any impending Russian attack, and was not afraid of the consequences of a temporary want of success. He felt that Germany was just as much dependent on us as we were on her, and that Bismarck would in his own interests be compelled to consider our wishes and secure us for his ally.

Andrássy's resistance had its reward. Bismarck wrote to the Emperor William, with the simplicity and sincerity which characterise true greatness, that he " could not withstand the arguments of Andrássy, for they were absolutely sound."

But the Emperor's mind was not so quick as his illustrious Chancellor's to grasp the situation. He

reminded the new Bismarck of the traditions of the old
Bismarck ; he attributed his grand triumphs to the
friendship of Russia and was indisposed to relinquish it ;
he saw therein the old Austrian mentality : he feared
revanche for Königgrätz, and thought it not impossible
that we, relying on England and France, might have
designs on Russia, as was tendenciously asserted in
St. Petersburg.   Yet if in spite of all this it were necessary
to conclude an alliance with Austria-Hungary, it must
only be a general alliance against all and sundry and
not one specially directed against Russia. In his
opinion, the advantages to be derived from the treaty
would be unequal if Germany on her part had to defend
the Dual Monarchy against an attack from Russia,
while Austria-Hungary could remain neutral in case of a
conflict with France.   He failed to realise that parity was
ensured by the fact that Russia menaced Germany just
as much as ourselves, and that both contracting parties
engaged to assist each other in the case of a common
danger.   In vain did Bismarck point out to the Emperor
that, according to the terms of Andrássy's draft, in the
event of an Italo-Austrian war Germany would not be
obliged to help ; the old monarch was at a loss to
understand that, while by the terms of Andrássy's draft
Germany had not to draw the sword, in accordance with
Bismarck's she would have to do so.   Equally in vain
was it that Bismarck assured William that in the event
of an isolated attack by France, Germany would need
no assistance from anyone—just as Austria-Hungary
would need none against Italy alone—but as soon as
either had to face a coalition the treaty would come into
force.   Thus the aid would be lacking only when it was
not required. Moltke was likewise unsuccessful in
convincing the Emperor that, according to the geo-

graphical and military situation, the Austro-Hungarian power çould be really effective only against Russia and not against France. William was obdurate and closed his ears to the advice of his famous Ministers. He insisted that it would be an act of disloyalty to the Czar to make a secret treaty behind his back, when he had so shortly before met his Imperial Majesty and exchanged vows of friendship with him. This was a truly honourable sentiment on the part of William I, but it is to be regretted that he manifested no such fine scruples against a secret agreement with Russia behind the back of Francis Joseph (1887).

Eventually the old Emperor, though unconvinced, was silenced. Bismarck and the entire Cabinet offered their resignations. The conscience of the venerable monarch would not allow him to part with Bismarck, his trusted, albeit troublesome, adviser, the Germans' pride, who had made him the foremost among the world's rulers.

Thus, after all, Andrássy's draft was signed (7th October 1879), and that treaty concluded which for a period of forty years determined the trend of European policy and continued to be its most important instrument, until it was overwhelmed in the sea of blood it had been intended to prevent. To throw it overboard became the tragic duty for me (1918)—for me, who had clung to it to the last, not only because I saw therein my father's glory, but also because I regarded it as a wise and grand work, which had well served our interests for so long.

Andrássy vacated his responsible office on the very day on which the treaty was signed, and by his resignation the direction of the foreign affairs of the Dual Monarchy was abandoned by the only man who could influence Bismarck, cross his will, and get him to take a way he disliked—and all without forfeiting his confidence and friendship ; the only man who could co-operate with the Iron Chancellor without becoming a mere dependent on him.

4. Characters of Bismarck and Andrássy
contrasted

Before proceeding further I would like to deviate for a moment to sketch the political characters of Andrássy and Bismarck by drawing a parallel between the two statesmen. While there was much resemblance between them, there was also a wide difference.

Bismarck was at the head of a greater Power than his colleague's, he remained for a longer time in office, he achieved more important successes, he left deeper prints on the scroll of world-history, he manifested his genius on more multifarious occasions than did Andrássy, though the foreign political campaign of the latter in the Eastern Question might justly be recorded by the side of Bismarck's most brilliant exploits.

Both men equally were led by their convictions, their patriotism, their sense of duty ; the highest court of appeal in the case of both men was their conscience. Neither could have sustained the burdens of public life, the onerous task that engaged their entire energy, if they had not possessed the absolute conviction that what they were doing was the only right thing and the best for their respective Fatherlands. Both could undertake only what their conscience approved ; both were ready to face unpopularity, loss of place and power and favour ; both would feel dispirited and weak if dissatisfied with themselves—in vain would be the applause of their people or the honours of their sovereign.

A rare example of this sense of duty and conscientiousness was furnished by Bismarck when, though persuaded that he could win splendid renown, that he could again break France, and humble Russia—the only undefeated Great Power—he resisted the temptation afforded by these grandiose prospects worthy even of a Napoleon, and plodded on along his thorny path for the preservation of peace.

Similar unselfishness on the part of Andrássy was demonstrated when the Russian armies lay bleeding in the Balkans and before Constantinople. Though absolutely certain that his intervention in the struggle would mean a brilliant victory, yet, like the German Chancellor, he resigned the dazzling rôle with the glorious reward which even in these days can be won only by the aid of Mars, because, in his opinion, war at that time was not in the interests of his country : victory would be followed by a series of wars of revenge until the weakened Dual Monarchy became exhausted and fell an easy prey to its foes.

Both men were Nationalists from top to toe. Bismarck once retorted to an opponent that " if he ever sold his soul to the devil, it would have to be a German devil." It was a feature of his fervent race-consciousness that, as I heard from his family, when during his last illness he had the biography of Napoleon read to him, he requested the gloomy episodes of Jena and Eylau to be omitted, because (he said) " they distressed him too much " ; though after Sedan he would have been just the very man to recall with equanimity that seemingly long-bygone age. Bismarck was essentially a Prussian, but of the rarest and worthiest type. He understood

Europe and the foreign mentality. His manners were international—they fascinated by their charm : qualities seldom found in the average Junker.

Andrássy was an out-and-out Hungarian. His countenance was typically Magyar. He ardently loved his race, and took pride in being a Hungarian. He entered the common Austro-Hungarian service not out of a hyphenated (i.e. Austro-Hungarian) patriotism, but because he believed he could be useful to the Hungarian half of the Dual Monarchy under the conditions then prevailing. He changed his views in many respects during the course of his diplomatic career, but his chief motive in all his actions was a specific Hungarian patriotism, whether at the Hofburg at Vienna in the common cabinet councils, or at Isaszeg, where he fought as a *honvêd*, or under the walls of Buda, where he was struck in the breast by a spent Austrian bullet. During his residence at the Ballplatz[1] he brought up his children in the most uncompromising Hungarian patriotism. He had, however, certain qualities not usually found in Hungarians : he was a man of a broad European outlook ; he was capable of regarding every political question in its international aspect, though the chief shortcoming of the Magyar race is its absorption in the " Hungarian world," i.e. its lack of interest in what is going on across the frontier. Unfortunately this is true even to-day, when the blunders of foreign policy have brought us to a critical pass and when only a sound foreign policy can save us.

Both Bismarck and Andrássy were strenuous workers. They regarded a problem from every point before taking action, but their decisions once taken they never deviated

---

[1] The Austrian Foreign Office at Vienna, formerly the palace of Kaunitz and Metternich.

from, but followed calmly and with bulldog tenacity to their final results.

Even genius cannot dispense with hard work; it might even be stated as an axiom that one of the chief constituents of genius is the ability to perform more work and that more intensively than the ordinary man —to put forth more energy—to take an idea and brood over it, following it to its ultimate consequences—the ability to analyse facts and get at the essence of things with greater efficiency than the average human brain.

It used to be said of Andrássy that he was frivolous and superficial. I have seen many statesmen at work, yet never one who has acted after so much serious consideration, discussion, and conscientious deliberation as he; never one who devoted all his energies and his health and strength to the discharge of his duties as he; who spent so many sleepless nights before taking a grave decision as he. He often stated that he had lain on the hard, cold floor in order to cool his body heated after excessive mental effort; only thus could he obtain a little much-needed sleep.

In every line of every project of Bismarck's can be felt the conscientious deliberation, the thoroughness, so characteristic of the man. He always considered the most widely different contingencies, set out from the worst premisses, and decided only after such exhaustive analysis. This nerve-racking labour undermined even his robust constitution.

Real practical statesmanship is a rare gift of the gods. There are many men who dare, simply because they are purblind and lack the insight to perceive the dangers ahead, into which they are madly rushing, like the Gadarene swine; or else because they are irritable and lacking conscience. Also there are not infrequently

some who, being profound, see the vital part of things
and are thus able to discern all the possibilities, to balance
the advantages and the drawbacks, but, having a too
critical brain, dare not shoulder responsibility, on account
of the risks contingent upon every human enterprise, and
especially so when it is the question of grave political
operations with human material.

But neither of this type of statesman can be a provi-
dential leader. The hesitating sage may be an acceptable
adviser for the man of action ; he may be a good thinker,
writer, and orator ; but he would prove a dangerous
leader in a time of crisis, because such a man's decisions
are always made too late. Precipitation and hesitation
are equally the foes of success. The thoughtlessly rash
man may sometimes have astonishing success and be of
more use to his country with his strong will and lightning-
like decision, if only he can unite those qualities with a
certain *savoir faire*, than the halting, wise man. This
notwithstanding, such a statesman may prove very
dangerous and lead his country into a morass whence
it may be impossible to extricate her.

Fortune's best gift to a nation is a leader who sees,
knows, and yet dares ; who chooses the way of least
risk, who weighs the consequences, considers everything
before making up his mind, and then, shouldering the
responsibility for the not impossible contingency of failure,
steers his course boldly and firmly, amidst the rocks and
shoals.

Such a statesman was Bismarck ; such also was
Andrássy ; and such an one must be every true practical statesman.

Both of them were honest and sincere ; they repudiated the saying of Talleyrand, that " words—
especially those of statesmen—are intended to hide

the thoughts." In their view, the chief art of politics is to form the right conception, that corresponding to the actual situation, which on that very account can be acknowledged ; then the energetic, bold, prompt action—and not the skilful use of subterfuge and trickery.

Of the two men, however, Andrássy was the more idealistic. Bismarck was a man of muscle and brawn, the embodiment of animal strength even to the point of roughness, except that interest and insight added moderation and refinement to the natural inflexibility of his character. To the power and decision of Andrássy were added nobility and refinement, as human qualities equivalent to power, as innate instincts which could be suppressed only momentarily at the behests of his country's welfare. He brought with him into the realm of politics that chivalry which formed one of his brightest attributes.

Bismarck believed himself raised up by Providence to lead Germany in the path of progress towards perfection. Though directness accorded with his vigorous nature, knowing neither fear nor ruth, and though he considered straightforwardness in politics the better way, yet, if necessary for the successful performance of what he conceived his sacred duty, he would stoop to trickery, lying, and even insolence—all things of which Andrássy was utterly incapable. Bismarck's maxim was to be to a gentleman a " *gentleman et demi,*" but to a pirate a " *corsaire et demi.*" He held, like Cavour, that a minister should be prepared to sacrifice even his personal honour for the sake of his Fatherland. Theoretically Andrássy too accepted that view, yet he could never belie his nature : he was chivalrous and straight in all his acts. Czar Alexander was no more than just when he said of the Hungarian statesman: " Andrássy is too proud to deceive." Bismarck's nature was suspicious; he had a contempt for mankind in general; he suspected ill-will in everyone holding opinions different from his own, or who thwarted him; he was constantly seeing intrigue, envy, malice, and hatred. In the political arena he was unrelenting. Not satisfied with putting his opponents *hors de combat*, he would break them, and had no mercy on the weaker beaten to his knees. He gave full rein to this unamiable propensity, especially in home politics, where in consequence the situation sometimes became very bitter, and the Chancellor, in spite of his victories and unprecedented fame, would find himself surrounded by a host of ill-wishers and foes. He saw in his personal enemies, enemies of the Fatherland, which was a dangerous and harmful attitude in a statesman; since a man denounced officially as disloyal, and held up to public opinion as disloyal, may easily end in becoming so.

In many respects the two statesmen held differing views with regard to their ministerial posts. Bismarck was full of self-complacency, he was self-willed and tyrannical—even towards his Emperor. Yet in spite of all he modestly considered himself a mere official, a humble servant of his sovereign, and was not in the least embarrassed when his services and efforts were recognised by special rewards. I happened to be in Berlin on the occasion of his jubilee, when there was a public subscription for a testimonial to the Chancellor. Some individuals—among them certain who, like Bleichröder, had business relations with the State— gave an immense sum for this object. Andrássy was puzzled about the affair: he could not understand it at all. He considered himself a *grand seigneur* rather than an official, and declined even the pension he was entitled to on quitting his post ; and when, on the occasion of the meeting of the Emperors at St. Petersburg, he heard that it was proposed to present him with a diamond-studded snuff-box, he did his best to escape it. It was repugnant to his self-respect to receive valuable gifts from sovereigns when he could not return the compliment.

A special chapter of Bismarck's life-story might be devoted to his remorseless war on women who dared to cross his plans ; it made no difference though they belonged to the Royal Family. He was ever on the alert to guard his sovereign from all outside influences, and he even managed to make him subservient to his will. Bismarck's domineering, unforbearing disposition is illustrated also in the fact that, finding that William II desired to get rid of him, he refused to resign and forced upon the young sovereign the tremendous responsibility before history of dismissing from his high office the greatest statesman that Germany has ever known or is ever likely to know. Andrássy would never have done such a thing : once he were convinced that he had lost the confidence of his monarch, no chains would have been strong enough to bind him to the velvet chair.

Andrássy was an optimist with regard to his fellowmen ; at least he was far more considerate of them than was his illustrious friend. His view in this regard may be gathered from the answer he once gave to the question : " What is your chief source of pride ? " He was proud to say that, knowing men, he could yet love them. It is doubtful whether he had any real enemies—an unusual situation for a man of strong character like Andrássy. He bore no lasting malice or bitterness against anyone. His personal charm won all with whom he came into contact—to a certain extent even his opponents. He was successful in his dealings with men, perhaps on account of his suavity of manner and personal influence. In the case of persons with whom he was in constant touch, he knew as a rule how to stimulate their better sentiments, and thus he got more loyalty than usually falls to the lot of a statesman.

Both men appear to have been special favourites of Fortune. Yet may we talk of accident as one of the factors in the making of history ? Is it not depreciation of great men to say or suggest that their success was due, if only partially, to the caprice of the fickle Goddess ? Not so, in my opinion. The fortuitous plays a great part in all our affairs. Men, however great, are not omnipotent ; they cannot make something out of nothing, nor even create the milieu, the conditions, under which they are to work. They can neither choose circumstances nor fashion them to their taste. They cannot change the abilities of their superiors, colleagues, subordinates on the one hand, or of the sovereigns, ministers, and generals of the enemy on the other ; although these factors undoubtedly affect in a great measure the success or failure of their plans. Possibly all these circumstances are the inevitable consequences of Nature's immutable, eternal law, links in the chain of cause and effect ; but this does not alter the fact that, from the view-point of those playing the game, these events may be regarded as the fruits of the fortuitous. Who can deny that some statesmen and generals are constantly favoured, while others are doomed to ill-luck—to the frustrating of their most excellent schemes by circumstances entirely beyond their control ? This does not detract from the merit of the latter. Without merit, any lasting and true success is as little to be expected as without the favour —or at least the neutrality—of Fate. The really great statesman is he who can so use his opportunities as to get the utmost profit out of them, he who can best parry the rude buffetings of disappointment and misfortune. The essence of the political and military art is to seize opportunity by the forelock, exploit it, reduce adverse consequences to a minimum. Life itself is a sort of gamble, in which the winners are those who know how to bring skill to the aid of chance.

It is indisputable that Bismarck could never have reached the lofty heights that he did if Roon had not reorganised the Prussian Army, if Moltke had not been the greatest strategist of the age. Yet notwithstanding these, Bismarck's whole career hung on a thread : he could never have achieved his brilliant successes without the helping hand of Fortune. In spite of the military genius of Moltke and Roon, the battle of Königgrätz would have been lost if the Crown Prince had arrived but a few hours later—Frederick's arrival in the very nick of time was a circumstance which Bismarck could not control ; it was a fortunate accident for the Chancellor. Moreover, how fortunate it was for Bismarck that he was born to serve such a magnanimous Emperor as William I, who tolerated his domineering, his rudeness, his tyranny, because he perceived that the often odious Junker's place could not be filled by another ! Again, how much Bismarck owed to Napoleon III's vacillating and idealistic temperament, and his (Napoleon's) period of bad health—to Beust's and Gortchakoff's weakness and vanity—to the circumstance that they were witty diplomats rather than men of action ; that

4

Benedek was a mediocre general; that in 1870–1 there was no Frenchman worthy to be the successor of Turenne or Bonaparte! In any sphere Bismarck would have been an interesting, brilliant figure for the contemplation of posterity; but born under a different star, he might have been only another Alberoni or Radowitz, and not the illustrious founder of German Unity.

Andrássy owed much to his being a contemporary of Francis Deák, the Hungarian statesman, who was his ideal complement and who, with his unprecedented popularity and fame, supported him and yielded up to him that leadership for which he had no truer vocation than had the great jurist. Andrássy owed much, too, to the sound common sense and perspicacity of his sovereign, Francis Joseph, who understood *au fond* the policy of Andrássy and supported him loyally, though at considerable personal sacrifice, as Andrássy's counsel often brought him into conflict with his traditions and natural sentiments; the sovereign who could appoint him—a revolutionary sentenced to death—as his minister, although the impulsive personality of the minister was not congenial to the monarch. And how much Andrássy owed to Queen Elizabeth, who with womanly intuition understood the Hungarians and interceded between them and their King!

Neither Bismarck nor Andrássy experienced such a reverse of fortune as that which befell Napoleon I. The foundation laid by the great Bonaparte could not have endured, because it was designed for a superman like himself and was useless to a mediocre person. However, his world-empire fell to ruin during his own lifetime like a house of cards, and he was destined to end his existence in exile, simply because his legendary luck forsook him at several critical moments, through no fault of his own. The excessive severity of the Russian winter of 1812 ; the failure of the Russian generals to engage him in a decisive battle, according to plan, near the frontier ; the devastating conflagration in Moscow ; his desertion by his Saxon allies at Leipzig ; the defection of Ney and Grouchy in his final campaign, which caused the French reinforcements to come too late on the afternoon of Waterloo, while Blücher appeared on the French left wing—the fact that, as Lloyd George said in a speech, " Wellington realised too late that the battle had been lost " : all these circumstances contributed to and finally culminated in the tragedy of St. Helena. Nevertheless it must be conceded that Napoleon tempted Providence, and that his temerity exhausted the patience of his presiding genius (*dæmon*) ; while, in the case of both Andrássy and Bismarck, Fortune continued to befriend them because they were not too exacting in the demands they made upon her. They, too, had faith in their stars and in a good Providence which had bestowed power upon them. They did not, however, abuse the gift, and therefore were not punished with its withdrawal, as was the great Bonaparte.

Andrássy and Bismarck will descend to posterity as the founders of the same system of foreign policy, yet their conceptions were entirely different as regards both home and foreign policy. Bismarck's cherished idea was the Alliance of the Three Emperors ; that of Andrássy was the Dual Alliance—a sort of weapon presenting a defensive edge towards Russia. Bismarck accepted Andrássy's theory only when he saw he could not do otherwise—that is to say, when during the Oriental crisis the Czar turned his back upon him. He hoped, however, that the severance of the friendship of the three

Emperors was temporary only, and would be resumed as
soon as the Czar—thwarted and terrorised by that same
Dual Alliance—was brought to see his error. In the
eyes of the Iron Chancellor the Dual Alliance was merely
a kind of stepping-stone to the resumption of the Three
Emperors' Alliance.

Andrássy, on the other hand, from the beginning
regarded the Dual Alliance as his goal; and when he
had attained it he desired to break with the Alliance
of the Three Emperors for good and all. He said he
" could relish nothing served up by the Alliance of the
Three Emperors." He was anxious to complete the
Dual Alliance and assist it to predominance, instead of
including the Czar, by an entente with Great Britain.

He strongly believed that an intimate relation with
England could range Italy on our side, divert the Muscovites for ever from their Balkan ambitions, and render
the result of the Berlin Congress (i.e. our footing in the
Balkans) firm and durable. Bismarck too was wary of
coming into opposition with England. In a case of
imminent danger he was willing to conclude an alliance
with her, though he preferred the friendship of the
Russians to that of the English, and had he freedom of
choice he would have chosen Russia. He was always
afraid of England exploiting Germany, using her to get
the chestnuts out of the fire and then leaving her in the
lurch. He wanted a permanent alliance, and this he
thought he was unlikely to obtain from a parliamentary
England. Yet Andrássy, in their final negotiations,
appears to have won over Bismarck for the English
orientation. This would appear from the fact already
alluded to, that at this time Bismarck approached
London, and also that the two statesmen, meeting at
Salzburg and Vienna, agreed to try to gain England for

their policy. At that period, however, the German Chancellor was not drawn towards England of his own free will, but rather impelled thither by pressure of the general situation. He would have joined St. Petersburg, though he would have quarrelled with it ; and though he could not trust England, yet he would go with her, co-operate with her (as at the Berlin Congress), and solicit her help. Andrássy, on the other hand, from the very beginning, saw in Great Britain the natural friend and ally of Austria-Hungary and Germany.

A very important—perhaps the most important—question for the future was, which would triumph in the end—the powerful, inflexible will of the Man of Iron ? or the general circumstances favourable to Andrássy's conception and which at the time of his resignation were ready to assert themselves ?

CHAPTER II

FROM THE AUSTRO-HUNGARIAN ALLIANCE WITH GER-
MANY UNTIL THE BULGARIAN UNION (1879–1885)

1. Gladstone's Estrangement from Germany

NOT long after the Berlin Treaty and the conclusion
of the Dual Alliance three events occurred to
change the aspect of the political situation. The
first was the alteration in the foreign policy of Great
Britain which led to her adventure in Egypt; the
second, the more vigorous French colonial policy; and
the third, the awakening aspiration of Germany for her
" place in the sun." In consequence of these events the
situation overseas came into the limelight, more intensely
affecting the relations of the European Powers to each
other than had been the case in the preceding decades.

The change in the British policy was brought about
by the general election of April 1880, which overthrew
Beaconsfield, the imperialistic co-worker with Bismarck
and Andrássy, and put into power his great opponent
Gladstone, whose policy differed entirely from that of
his predecessor. Beaconsfield and Salisbury, the leaders
of the Conservative England, became in August 1879 so
Germanophil that they declared in Rome that, should
Italy assist Russia against Germany or Austria-Hungary,
England would regard it as a *casus belli*; and, on the
other hand, they promised Bismarck that in the event
of the Franco-Russian allies getting embroiled in war
with Germany or Austria-Hungary, England would take
the side of the latter, i.e. the Central European Powers.
The Queen held the same views as her ministers, and

even the Prince of Wales himself—afterwards Edward VII —the inventor of the " Einkreisung," adopted the standpoint of the Conservative Government. Beaconsfield said of the Prince that " though he was fond of the French women, he was so Russophobe that he would gladly break with the French rather than hold with the Muscovites." Gladstone, however, brought into the Cabinet quite the opposite political sympathies and tastes. The fall of the Conservatives in itself meant that the nation had got tired of Beaconsfield's imperialism, which had brought her into antagonism with Russia, involving her in the danger of war.

Moreover, Gladstone, owing to his political past, intended to strike out into new paths. As a member of Palmerston's Cabinet he had represented the idea of Italian unity with great zeal against Austria, and his old Austrophobia again asserted itself as the result of our Eastern policy, which he regarded as anti-Christian and contrary to the interests of civilisation, since it attempted to reconcile the interests of Christianity and civilisation with the bolstering-up of Turkey—a State that he passionately detested. At the previous election the famous orator and agitator was carried away by his anger so far as to use expressions so offensive towards Austria-Hungary that he had, as Premier, to withdraw them. With the Turks he dealt even more ruthlessly ; he told them plainly that they had better pack up and clear off to Asia, " bag and baggage."

Bismarck and Gladstone could scarcely understand each other. In these men two diametrically opposed political views were personified in two perfectly different individualities. Bismarck and Gladstone had widely different notions of the aims and ethics of politics. These two giants had also different political talents.

Gladstone maintained that the statesman was the servant of the people. According to his creed, all parties, all statesmen, existed but to enlighten and win over the people, and to fulfil or still further enlighten and influence the national will as revealed through the ballot-box. On the other hand, Bismarck's highest conception of his duty was to serve the Fatherland, if possible *with* the people, but if need be against them.

According to Gladstone, the King must not interfere in affairs of government, this being solely the right and duty of the people and the ministers who are responsible to them.

According to Bismarck, however, the King ruled by divine right and the ministers were merely his servants and responsible to him alone. If the convictions of the leading statesman came into opposition with the will of his sovereign, there was nothing for him to do but retire. The majority of the people, however, must serve the interests of the country; if necessary they must even be compelled to do so. The will of the majority produced no impression on the Prussian Junker. To him it was a matter for surprise if a few persons were found capable of understanding the national interest; how then could it be supposed that the uninstructed and impressionable masses could understand it? A highly popular policy he *ipso facto* regarded with suspicion.

Gladstone considered it a serious crime for a statesman to resist by force the will of the people, or act contrary thereto. To gain popularity was one of his chief ambitions. Bismarck, on the other hand, held in contempt the man who would violate his conscience for the sake of popularity or in subservience to the national will.

Bismarck's power was built up on his conflict with the parliamentary majority, when he fought by his

King's side for the extension of the army. Gladstone's success was based on his ability to adapt and trim his views to those of his times, so that, from a Conservative, he could become a Liberal when the star of Liberalism was in the ascendant.

Gladstone was *par excellence* an orator—perhaps chiefly an orator. Bismarck spoke badly, found his expressions only with difficulty, frequently hesitated. Just as an overcrowded hall empties itself but slowly on account of the multitude thronging out, so Bismarck was prevented from expressing his thoughts fluently and with ease by the very redundancy of his ideas. Before he had finished one thought, another would come surging upon his lips. Gladstone's speeches fairly lifted his audiences from their feet ; but when read in cold type they failed to arouse any enthusiasm. With Bismarck, however, the contrary was the case : his speeches were far more captivating when read than when delivered. Macaulay, the great English historian, wrote of " young Gladstone " that he had " one dangerous quality, i.e. his eloquence," which was too majestic, and its very sublimity enabled him to dispense with lucidity. All Bismarck's utterances were crystal-clear, razor-edged, precise, free from mere verbiage ; they were not the outcome of sentimentality, nor likely to create it in others : in his speeches it was his intellect appealing to the intellects of his hearers.

Bismarck was essentially a man of action rather than of words. One-sided, eminently practical, his education was chiefly in the sphere of history and politics. Gladstone was a belletrist, a philosopher. Whereas Gladstone was a home politician, Bismarck was pre-eminently a foreign politician.

Gladstone's ruling ambition in internal politics was to deliver the oppressed, to improve the economic situation of the country, and to extend its constitutional liberties. Bismarck's aim, on the contrary, was to erect a powerful monarchical State, strongly and soundly to develop the German and Prussian race. These two sharply contrasting life-objects are by no means merely the result of different personalities, but also of different environments. That favoured land guarded by the encircling sea, the cradle of liberty, supported by its proud traditions, was in a position to serve ideals far different from those of the Continental State surrounded by jealous foes, created by kings and defended by armies, whose position as a parvenu Power was still regarded askance by the world without.

Gladstone sought to enforce right and justice in foreign politics too; while Bismarck disdainfully—sometimes even cynically—observed that "the sufferings of other nations left him cold," that he would "consider it a crime to jeopardise the least German interest for the sake of the rights of aliens" or for "the peace of others"; his "sole guiding rule was the welfare of his own Fatherland and his sovereign's honour."

Gladstone's school is certainly a more agreeable one than that of Bismarck. Its single great fault is that it is sincere only in very rare cases, and that it can be sincere only in such cases. To-day the "sacred egoism" of nations is so strong, and the service of their own country the only recognised duty and desire of statesmen, that the slogan of "Right and Justice" is often no more than a cloak to hide national selfishness and greed. Even where it is otherwise, some more alluring catch-phrase unconsciously and involuntarily comes under the influence of national interests, since

the average mind can conceive as " right and just "
only such things as are useful and profitable for itself.

The political idealist, actuated by noble motives,
is often more dangerous than the political realist with
his policy rooted in self-interest. It is possible that
a genuine Utopia may cost too much blood. The
idealist has usually a finger in every pie and meddles
with affairs that do not concern him—which, moreover, he is incapable of understanding. The more of
an idealist he is, the more tyrannical, the more impatient,
he will be. He will seek right and reason by violence
just because of his excellent intentions. The danger of
clashing interests remains even when the cause is led
by idealists ; and to this peril we may add those of the
idée fixe, insurmountable prejudices, and the conflict
arising out of the desire to confer blessings upon others.
Apart from the infatuation of ambition, egoism, national
and individual, will often don the disguise of humani-
tarianism and zeal for righteousness. Even the most
coldly calculating statesmen will often prate of " right
and justice."

History, at any rate, fails to show that much good
was ever done by the alleged intentions of men in the
possession of power to secure the cause of justice and
humanity instead of the " sacred egoism " of the nation.
King Henry IV of France and his minister Sully perhaps
sincerely desired to reform Europe along the lines of
right and justice ; but who dares deny that if the King
had attempted to carry out this grandiose scheme, rivers
of blood would have deluged the whole European
Continent ; while in the best case—in the event of
success—a merely transitory French supremacy would
have been the sole tangible fruit of this beautiful dream.

Political idealists should bear in mind that Napoleon I

justified his interminable wars, dreadful devastations, and unexampled aggressions by his intention to secure to Europe a régime of peace and righteousness. He expressly avowed that, when finally victory had crowned his arms, all the great international problems would be solved by congresses and conferences in accordance with the principle of justice. The rôle proposed for the League of Nations to-day, Napoleon would assign to an alliance of sovereigns—of course on condition that *he* should be recognised as the most potent and exalted among them.

Napoleon III was far more idealistic than his grand-uncle Napoleon I. I consider the former the most idealistic among the leading statesmen of modern times. He opened up the widest field for lofty ideals in practical politics ; he waged a war for the unity of a foreign nation ; he proclaimed from the throne that the fate of nations must not be settled without those intimately concerned being consulted. Yet even he looked at world-events through egoistic spectacles, and saw his duty to humanity only where the interests of his country were at stake. Certainly he served the cause of justice, but only where it was, in his opinion, useful for him and his people. For example, he considered Italian unity useful ; he made war and shed French blood in its behalf ; only, however—be it noted—in behalf of *Northern* Italy. For the " greater Italy " ideal of Garibaldi he was not enthusiastic : that was not compatible with French interests. As for German unity, he feared it, and did all he could to thwart it. The true cause of the war of 1870–1871 was Bismarck's conviction that the French would never be friendlily disposed to the idea of German unity, and that the only road from Berlin to Munich was via Paris.

Napoleon loudly advocated the principle of the *plébiscite*. Only, however, in those cases where he knew in advance that the result would be favourable from his point of view. He demanded the *plébiscite* in the region taken from the Italians because he had already arranged for the necessary majority; but he considered the popular sanction quite superfluous when he wanted to get possession of the left bank of the Rhine, and also Belgium, well knowing that there was no prospect of a majority for him in either of those quarters.

In spite of his idealism, Napoleon III engaged in three European wars, i.e. the Crimean War (1854), the Italian War (1859), and the German War (1870). Besides these, his calculating egoism contributed to a fourth—the Austro-Prussian War of 1866.

With the exception of Napoleon III, Gladstone was the most idealistic political leader. Yet notwithstanding his noble principles, Gladstone too became a conqueror. He reduced Egypt to subjection to England by force; he had Alexandria (an open port) bombarded; and he embarked on the disastrous campaign against the Boers for the maintenance of British suzerainty, though only a short time before he had declared that he disapproved of the suzerainty, which (he stated) "had been acquired by unlawful means and was moreover useless." The consequence of his idealistic intervention in the interests of the Bulgarians was the sanguinary Russo-Turkish War in which England herself barely escaped getting embroiled, in spite of Gladstone's excellent intentions.

The single act of his really in keeping with his principles, the solitary unselfish step he ever took in the course of his long political career, was the cession of Corfu to the Greeks—a proceeding which inflicted immense injury upon Great Britain. In the late Great War the possession of that island would have been of incalculable value to the British cause.

Wilson, too—the last great political idealist—perpetrated a tremendous wrong upon humanity. From the sublime character of his professed principles and the profound depth of his convictions, he had the temerity to entangle his nation in the most gigantic war ever yet waged and at the subsequent Peace Conference to sit in judgment upon the living and the dead ; uninformed, having no competent knowledge of the situation, to decide the fate of nations—in short, to inflict tremendous ruin in the name of justice. In the European labyrinth of geography, traditions, the manifold historical and economic interests, and national sentiments, Wilson, intoxicated with the new wine of his Fourteen Points, succeeded in working as much mischief in Europe as an infuriated elephant let loose in a carefully tended flower-garden.

The Great War was a stupendous event that must shatter one's confidence in the efficacy of an idealist policy. We witnessed such a confused conglomeration of the most hyper-selfish imperialistic motives allied with the purest, noblest, and most exalted, that faith in the triumph of right and justice could not help taking to her death-bed. Who could believe in altruism, when on every hand were heard " the rights of the small nations," " self-determination," and other shibboleths, glibly pronounced by the very people who kept—nay, still keep—millions under the yoke ?—when those who reiterated " a just peace, without penalties or annexations," have crippled, mutilated, and sentenced to the (economic) galleys, to drag out a weary existence, all

the defeated nations, by virtue of instruments miscalled
" Peace Treaties " ?

After such disenchanting experiences, Bismarck's
philosophy (cold as it is) is more acceptable to me than
Gladstone's ; and I am disposed to believe in those
politicians who confess *sans phrase* that they are concerned only with their own country's cause, in preference
to those who are constantly preaching peace and justice
and denying their national egoism.

To-day also I see the highest and most salutary
service for humanity at large in the apparently narrower
sphere of service for one's own people. The cause of all
mankind can be served most effectually by the uplifting
of individual nations. Progress towards an age more
perfect and nobler than the present can only be achieved
by driving out the ravening wolf from the heart of man
by the power of Christian morality, and implanting in
its stead a sense of justice and respect for inalienable
human rights, so that the observance of those principles
becomes the true interest of the State.

The only thing I regret and disapprove in Bismarck
was that his patriotism was so often mixed with
cynicism, and his expression thereof always with an
intentional rudeness. While it was certainly a great
advantage for England and France to pretend to humanitarian justification for all their most imperialistic
designs, it was detrimental for Germany that Bismarck's
attitude gave an egoistic appearance even to the most
pacific and most moderate steps he ever took, and that
since he passed from the scene they only were regarded
at Berlin as real statesmen and worthy disciples of the
Iron Chancellor who followed a similar policy of harsh-
ness and contempt for mankind in general—who affected
to despise public opinion and to be ashamed of and

disapprove every policy that was not uncompromisingly realistic. This tradition and Bismarck's language became positively noxious after Germany, from being a Continental Power, had attained the dignity of a World Power. This fact itself naturally created much jealousy. She came into conflict with new spheres of interest, and in Berlin the itch for the limelight became ever greater and caution ever less. Bismarck's ponderous manner of speaking and realistic doctrine facilitated the formation of that general world-coalition under whose united blows the mighty German Empire collapsed.

The contrasting mentalities of Bismarck and Gladstone also led to personal antipathy. At any rate, Bismarck severely condemned Gladstone and pronounced him a danger to the community. He exclaimed (à propos of a note in which a certain Russian minister was styled a humbug and fanatic): " *Then he is like Gladstone !* " The German said of the Englishman that " he would ruin his country and jeopardise the world by his radical domestic policy on the one hand and his pandering to revolutionary Pan-Slavism on the other." Young Herbert Bismarck wrote with profound contempt of the British Premier that " *It is not worth while to discuss foreign politics with him* " (i.e. Gladstone) : " *he knows so little about it.*"

Nothing could be more natural than that the England of Gladstone and the Germany of Bismarck should become estranged from each other.

The new orientation of England became apparent first of all in the Balkan Question, towards which she began to manifest a changed attitude. Whereas formerly Great Britain, in both the drafting and the execution of the Berlin Treaty, had taken the side of the Turks, Gladstone now came out as the advocate of Russian aspirations. Bismarck maintained a cautious defensive against this new manœuvre of England. He would not, however, allow himself to be provoked into opposition to her. He did everything in his power to frustrate any intimate co-operation of England and Russia, lest the two rivals should get accustomed to each other in their struggle against the third; well knowing that a common foe can the most easily make friends with his old antagonists.

I have no desire to enter into particulars of these diplomatic intrigues; sufficient to emphasise that Bismarck attained his object, and in the two chief problems of the day—the Albanian and the Greek Questions—he managed with consummate skill to effect a compromise without the Anglo-Russian and the Austro-Hungarian attitudes coming into sharp opposition. He moved so skilfully that he won even the confidence of Turkey. Though shortly before he had stood for the policy of carving up the Ottoman Empire, he now cast his whole weight in the scale for the Padishah, and thus brought the Sultan into the German sphere of influence.

2. Improvement in the Strained Relations between Germany and France

England's alienation from us—a political event of far-reaching importance—had naturally a visible influence upon the French policy of Bismarck. While in the preceding years the German Chancellor had attempted to stifle the spirit of *revanche* by means of bluster and terrorism, he now laid himself out to gain the good-will of the French people and thus appease them as far as possible. And in this more benign method he succeeded.

Up to this period France was fascinated by the

5

Rhine to the exclusion of everything else. Since the *débâcle* of Napoleon III, all eyes were turned towards Alsace-Lorraine. Public opinion and even experienced politicians were afraid of that " devilish Bismarck." They lived in constant perturbation lest this new " Antichrist " should avail himself of some excuse to strike them again to the earth and thus retard their ultimate recovery. At the time of the Berlin Congress, however, this feeling had already somewhat subsided. Bismarck had succeeded in creating in the minds of the leading French statesmen the confidence that they might safely engage in colonial enterprises so far as he was concerned. And it was a stroke of luck for Bismarck that simultaneously with the accession to power of Gladstone, when a hostile England would have done much to accentuate the hostility of France, French public opinion took a decidedly friendly turn towards Germany. The French Premier, Jules Ferry, the most practical, the boldest, and most energetic statesman of the Republic, understood Bismarck, credited his pacific intentions, and dared to direct his (Ferry's) attention to the acquisition of the rich country of Tunis. (March—May 1887.)

The German Chancellor now quickly seized the opportunity thus presented. Not for weakening his rival, not for embarrassing France ; but, on the contrary, he made an effort to conciliate her and attach her more closely to the Fatherland. With this object he promoted the colonial ambitions of Ferry to the utmost of his power, and Germany became a sort of rearguard of France. German diplomacy undertook to reassure Turkey and Italy, whose trade-routes were thus crossed by the French advance. In Morocco, too (May 1880), Bismarck espoused the French cause : he was willing to support France even to an extent where Bülow and Bethmann-

Hollweg went to the brink of a war in defence of German interests.

The German Chancellor made it clear that he would welcome the spread of French influence on the Latin race and would not look unfavourably at the conquests of the French overseas. This consummate political schemer was aware that to place warnings in the way of his defeated neighbours, whether on the Rhine or elsewhere, would but fan the smouldering embers of revenge and perhaps lead to another war ; while the successes of France abroad would divert her thoughts, for the time at least, from the soreness of Alsace-Lorraine.

To our age belongs the honour of creating a precedent for the policy of thwarting a defeated enemy everywhere, in all his attempts to recover, to regain his health and strength—a policy supported by not a few specious arguments, but which is nevertheless bad and recoils on the whole of humanity. Even the victor is swept away by the great moral and material avalanche inevitably caused by the demolition and wrecking of serious factors in the civilisation and progress of Europe.

In the Europe of to-day it is impossible with impunity to condemn nations to perpetual suffering, misery, or slavery. A nation can get rid of her dangerous criminal members by executing them ; an individual of his enemy by killing him ; but it is impossible to eliminate entire nations from the ranks of the living. A guillotine or a poniard for decapitating or stabbing a whole nation has yet to be invented by our scientists. The moribund nation, unable to survive, will always be a source of infection for her neighbours—if not otherwise, then by spreading the deadly diseases of Bolshevism and Anarchy.

All the methods of murdering nations hitherto applied

have failed to stand the test. The Jews were dispersed,
yet they have retained their power, and to-day they are
even an organised State. The Poles were separated,
the Serbs, Greeks, and Bulgarians subjected to alien
tyranny—their very names for a time erased from the
map—yet these persecuted pariahs have seen their
resurrection, they have proved stronger than all the
treaties made for their annihilation ; all the paper pacts
against them have proved no more durable than such
material usually is.

Bismarck was cognisant of these things. The inveterate foe of France, he was urged by his nerves or his
sentiments to drastic measures, yet his wisdom withheld
him from attempting to frustrate a nation's natural
development, her economic reinvigoration and independence. Bismarck therefore kept aloof from the merest
semblance of meddling with the internal affairs of France.
When Gambetta became Premier (November 1881)—
Gambetta, the uncompromising representative of *revanche*
whose dissentient compatriots declared " *Gambetta c'est
la guerre !* "—the Chancellor proclaimed that he should
respect French independence. And when somewhat
later (18th November 1883) the Legitimists sounded him,
he emphatically assured them that he should never make
war on France on account of her form of government,
though he thought a kingdom instead of the Republic
might eventually lead to war, as the former would the
more easily obtain allies and would not disintegrate the
country so much as the latter. He would by all means
respect the right of France to settle her own form of
government. " Should she become a kingdom, he would
have less confidence in the preservation of peace ; but
at any rate he would wait and see whether the new
régime did really mean war. But in any case, he repeated,

he would never interfere in the internal affairs of the French people " (26th January 1884).

In many respects Bismarck was a man of brute force, a believer in the efficacy of " smashing a way through "—and for this we hear him loudly condemned even at this day. But, for that matter, many blatant apostles of " freedom," of the " right of self-determination " and " human solidarity," are disposed to follow the example of this out-of-date, retrograde old statesman. The old-fashioned Man of Iron paid more respect to the rights of others than do the modern tribunes of the people, who would make a *casus belli* of the question as to who is the rightful King of Hungary according to the millennial constitution ; or than do the ranters about Wilsonian principles, who restrict our self-determination by means of that very violence and brute force they denounce as so criminal when directed against themselves, because we are weak, and at the same time approve and applaud the right of the Bolsheviks to massacre millions, to wage universal war on the bourgeoisie, and to set up the most awful reign of terror that this world has ever experienced, because they are strong !

3. EXTENSION OF GERMANY'S COLONIAL EMPIRE

The progress of France in Africa was followed and counterbalanced by the British venture in Egypt (where Gladstone, so to speak, came a cropper over his own principles)—an enterprise not methodically prepared by the accumulated wisdom of Downing Street, but improvised by the imperialism in British blood and the admirable initiative of the Briton himself. This imperialistic instinct, by a quick stroke, lays prostrate the Egyptian national movement struggling manfully against European influence, hustles aside the French, who hitherto were understood to enjoy the same rights, and makes the British nation the real lords of the land of the Pharaohs (September 1882).

This bold move became in time an immense advantage for England ; it won for her the *point d'appui* which enabled her to display a tremendous power during the Great War, securing her uninterrupted communication with India ; though this at first involved the British Empire in serious danger, since it put her at variance with her chief ally, France, who could not look on coolly at England establishing herself by force and injustice just where her own colonial appetite was so great, when she contemplated the foundation of an overseas empire on the banks of the Nile in fair Egypt, on the former battleground of Napoleon, to which she was attracted by many traditions and not a few real interests.

What ought Bismarck to do in this situation ? Should he stand by the French ? Should he bid for their good-will by adopting a decided anti-British attitude ? Should he try to humiliate England ? should he imitate Palmerston, who was so fond of driving his opponent into a corner, to publicly humble him ? in order to enhance the glory and prestige of his country —as, for instance, on account of the Egyptian imbroglio he had humiliated France in 1840 by causing the fall of Thiers ? Why should Bismarck not trip up Gladstone, to punish him for his Germanophobia ?

Or should he proceed later, as Germany did in the case of Morocco, by demanding compensation for Egypt, and on principle refuse to permit others to divide up and apportion continents without reckoning with him ?

As Prussian Minister, when he had desired to upset

the existing balance of power, he did not scruple to exploit the Anglo-French dispute to its lowest depths.

But he no longer thought of Cæsarean operations, attended with such grave risks; he was now as cautious as formerly he was bold. He frequently changed his instruments, adapted them to the changed and changing situation; but his chief aims were rigidly consistent; they were never modified to suit merely passing needs.

And his dearest wish was now to preserve peace, to isolate France and avoid antagonism which might raise up enemies for Germany and friends for France.

With this object in view he desired to make use of the Egyptian question in the first place for keeping the Anglo-French quarrel alive, well aware that as long as Paris was afraid of the English, Germany had nothing to fear from the French.

Bismarck, however, abstained from inciting anyone to war, as Napoleon III incited Prussia and Austria in 1866, as now war might disturb the balance of power in a way the consequences of which were unforeseeable and incalculable, while he was satisfied with the actual state of things. The French Emperor, too, had fared badly, for the war he desired had disappointed his hopes.

Equally Bismarck was unable to make up his mind to afford prompt and vigorous aid to the Quai d'Orsay and thus win the friendship of France. He feared lest by doing so he should make an enemy of England without success in winning Paris and making her forget Alsace-Lorraine. He thought that the alarmed English Cabinet might relinquish its autocracy in Egypt and itself make advances to Paris. He was apprehensive of the Anglo-French condominium in Egypt, the alliance of the two Western Powers, the victim of Gambetta's policy. Bismarck forbore to take any particular line of action, or to play any leading rôle in the question ; he feared lest open intervention would dispose France and England to settle their dispute and become reconciled. Subsequent developments fully justified his cautious attitude. Under his successors the active intervention of Germany in the colonial question, together with the extension of her navy, drove the Anglo-French antagonism into the background : Egypt and Morocco, formerly the hotbeds of strife in Bismarck's time, now became the nests of entente.

Bismarck approached nearer to England. He reassured Gladstone. In London (September 1882) he stated his willingness to agree to anything England desired in the country of the Pyramids. All the same he fought shy of exposing himself for the sake of England ; he would not risk arousing the antipathy of the Anglophobe nations, and in particular he would not be a party to the humiliation of France. Being anxious for the success of his work in Russia, he feared that an alliance with London would create a bad impression in St. Petersburg and render difficult a smooth running of the new relations, for the Russians were strongly opposed to the occupation by the British of strong positions near Constantinople, the hub of the Mohammedan world. They would look askance at Bismarck in this matter harnessing himself to the car of Great Britain. Bismarck gave therefore an evasive answer (4th September 1882), when Gladstone, seeing that without the good-will of the Germans he might have to face grave dangers, asked whether the Empire was disposed to conclude an alliance with Great Britain.

By such astuteness Bismarck reached his aims :

he improved his relations with England ; the Anglo-French antagonism became more and more acute, without either Russia or France gaining any valid excuse to charge Germany with hostility towards herself, and without the Anglo-German *rapprochement* driving Paris and St. Petersburg into each other's arms.

An entirely unforeseen circumstance, however, jeopardised the stability of this pleasing edifice, which might easily have driven Bismarck willy-nilly to an anti-English attitude.

Apart from his prime object, which was the improvement of his relations with the Great Powers, there was also a second consideration.

French success abroad, the strengthening of British power in Egypt, the colonial ambitions of Italy, all had a repercussion in Germany: The rising generation of Teutons longed to see the flag of the Fatherland waving over the shores of Africa and Asia.

The old Chancellor condemned the aspirations of the colonising " Jungen " : he wanted no colonies, which might necessitate the modification of his continental policy, and possibly involve him in wars abroad and political campaigns at home. In spite of this, however, he held that Germany had a right to and an interest in the possession of modest colonies, about which he hoped there would be no difficulties raised, in return for his diplomatic complaisance over Egypt.

But Gladstone perpetrated an amazing blunder. Instead of promoting the German co-operation, which he so ardently desired, by acquiescing in the really moderate demands of Bismarck, he frustrated Germany's efforts at expansion—or rather he winked at his subordinates doing so. In this he was scarcely actuated by any conscious political aim, for at this period Gladstone felt the need of German assistance : it was rather that he gave full rein to that instinctive jealousy which the English always feel against any Power than themselves daring to acquire possessions overseas. His attitude, however, was none the less wrong. The situation of Great Britain was now too serious to let loose British imperialistic instincts in all directions. The British arms had sustained defeat in the Sudan (November 1883) ; their advance in Egypt was everywhere accompanied by jealousy : in St. Petersburg it was feared lest England should control Constantinople and the Dardanelles via Egypt, even more strongly than formerly, consequently the people on the banks of the Neva were considering what would be the most effective counterstroke.

They would try to get to India across Central Asia. In spite of Gladstone's Russophilism (or perhaps counting on that very fact, and on the known weakness of the English Premier), they attempted to occupy a position in Central Asia capable of off-setting the new accession of British power in Suez and rendering it possible for the Czar to humble another Palmerston or Beaconsfield. The Autocrat was anxious to increase his influence in Afghanistan equally at least with that of England on the Nile. The stronger England might be near Constantinople the closer the Czar desired to get to the Himalayas. Though his policy was as yet in an early and undeveloped stage, its effects could already be discerned, and Dilke, as early as September 1882, complained to Herbert Bismarck about the Russian offensive in Asia.

The situation of England was not improved by Jules Ferry — luckily for Bismarck — becoming Premier of France (February 1883). This was the man who had the courage to go hand in hand with the German Chancellor and by his assistance to acquire Tunis. It would now be seen whether Ferry, supported by the Germans, would be able to weaken the British supremacy in Egypt. Would Bismarck foreshadow an eventual Anglophobe policy by concluding a definite peace-pact with Paris under the leadership of Ferry, and thus cause England to find herself up against a united Europe?

This danger was all the more imminent as the European conference (28th June to 2nd August 1884), whose business it should have been to improve the financial situation of Egypt, failed to do so, on which the Egyptian Question became once more acute.

Bismarck felt his power. He acted with ruthless vigour (spring 1884). He took no pains to soften his voice. He, in a manner of speaking, levied blackmail ; played *à deux tableaux*. He stoutly declared that if England would not help him to satisfy his colonising aspirations, he would turn his back on her (April 1884—January 1885). He was willing to make terms with England, but if she were adverse to him he would throw all his weight into the scale with France against England. Hitherto it had not been for his own interests in Egypt that he had sided with the English, but because he hoped that his attitude would induce England to adopt a pro-German policy. If he were disappointed in this respect, it was in his power to change his policy without the least difficulty or drawback.

Bismarck, however, merely cooked a small joint at this large fire. He blustered and thundered, convinced that a display of energy would enable him soon to reach his goal—that England would not risk losing Egypt for the sake of Angra-Pequeña. The English attitude was offensive to him ; nevertheless he wished to avoid offending British public opinion. He would not take any undue advantage of his favourable situation. He was not afraid of quarrelling with Gladstone, but he wished to avoid seriously wounding the *amour propre* of the British people, who after all were the real rulers of England. His simulated rage did not carry him a hairbreadth further than he intended to go. He emphasised the possibility of co-operating with Great Britain in the future whenever he wished to do so ; he would leave no thorn in the side of England. For the moment he would not enter into alliance with her, but he wished to leave the way open to do so at any time in the future.

His ideas are best illustrated by his attitude in the Heligoland affair. On the occasion of Gladstone's friendly overtures Bismarck took the opportunity to hint at the exchange of the island, then in the possession of Great Britain. He argued that the island was of no use to England except in the almost unthinkable event of a war with Germany, while it was invaluable for the Fatherland in that it increased the defensive power of the Empire and guarded the estuary of the Elbe against attack. He, however, dropped the project on perceiving that the British people were averse to it. He would not acquire it by any sort of violence or pressure, lest he should provoke ill-will. Notwithstanding his secure tenure of power, his only aim was to preserve the actual colonial possessions of Germany from being jeopardised by a quarrel with England. With this object he made to France even more important advances than before. He launched at Paris (4th August 1884) his schemes for a coalition (as in the eighteenth century) of all the other States against the maritime supremacy of Great Britain, with the slogan of "armed neutrality." France, the second naval Power, was to be appointed to the leadership of this coalition, and thus she would play a predominant part in the world-situation. Evidently Bismarck designed to use France as a battering-ram and to egg her on to a more intensively Anglophobe policy. In this he failed, however. Jules Ferry was not disposed to burn the bridge connecting him with *Albion le perfide.* He was too astute to be caught napping. His new-found friendship with the Germans did not blind him to the fact that Germany was the chief enemy of France. In spite of all, Bismarck succeeded in creating a co-operation between the Germans and the French—a thing seemingly impossible, and which enhanced accordingly the prestige of Germany in London. Ferry undertook (October 1884) to take no step with regard to Egypt without first consulting Germany. In the Congo Question Bismarck acted in concert with Ferry, and by their united pressure wrung concessions from England.

The tempers of the two antagonists improved so much that Barrère, a French diplomat, remarked to Herbert Bismarck that a "Franco-German alliance would be an excellent thing for them " (the French), and Camperon, the French War Minister, even dared to express to the German Military Attaché the opinion that " a Franco-German Alliance could dominate the world and preserve peace ; it would only be necessary to let bygones be bygones."

Realising this situation, Britain had to yield. She had never manifested an open opposition, and had only played her cards behind the scenes to frustrate the colonial expansion of Germany. The British Premier shifted the responsibility for the Government's actions first on to the Foreign Secretary, afterwards on to the Secretary for the Colonies, again on to the local officials, later on to the individual colonies, until finally (7th March 1885) after the negotiations acrimoniously carried on by Herbert Bismarck, the Chancellor triumphed. England agreed to accede to all his concrete demands, while Bismarck, on his part, once more agreed to back the British schemes in Egypt.

A piquant incident occurred during these negotiations. Dilke publicly announced (5th October 1884) his intention of repudiating the international agreements on the plea of necessity! Herbert Bismarck was inexpressibly shocked, and pointed out that " if a State thus broke her solemn engagements, no treaty would be worth the paper it was written on, and the entire structure of international law would fall to the ground."

Ah! but a few decades later, at a much more tragic moment, when the destiny of the European Continent hung on a breath, it fell to the lot of a certain other German statesman to make a similar declaration to that of the Englishman. Then did not the English people wax wrath! Such an unheard-of thing! A solemn treaty a mere scrap of paper!—as though such an announcement were the grossest insult to that nation one of whose ministers had been the first to propose it!

Bismarck won in the battle of politics begun by Gladstone. The defeat of the British statesman was not limited to his having to give way on the question of the German colonies; the world-position of Great Britain was shaken when amidst her difficulties in Egypt she chose to fall out with the mightiest factor on the Continent. While Beaconsfield, in friendly relations with Andrássy and Bismarck, was able to stop the victorious Muscovites at the very gates of Stamboul, Gladstone alienated Germany and thus became powerless to prevent Russia approaching India. Nothing remained for him but to sign the most unsatisfactory agreement at the foot of the Himalayas. His own policy was turned against him. He had coquetted with Russia, and now she had him in her toils: he would be hard put to it to avoid war with her. He had fulminated against the Turks, yet now his only hope of rescue from his miserable plight lay in the objects of his erstwhile scorn allowing the Straits to be opened for him, in order that the mighty British fleet might reach the Black Sea and come to grips with his redoubtable foe. But how dare he hope for this when, as Bismarck said, "he had stupidly squandered the traditional influence of Great Britain over the Sublime Porte"? How could he expect to find his way out of the labyrinth, when Turkey could only be induced by the pressure of Kálnoky and Bismarck to alter her anti-Gladstonian course; and Bismarck, owing partly to the policy of Gladstone, was far nearer to Russia than to England, and consequently advised entirely to the contrary (March—June 1885)? How could Gladstone hope to attain his object when even France had been alienated from him by his policy in Egypt, so that no one accepted his attitude? He had isolated himself, and so had lost the game, besides having the mortification to see that he had "backed the wrong horse."

In contrast with Gladstone's failure, Bismarck was successful all along the line. He pulled off all his colonial demands. He brought it home to England with the logic of cold facts that she could not do without him. For Gladstone's failure British public opinion did not blame Bismarck, but rather the ineptitude of its own Government ; so that the co-operation of England with Germany soon came once more within the purview of practical politics. And while the road between Berlin and London remained open, and while the relations between Berlin and St. Petersburg became more and more amicable, barriers were erected between London and Paris as well as between London and St. Petersburg. Thus Bismarck accomplished his prime object and also his secondary aims. He strengthened his diplomatic position in Europe, set France and England at loggerheads, and obtained the colonies he coveted.

4. Renewal of the Three Emperors' Alliance

Amidst the daily events of the political world Bismarck worked indefatigably, utilising those events for building a system of alliances suitable to preserve peace as well as to safeguard the spoils of Germany's last war—i.e. Alsace-Lorraine.

The alliance with us was insufficient for him. He returned to his old pet scheme, the Alliance of the Three Emperors—not, however, instead of, but as a complement to, the Dual Alliance. He desired to renew the Alliance of the Three Emperors separately from the Dual Alliance of 1879, since, in his belief, this would form a more effectual guarantee of peace, to which he staunchly adhered, as owing to the spread of Socialism he was afraid that a world-war would sweep away the existing social order. As he subsequently declared (1887), " the defeated nations would hereafter hold their Governments responsible for their misfortunes. A defeated Russian autocracy would be superseded by a republic ; a defeated Austria-Hungary would dissolve into a number of small republics ; and even in a defeated Germany the monarchical principle and middle-class society would be imperilled.'' Further, Bismarck adhered to the Three Emperors' Alliance because he expected therefrom a strong domestic policy which would drive the beasts of Revolution and Radicalism back to their lairs and prove an impregnable bulwark of Conservatism.

Was Bismarck right ? Which was likely to prove the more effective in counteracting the spirit of destruction : force ?—or gradual progress towards liberty and self-government ? The iron hand of an autocrat ?—or real constitutional life ?

I do not propose to discuss this interesting problem ; but merely to emphasise that though revolutionary propaganda should be met with vigorous repression, and though at the proper time stern measures are inevitable, yet the sole remedy against revolution is personal liberty and respect for law founded on a suitable autonomy.

The famous Junker statesman saw in Gladstone's rash reforming spirit the harbinger of revolution ; he considered France, Italy, Spain, and England as democratic States, the sure and certain victims of revolution ; and thought that the dominions of the Emperors alone were safe from that scourge.

Events, however, have proved to the contrary. Parliamentary England, Italy, and Spain are monarchies still ; France is the most conservative of European States ; Italy the sworn foe of Bolshevism ; while the thrones of the Three Emperors have gone down before the onslaughts of revolution. In spite of all, revolution has proved the most disastrous in those countries where the people enjoyed the least liberty !

6

If anyone should seek to explain this fact by the circumstances that the most autocratic States happened to be those defeated in the Great War, my answer is: Italy, France, Belgium, Serbia, and Rumania also came very near final disaster without the critical military situation destroying their home fronts; while in the territories of the Three Emperors it was the internal disintegration that was the principal cause of their absolute military collapse. And the explanation is easy. The necessary repressive measures are much easier of application in a country where order is maintained by a broad-based Government, supported by wide strata of the population—by an active law-abiding people—than where the government is vested in a few autocratic ministers, relying on the passive obedience of the general public. The Czarist régime failed to prove itself a conservative factor. On the contrary, it was Czarism that paved the way for the bloodiest and most devastating revolution this world has ever seen. The absolute power wielded by the Czars sowed the seeds of Bolshevism, the dragon's teeth of Red terror. One extreme engendered another, tending downwards towards Avernus. Only in a social order based on blind obedience, such as was Czarist Russia, could Leninism take root and blossom—that Leninism which is but an Asiatic form of Czarism plus Anarchy. The Russian people could never have escaped their present tribulation by the reactionary measures of Czar Alexander III and Nicholas II—nothing less than systematic reforms, far-reaching and drastic at the proper time, could have saved them.

But to take up again the thread of the relation of events. Badly as Bismarck needed the Alliance of the Three Emperors, he did not hurry it on. He patiently waited. He knew that if one runs after an alliance, or solicits the friendship of others, he usually finds himself at a disadvantage. Though it is true that in 1879 Bismarck took the initiative with regard to us and made overtures to Andrássy, the circumstances were quite unusual. At that time he envisaged the possibility of an immediate attack. He was afraid that if Andrássy resigned before the conclusion of an alliance he might have difficulties with his successor. Now, however, the situation was different : he had in his pocket the assurance of the Dual Alliance ; he had no longer any cause for fear from any quarter. To run after the Russians would be construed at St. Petersburg as a sure sign of his weakness. He knew that he could accomplish his object of restoring the Alliance of the Three Emperors if only the Czar had learnt his lesson from the past, was duly impressed by the Dual Alliance, feared the spread of Nihilism and the revolutionary spirit in Russia, and looked for aid to his two great and conservative neighbours. In that case he felt convinced that the Czar would knock at the door of Berlin.

And this actually came to pass. The Czar took the first step towards Germany. But no sooner had the Autocrat done so, than Bismarck proceeded in the matter with great vigour and re-established the Alliance of the Three Emperors at Vienna (18th June 1881). Haymerle, like his predecessor Andrássy, showed a preference for the Dual Alliance, but he had not sufficient courage openly to contradict the Chancellor. Had he done so, it would have been in vain, for Bismarck had a poor opinion of Haymerle.

When the Chancellor first met him, he remarked that he had much difficulty in understanding his reasoning, for he was by no means lucid. When they differed with regard to Egypt, Bismarck dryly observed that

" people in Vienna could not see more than a few days ahead." Later on, in conversation with a British statesman, he referred with raillery to the vacillating character of his Viennese colleague, who—Bismarck said— " always uttered an emphatic ' No ' twice on getting up in the morning in order to fortify himself against committing himself to anything during the day." When Haymerle addressed a sharp note to Berlin on the economic treaty, Bismarck flew into a rage and replied that " Germany was great enough to tolerate such insolence for a while, but if Vienna dared to treat the minor Balkan States in a similar fashion, she must not be surprised to find herself surrounded by enemies." It is regrettable that our diplomats not infrequently justified Bismarck's scathing remarks by combining a pusillanimous action with a braggart pen ; too few of them have acquired the art of true statesmanship, of uniting the *suaviter in modo* and the *fortiter in re*. I hope my Hungarian compatriots have not inherited this unfortunate trait, but may they ever remember that only a combination of lofty courage and never-failing courtesy can avail us in our present difficulties.

The new Three Emperors' Alliance was different from the old one. Unlike the former, it was not entirely based on conservative principles, but stipulated a common policy in regard to the Balkans, whereby we lost the opportunity of exploiting the advantageous situation conferred upon us by the Berlin Treaty and our alliance with Germany for extending our economic and moral influence over the Balkans and finally supplanting the Russians. Likewise the new treaty differed from the old one, and was unfavourable to us in so far as it was directed against England ; as in the affairs of the Straits, *expressis verbis* at least it took up a pro-Russian, anti-British attitude, although in the East the interests of England were more identical with ours than were those of Russia, and England had never been in our way, while Czardom signified a positive danger for us.

The aspiration of Russia has ever been, and always will be so long as she is a Great Power, to have a right of way for her fleet through the Dardanelles to the Mediterranean and the Adriatic, but at the same time to close the Straits for foreign vessels and thus preserve the Black Sea coast immune from attack. This beautiful dream very nearly materialised when the great Czar Nicholas I espoused the cause of Sultan Mahomet against Mahomet Ali, Pasha of Egypt, and in reward for his valuable services the Autocrat demanded that the Padishah should, whenever required, open the Dardanelles to him but keep them closed against all others—in short, that the Sultan should fill the post of gatekeeper to the Czar.

A conspicuous instance of the durability of interests wherein geography and power are related is furnished by the fact that both Lenin and Tchitcherin in altogether different circumstances attempted Nicholas I's temporary achievement, and that Mustapha Kemal indeed undertook, like Sultan Mahomet, to guard for a time the south-western gate of Russia in return for Russia's assistance in his revolutionary schemes.

At the time of the formation of the Three Emperors' Alliance, however, the Russians, under the effect of the Berlin Treaty, were of necessity more modest. They could not think of monopolies ; they had to be satisfied with the closure of the Straits being made an international obligation on the part of Turkey—an obligation from which, without the consent of all the signatory Powers (of whom Russia was one), Turkey could not deviate. Yet even this less pretentious demand was contrary to the views of England : she desired to make the opening and the closing entirely a matter of the Sultan's " free will "—which, in plain terms, meant that Britannia would be able to rule the waves of the Black Sea by cajoling or intimidating the Sublime Porte as occasion required.

On this question the Alliance of the Three Emperors adopted the attitude of Russia, and declared that, should the Sultan open the Straits without the consent of Europe, he would forfeit the defence guaranteed to him by the Powers signatory to the Berlin Treaty.

In the Balkan Question the allies agreed to respect each other's rights and interests, and to come to an agreement with each other prior to any alteration of the *status quo*. Besides these general obligations, the allies also agreed on certain definite questions. They recognised the right of Austria-Hungary to transform the occupation of Bosnia-Herzegovina into an annexation ; they engaged not to prevent the union of Bulgaria and East Rumelia if the desire were mutual and spontaneous. Further, they bound themselves to oppose the occupation of the Balkan line by the Turks, though the latter were accorded that right by the Berlin Treaty ; and, moreover, to protest in the case of Bulgaria attacking Turkey or reviving the Macedonian Question.

Thus Bismarck's work was complete. He had renewed the Alliance that he considered best for his Fatherland, but which had hitherto been prevented by the crisis in the East. Andrássy's achievement, the Dual Alliance, continued, though with an addition desired by the German Chancellor but not by him (Andrássy). The questions remained, with what spirit the dead letter of the Alliance would be animated ; whether a common policy for the

Balkans by Austria-Hungary and Russia would not again be found impossible ; and whether the clashing interests which had once before wrecked the Alliance of the Three Emperors would not again become acute ?

Which would prevail—the dead letter or the living spirit ?

5. THE TRIPLE ALLIANCE

The colonising successes of the French, especially their acquisition of Tunis, gave Bismarck the opportunity for a new alliance. Italy had long cast covetous eyes in the direction of the port of Bizerta and its valuable hinterland. She looked on enviously at the progress of France and sought Germany's assistance in checking the further expansion of her Latin sister.

Bismarck had little confidence in an Italian alliance. He considered the Italian Government weak, incapable of carrying out an unpopular policy and executing a treaty denounced by public opinion (October 1880). He could not believe that Italy would dare to draw the sword against France (December 1881). He did not rate very highly the military strength of Italy. In spite of these drawbacks, however, the Chancellor desired the alliance.

To decline the treaty would weaken the monarchy in Italy, whereas the proposed alliance would strengthen it. The far-seeing statesman perceived also that refusal would cause Italy to make overtures to France ; and that in the event of war the mere ill-will of the Italians would lock up the Austro-Hungarian armies on the Isonzo and thus prevent their operating on the Vistula.

And as Bismarck held that if he wanted to get something out of the Italians it would be a mistake to run after them, he first adopted an attitude of indifference towards the Italian approach, and proposed as a preliminary that they should first of all come to terms with Vienna and abandon their irredentism.

Kálnoky, Austro-Hungarian Minister for Foreign Affairs—who succeeded Haymerle—was less exacting than Bismarck : he did not insist on a formal repudiation by the Italians of their irredentist claims. Such moderation brought to birth the Triple Alliance, consisting of Germany, Austria-Hungary, and Italy (20th May 1882), side by side with the previously existing alliances—that of the Three Emperors and the Dual Alliance.

The terms of this later treaty were especially onerous for us, for they bound us to render military aid to Italy in the event of her being attacked by France, while Italy undertook no similar reciprocal obligation towards any party, promising us military aid only in the event of our being attacked by a coalition of Great Powers. That which William I erroneously saw in Andrássy's Dual Alliance, on account of which he so long declined Bismarck's advice, we had now accepted with regard to Italy, by shouldering unilateral burdens. It is astonishing that Kálnoky neglected to insist on the demand that Italy should support us in case of a Russian attack.

Germany fared much better by the treaty, for in return for the assistance she was bound to render against France, Italy undertook a similar reciprocal obligation towards Germany.

For Italy the treaty was a splendid bargain ; she was to be protected against France by both Germany and Austria-Hungary, while Italy had merely to assist Germany, and that only against France ! This is all the more inexplicable, seeing that Italy was the petitioner, as well as the weaker party, as she stood alone against the already existing Dual Alliance.

By this treaty the Dual Monarchy abandoned the principle she had hitherto unswervingly followed, of not pledging herself to armed assistance against France.

With regard to the bitter Magyarphobe spirit now manifested by some of the French, it is worthy of note here that the Hungarian nation always took the view that we should not engage ourselves to fight against France. Andrássy advocated this view, and adhered to it so tenaciously that, failing its acceptance, he was unwilling to conclude the Dual Alliance. When concluding the Triple Alliance, Kálnoky was prevented from undertaking more extensive obligations against the French by Hungarian public opinion swayed by the traditions of Andrássy.

For without doubt, but for the Hungarian public opinion the Foreign Minister would have gone further than he did. At first he contemplated an alliance of a general character between the three Powers, which would have pledged the parties to common united action against any attack, including the case of an attack on Germany by France. Later the Foreign Minister would have consented to the *casus fœderis* being an attack by France simply, irrespective of whether Germany or Italy were the victim of French aggression. Finally, he did not conclude any such agreement because, as he said, the Hungarians failed to see how France could imperil the Dual Monarchy and consequently they were unwilling to engage themselves against France. For the sake of completeness I would add that the Francophil attitude of Hungary was apparent even at a later period. For instance, when it became a question of prolonging the Dual Alliance (Austria-Hungary and Germany), Bismarck proposed to extend the *casus fœderis* to include French aggression. This Kálnoky rejected on the ground that the Hungarian Premier, Coloman Tisza, had announced that in that case Hungary would decline to prolong the treaty. Kálnoky told the Germans that the idea of the French ever coming into conflict with Hungarian interests was a contingency that no Hungarian brain could take in (27th February 1883).

6. SERBIA AND RUMANIA JOIN THE TRIPLE ALLIANCE

Bismarck and Kálnoky extended their system of alliances also to the Balkans. The strong can always find friends ; the weak alone have any difficulty about that. The Greater Bulgaria conception of Ignatieff and the Peace of San Stefano estranged the Serbs from the Russians, and the course taken by the Berlin Congress convinced Milan Obrenovitch that the will of Austria-Hungary would prevail in the Balkans, particularly in the west thereof, where, owing to the occupation of Bosnia-Herzegovina, our army occupied a predominant situation. At Berlin that gifted Prince saw also that Austria-Hungary was disposed to agree to defend the interests of Serbia. He was indebted to Andrássy that the Berlin Congress granted him more than he got from the Russians at San Stefano. In consequence of these experiences Serbia aligned herself with Austria-Hungary, and a treaty was accordingly concluded between the two neighbours (28th June 1881). We promised Milan to recognise his kingly rank should he eventually assume it, and to place no obstacle in the path of Serbian expansion southward, but, on the contrary, to promote it. In return the Serbs undertook to stop their irredentist propaganda.

Serbia, in engaging to conclude no political treaties without our consent, became completely dependent on us. It is true that a few months later (1st October 1881)

Milan explained this unusual and, for him, humiliating condition to the new Serbian Minister as that it merely bound the Serbian Government to conclude with foreign Governments no treaties such as would be in opposition to their agreement with us. This explanation, however, seems to have been a piece of guile to mislead the Serbian Minister for Foreign Affairs, since Milan (October 1881) renewed, with binding force, his obligation not to conclude any treaty whatever with a third party without our consent (*vide* Pribram : *Die politischen Geheimverträge Oesterreich-Ungarns*), and solemnly declared that he would keep his princely word.

Serbia was followed by Rumania. Bratianu, the enlightened father of the present Rumanian Premier, recognised that Rumania's real danger lay not in the numerically small Hungarian nation, but in Pan-Slavism. He saw that Rumania must lose her independence if Russia held the hegemony in the Balkans, if she obtained a permanent influence in Bulgaria : for thus Rumania would become the highway between St. Petersburg and Sofia, which the former would have at all costs to secure for itself. Bratianu stated that the support of Austria-Hungary and Germany would be the only safeguard of Rumanian independence. Though, like a true Rumanian, he never gave up the idea of expansion, yet he assured us that Transylvania was not in his mind, since, as he admitted, it had never been Rumanian territory ; but rather Bessarabia, of which the Muscovites had deprived their Rumanian ally some years previously. Bratianu called personally on Bismarck ; on whom, however, he does not appear to have made a good impression. The Chancellor wrote of him that " he is too garrulous." Nevertheless Bismarck concluded—in spite of his scant confidence in Rumania—that he must come to an understanding with him. In a very literal sense he saw into the future when he said that by means of a treaty it would be possible to bind the Rumanians to the end of King Charles's reign at least! Accordingly, Kálnoky and Bismarck concluded with Bratianu a defensive treaty directed against Russia.

As in 1879, however, the German Emperor's Russophil sentiments awoke once more, and he was most reluctant to sign a treaty obviously directed against Russia. Now Vienna obediently departed from precedent and yielded. She allayed the conscientious scruples of the old Emperor at the sacrifice of her own interests. While we on our part (to avoid naming the Russians) undertook to defend her against aggression from any quarter—thus binding ourselves to defend her against Bulgaria, Serbia, and Turkey also, and implicating ourselves in the quarrels of the Balkan States—Rumania, on the other hand, was bound to render us assistance only in the event of our being attacked by one of her neighbours—i.e. Russia, Bulgaria, or Serbia ; in all other cases she was to remain neutral.

7. The Weakness of 'Bismarck's System of Alliances

The object of the system of alliances formed by Bismarck in the period 1879 to 1884 was the maintenance of peace, and its character was defensive. But the methods he resorted to were various and even inconsistent. Firstly, the treaties were intended to erect a bulwark against east and west—i.e. against the single or combined attacks of France and Russia ; while, secondly, they were to isolate France by winning over Russia.

It was a complicated affair. It could hardly have been otherwise. Such varying aims could be safeguarded only by a complicated system. It was based on five separate treaties entirely independent of each other and expiring on different dates. And six sovereigns were involved : those of Germany, Austria-Hungary, Italy, Russia, Serbia, and Rumania ; on each of whom were imposed different obligations. Some of these rulers, though they had concluded no treaties with each other, found themselves in a certain relationship, merely by virtue of their agreements with third parties ! The final results of the system may be summed up as follows :

In the event of France attacking Germany, Italy alone must assist the latter ; in the event of France attacking Italy, both Germany and Austria-Hungary would have to go to her aid. In the case of Russian aggression against Germany, Austria-Hungary, or Rumania, all three Powers were bound to stand together. A similar obligation existed also in the case of Austria-Hungary and Germany in the event of either of them being attacked by a third Power, if Russia joined the latter or threatened military measures. Should Serbia attack Austria-Hungary, a *casus fœderis* would thus arise for Rumania and Germany. The most effective defence fell to the fortune of Rumania, she being the only State which, in the event of attack, could depend on the support of the two Great Powers, Austria-Hungary and Germany. If Germany, Austria-Hungary, and Italy were attacked by two or more Powers, then these three States were obliged to stand by each other.

Benevolent neutrality and moral support were promised each other by Germany, Austria-Hungary, and Russia in respect of any wars against a Great Power without regard to the question of who was the aggressor. An exception to this, however, was made in the case of a dispute with Turkey, against whom the obligation could apply only if an agreement had previously been concluded by the Powers with regard to the war aims. Austria-Hungary and Serbia promised each other mutual support in all hostilities without exception. A similar obligation obtained in the case of Germany, Austria-Hungary, and Italy if one of them should be attacked by two or more Powers, or if one of them should deem it necessary to declare war on some Power on account of actions menacing their own safety. An exception to this was made in the case of Great Britain, against whom Italy was, by virtue of a special agreement, released from all obligations.

The contracting parties engaged themselves to pursue a common policy in exceptional cases only. Germany, Austria-Hungary, and Italy on the one hand, and Austria-Hungary and Rumania on the other, were bound to discuss with each other all political and economic questions that might arise, and to support each other's policy in so far as it was compatible with their own interests. A more particular limitation was contained only in the Alliance of the Three Emperors and the Austro-Hungarian-Serbian Treaty for the precise purpose of eliminating antagonisms arising from conflicting interests.

By such a complicated structure Bismarck constituted himself master of Europe. As in the past Napoleon I, Metternich, and Napoleon III, it was now his turn to direct European politics. Not only his personal influence but his peculiar fame as a statesman and diplomat earned for him his unique position. Not only the unchallenged superiority of the allies and the absence of any counter-alliance, but also the fact that Germany was the most favourably situated Power within the Triple Alliance, gave that Power and its Chancellor the decisive voice in the affairs of the Continent. Germany formed the connecting-link in the chain of alliances, she being nearer to all the others than they to each other.

Austria-Hungary fared scarcely so well in the new system. It may even be said that the Dual Monarchy fell considerably from the lofty position she had held up to the time of Andrássy's resignation. The decisive influence we exercised on the Balkans during the Congress enhanced our prestige to a remarkable degree. The hopes and fears of the Balkan peoples were beginning to be centred in us. They saw us with free hands to assert our rights and protect our interests in the East ; they saw, moreover, that we were strongly backed by the principal Powers. They saw England following an Oriental policy identical with our own, while Germany supported us so vigorously as even to cause the Czar to cool towards her. Now, however, the peoples of the East began to observe that we were again seeking the friendship of the Russians ; that we intended to pursue a policy parallel with that of the Czar. This brought into the foreground the question whether we should not have eventually to pay for this by the sacrifice of either some of our own Oriental interests or those of our Balkan friends. The suspicion was aroused in some of them that the Pan-Slav idea would be strengthened by the fact that the Western Powers sought the friendship of the Czar.

But the structure had serious weaknesses even from its creator's point of view. Such were, e.g., the careless draftings of the treaties. On the conclusion of the Italian Alliance Bismarck announced that he was not responsible for the text ; nevertheless he accepted it, as it would be a mistake to reject the essence on account of the imperfection of the form. In international law, where the execution of a treaty depends entirely on the good-will of the contracting States, words have less importance than in civil contracts, where the will of the parties must be carried out according to the words, which in the event of dispute will be interpreted by an impartial court of justice placed above the contracting parties—in some cases even against the will of one of them. Notwithstanding, a faulty text in an international agreement is injurious, as it tends to laxness in its execution. An obligation clearly set forth in unambiguous terms is not so easy to wriggle out of as when the text is carelessly drafted and susceptible of misinterpretation.

However, the real Achilles' heel of the achievement lay in the fact that the alliance of Italy and Austria-Hungary on the one hand, and of Russia, Germany, and Austria-Hungary on the other, was not in keeping with the sentiments of the peoples concerned ; it was an artificial plant, having no root in public opinion.

Italy could never forget the rôle played by the Habsburgs in the past, nor in her heart of hearts become reconciled to the frontiers laid down in 1866. Though we had no hostile intentions towards Italy, though Francis Joseph had generously abandoned all ideas of revenge together with the dominating position he had enjoyed in Italy, yet in Austria there was still great bitterness against the foe of 1848, 1859, and 1866. The Italian alliance was a sort of *mariage de convenance*, and in Vienna regarded as on the whole degrading and unnatural, while in Rome it was considered a fetter demanded by necessity. The political temperament of the Italians generally was not in accord with us. We were thoroughly conservative ; Italy desired to expand. We were perfectly satisfied with the *status quo* in Europe and the Mediterranean. But Italy decidedly was not ; for her the *status quo* was simply a necessary evil, which had to be made the best of. If we acquiesced in the Italian aspirations, we might only saddle ourselves with awkward complications, aims far from our mind. By restraining our ally we should alienate her, and might drive her into the opposite camp, there to seek opportunities for expansion. Andrássy disapproved of the Triple Alliance ; he was not familiar with its contents, but was nevertheless convinced that it had an anti-French edge (a thing he wished by all means to avoid) and therefore would lead to a Franco-Russian alliance. He too attached immense importance to the friendship of Italy, but was of opinion that this could be secured better by proceeding in harmony with England than by a written treaty with Rome ; the desired result could be achieved sooner by good relations with Great Britain than by a definite alliance with Italy.

The awkward position of Russia in the Alliance was apparent in the fact that while one of the treaties bound her and her two neighbours to follow a friendly policy, in the other treaty the same two neighbours were arrayed absolutely against her.

Czar Alexander III very pertinently asked what was the value of friendly relations as regulated by treaties two of whose members were already in hostile alliance against the first ? Did not this show that between the allies there was a lack of confidence and

7

a conflict of interests which annulled the real value of the contract ?

A further embarrassing feature of the Alliance was that the treaties in their entirety were known only in the Wilhelmstrasse and the Ballplatz, the rest of the allies being acquainted only with the documents they had themselves signed. Would such a system be able to stand when questions came up for debate in which the interests of the several allies were found to be opposed, if the Eastern Question should lead to complications ? And would the *rapprochement* of Austria-Hungary and Germany to Russia not induce in the Czar's Government a course of conduct calculated to raise just such questions ? Our strong defensive position at the Berlin Congress and the hint of the Dual Alliance would have depressed, and perhaps in due time even suppressed, Pan-Slavism. Would not the surrender of this position and the renewal of the Three Emperors' Alliance mean the ascendancy again of the traditions of Peter the Great ? Would not that Alliance attract to it all those dangerous animosities which aforetime had rendered the Alliance impossible, and which Bismarck had attempted to prevent by this later Alliance ?

CHAPTER III

FROM THE EAST RUMELIAN CRISIS TO THE FALL OF BISMARCK (1883–1890)

1. The Growth of Revanche in France

THE year 1885 was a turning-point in the political situation. The influences discussed in the preceding chapters—influences which in some measure altered the relations of the European Powers to each other from 1879—now ceased, and the circumstances resulting from the Peace of Frankfort and the War in the East once more asserted themselves. Important permanent interests and intellectual currents proved stronger than passing passions and the will of individuals.

France again became what the annexation of Alsace-Lorraine had made of her. The nation could not follow Jules Ferry along the path of *rapprochement* with Germany. Though the great German Chancellor had, by his diplomacy and real services rendered to France, got nearer to some of her leaders, he was nevertheless unable to get any nearer to the French national instincts. Had such a thing been at all possible, the *sine qua non* thereof would have been a lustre in Bismarck's home policy as brilliant as in his foreign ; that is to say, he would have had to succeed in conciliating the population of Alsace-Lorraine and winning their loyalty under the new conditions. But so long as murmurs and complaints reached Paris from over the new frontier, neither Tunis, Morocco, nor the Congo could heal the bleeding wounds freshly inflicted, and the Peace of Frankfort was like a millstone round the neck of Germany and indeed of all Europe.

To-day also the situation is similar. A durable peace, sincere friendship between victors and vanquished, can never be reached until the rights of the minorities have passed from the stage of paper to that of reality. So long as Germans, Hungarians, Slovaks, Turks, Bulgarians, and others have cause to fear for their language, culture, and property in the series of new Alsace-Lorraines created by the various peace treaties, neither the Great Entente, Little Entente, League of Nations, economic boycotts, nor any treaties can end the tension now prevailing. Would that the political leaders of to-day might only study world-history! On the same rock that wrecked the mighty genius of Bismarck will also split the schemes of our modern imperialists.

Ferry at the height of his success was swept away by an unfortunate, albeit transient, military accident (31st March 1885)—anxiety lest further colonial enterprise should allure the power of France overseas, weaken her on the Rhine, and thus under these influences cause her to forget her most sacred duty to Alsace-Lorraine. A victorious ultra-nationalist and chauvinist movement was led by " Clemenceau the Tiger," who, it must be admitted, felt with the keenness of a great patriot the defeat of his people and the mutilation of his country ; who lived but for the fulfilment of *revanche* with admirable consistency, until in his old age he not only saw it but himself to a great extent achieved it. It was given to this obdurate man not only, like Moses, to see the Promised Land, but to enter therein and plant his standard on the soil for which millions of hearts were yearning.

Which was right in the question of the colonies ?

Whose views were justified by subsequent events—Ferry's or Clemenceau's ?

It cannot be denied that the French colonial empire, founded by Ferry with so much pains, did not hinder the *revanche*—on the contrary, it promoted it. The fears rife in certain quarters lest these colonies should play a rôle similar to that played in Mexico in the time of Napoleon III—lest they should demoralise the army and render it incapable of performing its duty in Europe—proved groundless. Indeed, the African negroes proved valuable auxiliaries on not a few critical occasions during the course of the World War. It might even be said that to a great extent the fate of the war was decided by the extra-European forces—those of the United States, Japan, and the Entente colonies—since on the European continent the Central Powers were undoubtedly the superior. Ferry was, moreover, justified by events, as Bismarck had no intention of taking advantage of the momentary weakness caused by the colonial question to begin another war. In fact Bismarck, having succeeded in alienating France from England and Italy, had no thought of ensnaring or injuring her further, as Clemenceau believed.

It is, however, equally certain that this favourable result was not a mere matter of course ; if events had taken a different course, the colonies might have seriously hampered the subsequent achievement of the *revanche*. Had the idea of preventive war asserted itself in Germany, France might have had to pay dearly for her colonial policy, as the risks of German aggression were on more than one occasion increased by the enterprises of the French overseas. I will even go so far as to assert that if, when the day of reckoning arrived, France had lacked the support of Great Britain and had her enemies been stronger on the sea, the forces in the colonies would have been wanted very badly on the battle-fields of Europe. Thus Ferry's enterprise was exceedingly risky, though in the long run, owing to his luck and the skill of his successors, it proved for the good of France.

But the same may be said for nearly every great human undertaking. The very best mind is so limited that it is incapable of foreseeing every result of its actions. The wisest and most correct combinations even may turn out badly if, in consequence of error and ill-luck, the subsequent developments take a wrong direction. I say this, not to encourage men of action to heedlessness: I only wish to point out that in all mundane affairs it is impossible absolutely to exclude the element of chance, all uncertainty ; there is always the unknown quantity to be reckoned with, and the man who is unwilling to take risks ought never to enter the political arena.

The French elections (October 1885) proved a victory for the Germanophobes. Immediately afterwards Clemenceau secured the portfolio of Minister of War for General Boulanger—the advocate of the doctrine that only by a vigilant anti-German policy accompanied by the piling up of armaments could the dignity of the French nation and her safety be preserved ; that France should be prepared for an attack by Germany at any moment, and therefore desist from wasting her energies in unprofitable and embarrassing enterprises abroad.

I do not know whether Boulanger really thought that the time for *revanche* had now come, but it is certain that he lived in the hope of it and directed all his attention to arousing his nation to the imminence of the great reckoning day. Boulanger himself was but a mediocre man : the power and influence of politicians, however, is not always in proportion to their personal value, their spiritual and moral worth, but more often than not to the currents and ideals they represent; it depends largely on the disposition of the public for the time being. The popular *" Brave Général "* understood the soul of the French people, and himself shared it. With his martial figure and air, astride his white steed, he constituted excellent propaganda material, impressing the Gallic mind with the idea that he was another Man of Destiny—to avenge Sedan and restore the faded *gloire* of the French nation. This superstition secured his political influence for a number of years. The shafts aimed at him by statesmen far more capable than he failed to pierce the armour of his popularity. When he fell as minister, he became even more powerful as a party leader. The elections proved his popularity to be so great that the entire republican system was shaken to its foundations by it. After his fall, learning of the Government's intention to arrest him, he fled discouraged; but when he disappeared from the political stage he had already created a public opinion which rendered a policy according to Jules Ferry impossible for a generation. The " Boulanger disposition " of the French people on the occasion of the Schnäbele frontier incident (April 1887) nearly precipitated war and made Franco-German antagonism once again the chief and most potent factor of the international situation.

This neither took Bismarck by surprise nor found him unprepared. He had always borne the contingency in mind, and never had much confidence in the durability of Ferry's régime. When the tension was renewed, the Chancellor immediately reverted to his previous policy. He did not insist on co-operation. His aim was now to stave off the French attack as long as possible—to

temporise. His attitude towards Paris was usually one
of frigid politeness, avoiding all provocations ; sometimes
he was even amenable, as in the Schnäbele incident. At
other times he was inflexible and could menace—as in
his speech of February 1887, in which he announced that
if ever it fell to his lot to defeat France again, he would
utterly crush her and effectually prevent her for all
time from being a danger to the Fatherland.

It is possible that for the moment the speech had
the desired effect. But the time came, after long
years, when it proved a disadvantage. In the World
War it was seized upon by the German and the French
nationalists and chauvinists as a pretext for cloaking
their severe peace conditions—although the speech
had been delivered for the sole purpose of scaring the
French out of their warlike attitude, as Bismarck
explained in London and St. Petersburg and also to
Count Waldersee, Deputy Chief of the German General
Staff. The Chancellor's real convictions were summed
up in the words that " it was impossible to destroy a
nation of forty millions with the talents and self-consciousness of the French ; and therefore, in the event
of another German victory over them, a peace as lenient
as that he made with Austria-Hungary in 1866 would
be advisable."

However, the feasibility of Bismarck's chief aim—
the safeguarding of peace and German supremacy—
depended not so much on the effect of this speech and
the details of the policy to be pursued towards France,
as on the willingness of Europe to tolerate the supremacy of Germany ; it was a question whether the other
Powers would not instigate France—whether an anti-
German disposition would not take root there—against
the predominant Power.

2. SALISBURY'S LETTER TO BISMARCK

It was of the utmost importance for the world-situation that the second chief event of the year 1885 was the swing of the pendulum of British policy away from France and towards Central Europe led by Germany. Peace was the securer for the fact that, while France was worshipping at the shrine of Mars Ultor, in England the Germanophil spirit had taken root and was spreading.

When Gladstone had ridden to victory on a tremendous wave of popularity, Bismarck shook his head, believing it impossible to depend on England owing to her foreign policy being rendered unreliable by the caprices of public opinion. Subsequent events, however, testified to the contrary. It became clear that such disturbing circumstances and fleeting changes of the popular humour could not for long sway the British people, so famous for their common sense, and divert them from the path of their traditions and interests. Above all, a temporarily estranged Power will not do violence to her self-consciousness, nor provoke by a policy that might jeopardise it. As Bismarck guarded against this, England soon returned to the policy dictated by her then existing interests. As we have seen, Gladstone himself discovered that his Germanophobia was a mistake and offered an alliance to Bismarck. The other liberal leaders of foreign policy—Chamberlain, Dilke, Rosebery, Harcourt—all united in condemning the out-of-date policy of their chief. One of the best authorities on foreign politics in the Liberal Party, Lord Rosebery, who subsequently became Premier, characterised Gladstone's orientation as an attempt to make friends with Russia, which however proved impracticable. This Russophilism became quite discredited by Gladstone's policy. The consequences thereof were isolation, a barely averted war with Russia, and the return of British public opinion to the old path. The failure of its foreign policy even formed one of the causes of the downfall of the Liberal Party. Therefore it was natural that Gladstone's successor, Lord Salisbury, when he became Premier (July 1885), should return to the traditions of the Conservative Party and its late leader, Beaconsfield, and desire the friendship of that confederation of States which constituted the natural support of Great Britain, and which, while the strongest military Power on the Continent, formed no menace to the security of the British Isles, like their next-door neighbour in the times of Louis XIV and Napoleon I ; nor threatened India, as Czar Nicholas I had done ; nor yet was ambitious to challenge the British sea-power, like Spain, Holland, France—or in our own day William II, thereby manifesting the English blood in his veins.

Salisbury had hardly taken the seals of office when he wrote to Bismarck (July 1885) in terms so cordial that his colleague, Lord Randolph Churchill, saw in the letter the suggestion of an alliance, and had Bismarck wished, it might even have led to an alliance. Unfortunately Bismarck did not then entertain the idea. Loyal to his former creed, he attached greater importance to keeping the good-will of Russia than to obtaining that of England. But though, owing to the Chancellor's lack of interest, the change in British policy failed to lead to a formal Anglo-German Alliance, it at any rate had the valuable effect of bringing England nearer to us. The impression was produced that probably the greatest navy and the most efficient army

in the world would co-operate in preserving peace.
If Boulanger had any thought of attacking us, this
reflection must have cooled his courage and caused
him to think twice about it. At the same time German
supremacy aroused no ill-feeling anywhere such as
might endanger peace.

For this happy result we are indebted to Bismarck's
wisdom and moderation, and especially to the fact
that he never hankered after cheap laurels by diplomatic coups, lest the humiliated (though not defeated)
party should become an enemy of Germany. He had
the laudable habit of never standing in the way of
others, unless important national interests left him no
alternative. On the contrary, he was always ready
to flatter the vanity of other nations, to encourage with
words their desires for expansion, so that they might
not see in him an obstacle to their aspirations and thus
turn against him. The Iron Chancellor usually welcomed any ambitions not directly opposed to the
interests of the Fatherland, for they generally set the
Great Powers at variance and drove them to seek the
good-will of Germany.

He was very far from the purblind mentality so
common since the World War, which leads victorious
States to exploit their conquests to the utmost, without
regard to reason or humanity—for which those States will
yet have to pay dearly, as the Greek Venizelos already
has done. Bismarck was never overcome by vanity ;
he was not affected by considerations of prestige, like
Napoleon III, and to a certain extent also William II.
His fame was so genuine, so great, while he regarded
Germany as so powerful, that he could clearly distinguish the permanent and abiding from the superficial
and evanescent ; he was never deceived by appearances.

He was great enough to be moderate when he saw it was to the interests of the country to be so. He never unduly or wantonly flaunted his dominant position, nor strove to play the leading rôle for its own sake. He preferred to shift the burden to another's shoulder unless the welfare of Germany necessitated his bearing it himself. He never meddled in affairs which were not directly his, lest he should create enemies which he might otherwise avoid.

Bismarck said of Napoleon III that " people attributed to him everything that happened in the world, even holding him responsible for the bad weather in China." Not being ambitious to occupy a similar position, the Chancellor preferred to avoid becoming so unpopular and disliked, as a man usually does who holds so much power in his own hands.

Bismarck promoted the progress of Austria-Hungary in the Balkans, assisted the colonising aspirations of France, encouraged England in Egypt (he refrained from humiliating Gladstone over Egypt), notwithstanding his antipathy towards the British statesman and his secure position of power), and supported Italy in Africa and Albania. This procedure succeeded in getting England, Russia, and Italy involved in disputes, which enabled Bismarck to set Ferry against Gladstone, to gain over Italy, and even to come to an understanding with England in spite of the Gladstone episode. The rising States saw no obstacle in the envy or insatiability of the Germans.

If the Iron Chancellor had acted otherwise, had he always domineered, had he thwarted the projects of other nations, had he demanded—with the excuse of preserving the balance of power—compensations for the conquests of others, had his policy been to have a finger in every pie, then the Entente would have been formed even in his lifetime and the situation would have been changed to his disadvantage. His successors in office also did not want war, they also pursued no aggressive policy, but they were unable to maintain that appearance of pacific moderation which renders an attitude of superiority tolerable.

3. THE BULGARIAN CRISIS AND THE GREAT POWERS

The third important event of the year 1885 was the recrudescence of the Eastern Question. Though in a new form, it was essentially the same, for Russia was now again contending for supremacy in the Balkans. This time, however, the Czar was not concerned with Turkey, but turned his efforts against Bulgaria, which he had founded.

Russia had always looked askance at a free Bulgaria : she desired a subservient and grateful Bulgaria, which should be an advance-guard of Czarism. No sooner did Russia perceive Bulgaria aspiring to independence than she turned against her. The weapons of the Autocrat were plots, incitement to revolt, and undermining the national sentiment, all in the name of Pan-Slavism and Orthodoxy. Such weapons, however, are double-edged. They wound not only him against whom they are directed, but also the wielder himself. During the Great War the Autocrat of All the Russias, representative of the principle of despotic authority, had to pay the penalty of the intrigues committed for decades by his officials in his name. By such tricks abroad and its reactionary methods at home, Czarism played with fire and was finally consumed in the resultant holocaust.

By a wrong provision of the Berlin Treaty a special

weapon against Bulgaria was given to Russia. Instead of one strong Bulgaria, the Congress created two which were too feeble to thrive, and consequently the people were discontented. Beaconsfield was chiefly responsible for the blunder, since it was he who, with Andrássy, frustrated the foundation of the Bulgaria of Ignatieff because it was considered too great ; but who, in spite of Andrássy, formed two small States out of the territory. Either of these extremes would have had precisely the same result : a Bulgaria too large would have come under Muscovite tutelage because of her size, and the two small Bulgarias because of their inability to stand alone. The former would have had to seek the protection of Russia from her many jealous foes, as well as to fulfil the demands made upon her by her size ; while the latter had to apply to the Czar for the revision of the impossible frontiers forced upon her. Ignatieff's Bulgaria could not have contended with her enemies except with Russian support. So near to Constantinople, with her too numerous Serbian, Greek, and Turkish subjects, and struggling with initial difficulties, the new State would have been powerless against her hostile neighbours, Turkey, Serbia, Rumania, and Greece, without the active assistance of the Czar. And the two Bulgarias born of the Berlin Treaty could look for union only to the same imperial source, since it was against the Czar's will that Bulgaria had been divided, while he further stood for the idea of revolution in the East. What is more, Russia intended to exploit this advantage. She was ready to play the part of conciliator. She had already taken the first step towards upsetting the Berlin Treaty.

The Czar had renewed the unpopular Three Emperors' Alliance, partly with a view to regaining in the Balkans the power he had lost a short time before through the action of the two other allies, and partly to restore with their aid the interrupted union. This alliance could by no means have been forgiven by Pan-Slav public opinion unless it demolished, partially at any rate, the work of the Berlin Congress. Czar Alexander took the first steps in this direction by persuading his two imperial friends to adopt the union, in principle at least, and also by having it advocated by his agents on the spot.

There was one circumstance, however, which restrained him from any rash action. As the Battenberg Prince of Bulgaria failed to prove himself a docile viceroy of Russia, but kept loyal to his oath to serve the cause of the Bulgarians, the Czarist Government, counting on Bismarck's assistance and Kálnoky's complacency, proposed to dethrone the ingrate Prince before the union was carried into execution. They aimed at presenting the union to a Bulgaria they were satisfied with.

In this, however, they were forestalled. The union became a *fait accompli* ere Russia had time to transform Bulgaria according to her taste or to break Battenberg. What the Czar intended to perpetrate for his own glory and profit, Prince Alexander achieved by way of a revolutionary coup. He proclaimed Bulgarian union (20th September 1885); and thus the seed sown by Russian hands and watered by Russian gardeners yielded fruit that was bitter in their mouths. The situation was complicated by the fact that Serbia and Greece, jealous of the sudden access of power and territory of Bulgaria, demanded compensations.

The trend of foreign policy during the following years was due to this event, which formed the subject of diplomatic wrangling. Under its influence the Concert of Europe underwent an unprecedented change. As by the touch of a magic wand the policies of almost all the

Cabinets were modified, and the Great Powers, like the partners in a quadrille, changed places.

The situation of Russia became exceedingly difficult. She saw herself obliged to thwart the very thing she had herself prepared; she had to defend what she had condemned; she had to compel Christians to submit themselves to the supremacy of the Sultan, though only a short time before she had resorted to bloodshed to deliver them from the Ottoman yoke. The very thing that Russia would have greeted with jubilation as justice and the will of the people, if wrought by Kaulbars or Enroth in her name, she had to pronounce breach of treaty obligations and revolution because it was the work of the anti-Russian Alexander of Battenberg.

The newly elected British Government also got into an awkward position. Salisbury had been Secretary of Foreign Affairs in the Cabinet which created East Rumelia and demarcated the Balkan frontier in order to keep the balance level between the East and Turkey. Must he now come into opposition with his former self ? Should he now destroy what he had formerly built up ? Or must he subserve the policy of the Czar, encompass the fall of Battenberg, and thereby thrust Bulgaria back again under the tutelage of Russia? Consistency in form would be inconsistency in essence; for the English Conservatives in 1878 objected to " Great Bulgaria " out of fear that Russia would thus increase her power and influence in the vicinity of the Dardanelles and the Bosphorus. If England under the changed circumstances now demanded what she had insisted on at Berlin, she would jeopardise the object she strove for both then and now—namely, that Constantinople and the Straits should be surrounded by Powers independent of Russia.

The Sultan, too, was on the horns of a dilemma. He

must either sanction the revolution directed against himself, or comply with the wishes of Russia and throw over Battenberg, who had emancipated himself from her thrall.

Austria-Hungary was somewhat better situated, though she, too, at the Berlin Congress, had voted for East Rumelia ; but only for the sake of England and against Andrássy's inclination. Austria-Hungary's sanctioning of the union was the less inconsistent as, in the Three Emperors' Alliance, Kálnoky, under the impression that Greater Bulgaria would be more independent of Russia, in signing the Alliance of the Three Emperors, accepted the idea of the union of the two parts. Notwithstanding this, however, our position was neither simple nor easy. It was difficult for us, on the one hand, because, according to the provision of the Three Emperors' Alliance, we had to consider the interests of Russia in the Balkans, and on the other hand, because, according to the clause in the treaty with Serbia, we had promised to support the expansion of that State southwards. If we stood by Milan and his anti-Bulgar policy, we should miss the opportunity of winning the good-will of Bulgaria ; if, on the other hand, we left Milan in the lurch and broke our promise to him, it would prove that it was bad business to go with us, while at the same time we should endanger the throne of our ally.

How did the various Cabinets act in such moments of grave difficulty ? England and Russia conformed most completely to the new circumstances.

Salisbury was not the excellent party leader and brilliant orator that his opponent and predecessor Gladstone had been ; he had not the genius of Disraeli ; but he had more of the English common sense than the pair of them, while he was not, like them both, under

8

the disturbing influence of personal vanity. This fact was of immense value. For Bismarck was right when he said that "the true value of a statesman is the residue of intellectual faculty and power remaining after the subtraction of his vanity." Salisbury proved the truth of this. At the decisive moment, of all statesmen in responsible positions, he was perhaps the first to discern the right way when, breaking with his past, he stood by the union. In so doing he not only served the cause of Great Britain abroad, by weakening the Russian influence near Constantinople, but at home too, by basing his genuine profit on pleasing, insinuating argument—the right of nations to their self-determination and the great force of the *fait accompli*—when he convinced both the imperialists and the idealists among his countrymen at the same time. He made a clever move against the Russians and disarmed Gladstone at the same time. To the idealism of the latter the new policy was much nearer than that represented by Disraeli and Salisbury at the Congress.

Russia also broke with the past. Unfortunately for her, however, the step was prompted by the wrath of the offended Autocrat, rather than by her real interests. Giers, the honest bureaucrat, the humble servant of his master, obstinately turned upon Battenberg and attempted to enforce the *status quo ante* with the mental reservation that the union should be realised later by the Czar himself in the interests of a régime dependent on Russia.

Kálnoky approximated to Salisbury's view. His first idea at least (29th September 1885) was to protest against the union effected by violence, but to sanction it by virtue of a new international agreement. The situation was doubtless facilitated for him by the fact that his predecessor, Andrássy, was in accord with him. The ex-Foreign Minister, who was painfully aware that the Alliance of the Three Emperors had turned the attention of the East once more to the Czar and shattered the favourable position of power he had acquired, saw that now was the time to repair the error we had committed. Only we must take advantage of the even greater mistake made by Russia turning against her own work.

Andrássy explained his policy in a memorandum submitted to the Emperor-King Francis Joseph (24th November). Like Kálnoky, he would protest from the legal standpoint against the violence committed, but at the same time he was for recognising the union. As at the Congress, he still held that Bulgaria should be made perfectly independent in order to avoid quarrels with the Porte. He suggested a certain rectification of the frontiers in favour of Serbia and Turkey, granting the latter the small part of East Rumelia populated chiefly by Mohammedans. The main difference between the projects of Kálnoky and those of Andrássy was that, while the former sought a solution within the Alliance of the Three Emperors together with Russia, the latter considered the Powers signatory to the Berlin Treaty the competent Court, and claimed the initiative for Austria-Hungary. Andrássy contended that Europe was the sole rightful as well as the most suitable judge of the matter. He believed implicitly that England, Italy, and France would accept his view, that Germany would not quibble over it ; while, on the other hand, he was afraid lest, within the Three Emperors' Alliance, Bismarck should vote in favour of the Czar and against us.

But this accord in the views of Kálnoky and Andrássy had no effect ; for while Andrássy was writing in that sense, Kálnoky had abandoned his original intentions and was listening to Bismarck, who regarded events from an entirely different angle. As with Tunis, Morocco, and Egypt, the fate of Bulgaria had no interest for the German Chancellor. He desired to exploit the Bulgarian Question without regard for justice or the interests of the peoples concerned, simply that he might maintain and strengthen his position among the Great Powers and keep France isolated. As in the past, now also he took advantage of the ambitions of others in order to exploit the complications he foresaw would arise. Firstly, he succeeded in alienating France and Italy over Tunis; next, England, France, and Italy over Egypt; and now he was hoping to estrange Russia from France over Bulgaria.

During his visit to Paris the Emperor Napoleon III justified the Crimean War before him, by pointing out that he could not allow the Russian fleet to play in the Mediterranean a rôle which rightly belonged to France. Bismarck hoped that the French Republic would neither approve of Russia laying hands on the key to the Mediterranean, the Dardanelles. He especially hoped that the forward movement of Russia in the East would put a stop to the *rapprochement* between the French and the Muscovites. There was, however, a wide difference between the case of Tunis and Egypt and that of Bulgaria.

Whereas Bismarck had formerly been quite indifferent as to whom the French and English schemes backed by him came into opposition with, his whole system might now be wrecked if Russia came into collision with Austria-Hungary—if he had again to choose between the two Emperors—if the friend he had neglected were to become his foe—if the Three Emperors' Alliance went to pieces on the rocks of the

Balkans ere the Russian and French ambitions in the East had had time to clash with each other. Bismarck certainly wanted the Czar to quarrel with *France* over the Balkan affair—but not with *us*.

Consequently he desired to bring about an agreement between Austria-Hungary and Russia, and with this object he urged us to obsequiousness. He acted differently from this in the seventies, when in a similar situation. Then he did not dream of coercing Andrássy to adopt his foreign policy, well knowing that the Magyar magnate was difficult to handle, as he would resign his post rather than undertake the responsibility for a policy he disapproved, and that the changing of Austria's Foreign Minister would be more damaging for Germany than letting Andrássy go his own way. Now, however, Bismarck did not consider Kálnoky capable of such independent action ; he had no misgivings about the consequences of his pressure on Vienna ; his sole fear now was on account of the Russians—they were his only anxiety. He sought to avoid the development in that quarter of a disposition like that of 1879 which had forced him to conclude an alliance with us.

This event forms a classic illustration of the importance of the personality of the leading statesman, and the caution with which we should receive the attempts of a Foreign Minister to justify his failures on the ground that they were inevitable ; for the skill of the leader is one of the most important factors in any and every situation ; the mere opinion of his talents entertained by his friends and enemies has a considerable influence upon the results of his actions. Not only are the staying power and will-to-victory of the nation influenced by the personality of the man who guides the ship of State, but, on the other hand, the attitude

of other nations towards it—their pride or humility—
is also influenced by the prestige of the competitor and
the opinion held by others with regard to him.

That which Kálnoky failed to achieve—that which
the situation rendered impossible for Kálnoky because Bismarck understood his limitations, knew exactly
what he would dare and would not dare—could have
been accomplished by Andrássy. Under the latter's
leadership the Dual Monarchy would probably have
acquitted herself very differently in the political arena.

Consequently Bismarck paid little attention to the
Austria-Hungary of Kálnoky and adopted the Russian
attitude against him. He would have preferred the
union of Bulgaria and East Rumelia undone : whence
he thought would follow the disarmament of Serbia
and Greece, the satisfaction of the Czar, the safeguarding
of the peace of the Balkans, and the fall of Battenberg,
whom the Chancellor now detested more than ever
since, notwithstanding his shaky political position,
he had dared to aspire to the hand of Princess Victoria,
granddaughter to the German Emperor.

It was a tribute to the Chancellor's immense power
that at the meeting of Ambassadors at Constantinople
(November) the European States decided in accordance
with his views and that Kálnoky—in spite of himself—
adopted his attitude. But all in vain ; the question
remained unsettled. England declined her consent,
and without England the Sultan (in whom was invested
the execution of the decision) dared not move.

Amidst this diplomatic bickering the cannon of
Milan began to roar. He had the peculiar advantage
that both rivals, Russia and Austria-Hungary, regarded
his adventure with equal pleasure, though for different
reasons. Both desired Milan's victory and believed

in its certainty. Both opponents put their money on
the same horse, and felt sure of winning, though they
intended to use their gains for different purposes, i.e.
Russia to damage Austria-Hungary, and Austria-
Hungary to damage Russia.

Kálnoky hoped that Milan (and through him Austria-
Hungary) would obtain the leading rôle in the Balkans
and that at the same time Bulgaria would get such
favourable peace terms as would attach her to us. On
the other hand, Giers hoped that victory for Milan
would seal the doom of Battenberg, when Russia would
step in to the rescue of Bulgaria and give her a government under Russian protection.

They were both disappointed, however. Serbia
was defeated by the Bulgarians under Prince Alexan-
der of Battenberg at the decisive battle of Slivnitza.
Kálnoky intervened with an attempt to bring about
an armistice to be followed by peace. The rôle the
Czar coveted in Sofia now, much against our will, fell
to us—to defend Serbia. The Ambassador of the
Dual Monarchy, the brilliant but shallow-minded
Khevenhüller, put a rash interpretation upon the
intentionally vague and ambiguous instructions of
Kálnoky and checked the Bulgarians by pure threats.
Subsequently the Foreign Minister endorsed the atti-
tude of his delegate and thus obliged himself to oppose
Battenberg by force of arms in the event of his prose-
cuting the war further.

With this the Oriental Crisis entered a new phase.
What would Russia do if our troops defeated her former
protégé Bulgaria, whom she hoped eventually to win
over to herself ? In the event of our army appearing
in the Balkans, would not the Czar be obliged to occupy
Bulgaria in order to restore the balance ? Would not

the Serbo-Bulgarian campaign be thus transformed into a duel between Austria-Hungary and Russia ?

At any rate, Bismarck feared so, and roundly denounced Kálnoky's policy. With prophetic vision he advised us to beware of pandering to Serbia's megalomania, which in changed circumstances would cause her to pursue in the Bánat of Hungary the same irredentist policy now preached by her with our encouragement in Bulgaria. Serbia—he warned us—would manifest no more gratitude to us than she did to Russia. His chief objection, however, was that the procedure of our Foreign Minister was not in harmony with the spirit of the Three Emperors' Alliance. He considered it an alarming step on the part of Kálnoky to threaten Prince Alexander without first consulting Russia ; and he would regard our one-sided military action in the Balkans as a simple breach of treaty. For the agreement obliged Austria-Hungary to respect the interests of Russia in the Balkans, and prescribed that any change in the territorial *status quo* of Turkey should only be effected by mutual consent. And Bismarck interpreted the temporary occupation of Serbia as such a change in the *status quo*. Would Kálnoky not consider—he asked—the occupation of Bulgaria by Russia without the consent of Austria-Hungary a breach of treaty ? The dissatisfied Chancellor also blamed our policy for driving the Bulgarians—who had proved themselves the stronger antagonist—into the arms of Russia without making sure of the Serbians : for these latter, if we delivered them, would certainly declare that they would have won but for the interference of Austria-Hungary.

But more effective than all these arguments was Bismarck's statement that he would not consider himself bound to help us if we got entangled in a war with Russia on account of the mistake of Kálnoky.

This hint caused Kálnoky to execute, as it were, a fighting retreat. He admitted that Bismarck was in the right. In spite of all his previous arguments to the contrary, Kálnoky condemned his own action in acknowledging that, according to the terms of the treaty, he would have been compelled to agree with Russia before proceeding with his intervention.

Undoubtedly the Alliance of the Three Emperors was a serious burden, and it was a difficult matter to square our former conduct with that clause of the treaty which obliged all the parties to respect each other's interests. Yet Bismarck overshot the mark by interpreting our projected military measures in Serbia as a territorial change with regard to European Turkey, as referred to in the treaty of the Triple Alliance; for there was no territorial change whatever contemplated, but merely military action for the purpose of defending the territorial *status quo.*

Fortunately for Kálnoky, however, peace was concluded between the two belligerents on the basis of the *status quo ante* before he had to make a final decision as to whether he should, under pressure from Bismarck, abstain from carrying out his severe threats, or defy the Chancellor. Hereupon the acute conflict between Austria-Hungary and Russia ceased, though the Bulgarian problem with all its complications remained.

Battenberg's victory failed to save him. Shortly afterwards he fell a victim to a Russian military conspiracy: he was captured and forcibly removed from Bulgaria. This knavery, however, had only a short-lived success. It rather conduced to Prince Alexander's greatest triumph. His people loyally supported him and

fetched him back. But alas! at this trying moment
the Prince lost his nerve, and with that the game, for
he ended his career by placing his abdication into the
hands of the Czar (7th September 1886). Prince Alexander possessed many fine qualities. He was a good
soldier and a skilful diplomatist under difficulties ; but
his end proved that he lacked tenacity, the resolute will,
and the iron nerve, without which great deeds, such as
the successful leading of a nation in times of storm and
stress, are impossible of achievement.

Battenberg himself was responsible for the fulfilment
of Bismarck's prediction that " his reign would become
a pleasant memory of his youth."

Regarded, however, from the standpoint of world-
politics, this tragedy meant no real change. It brought
no solution to the problem. Battenberg's place was
taken by a strong man, Stambuloff. This muscular
Bulgarian was the first representative of the great
political talents of his nation. He championed the
cause of his country's independence against Russian
aggression, and, backed by the bulk of his compatriots, he
succeeded in maintaining the union until the Sobranje,
under his leadership (7th July 1887), elected another
prince in the person of Ferdinand of Coburg, who, more
skilful and able than his predecessor on the throne,
steered his course safely through the treacherous cross-
currents and whirlpools of Oriental politics and finally
succeeded in fixing his rule firmly on the country.

For a while, however, each player on the diplomatic
chessboard continued his previous game. Russia carried
on her campaign against the Bulgarian union, against
the regency of Stambuloff, and later against Coburg—
against everything that could strengthen and stabilise
the union effected without her consent. Giers would

have liked a Russian Governor to prepare the election of the Sobranje and place on the Bulgarian throne a prince amenable to the Czar—to make the union legal under Muscovite protection. All his efforts were vain ; his paper protests were of no use, for there was no one to enforce them. The situation of mighty Russia was similar to that of France after the armistice of Villafranca.

Napoleon III, before drawing the sword against Austria in 1859, promised the Italians full liberty from the Alps to the Adriatic. After Solferino, however, he stopped half-way—at the Mincio instead of the Adriatic. But he omitted Italian patriotism from his calculations —he forgot that he had to reckon with the indefatigable Victor Emmanuel, the great Cavour, the heroic Garibaldi. The Italians worked on to cement the unity of their country. They resolved to finish without Napoleon's aid the task they had begun in co-operation with him—if need be, even against him. The French Emperor was furious, but he could not go against his own programme and his own protégé. Thus he was compelled to allow the work begun by him from egotistic motives to be finished without him and at the cost of his prestige. Like the new Czar, Alexander III, Napoleon III found England in his way. England there and then took over the rôle relinquished by France and Russia. England protected Piedmont and Bulgaria ; and England reaped the harvest from the seed sown by the French and the Russians.

The two events differed only in so far as Napoleon III adhered to his original view more steadfastly than did Alexander III ; since the former would not permit Austria to use armed force against the Italians to exact the peace conditions he had imposed upon them, whereas the Czar came into such opposition to himself that he was even willing to resort to the Turks to frustrate the union of Bulgaria.

This difference, however, had no decisive consequences, for the Sultan was ill-disposed to be the catspaw to take the chestnuts from the fire for the Czar. The Sublime Porte distrusted the Autocrat and saw quite clearly that, after Battenberg, Stambuloff and Coburg also would have to yield to the Russians if the Padishah himself took a Russian general to Sofia ; in which case not only Bulgaria but Turkey too would become a vassal of the Czar. Consequently the Russian policy was unable to assert itself. It contented itself with a mere diplomatic action when it was seen that the *status quo* could only be changed by force of arms. As on Italian territory, also here the *fait accompli* proved stronger than law, the only trouble being that (the Czar's antipathy to his own former programme being more deeply rooted than was that of Napoleon III—as the Czar displayed a more obstinate resistance against the Bulgarians than did Napoleon against the Italians) the legal recognition of the *fait accompli* took longer in the case of the Balkans than in the case of Italy, and the estrangement between the Russians and the Bulgarians was more profound than that between the French and the Italians.

After the final fall of Battenberg, Bismarck continued his old game. As in the past, he backed Russia. He sought to persuade his two friends to divide the sphere of influence—the west of the Balkans to fall to Austria-Hungary and the east to Russia. He had plenty of arguments for his idea. Was he ever at a loss for arguments to prove anything that his interests required ? According to him, the division of power in the Balkans was the direct logical consequence of the Berlin Treaty as well as of the renewed Three Emperors' Alliance. This interpretation was, however, quite arbitrary. While it is true that Bismarck advocated the division in question under the Foreign Ministry of Andrássy, it is equally true that the latter never accepted, and that Bismarck himself did not insist. And if we admit that the mission of the Russian General Sumarokoff, prior to the Russo-Turkish War, had reference to such a division of power, it never went beyond the stage of a desire. As we have said, Andrássy never accepted the suggestion. And even if, before the Russo-Turkish War, an agreement was come to between the two empires which confined the operations of the Russian army to the west, stipulating that it should not cross the Serbian frontier, that also is no proof that it had reference to anything but military operations, becoming invalid at the end of the war and never contemplating a permanent division of power at the expense of the Porte. Neither did the Berlin Treaty contemplate Bulgaria belonging to the Russian sphere of influence. For it was on the very account of Bulgaria that desperate conflicts had taken place between Russia and her enemies ; that the Berlin Congress altered the Treaty of San Stefano, which (i.e. the treaty) accorded with the views of Russia. It was Bulgaria that it divided and reduced, contrary to the will of the Czar, at the time of the occupation of the country by the Russian forces. How could all this have happened if at Berlin we had recognised Bulgaria as being within the Russian sphere of influence? We may observe, in passing, that Bismarck never produced a single document or *viva-voce* declaration to support his contention.

The German Chancellor entirely misinterpreted the foreign policy of the Austro-Hungarian Monarchy under Andrássy's direction. Not the division of the Balkan Peninsula, but the very opposite thereof, was our intention. After Plevna and San Stefano, Andrássy avoided a military solution of the problem, in spite of his firm confidence in our victory, because he believed himself able, by a proper policy, to attain without war our chief aim in the Balkans : the abolition of Russian supremacy. This was at the back of Andrássy's mind when he had inserted in the peace treaty everywhere the words " *the rights of Europe* " instead of " *the rights of Russia* " ; when he strove to create a Bulgaria independent and contented ; and attempted to conclude a system of alliances to secure us a free hand in the Balkans, enhance our prestige there, and counterbalance the Russian advance. That he tolerated for the time being the Russian possession of certain powers acquired by them through their victorious campaign by no means signified that he recognised them as permanent and indefeasible rights, but that he thought it better to wait patiently for the inevitable reaction against Muscovite tyranny and the desire for liberty on the part of the people concerned. His chief aim—the elimination of the last remnant of Russian influence—remained unchanged.

Moreover, there is no proof that the Dual Monarchy since Andrássy's resignation had accepted the idea of division into spheres of interest. The Three Emperors' Alliance had no intention of according privileges to us in the west and to Russia in the east of the Balkans, while it recognised our right to annex Bosnia-Herzegovina and in certain contingencies accepted Bulgarian union. Kálnoky justly pointed out that Austria-Hungary had acquired no rights by virtue of this agreement, which had merely recognised the situation created by the Czar at Reichstadt prior to the Berlin Treaty. Neither did Russia acquire any privileges in Bulgaria, for the Czar had, in the treaty, just the same rights as the other parties to the alliance. All special rights and privileges were excluded by the text of the treaty, which supported a union created solely by internal natural development, thereby denouncing the legality of any union resulting from foreign influence, whether Russian or other.

But Bismarck advanced political arguments also to justify the division into spheres of interest. He asserted that the military position of the Dual Monarchy with regard to Russia would be improved by the occupation of Constantinople and Bulgaria by the latter; as Russia would, on the one hand, come into conflict with Great Britain, and perhaps even with France (Bismarck's fervent hope); and on the other hand, the forces engaged in the Balkans would be lacking in Galicia, so that we could easily cut off from their base of operations the Russian troops that had advanced towards the Straits.

These arguments of Bismarck were just as fallacious and futile as his others had been. If Austria-Hungary had given Russia a free hand, the occupation of Bulgaria could have been effected with but a small force, and without such a prolonged campaign as would have exhausted Russia there and considerably weakened her on the other fronts. In that event England would not have been in a position to cause Russia any serious trouble; for—by herself—she would never have undertaken hostilities on behalf of Bulgaria, and would have been obliged to come to terms with Russia, as we also had. Further, had the Russophil party in Bulgaria come into power, Russia might easily have put the Bulgarian troops under Russian officers, to train them and educate them in the Muscovite spirit, and thus get us between two fires.

Our influence in Serbia would not have provided a satisfactory equivalent nor restored the balance of power. Our influence in Serbia could never have taken such deep root as did Russia's in Bulgaria, especially if the Muscovites had succeeded in presenting the latter with the coveted union after the failures of their bid for independence. Bismarck himself emphasised this fact when he stated that the Russian influence could be extended to Serbia even more easily than to Bulgaria. The natural yearning of the Serbs for the deliverance of their brethren scattered throughout Hungary, Bosnia-Herzegovina, and Turkey; the slogan of Slavdom and Orthodoxy; the fascination of the " rolling rouble "; the astute Russian diplomacy— specially adapted for the Balkan situation—all these constituted powerful weapons of the Czar in Serbia; so that Russian supremacy in Sofia and the Straits would sooner or later have meant Muscovite hegemony over the whole Balkan Peninsula. The Russian triumph in Sofia would have had a moral influence extending throughout the region.

Would Bismarck have preserved his equanimity if France, for example, had driven a wedge into Denmark—or Poland—and assumed the military power there? Would it have been any adequate consolation to the Chancellor to be told that the French forces in Denmark—or Poland—would correspondingly weaken Gallic armies on the Rhine? Certainly not. When the interests of the Fatherland were in question, and when his own reputation was involved, Bismarck thought quite otherwise than when he had simply to advise. Then his utterances were not scientific disquisitions for arriving at truth, but political actions intended to arouse, to intimidate, or to convince, as the circumstances required.

The only unanswerable argument of Bismarck was that, if our non-consent to the Russian occupation should lead to war, the *casus fœderis* fixed in 1879 would not become operative. It was possible to challenge the justice of that statement, but after all, the importance of the pronouncement was not dependent on its abstract truth but on the will behind it. The Chancellor was within his rights in interpreting the obligations of the German Empire, and therefore his view prevailed in this case.

Yet notwithstanding all these arguments, the pressure he brought to bear, his extensive authority and power, Bismarck failed to score a decisive success. Nowhere outside Germany was this theory accepted. He failed with the Czar, who was bored at the repeated requests that he would safeguard our interests in Serbia (November 1888). He had no better success with Russian public opinion either. Herbert Bismarck was right in asserting that most Russian statesmen wished to subject the whole Balkan Peninsula to Muscovite rule. To which remark his father added sarcastically: " Including Bohemia ! "

Neither did the Chancellor succeed any better with us. Even the obsequious Kálnoky left him in the lurch. Our Foreign Minister did not share Bismarck's views, and produced serious arguments against them, though he would probably have yielded to his more powerful colleague had he not been subjected to counter-pressure. The proud Austrian noble was a man of common sense, an experienced and shrewd diplomat with excellent accomplishments, but he lacked initiative, courage, suggestive ability, and consequently he involuntarily came under the influence of the superior individuality of Bismarck. He must finally have suc-

9

cumbed to it but for the counter-pressure of Andrássy and the Hungarian public opinion which forced him into the opposite path.

Hitherto there had been differences of view between Andrássy and Bismarck, but so long as both of them were in office they had generally agreed in the end. Now, however, personal communication was inadequate to bridge the gulf of antagonism, and they came into violent conflict. Andrássy no more desired war than did Bismarck, but was convinced that it was easier to avoid war by an independent Eastern policy than by truckling to the Russians. He believed that were Austria - Hungary — supported by Germany, Great Britain, and also Italy (who could be relied upon in this case)—strenuously to resist the Russian expansion, were Pan-Slavism to be disappointed in Bulgaria and find that the Balkan nations desired their independence, then the Muscovites would turn their attention to Asia, where they had more at stake than in the Balkans, while they would not have the courage to attack us. France might be expected to restrain Russia to her utmost, having no mind to expose herself to the united power of Great Britain, Germany, and Italy in the cause of Pan-Slavism.

Division into spheres of interest—Andrássy held— though it might postpone war, would not render it any the less inevitable. It would simply be the means of creating new antagonisms. The eastern and western Balkans constituted a single political unit in a certain sense coherent, and if Russia should become master of the strong strategic base of the Black Sea, her progress could not be arrested by any artificial paper frontier : like an ink-blot on a piece of blotting-paper, it would spread until it had covered the whole region.

If we permitted this hypertrophy of power by Russia, we should become her slave; if we now fell without striking a blow, we should later have to shake off our fetters by fighting under conditions far less favourable. At the fateful moment we should find ourselves between the devil and the deep sea—attacked from Warsaw and the Belgrade-Cettinje line, and with disintegration at home.

It was Andrássy's deep-rooted conviction that the fate of the Dual Monarchy would be decided in the Balkans, that her vitality and strength would be increased by the absence of Russian rule in the Balkans and the dependence of the Balkan peoples on us; while, on the other hand, our existence would be jeopardised should Russia manage to get us between the Slav shears and be able to count on the obedience of the Balkan nations, whose racial kinsmen were very numerous in the Dual Monarchy. The recent fate of the Monarchy has proved that Andrássy was right. Its existence hung by a thread from the moment when the influence of Russia on the Yugoslavs was definitely established.

Andrássy was convinced that Bismarck could be won over to the more active Eastern policy of Austria-Hungary. He knew from experience that the Chancellor had really no confidence in Russian friendship, and was unwilling to be left to the tender mercies of the, at bottom hostile, Muscovites as his chief supporters. Though aware that Bismarck would domineer over us as far as he dared, Andrássy implicitly believed that, if only we stood firm, the Chancellor would eventually choose the more reliable friend of the two, as in 1879, when he supported us without any obligation on his part and even against his real inclination.

Andrássy also believed that in the event of Russia

incurring the risk of war for the attainment of her
ambitions, we should be victorious. He considered
the giant with the feet of clay to be corrupt, disor-
ganised, anæmic from the blood-sucking of the revolutionary vampire. He knew that she would nowhere
find sufficient allies to conquer the Central Powers
supported by Great Britain.

The correctness of this forecast seems to be proved
by the fact that Moltke, the famous strategist, and his
Chief-of-Staff, Waldersee, at the end of 1887 held the
same view and advised the provoking of a war then on
the ground that the conditions of victory would never
again be so auspicious as they were at that time.

On the basis of this conviction Andrássy expected
more energy and initiative on the part of our Government.   He foresaw that if Europe failed to bring
the question to an issue on account of Russia, the Prince
of Bulgaria would sooner or later be compelled to make
a pilgrimage to St. Petersburg (which Ferdinand actually did in 1896, when he won, at the cost of his son's
religion, that recognition which the united good-will of
Europe failed to procure for him).   To avoid such a
humiliation Andrássy advised the recognition of the
new Prince and the fulfilment of the union in the Concert of Europe.

In this Andrássy was supported by the majority of
the Hungarian public.   The opposition, led by Count
Albert Apponyi and Szilágyi, entirely agreed with
him ;   and even the Premier, Coloman Tizsa, with
his infallible tactical sense, perceived that it was a
matter that must be reckoned with.   Thus the defence
of the independence of the Balkan nations became the
watchword of the entire public opinion of Hungary.
Kálnoky, his hands strengthened by this movement—

or perhaps forced by it—abandoned the idea of spheres of interest.

Nevertheless Kálnoky was far from following Andrássy's policy. The official policy was the *via media* between the policies of Andrássy and Bismarck—skilful manœuvring between the pressures from each side. Kálnoky referred the Hungarians and Andrássy to Bismarck—Bismarck to us; he identified himself with Andrássy's policy so far as it prevented Russian aggression and military occupation, and openly proclaimed that the independence of the Balkan peoples was his object. But he limited himself to defence and made no attempt to settle the Bulgarian Question positively; he did not even object to the efforts at solution on the part of the Russians, in the hope that they could not be executed without force, to which he thought the Russians would not dare to resort. Kálnoky, however, made no attempt to exploit the opportunity of ousting the Muscovites from the Balkans and solving potential questions according to his own will and the interests of the peoples concerned. He contented himself with the negative success of maintaining the *status quo* disapproved by the Russians, so that the Czar might not ultimately triumph and we, on our part, might avoid an intolerable situation.

Even so, Bismarck was dissatisfied and angry with the Hungarians, and with Andrássy especially. He had got so used to reliance on Vienna, he held us Hungarians (and quite rightly) primarily responsible for the independence of the Dual Monarchy. He charged us with seeking revenge for Világos (1849), forgetting that if such had been the Hungarian mentality Andrássy could have attained it more easily after Plevna than at the time referred to. Bismarck retorted (September 1886) that he had concluded the alliance with the

Emperor, and not with men like Apponyi and Irányi, the Hungarian Winthorst and Richter. This was a most scathing denunciation from Bismarck, for the individuals mentioned were doughty opponents whom the Iron Chancellor would never forgive; they were the standard-bearers of Catholicism and Liberalism, preachers of doctrines and principles which the ultra-Protestant and autocratic Bismarck held in abhorrence. He objected to subordinating the German policy to Hungarian " Strebers " (pushful persons—a term of contempt); suiting it to the convenience and tactics of the Hungarian parties and the tomfooleries of the empty-headed chauvinistic Hungarian Parliamentarists. Now — he said—the extravagant rôle played by the Hungarian Parliamentarists was revenging itself: ignoring the fact that he himself, by his destruction of Austrian Absolutism (1866), had put those same Hungarian Parliamentarists into the saddle and given them his blessing.

When the Czar enquired of Schweinitz (August 1887) whether Bismarck still entertained his former high opinion of Andrássy, the Ambassador returned an evasive answer. Bismarck would probably have replied with strong language; at any rate, his opinion certainly was changed. According to him, Andrássy's attitude had wrought great mischief. He directly accused him of political ambitions. He attributed his policy to a desire for power and place. Such a charge was in keeping with the character of the old tyrant, who could brook no contradiction. How could Andrássy have been animated by a desire to win back a post he had quitted at the first favourable opportunity entirely of his own free will? He was ever actuated only by the firmest conviction that the interests of the Dual Monarchy demanded the policy he pursued—the legal sequel to the policy that had led to the treaty of 1879, and that as Foreign Minister he had pursued even to Bismarck's satisfaction. He would of course have undertaken, if necessary, to carry out his programme, but only if Francis Joseph had invited him to do so. The personal relations that had arisen during the long period of service alone rendered it impossible for him to coerce the Sovereign by the weapon of Parliamentarism to accept his (Andrássy's) policy.

But Bismarck, in spite of his bluster, found himself unable to carry through his programme. In December 1886 he stated officially that the " spheres of interest " idea had been rejected by Austria-Hungary and Russia alike, and that although he would eventually recognise in Serbia the Austro-Hungarian, and in Bulgaria the Russian, demands, he did not intend to try to obtain other converts to that doctrine.

4. The Agreement between England, Italy, and Austria-Hungary

When Bismarck saw that the scheme of spheres of interest had failed to put an end to the Austro-Hungarian and Russian rivalry in the Balkans, and that his pet idea, the Alliance of the Three Emperors, had come to be a mere empty form, he concocted a new and most ingenious plan. He was no Rechthaber, he had none of that vanity often associated with authorship, his actions were always such as the actual circumstances rendered necessary or advisable. He had several irons in the fire at once, and as soon as one grew cool he took up another which he had been keeping warm for the occasion. As soon as he realised his inability to bring the views of the two Emperors into line so that he need not fear conflict between them, he revised his entire plan of action and, with a twofold purpose in view, elaborated a new grouping of States.

One of his aims was to strengthen Austria-Hungary in view of a potential conflict, another to preserve Germany's freedom of action as long as possible, so that he might enjoy cordial relations with St. Petersburg till the last moment and frustrate the Franco-Russian Alliance in spite of the disunion between Russia and Austria-Hungary. It is illustrative of Bismarck's conscientiousness and sense of duty that, notwithstanding his strong subjectivity and passionate nature, while strenuously combating the political ideal of Andrássy, when he perceived that he could not completely defeat it he cast round for a means of exploiting it in the interests of the Fatherland. And this means he found in the alliance of Austria-Hungary, Italy, and Great Britain in defence of their common interests in the East. Though Germany remained outside, yet she gave the alliance her tacit goodwill and blessing.

Bismarck, indeed, was towards us the *deus ex machinâ*. Only a short time previously he had brought us into closer relations with the Russians and won for us the alliance with Italy ; now he desired to get Italy and England to support our Oriental interests. He was well aware that Italy would regard with some uneasiness the flag of the great Slav Power in the Mediterranean and the Adriatic, that the tradition of Cavour, who had participated in the Crimean War, was partly on that account still alive in Rome and that therefore Italy would be willing to challenge the supremacy of Russia in the East. But he knew further that we could, apart from that consideration, depend upon the Italians : the alliance with Italy would be reliable if only she could count on England too. Therefore, with a view to realising his project, he must first of all bring about amicable relations between Rome and London. With that object he used the lever first against the Consulta : he recommended the Italian Government to take steps to win England permanently (December 1886).   He emphasised the reports of military experts, according to which Italy would find herself in a grave dilemma on the French front, if she were obliged to storm the hills and defend her own long coast-line at the same time, unless she had command of the sea and were able to get round the Alpine forts by water, by effecting a landing at Marseilles.   The Anglo-Italian conversations thus begun soon came back to their originator.   That is to say, England naturally applied to Bismarck for information regarding the suggestions of Italy, since the German Chancellor was the most powerful man on the Continent, the very man with whom Salisbury desired to be on good terms, and who seized the opportunity thus presented for realising his own scheme.   In eloquent terms he explained to Sir Edward Malet, the British Ambassador (3rd February 1887), that England could not afford to isolate herself from the great European problems, since, if she did, no one would mind her, no one would consider her interests, and consequently she would be left out in the cold.   If England were indisposed to render reciprocal services, Germany would have no alternative but to support the French in Egypt and the Russians in the East.   " Germany," said Bismarck (and subsequent events proved him perfectly right) " must be in close touch with either England or Russia." If England cannot be approached, he must gravitate towards St. Petersburg.   Neither could Austria-Hungary oppose Russia unless she could rely on England and Italy ; the latter being needed by the Dual Monarchy also for the second important reason that, without British naval support, Italy could not risk exposing herself and her lengthy littoral for the sake of her alliance with Austria-

Hungary. The Chancellor clinched his arguments with the promise that if England would support him, she would find willing co-operators in the Central Powers, and moreover Germany, in the event of the Oriental crisis, would undertake to coerce France to keep neutral and thus save England from the only serious danger that would menace her.

These arguments went home to the English with convincing force. As Salisbury keenly desired the help of German diplomacy in the Egyptian Question, which was again becoming complicated, he asked Bismarck whether he was prepared to afford the same support if he (Salisbury) adopted the standpoint desired by the Chancellor. Bismarck's answer was an unreserved and unequivocal affirmative. He had at first used Egypt as a means of alienating England and France in order to obtain England's good-will in the matter of the German colonies, but now he exploited the difficulty on the Nile in order to induce England and Italy to support the Balkan policy of Austria-Hungary. In his zeal to win Salisbury, the Chancellor even engaged not to use his influence at Constantinople in favour of the Russians.

Further than this, however, he made no promise to the British Premier regarding Bulgaria, and candidly confessed to him that he should persist in his plan of spheres of interest. In regard to Serbia he adopted the Austro-Hungarian, in Bulgaria the Russian, and in Egypt the English attitude.

This should not appear surprising, for he could not do otherwise without abandoning his scheme. It was on the very account that he desired to enlist England and Italy for our cause, that he might in the first place avoid opposing Russia and not be compelled to take sides at the beginning, as the prime object of the whole manœuvre was to furnish us with a rearguard without driving Russia into the arms of France by offending her at the outset.

Bismarck's assurance satisfied Salisbury. He concluded with Italy (12th February 1887) the agreement proposed by Bismarck, thereby becoming a sleeping partner in a mighty continental political firm.

He did not accept all the far-reaching recommendations of the Italian Premier, Robilant ; he declined to stand solid with Italy as regarded all wars against France ; nevertheless he bound himself by an exchange of notes, avoiding the appearance of a formal alliance. Therein the two Powers actually undertook to maintain the *status quo* on the shores of the Mediterranean, the Ægean, and the Black Sea ; to oppose all foreign occupation there—this being directed as much against French expansion in Morocco and Tripoli as against the Russian in Bulgaria. In their respective notes Italy promised England *expressis verbis* a free hand in Egypt and England the same for Italy in Tripoli.

However, this Anglo-Italian *rapprochement* was insufficient for Bismarck. From the beginning his real object had been to strengthen the Eastern policy of Austria-Hungary, and therefore he informed the Ballplatz confidentially of the Anglo-Italian Treaty concluded through his intermediary and suggested that the Dual Monarchy should join the alliance as a *tertium quid* (15th February 1887).

In making this offer Bismarck manifested a striking change of front. During the autumn of 1886, when a similar combination was mooted on the part of England, he had testily called it " Bauernfängerei "—an attempt to jockey him. For Kálnoky, however, who still entertained the suspicion felt by Bismarck so shortly before, the plan seems to have had some difficulties. This would appear from the Foreign Minister's statement that he was willing to agree with England only when circumstances rendered such a step necessary. It is somewhat astonishing to find that he should consider such valuable advice rather as an evil pressed upon him than as a positive advantage.

Bismarck did not care to make himself conspicuous in the negotiations. If Russia were to discover that he had brought about the arrangement, he would expose himself to the vengeance of the Czar and find himself metaphorically in the first-line trenches, where he had no desire to be. Neither did the Chancellor wish to play the principal rôle as intermediary, lest his doing so should render it impossible from the beginning to settle the Eastern Question separately without the participation of France (11th March), a plan which would be frustrated if his secret were known on the Neva. He thought the best thing for Austria-Hungary to do would be—as he had so often urged before—to adopt the Russian attitude in Bulgaria. If, however, she were unwilling to do that, the only other thing he could advise would be to agree with England and Italy. Kálnoky did not long hesitate, but signed the pact with England and Italy on 23rd March 1887.

The contents of this Triple Agreement are more ample than those of the Anglo-Italian Double Agreement, the aim of the latter being the maintenance of the *status quo* " on the coasts " only, whereas the former provides for the preservation of the *status quo* on " all the territories and regions adjacent to the coasts."

For this achievement the credit is due to Bismarck ; it is the proof and the fruit of his intellectual elasticity, his skilful opportunism. He was listened to alike in

Rome, London, and Vienna ; his influence was felt in all three places ; his advice was solicited from all quarters, and, what is more—it was even followed.

5. Renewal of the Triple Alliance

Now began the onerous labours of the negotiations for the renewal of the Triple Alliance : Germany, Austria-Hungary, and Italy.

Robilant, the Italian Premier, and Kálnoky took opposite sides, the former stipulating for a new agreement and the latter standing out for the prolongation of the life of the old one. Bismarck acted as umpire in the dispute ; he was not unbiassed, however. The Italian manifested more decision of character : he was the more resolute, more fascinating in his manner ; and therefore Bismarck, not desiring to fall foul of him, deferred to him, admitted his premisses, brought pressure on us in his interests, and in general was complaisant towards him. The eminent judge of mankind once more cut his cloth according to his colleague's yard—and again at our expense.

Robilant opened the negotiations with consummate adroitness. He boasted of offers he had received from the French, and made much of the circumstance that Italian public opinion was displeased with the Triple Alliance and could only be won for it by its securing to Italy not only a favourable defensive position, but also the opportunity to prosecute her policy of expansion.

In this Robilant was quite right. It was true that the Italians could not easily be won for friendship with us.

Apart from the question of her integrity, Italy was offended with us on account of Francis Joseph's neglect to return the visit of Victor Emmanuel to Vienna, the Austro-Hungarian Monarch's regard for the Pope causing him to avoid visiting Rome.   During Andrássy's ministry the Emperor visited the ceded territory, but since the former's resignation nothing of the kind had taken place.   In such circumstances the Alliance could be made popular in Italy by tangible results only.   If, in spite of the Triple Alliance, Italy were to suffer from further French successes in Africa, the Alliance would be killed by the general antipathy.

Robilant therefore proposed to extend the *casus fœderis*, at the expense of the hitherto purely defensive character of the Alliance, to the contingency of Italy making war on France on account of her expansion on the coast of Africa.   He further insisted on our engaging to follow a common policy with Italy in the Balkans, lest Italy should be unexpectedly faced by the Three Emperors' Alliance with disagreeable *faits accomplis*.   The treaty should set forth that it was the mutual object of the contracting parties in their Eastern policy to preserve the *status quo* ; and that if its modification in respect of the Asiatic and Ægean coasts or the Turkish islands should at any time become necessary, the same could be effected only by mutual consent on the basis of compensation.

Kálnoky's idea—the maintenance of the original treaty—would have been more favourable for us.   But as Bismarck declined to support it, the former soon withdrew it, and accepted the amended treaty, though he would have liked to change certain particulars of the Italian project.   Our Foreign Minister was willing to accept Robilant's demands with regard to France on condition that Italy should agree to defend us against Russia, thus making amends for the omission in the original treaty.   He accepted also in principle the Italian proposal on the Eastern Question, but suggested certain modifications. He approved the common defence of the *status quo*, and was even willing to extend it from the coasts to the entire Balkan Peninsula, pointing out that the interests of Austria-Hungary were more endangered there than on the coast—this, however, only on Italy agreeing to relinquish her claim to compensation, since he saw in that a real danger and the source of endless complications.

Owing to Bismarck's insistence, the agreement was after lengthy negotiations concluded. Robilant yielded on the African Question, though we got no fresh assurance of aid in the event of Russian aggression. This compromise was brought about by the Chancellor, on this occasion, exceptionally, at the cost of sacrifices on his own part, in undertaking for himself alone the obligation that Robilant had stipulated also for us—to assist Italy in the event of her waging war with France on account of her expansion in North Africa. Bismarck explained his complacency in this matter by the statement that he undertook no more than his interests compelled him ; for whatever might be the cause of the conflict, as soon as France and Italy came to blows, the interests of Germany necessitated the victory of Italy.

But in the agreement regarding the East we got decidedly the worst of the bargain. The final result was even worse than if we had accepted the original Italian proposal ; for the Italians adopted our own recommendation that the *status quo* be extended to the entire Balkan Peninsula, instead of merely to the coast, while we accepted the principle of compensations notwithstanding we had proposed the extension in the hope that the compensations question would be dropped. Kálnoky perceived the drawback and would have preferred the original Italian proposal. But it was too late. Bismarck pressed him so hard that Kálnoky was obliged to sign the text he had hitherto refused. He was not even permitted to get his modest desire that any compensations exacted might be effected from foreign territory only, and not from that of the contracting parties. The Chancellor defeated our proposal with the jest that " such a thing would not do : it would be like unconditionally trusting your gambling partner with the bank and at the same time requiring his word of honour not to pick your pocket."

And yet such an agreement would have been advisable, though it might have failed to be adequately effective. It is conceivable that a gambler willing to entrust the bank to his partner might consider the contents of his pocket his own property by a prescriptive right superior to any treaty.

This unfortunate treaty was avenged at the outbreak of the World War. In consequence of its bad, careless, and faulty drafting, Italy was in a position to demand that we should arrange with her, before every military operation in Serbia, regarding the compensation to be awarded her. And it was owing to this defective instrument that the hesitation of the Dual Monarchy to concede the said demand was construed by Italian public opinion as an offensive and provocative breach of treaty—a construction which the Jingoes did not fail to exploit to the utmost.

When during the war this came to my knowledge, I was surprised at what appeared to me the shallowness of the Italian argument. To-day, however, knowing the antecedents better than I did then, I must admit that the Italians were not without justification for their standpoint.

The argument that, according to the treaty, Italy

could demand compensation only if our operations took place on the Turkish coast, looks very feeble when we reflect that it was no accident that the agreement was extended to the entire Balkan Peninsula—to which Serbia also belonged ; there was no error in the drafting, but it was done at our own proposal, because we considered the Turkish coast not a sufficiently wide sphere and intentionally contrived to include in the treaty not only the littoral but also the hinterland.

Our further contention that " temporary occupation in war-time signifies no territorial change and therefore cannot be made by Italy a basis for compensation " was rendered nugatory by Bismarck's interpretation, which, as we have already seen, regarded the temporary occupation of Serbia as a territorial change.

Without this explanation it would have been unjust to reproach Kálnoky for accepting the carelessly drafted treaty instead of insisting on the elimination of the absurd proviso that in a war actually in progress the enemy could not be attacked on his own ground, his defeated troops followed across the frontier without the previously obtained consent and satisfaction of a neutral State. But in view of such antecedents the acceptance of such a nonsensical text is seen to be a prodigious blunder, incomprehensible in a statesman. After the interpretation of Bismarck, the Italian interpretation could not very well be regarded as an absurdity against which it was not necessary to defend ourselves. Our blunder was all the graver as, according to documentary evidence, Kálnoky could have been successful, since at the beginning Italy did not insist so strongly on the principle of compensation, but rather was solicitous about getting more support in North Africa than formerly; in the Balkans she was merely con-

10

cerned in preventing Austria-Hungary from confronting her unexpectedly with unilateral conquests.

Our position in the negotiations was generally favourable. We were not bound to conclude agreements at any price. The relations between Italy and France were at that time so hostile that we had no fear of Rome changing places in the world-order by joining France, as she subsequently did. Kálnoky's responsibility is even more aggravated by the circumstance that he could have rendered our tactical situation much easier by making the Balkan Question one of those to be discussed with the English ; for England would certainly never have agreed to compensations the object of which was not apparent and which might tie her hands in the event of a war.

At all events, it cannot be denied that the Triple Alliance, as concluded, was the loss of another part of the precious heritage bequeathed by Andrássy.

The Alliance of the Three Emperors had already bound us hand and foot in the Balkans, where our fate was eventually to be sealed. Yet now we must don new fetters. Henceforth, no matter how urgent, how pressing, some defensive measure might be, we must first of all come to terms separately with two States whose interests were opposed, of which one was our chief rival, while the other was easily capable of becoming so ! Now in the Balkans we had got on a similar footing not only with Russia but also with Italy, though for neither of these Powers was the situation of the Peninsula so paramount, so vital as for us.

At this period (May 1887) Bismarck's powerful peace league obtained a new recruit, a most valuable one, owing to its geographical situation : Spain concluded an agreement with Italy in which the former engaged not to enter into any compact with France directed against Italy, Austria-Hungary, or Germany, especially with regard to the North African coast ; and also to enter, if necessary, into closer relations with the Triple Alliance in order to preserve the *status quo* in the Mediterranean (Pribram, *Geheimverträge Oesterreich-Ungarns*).

6. THE RUSSO-GERMAN SECRET TREATY

Scarcely had the old lion achieved his arduous task of renewing the Triple Alliance, scarcely had he secured once more the old line of defence against the French, than another delicate piece of work stared him in the face. The time of the expiration of the Three Emperors' Alliance was drawing near—that Alliance by virtue of which Bismarck attempted to make war impossible by the isolation of France.

The Three Emperors' Alliance was badly worn out by the course of events. Two of its members (the Dual Monarchy and Russia) were pursuing contrary policies and day by day violating their obligation to respect the interests of each other. Its predecessor (concluded in 1873) had been automatically ended by the Russo-Turkish War and the antagonism thereby caused between Russia and Austria-Hungary. Would the new Three Emperors' Alliance formed by Bismarck share the same fate ? Might not a new crisis arise in the East to prevent the renewal of the treaty ?

The German Chancellor had long foreseen this danger ; the leading motive of his whole policy was to counterbalance it, and to give the Eastern Question a direction which would facilitate the co-operation of these two allies. He desired to maintain his favourite scheme —the Alliance of the Three Emperors—even when all real co-operation was plainly impossible, sincerity being lacking. He would rather have a mere formal existence than a complete break-up. And seeing he could not manage even the former—that St. Petersburg was indisposed to conclude an alliance with us, that even Kálnoky's complaisance failed to disarm the Czar's court—when he had to decide whether to put an end to his connection with St. Petersburg or agree with Russia without us, Bismarck chose the latter course (10th January 1887).

At first he had no intention of concealing his decision. He informed Kálnoky (17th January) of his willingness to agree with the Russians if necessary without us. Later, however, he entirely ignored Kálnoky and did not inform him of his having opened negotiations with Giers, and concluded the treaty behind Kálnoky's back (15th June). He did not even condescend to mention the treaty after it had been concluded. He observed strict reticence towards everybody. The appendix to the treaty is marked " *très secret.*" Giers referred to it as " *la partie archi-secrète.*" Accordingly Bismarck advised Emperor William to answer evasively and conceal the truth if taxed by Francis Joseph with the matter.

This secret agreement bound the two parties thereto to benevolent neutrality in all wars, except in the event of France attacking Germany or Russia attacking us. Apart from these duo-lateral commitments, the treaty imposed unilateral obligations on Germany. Bismarck committed himself to the Russian policy in the Balkans. He recognised the historic right of the Russians in that region, especially their decisive influence in Bulgaria and Eastern Rumelia. He promised to object to any alteration of the *status quo* without Russia being first consulted, and even pledged the moral support and diplomatic assistance of Germany in the event of Russia considering it necessary to take possession of the key of her house—the Dardanelles.

7. BISMARCK'S EXPLANATION OF THE SECRET TREATY

By this agreement Bismarck entered upon untried paths, ways which were in opposition to the obligations he had taken to himself.   The secrecy itself was flagrantly opposed to the Triple Alliance, which provided that it was the duty of the Allies to inform each other of the plans of foreign States with regard to the *status quo* in the Balkans. Germany's obligation of benevolent neutrality towards Russia, if we attacked the latter, was a violation of Article 1 of the Triple Alliance Treaty, in which we swore eternal amity and declared we would never be privy to any agreement against any one of us. Such an obligation might also bring him into conflict with another obligation originating in the Triple Alliance, according to which he was bound to display benevolent neutrality towards us in the event of our attacking any Power (including Russia) owing to the Power in question menacing our safety by its behaviour (*vide* Article 4). The friendly contractual relations between us were violated by the very fact that Bismarck engaged to promote Russian schemes in which, as he well knew, we saw great danger and against which he himself had formed the Alliance of the Mediterranean Powers.   The treaty was unfair for Salisbury too. He—who had joined the Mediterranean Alliance because it had been proposed by Bismarck, because the latter had declared that he would not exercise in Constantinople any influence in a direction objectionable to the Alliance—might rightly have objected, if only he had been aware of it, to Bismarck having undertaken an obligation at variance with this promise to support the Russian plan. Salisbury —who signed the treaty on Bismarck's promise to keep France from intervening should England get entangled in a war with Russia in consequence of the treaty— would lose confidence if informed that his friend had wittingly allowed himself to get into a situation in which he would be unable to fulfil this promise. For the English Premier might justly have asked : How could Bismarck make a *casus belli* out of France's going to the defence of Russia when the Chancellor had himself adopted and would be compelled to support the Russian attitude ?

What was the object of this secret treaty ? What did Bismarck expect to gain by it ? Was it a change in the direction he had hitherto followed ? Did he perchance desire, as in 1872, to fix the centre of his defensive policy once more on the banks of the Neva until he had done with Gortchakoff, lost his confidence in the Russians, and found his chief support in us ?

All the signs pointed to the contrary. Bismarck deceived Russia rather than us and England. He did not wish to change the alliances. He was not in need of any support on the Neva. Russia remained his potential adversary, against whom he armed and whom he mistrusted. His sole desire was to maintain the contractual relations with her in order to avoid the raising of the *casus fœderis* against her which was fixed in several treaties which Bismarck considered binding and meant to enforce also in future. The secret pact contemplated no ally for the eventuality of war.

The agreement aiming at the prevention of hostilities was merely a compromise between enemies, nothing more. Bismarck's opinion was that the vital interests of Germany were bound up with our position of power. Lest the Czar might conclude an alliance with the French, which should result in a world war—a contingency which Bismarck with remarkable prophetic vision foresaw with horror as the prelude of a mighty social upheaval—he set himself to beguile the Czar with fine phrases and fair promises, the strict fulfilment of which would have brought him into conflict with his obligations to others. He had, however, no intention of keeping them strictly, or of rendering Russia any really valuable service. He was not going to leave us in the lurch for the sake of the Muscovites. He neither promised nor intended to render any positive military assistance ; he confined himself to diplomatic and moral support. And such elastic terms could always be interpreted by the wily old diplomat—who whenever necessary was a first-class sophist—in such a manner that he would get no trouble, Russia no profit, and we no harm therefrom.

The experienced statesman had no fear that within a measurable distance of time any decisive step would become necessary in which his tried skill would be inadequate to bridge the gulf of opposing duties. For the Russians themselves held that the solution of the Straits problem was unlikely to be arrived at within a brief period. The Ambassador Schuvaloff announced that the Black Sea fleet would have to be built twenty or thirty years before it was fit for a decisive action in the Dardanelles. Giers regarded the occupation of the Straits as such a remote contingency that the German promises with reference thereto had, in his opinion, no great value. Why, then, should not Bismarck promise for the next three years a platonic support that would probably not be required for several decades ?

Further, Bismarck foresaw that the Russian Government, owing to its indecision, would not resort to those means whereby it might attain its object ; he foresaw that the megalomaniac schemes of the Muscovites would only make them foes in the Balkans, and that they would certainly turn England and Italy—perhaps also France—against them. Why should Bismarck prevent Russia weakening herself and making a mess of her affairs, when he knew that he would get no thanks for so doing ? His good advice would only be resented.

Bismarck's mental reserve is manifested in his pencilled observations on the diplomatic notes. They are of decided importance, since they were intended for the guidance of the Foreign Office. For instance, one such marginal note states that it was superfluous to inform the Russians of the futility of their plans—German diplomacy should be confined to giving the Russians certain assistance in times of crisis. This dissimulation is also seen in his argument to Kálnoky (17th June 1887) : on the latter declaring his unwillingness to stand godfather to the still-born children of the Russian Government, Bismarck assured him that that was quite unnecessary, and it was one thing to promote the wild schemes of Russia and another thing to interfere to prevent her carrying them *ad absurdum*.

The Chancellor, with his cool judgment of the situation, calculated on the discomfiture of the Russians, and he had no mind to quarrel with St. Petersburg in order to save them from the fiasco. His dissimulation is again shown in his discussion with Kálnoky on the *casus fœderis* ; explaining his attitude to his own Foreign Office with the remark that he should only foster the Dual Monarchy's will for war if he were to clear up the question as to when he should support it— which evidently signified that such clearing-up would be favourable to the Dual Monarchy. On still another occasion Bismarck betrayed similar craftiness when he explained the pressure he had put on Vienna by saying that he had only meant it as an inducement for Austria-Hungary to arm (6th and 15th December 1887).

It is noteworthy that Bismarck did not say that he would not support us if we should be the attacking party —he only stressed the point that in that case he would not be bound to do so, because of his promise to the Russians and because it would be an incitement to us to war. The long and the short of it was that he reserved to himself all decision regarding the *casus fœderis*, on the ground of his considering the case upon its merits when it arose, without committing himself further in the meantime (19th and 20th December 1887).

The same spirit of dissimulation is shown in Bismarck's declaration that as soon as he saw that a Russo-Austrian war was inevitable, he would not take the *casus fœderis* too strictly, but would quickly mobilise and intervene (8th, 19th, 24th January 1888) ; and that in interpreting the terms of the alliance he should not be guided by the letter but rather by the fact that it was the vital interest of Germany to prevent our defeat (17th January 1888).

Everything that Bismarck did at this period was strictly in keeping with this fundamental idea. Whenever the Russians applied to him for active assistance he could always find a pretext for a *non possumus*. The kind of support he rendered to the Muscovites consisted of lecturing us on the innocuousness of the Russian policy and the errors of our own. He knew he could depend on us to receive his disagreeable scoldings with an appearance of respect, and he wanted to keep us from getting at loggerheads with Russia. As soon, however, as she wanted positive help, he took refuge in evasions.

This was quite consistent with his deliberate intention to avoid promoting the Russian policy and at the same time to eliminate antagonism between the Russians and ourselves, and to keep for himself as long as possible their good-will, lest the counter-attraction of Paris should weaken the connection resulting from the blood-relationship of the German Kaiser and the Russian Czar.

After the Anglo-Italian Mediterranean pact already referred to, Bismarck, on the ground of his promise to Salisbury, directed Radowitz, Ambassador at the Sublime Porte, to refrain from advocating the Russian attitude, as previously, but to appear indifferent and impartial (17th February 1887). And after the Russian secret agreement, too, Bismarck acted in the spirit of this instruction, notwithstanding it was a breach of the said secret agreement and the Russians demanded the promised aid. In short, the Chancellor acted in accordance with his promise to England and not with that to Russia in the treaty.

When the Ottoman Minister for Foreign Affairs (in order probably to sound Bismarck's real intentions, and to comply with the Russian demands only if the Chancellor seriously wished it) asked Bismarck to recommend in Rome, Vienna, and London the Bulgarian mission of Enroth, a Russian General, the Chancellor replied (3rd September 1887) that he would do so only if it were " officially and publicly " proposed by Russia and Turkey jointly, though he knew perfectly well that that was the very thing they sought to avoid, as they expected its success solely from Bismarck's initiative and did not wish to court its rejection.

Also when (December 1887) the Russians asked the Chancellor to support their action in Constantinople (where the counteraction of Great Britain, Austria-

Hungary, and Italy was encouraged by Bismarck and where his hitherto displayed reserve and caution strengthened the passive resistance of the Turks), the Chancellor ca'cannied, stating that he had no interests in Constantinople and that Russia should take the initiative. He might possibly help, but not lead. He was the less disposed to take any prominent part in the matter as the tone of the Russian press was then so unfriendly to Germany that any services Bismarck might render to Russia would only be construed as a sign of cowardice.

When Robilant demanded that the *casus fœderis* should be extended against France, Bismarck had consented, as previously mentioned, with the motivation that, no matter what had precipitated the conflict, he would not allow Italy to be defeated. On the very same ground it now became desirable that Bismarck should stand by us in any resort to arms in connection with the Balkan Question. The balance of power in Europe would just as certainly be shifted ; Russia would be just the same menace if she were to defeat us on account of Bulgaria and the Straits as of Serbia. In such an event Germany's interests would not be compromised by the cause but by the consequence of the war. Bismarck must surely have realised that.

I am sure that Bismarck was absolutely sincere in telling Salisbury after signature of the secret treaty (27th July 1887) that the alliance with us would be permanent irrespective of the fixed number of years for which it was concluded, for any German Chancellor who should abandon us for the Russians would certainly come to grief with his own people ; and also in writing to Emperor William I on July 28th 1887, when the ink was scarcely dry on the treaty, that the sentiments and

the interests alike of the German people rendered it
" impossible " for Germany to conclude a pact with
Russia which would imperil Austria-Hungary and that
the Fatherland would never sacrifice the Alliance with
the Dual Monarchy, deep-rooted in mutual sympathy,
for the friendship of Russia, which possessed no such
source of strength. Out of sincere conviction somewhat
later the venerable statesman, on the occasion of the
young Emperor William II's visit to St. Petersburg,
wrote that the German Emperor's conduct towards the
Russians ought to be subordinated to the consideration
of not breaking the bonds of friendship with Austria-
Hungary, as it was better and safer than that of the
Muscovites, since the former was dependent on Germany
while the latter were not ; moreover, the one already
existed, and the other had yet to be acquired ; and,
finally, Francis Joseph's pretensions were more modest
than those of the Czar.

If Bismarck failed to promise us unconditional assistance, as he did to Italy, his reasons for the omission
were purely tactical. He had no intention of doing
less for us than for Italy, in whom he had less confidence
than in us, and whose alliance he considered less valuable than ours. He promised the Ballplatz less than
the Consulta simply because he considered the first
promise disadvantageous and the latter indifferent.
He had at this time no reason for sparing France, and
therefore he could extend the *casus fœderis* against her
for the sake of the Italians ; but he was anxious to avoid
offending the Czar, and so he would undertake no new
casus belli against Russia in our interests. He expected
the France of Boulanger and Déroulède to pursue an
anti-German policy whatever might be the text of the
agreement with Italy ; and he thought it would drive

Russia into the arms of France if he openly declared at the outset against her Oriental ambitions, and bound himself in advance to solidarity with us absolutely unconditionally, even for the contingency of aggression on our part. This differential treatment was due also to the circumstance that Bismarck was convinced that Kálnoky would neither seek nor find the way to St. Petersburg, however dissatisfied he might be with Berlin ; while he was afraid that Robilant, if neglected, might easily win the friendship of the French, and accept it in lieu of that of the Germans.

We were absolutely at Bismarck's orders—we had no alternate choice, and therefore he did not spare us. But Italy might desert Germany, if she were disposed ; she could get along without us ; therefore Bismarck humoured her.

This policy does not appeal to one's sympathy ; it was not straight, yet it did not spring from vanity, nor from a desire for enhanced prestige or extension of territory, but solely from a laudable endeavour to avert a terrible catastrophe—that world war from the dire consequences of which all humanity is suffering to-day.

8. Scheme for an Anglo-German Alliance

The intentions of Bismarck at the time of concluding the secret treaty are illuminated as if exposed to a searchlight by his later actions. The supposition that he sought to make Russian friendship the basis of his political system is quite excluded by the fact that, after the treaty was signed, he thwarted Russia with the same pertinacity as before. Even now Bismarck was not content with allowing Russia to dash her head against a wall—he even took care to raise the wall for that purpose.

Salisbury (probably in order to discover whether the German Chancellor had any suspicion that if he made a *rapprochement* to Russia, Great Britain also might change the trend of her policy) had a conversation with the German Ambassador (17th August 1887) which gave the impression that instead of the previous Austro-Hungarian orientation England desired a *rapprochement* with Russia.

If the Chancellor really wanted to change his direction and incline towards Russia, he would have welcomed with pleasure the British Premier's implied hint. In the then state of affairs, however, he feared it. He wrote in a marginal note that "*primo loco* he desired the maintenance of the Anglo-Austro-Italian Agreement, and only in case that were impossible would he entertain Salisbury's idea." It was solely on that account that he did not speak openly against it, because then, he said, Salisbury would perceive that Germany could be intimidated by his coquetting with the Russians, and Bismarck was averse to placing in the hands of the British Government such a weapon to be used against the Fatherland.

Notwithstanding this, however, his every word was directed against an Anglo-Russian *rapprochement*. He openly warned the Court of St. James's that Germany must decline to have any hand in agreements antagonistic to us. He pointed out also that if England sought the friendship of the Czar, it might happen that Austria-Hungary and Turkey would forestall her and that Italy would incline to France. Germany, he said, would not be affected by this change of British policy, for she could revive the Alliance of the Three Emperors against western democracy. In the course of conversation Bismarck observed that he doubted whether

Russia would keep her promise, and especially recommended Salisbury, instead of changing his policy, to stick to the friendship of Austria-Hungary and Italy and try to approach St. Petersburg together with them.

Bismarck did his utmost to turn the attention of the British Premier to all points calculated to keep him from changing his policy; and Salisbury understood. Being aware that Germany intended to adhere to the old orientation, he decided to do the same (18th August).

That, however, was not enough for Bismarck. His entire political direction was marked by the fact that he was dissatisfied with having merely persuaded Salisbury not to change his policy—he was bent on increasing the power of the Mediterranean Entente protecting the Dual Monarchy. Influenced by his father's conviction that this Entente could be best completed by the co-operation of the Turkish army, Herbert Bismarck in London launched the idea of the Ambassadors of the Allied Powers at Constantinople endeavouring to gain over the Sublime Porte and emancipate it from the influence of Russia. And by virtue of this suggestion, the Ambassadors actually agreed upon the project of a new treaty.

According to this project, the Three Powers should jointly and severally declare that they would use all their endeavours to prevent the Sultan giving Russia any privileges in the Balkans and allowing Russia to obtain the same by force. If the Sultan should get involved in war with Russia on this account, the Three Powers should come to an arrangement as to the amount and quality of the assistance to be afforded him. They further decided that should the Turks yield to Russian pressure, the Powers should provide for the defence of their interests by occupying suitable positions (20th October 1887). This scheme, like most important political movements, came before completion to the Wilhelmstrasse, the centre of European diplomacy.   Before making his final decision, Salisbury applied to Bismarck—the virtual leader of the Continent—for a clear understanding, free from all ambiguity and subterfuge, as to whether he approved of the new grouping : whether the young Prince William would, in spite of his well-known Russophilism, follow Bismarck's policy.   The Chancellor, with the approval of the venerable Emperor William, was anxious to " encourage " his English colleague ; and so he sent to Downing Street an extract from the treaty of alliance between Germany and Austria-Hungary, thereby proving that Germany was attached to us by firm bonds which each Emperor must respect.

Besides this, the Chancellor in a lengthy private letter admirably summed up the reasons which rendered the anti-Russian grouping necessary in the common interest of both Germany and England.

In this document, which later became deservedly famous, the Chancellor explained that the Enperor, altogether irrespective of his personal tastes and inclinations, could at all times only follow a policy in keeping with the interests of Germany, seeing that it was solely with the consent of the millions of his people that he could resort to compulsory military service, and the German nation could not afford to permit the position of Austria-Hungary as a Great Power to be destroyed, since Germany could not do without her aid.   Without that she would be exposed to the risk of a coalition of France and Russia without any continental defence.   He explained that England, Austria-Hungary, and Germany were " saturated " (i.e. consolidated), while France and Russia were discontented, and therefore the former must be prepared against any outbreak on the part of the latter. France always had been—and was now—aggressive, and Russia was beginning to imitate the rôle of Louis XIV and Napoleon I. The revolutionary party wanted a war in order to exploit it for the overthrow of Czarism ; and on the other hand Czarism wanted a war in order to curb the revolutionary ardour by victory. Bismarck preferred to avoid war, but so long as Austria-Hungary and England did not change their direction, Germany would continue to be their trusty friend, ready to defend the independence and status of the Dual Monarchy as well as of England and Italy and prevent their defeat by French arms. But with Russia and against her natural allies (Austria-Hungary and England) Germany would never draw the sword.

He entirely approved the definite suggestion and advised his friends to form a coalition for the defence of their special interests in the East. He hoped that the alliance would be powerful enough to keep the Russian sword in its sheath, or, if drawn, to break it.

Bismarck prompted also the union of the Mediterranean Powers by advising his friend Crispi, the new Italian premier—an enthusiastic supporter of the Francophobe-Germanophil policy, a veteran revolutionary who carried with him into his new post all the fire and zeal of his youth—to agree with Kálnoky in regard to the Eastern Question. Crispi's confidence and courage were increased by the Chancellor's declarations that if the alliance formed by him between Italy, England, Austria-Hungary should get involved in hostilities on account of the Eastern Question, he would act as their rear-guard, prepared to intervene with arms, and that there was no cause to fear Russia, who had an Achilles'

11

heel in Poland. The foundation of an independent Poland under an Austrian archduke had already been decided upon, with a view to giving effect to the plan.

Our situation in the Great War would have been considerably alleviated if the successors of Bismarck had discerned their interests as quickly as did the Iron Chancellor and taken the way proposed by him. Instead of this, however, with what hesitation, shilly-shally, and vacillation they weakened that lever which Polish national sentiment might have afforded us!

Thus it was due to Bismarck's untiring energy that the new agreement between England, Austria-Hungary, and Italy was concluded—an improved and enlarged edition of the first agreement proposed and carried through by him. This new agreement was also, like the former, directed against Russia. Salisbury, in his note (30th November), emphasised that it would not be the least of Bismarck's brilliant merits that he had scotched Russian aggression. The contents of the treaty were identical with the proposals of the Ambassadors (December 1887), with the addition that, with regard to the defence of the Straits, it extended not only to the Balkans but also to Asia Minor.

This was, however, not the only achievement demonstrating that the great German strove, even after the conclusion of the Russian secret treaty, at the maintenance of our position ; equally manifest was the rôle he designed for the Fatherland if the alliance formed by him were compelled to attack Russia on behalf of its Oriental interests.

The General Staffs of Austria-Hungary and Germany attempted to make mutual military agreements which would soon have led to war. Moltke, swayed by the conviction that the Muscovites were preparing for hostilities, and that the military situation of the Central Powers could only become worse by waiting, wished to avert the threatened danger by prompt action against Russia. Bismarck, however, shook his head—not because he did not desire our victory, for he had invariably sought to make us strong, and urged upon us the necessity of increasing our army—not because he altogether condemned such a step, for he had stated (15th December) that if he were the leading minister of the Danubian Monarchy, with the prospect of being backed by England, Italy, and Turkey, he might even be willing to precipitate such a conflict—but because he intended a special rôle for Germany therein.

He thought (15th December 1887) that in such an event Germany should turn against France, not against Russia, and should intervene in an Oriental war only after she had settled accounts with the Gauls.

He desired to avoid a campaign on two fronts, and would prefer to use the undivided military strength of Germany first of all against France—and only after routing her, against Russia.

I am not competent to judge, from the military viewpoint, who was right—Bismarck or Moltke. But one fact is clear : that this conception of the Chancellor was not influenced by the Russian alliance, but meant as an execution of the Mediterranean alliance against the Russians, and had its roots in loyalty to us.

This conception, in my opinion, contained all the principles by which Bismarck was guided. He was chary of promises ; he promised us nothing ; he refrained from advising us to commence hostilities ; but if ever we found ourselves at war, he would fulfil his engagement as rearguard and keep France out. He would have done even more than he engaged to do : after defeating France he would have settled with Russia.

The same orientation is manifested in the fact that Italy at the same time became attached more closely to the anti-Russian coalition. Hitherto Italy, apart from the obligations upon her by the Mediterranean alliance, was not bound to assist Austria-Hungary or Rumania in the event of Russian aggression. Now, however, decided progress has been made in this respect. Italy joined the alliance of Austria-Hungary and Rumania (1888), and undertook that when the *casus fœderis* provided for in the treaty arose, she would immediately take counsel with us with regard to common action (Pribram).

Accordingly Bismarck did not become more Russophil but the reverse. The friendship of England was now more important in his eyes—the plan he had striven to carry out in 1879 in co-operation with Andrássy. This led to the new Mediterranean alliance. And this orientation became so valuable that, contrary to his former view, the Chancellor (11th January 1889), made to England a formal offer of alliance, for the contingency of an attack on her by France. He referred to the fact that such an alliance would render war impossible, since neither France nor Russia would dare to provoke hostilities if they were aware that England was with us ; and that, moreover, it would protect England from invasion, which, considering the present high development of science, would, failing the proposed alliance, be merely a matter of the weather and the number of ships in the English Channel at the decisive moment.

Salisbury, however, was indisposed for an alliance against France ; and thus it was no fault of Bismarck's that the friendship of England he had so carefully cultivated did not blossom forth into a closer political relationship.

9. THE FALL OF BISMARCK

The scheme for an alliance with England was Bismarck's swan-song in foreign policy. Even when issuing it, the Great Chancellor was on the eve of his fall; his fate was already sealed.

In theory Bismarck recognised one sole form of government—that of a monarchy in which the supreme leadership is vested in the sovereign; in practice, however, his own powerful personality led to this ideal being transformed into the omnipotence of the Chancellor himself.

William II, who had now come to the throne, in all the vigour and ardour of his gifted youth, preferred to rule according to the pure and undiluted doctrine of his famous political schoolmaster. The young Emperor's model was Frederick II of Prussia, who always undertook everything personally, and gave decisions and issued orders on every possible matter connected with the government of his country. Like his great ancestor, William II held the firm conviction that he exercised the royal powers and prerogatives by Divine right, considering himself responsible for his actions to God alone. In thus interpreting the rights and duties of his exalted station, the young Emperor left no place for the exercise of that authority which the famous Chancellor had wielded, by virtue of his commanding personality, by the side of the patriarchal William I and afterwards by that of the fatally stricken Emperor Frederick. The new Emperor William required an obedient instrument, a servant, not a tyrannical master such as the old statesman had always been towards everybody.

William II's lofty sense of duty, his personal ambition, irrepressible energy, his peculiar opinions on various matters besides home and foreign politics, which differed widely from those of the Chancellor, all combined to cause him to govern the empire inherited from his father according to his own views. And swarms of sycophants were not wanting to help by their flatteries to lead him into that fatal course.

The régime of Bismarck had lasted too long ; it was now out of date. It had been glorious, but remorselessly harsh towards the opponents of the Iron Chancellor, who had treated everybody with suspicion and intolerance. His enemies were compelled to denounce his methods, as otherwise they could not be sure that the " Bismarck era " would terminate even with his decease. They saw in his son Herbert a successor who was to be feared perhaps even more than the old man. Count Herbert Bismarck was gifted with a fresh and alert mind, broad experience, and an excellent capacity for routine ; he had been educated by the best teacher imaginable—his incomparable father ; he was a staunch friend, an implacable foe (especially towards his father's enemies) ; a pleasant, worthy, useful man : yet withal multitudes were anxious lest he should continue the régime of his father, with the inherited tyrannical tendency but lacking the exceptionally rare genius of the Teutonic Titan.

The young Emperor, easily influenced by flattery, was urged on all sides to get rid of his old Chancellor. But how was this to be done ? Bismarck stuck to his post with the tenacity of a leech. Though he knew he could never work with William II, yet he refused to resign—he would cast on his young sovereign the odium and the responsibility for his dismissal, before both his contemporaries and posterity. He considered it would be a dereliction of his duty to stand aside ; he was indispensable ; there was no other Bismarck at hand with his experience, his prestige, such a pillar of Germandom. Who can condemn him for this attitude ? Who can be surprised at his persistence ? Quite mediocre holders of power who are no Bismarcks very often think and act in this manner when the time comes for their retirement from public service. Hangers-on, who fall with them, proclaim the doctrine that the country will surely go to the dogs if others take the place of their chief and themselves, and they repeat it in season and out of season until they end by believing it. In the course of my own political career I have often observed that one motive for the stubborn clinging to office is the megalomania engendered by the flattery of toadies. As those about him stand to lose by the fall of their patron, and as he mistakes his clients for the nation itself, the falling leader is apt to regard his personal misfortune as a national tragedy. He discovers his error only when the anticipated catastrophe does not take place, when he sees that the world revolves as before and he does not appear even to be missed.

But Emperor William's position was rendered very difficult by the obstinacy of the old Chancellor. The sovereign himself had actually to dismiss—in plain terms, to " turn out "—the man to whom he owed his imperial throne, the founder of the empire, the man whom the entire German nation honoured as her most illustrious son.

The Bismarck era closed in depressing discord, amidst all the signs of human imperfection. The sun-flowers — the " mamelukes " — abandoned him ; like one of old, they denied their fallen lord. Those men who owed everything, emoluments and honours, to Bismarck now turned from him to the Emperor for confirmation in their offices. On the occasion of the wedding of Count Herbert at Vienna I witnessed not a few conspicuous instances of this shameful disloyalty, which justly aroused the indignation of his family.

On that occasion I realised for the first time in my life the depth of ingratitude, opportunism, time-serving, coat-turning, and utter lack of principle, under the crushing weight of which during the latest revolutions, the dynasties, rulers, and constitutions of so many States have been ruthlessly swept away ; and in their stead have been set up Governments supported by the faithful adherents of whatever party might be in power for the time being, together with the ever-numerous crowd of mean-spirited, backboneless place-hunters.

BOOK II

FROM BISMARCK TO BÜLOW

I. CAPRIVI (1890–1894)

CHAPTER I

RENEWAL OF THE ALLIANCE

BISMARCK'S successor, General Caprivi, aimed in every particular at following the path taken by that illustrious statesman. His chief object was the maintenance of peace and German supremacy bound up with it. He advocated peace, not only because Germany, as Bismarck had said, was " saturated " and had more to lose than to gain by wars, but also because William II was a peace-lover from his impulsive nature and warm heart, not to speak of his lofty sense of duty, as one may realise not only from his public utterances, but also from the private marginal notes he was accustomed to make on official documents. When, for instance, he was informed that the Italian Foreign Minister was surprised that the Kaiser, a young man, with such an immense army, had no warlike aspirations, he made the significant rejoinder that he " was not a *condottiere*, but a Hohenzollern." And when on 20th February 1902 St. Petersburg was disturbed, lest he should commit the " madness " of attacking Russia, William wrote that such an action would be " *meanness*," not " madness."

A simple event of this period is recorded that might perhaps have cast a shadow of doubt over his pacific disposition. This, however, was based on a misunderstanding ; it does not in the least prove any aggressive intention on the part of the Kaiser, but merely the will-to-peace of his ally, Francis Joseph. On the occasion of the military manœuvres at Szombathely, after exhaustive conversations had taken place between the two imperial friends, Francis Joseph observed to the German Ambassador that it was a mistake to belittle the power of the Russians, as the German Kaiser had done, for though not faultless, it might, if only numerically, prove a formidable factor. The aged ruler appeared anxious lest his young colleague should fail to take the Muscovite power seriously and decide on war without counting the cost. But the German Emperor wrote on the margin of his Ambassador's report of the incident, that Francis Joseph had misunderstood him. The words he had spoken in praise of the Austro-Hungarian troops were intended only to banish the pessimism of Vienna and not to incite his ally to war. He added that he could not help it if Francis Joseph, who had lost so many campaigns, interpreted an appreciation of his forces as the desire to start another war.

It seemed at first as if William II had attempted to put an end to the constant and deep-seated Germanophobia of the French, or at least considerably to mitigate it. He could not in the least be blamed for Sedan; he had various characteristics similar to the French; he entertained a lively sympathy for his genial Gallic neighbours, like whom he was often influenced by his sentiments: thus he had hoped to be understood in Paris. His amiability won all the Frenchmen with whom he had opportunity to come into contact. M. Jules Simon, the redoubtable leader of the Left, was quite charmed with the Emperor on meeting him at the Labour Congress at Berlin. Why might William not equally succeed in winning the whole French nation ? Of course the young Emperor had many flatterers. His attendants assured him, and even persuaded themselves, that he was capable of accomplishing whatever he would. It was therefore natural for him to think he could capture Paris by pacific means. A splendid idea! A noble ambition, worthy of a magnanimous young monarch! And at first sight the experiment seemed very promising of success.

The Emperor's participation in the mourning of the French people for the loss of their idolised painter Meissonier had a tremendous effect in Paris. Moreover, a benign influence was exercised by the German Government's alleviation of the passport regulations with regard to the annexed provinces, which had hitherto caused great friction and bitterness of spirit among the population affected.

Count Münster, Ambassador to Paris, on the 19th February 1891, reported that the French Germanophobia had visibly abated and that improved relations were apparent between the nationals of the two countries. The diplomats of the old school, however, were beginning to show anxiety for these new tactics of William II. Kiderlen, a chief-of-section in the Berlin Foreign Office, declared (18th April 1890) his fear that such coquetting with the French would lead to no good : it would only excite the jealousy of England and Italy, and thus bring about a *rapprochement* of the Powers with France.

But the Emperor continued the even tenor of his way. He chose his mother—Emperor Frederick's shrewd and tactful yet withal charming and high-souled widow (whose wondrously lovely, expressive eyes I recall even at this distance of time)—to promote a good understanding between the Teuton and Gallic neighbours in the sphere of culture. With this eminently worthy object the Empress-mother visited the French metropolis, to invite the co-operation of the French artists in a projected Berlin Exhibition. At first the lady, exalted as regards both birth and station, was cordially received, but ere long a reaction set in. The chauvinism of the French began to awake ; the artists who had promised their participation took fright and withdrew from the scheme, which resulted in a fiasco. At any moment a " regrettable incident " might have occurred. Even the contingency of war was not excluded.

Later also William II attempted to get nearer to the soul of the French by certain friendly overtures. He sent his representative to the funeral of Maréchal Mac-Mahon. In July 1894, after the assassination of President Carnot, he set at liberty two French spies. These things, however, were no longer regarded as signs of a policy but merely as isolated acts rightly intended to allay the violence of the contrasts.

Since the visits of the Empress Victoria (widow of Frederick III) to Paris, it was clear to William that the French would never become reconciled to the Peace of Frankfort, and that their Germanophobia was so deep-rooted that even those statesmen of the Republic who in their inmost hearts desired peace and friendship with Germany lacked the courage to proclaim their convictions and oppose the popular prejudice. Since that fiasco it became evident that the only policy open to Germany was that of Bismarck, and that the only right aim was to render the antipathy of the French innocuous, as Bismarck had done.

And the successor of Bismarck desired to use the same means as the Iron Chancellor. Under Caprivi, as under Bismarck, the Triple Alliance formed the basis of German policy, whose object was to maintain such a superiority of force as effectually to quench the thirst of the French for an eventual *revanche*.

But it was impossible to renew the Triple Alliance

without serious difficulties. As in the past, Italy now also expected to reap fresh advantages. Like Robilant, who in 1887 succeeded in improving the status of Italy within the Triple Alliance, now Rudini was out for new acquisitions without, however, the acceptance of new burdens. Up to that period Austria-Hungary alone was bound to co-operate with Italy for the maintenance of the *status quo* in the Balkans. In this matter Germany reserved for herself a free hand. Now, however, Rudini aimed at making Germany accept the same obligation and pledge herself also to protect the Balkan *status quo*.

And even that was not enough : he insisted on more favourable terms with regard to North Africa. Robilant had improved Italy's position there by inducing Bismarck to promise that he would support Italy if she were compelled to attack France over the question of her expansion in North Africa. Now Rudini went further. He desired Germany to support Italy even in the event of her demanding compensation for the expansion of any other Power in North Africa, should such demand lead to war—the excuse being the maintenance of the balance of power.

German diplomacy was not disposed to undertake either obligation. As to the Balkans, Marschall, the Foreign Secretary, pointed out the inexpediency of Germany binding herself in that manner, since by so doing she would be depriving herself of every weapon against the Magyar chauvinists if they should show a disposition to commit some crass stupidity, such as meddling in the Bulgarian Question. And Kiderlen, another leading light of the Foreign Office, said that such an amendment of the treaty would be equivalent to a written confession of the weakness of Bismarck's Balkan policy. Neither was Berlin disposed to undertake further obligations with regard to North Africa. For on the ground of the obligation demanded of Germany by the Italians, the former would be bound to assist the latter even in the event of their violating Turkish territory—Tripoli, for instance—though in the eyes of Berlin such a step would be sheer " brigandage and injustice." Such an alliance might even compel Germany to fall out with England for the sake of Italy—a prospect which Germany could not view with equanimity.

It would seem that a blunder on the part of the French made it easier for the friends to agree. The French minister Ribot, who, as we shall presently see, did so splendidly at St. Petersburg, made a sorry mess of things in Rome by his terroristic experiments. He attempted to force Rudini to betray the secrets of the Triple Alliance. He assured Rudini that not only would France not attack Italy, but would even engage to respect the *status quo* in the Mediterranean if only she (France) were satisfied that certain articles of the Triple Alliance were no more dangerous for France than the provisions of the Austro-German Alliance. If Rudini refused that satisfaction (that is to say, if he declined to divulge the secrets of the Treaty), then France might become disagreeable. Subsequently Ribot tried the same bluff on the King of Italy himself—with similar unsuccess. The King coolly answered that such a matter could not form the subject of a bargain and was beneath his dignity. Ribot then fell back on Rothschild. The banker-prince offered Italy a loan on generous terms on condition that Rudini would inform France in strictest confidence of the precise terms upon which Italy was bound to support Germany. To-day international loans have become the most approved means of suborning European States, but at that time the offer of a loan with such a degrading condition attached cut Rudini's sensitive conscience to the quick. Referring to the matter in conversation with the German Military Attaché, the Italian statesman said he had a great mind to kick out the " dirty Jew " who had dared to bring him Rothschild's message ; however, he was checked by the reflection that such an act would be unworthy of a Marchese di Rudini, so he let the man off with a good wigging, demanding of the emissary how he, an Italian, could lend himself to such a degrading mission.

These importunities on the part of France probably induced Rudini to be more complacent towards us. He dropped his Balkan scheme and made co-operation in North Africa contingent on a precedent formal agreement. And as the treaty set forth that England should be won for the North African agreement, it was impossible to represent the treaty as an anti-British instrument.

The renewal of the Triple Alliance was followed by the alliance with Rumania. At the negotiations in connection therewith the discontent of the Rumanians in Hungary caused trouble. King Charles manœuvred to get the party antagonistic to the Triple Alliance into power, in the secret hope that (as Bülow, who subsequently became Chancellor and who was at that time Minister at Bucarest, reported) the new Government would not last long and that after its demise the treaty could be renewed.

Emperor William was disgusted with King Charles's trick. He pronounced it " immoral "—a characteristic remark. It illustrates the Emperor's high sense of the duty of a prince ; but at the same time it shows that impatient, stern, superficial criticism he would often pass on actions differing from his own and which gained him many enemies.

12

In William's view, the minister is the instrument of the sovereign, the executive of the latter's policy; if the ruler has no confidence in a statesman, he ought not to invest him with power. But having once appointed a minister, the sovereign should identify himself with him. This is a fine, admirable principle, but only in a case where the prince himself rules and is master of the situation. In parliamentary government the sovereign is sometimes compelled to appoint a cabinet he considers harmful to the interests of the country, and in such circumstances it is no reproach for the sovereign to rejoice at its eventual fall, as he has done nothing derogatory to his constitutional duty.

However, the affair of the treaty was satisfactorily concluded without any change of parties. A change of persons sufficed. The policy of the Alliance was certainly strengthened by the treaty, signed by Bratianu the Liberal, being renewed by the Conservatives Catargi and Lahovári. We must here remember sympathetically Carp, who did so much to promote the conclusion of the treaty and stood by us so staunchly throughout his life. This exceptionally gifted and strong statesman became, during the war, a martyr for his principles. Rumanians to-day ought to feel proud of him, even though they may not be able to share his views. He was no time-server, but a real upright man among a band of opportunists— a credit to the country he loyally served.

The treaty was renewed (27th July 1892) without alterations of any importance.

Shortly after this success, this new consolidation of the east wing of the Central European front, the situation became stabilised also on the west. The Hispano-Italian Treaty was renewed, by which means that bulwark of Bismarck's defensive policy retained its old strength.

CHAPTER II

THE RUSSO-FRENCH TREATY

BISMARCK'S system had two main supports. One of these was the powerful continental alliance ; the other the cordial relations with the two great World Powers outside the alliance : Russia and England.

As we have already seen, Caprivi managed to renew the defensive alliances founded by Bismarck. But how did he fare with regard to that other legacy of Bismarck, the isolation of France ?

Let us first see how the relations with Russia developed. Bismarck had bound Russia by a secret treaty, obliging the Czar to neutrality in the event of a French attack, Germany to remain neutral in the event of an Austro-Hungarian attack, and to support Russia in the affair of the Dardanelles.

Caprivi was averse to such an alliance with Russia. He thought the obligations involved therein too onerous. The pledge with regard to the East was in conflict with the fact that Germany had already persuaded both her allies, Austria-Hungary and Italy, to conclude an agreement in order to counteract the Oriental policy of Russia. It was contrary to the promise and statement of Bismarck to Salisbury, when mediating in the interest of the treaties between England, Italy, and Austria-Hungary (1887).

Certain points of Bismarck's pacts for mutual security were in flagrant opposition to the terms of the Triple Alliance. The new Chancellor feared that Russia might, by publishing the treaty, at any moment wreck the

Triple Alliance and make Germany appear perfidious. Another argument against Bismarck's treaty was the fact that, in spite of its ambiguity, it could not even fully achieve its object. Though it might prevent the Czar from concluding a written treaty with the French Republic, Russo-French friendship became stronger day by day. The consciousness of a common fate had by this time brought together the two neighbours of Germany. Bismarck himself had no faith in Russian neutrality and set himself to prepare for a war on two fronts.

For this reason Caprivi wanted no secret treaty with the Muscovites. In all essentials, however, he adhered to the Bismarckian traditions and aims with regard to Russia. He desired to pursue the same course towards that country as did Bismarck, his aims there were identical with those of the Iron Chancellor, the sole difference being that he was unwilling formally to pledge himself to carry out his intention.

Like Bismarck, Caprivi recognised Russia's peculiar rights in Bulgaria and in the matter of the Straits, and declined to accept the standpoint of Austria-Hungary and England. We have seen that Italy's demand for the protection of the *status quo* in the Balkans was refused by Caprivi just as it had been by his more famous predecessor.

The new régime was quite as keen on securing the friendship of Russia as the old one had been. The young Emperor sent the Czar a message to the effect that amity with Russia was not only Bismarck's policy, but equally that of his grandfather William I and no less of himself. He advised Austria-Hungary to try to come to an agreement with St. Petersburg. At Köszeg, during the military manœuvres, he preached this doctrine to Kálnoky ; and when he saw a *rapprochement* between Vienna and the Nevski Prospekt he, in a marginal note, takes credit to himself for this happy fruition of his good advice. Let the Russians have Constantinople and the Austrians Salonica.

The new régime was perfectly right in pleading that it was unable to continue Bismarck's system, which was too complicated and involved the risk of Germany falling between two stools. For any man less gifted and less respected than Bismarck it would have been absolutely inadvisable to have followed his path. The attitude of William II was worthy of sympathy and evinced an upright character.

But it was a pity that by a faithful adherence to the former Russophil policy it was rendered exceedingly difficult to substitute the friendship of England for that of Russia, and to make the Triple Alliance as close as it would have been had its members pursued a concerted policy towards the East, and had England remained a reliable supporter of the Triple Alliance.

The results of this defect were the more damaging as Caprivi, in carrying out this policy, committed certain grave blunders which imperilled the friendship of Russia far more than the dissolution of the Bismarckian secret treaty by itself could have done.

According to the report of Schweinitz, Ambassador to St. Petersburg, Giers, the Russian Foreign Minister, who was no friend of the French orientation, attached great importance to the late secret treaty being replaced by another, no matter how vague it might be. Such a treaty, the consciousness that the names of the two sovereigns were signed to the same document, would—in the Ambassador's opinion—have kept honest Czar Alexander III from concluding a treaty with the French

Government. Caprivi, however, would not hear of it, and in fact declined to entertain an agreement of any kind, so that the slight thread connecting St. Petersburg and Berlin was snapped for ever.

The Chancellor had thereby overshot the mark. Schweinitz was probably right : the mere fact of an agreement between Czar and Emperor would have rendered a Franco-Russian pact exceedingly difficult. On the other hand, a treaty not in opposition to the Triple Alliance and not engaging Germany for any anti-English or anti-Austrian Oriental policy, as the Bismarckian secret treaty had done, would have presented no drawbacks nor imperilled the other friendships of Germany in the least. But the rupture of the treaties between St. Petersburg and Berlin removed all obstacles from the path between Paris and the city on the Neva and led to the Russo-French alliance (June 1890). The reluctance displayed by the Germans to conclude any treaties caused Czar Alexander III to suspect that Emperor William was preparing a war; consequently the former thought he had better agree with the French. His impression was confirmed by the unusually ostentatious publication of the renewal of the Triple Alliance.

Here I must place on record that, strictly speaking, the Triple Alliance was the first step to the dividing of Europe into two hostile camps. The 1879 pact between Bismarck and Andrássy cannot be so regarded ; not only because it was not *de facto* followed by the formation of an opposing group, but also on account of its content. The 1879 Dual Alliance was purely defensive—only against Russia. It did not affect the position of France as a Great Power. Germany acquired no ally against isolated France and left perfectly intact the natural superiority of the French over their weaker Italian neighbours. The case of Russian aggression only excepted, the Dual Alliance of 1879 was founded as a protection against a coalition. Thus it could not promote the formation of coalitions, but, on the contrary, it prevented their formation by providing in advance the means of defence against them.

The Triple Alliance changed all this. It secured for Germany the support of Italy, and for Italy the support of Germany and Austria-Hungary against an isolated France. It confronted a single attack on the part of either Russia or France with a coalition of the Central Powers. And this creation of a united front to repel an attack from either Russia or France caused both these Powers to form an alliance as a natural and logical counter-stroke. The Dual Alliance of Germany and Austria-Hungary was defensive only, whereas the Triple Alliance in certain contingencies supported the Italians also in an offensive against the French.

It is true that the Triple Alliance was secret, yet it constantly disturbed the Quai d'Orsay, for there it was felt that Italy's joining the Central Powers against the French gave the Triple Alliance a more dangerous character, as it meant a member who, since the success of France in Tunis, had followed a distinctly anti-French and pro-English policy.

This idea, as we have seen, was expressed by Ribot, the French minister, when at the renewal of the Triple Alliance he announced his willingness to change his attitude towards Italy and to give guarantees for the maintenance of peace, if only he were satisfied that the provisions of the Triple Alliance were not more menacing than the Austro-German Alliance. The French, however, failed to get such satisfaction, and thus their mistrust and nervousness were aggravated.

The announcement of the renewal of the Triple Alliance and the plain fact that England was in sympathy with it caused the necessity of a *rapprochement* to be felt in an increased degree at Paris and St. Petersburg, at the moment Russia's hands became definitely free and the relations fixed by treaties between Berlin and St. Petersburg were deliberately put an end to by the policy of Germany.

Thus in both Paris and St. Petersburg simultaneously the intention became ripe of giving the intimate relations which had so long subsisted between the two countries the form of a treaty.

Negotiations with this object were opened by Giers. But the leading rôle therein was of course played by the French Government, who were more interested than Russia in the conclusion of a formal treaty. An intimate friendship without a treaty would, in my opinion, have been of more use to Russia than the treaty ; for the latter when concluded did not bind France to render her any active assistance, since, according to the French Constitution, war could only be declared with the consent of Parliament and the Russian Government were unwilling to publish the treaty. The Czar had indeed said that the treaty would become null and void by publication.

Russia obtained no new advantages by the treaty. For long she had been aware that as soon as she could pick a quarrel with Germany the guns of France would go off of themselves and that the Republic would never look on calmly at a German war on the banks of the Vistula ; while Russia could easily keep out of a French war of revenge and need participate in a struggle for the Rhine only if her interests at the moment rendered it desirable for her to do so. The former " free love " had, as it were, placed at the Czar's disposal the forces not only of Russia but also those of France; so that he had two diplomacies, two armies, two navies, and two treasuries.

Giers suggested an agreement simply because he feared lest Germany might attack Russia at a time when France should have grown tired of the long waiting and her love have waxed cold just when her assistance would be most valuable and necessary.

Owing, however, to the above-mentioned interests, it is easy for us to understand that Giers desired to undertake as few obligations as possible and merely to declare that in the event of imminent hostilities the two Powers would enter into such negotiations as both parties might deem necessary at the time. But the French were not satisfied with this diplomatic " holy water "; such verbiage was no guarantee of the defence they required. They wanted more, and got it.

In the preamble of the agreement it was especially emphasised that the main object of the two signatory Powers was the maintenance of peace, and that the principal *raison d'être* thereof was, on the one hand, the renewal of the Triple Alliance, and on the other the fact that England had gravitated towards the said Triple Alliance. The document itself consisted of two parts: the first setting forth that the two Powers would negotiate on all questions involving the risk of war; while in the second part it was declared that in the event of one of the signatory Powers being in danger of attack, both contracting parties would come to an agreement with regard to the measures necessary to be taken. Here more than mere negotiations were in question. The contracting parties undertook a positive obligation to agree regarding the measures necessary to be taken. True, the treaty does not define a *casus belli*, but during the negotiations both the French and the Czarist Governments declared their intention of standing shoulder to shoulder in the event of war.

The alliance thus concluded was formally even more defensive than the Triple Alliance, which in the interests of Italy acquired a certain offensive edge ; the Russo-French pact, however, was wider in its scope than the Triple Alliance, being directed against all States without exception—against Japan and Great Britain equally as against us—whereas the Triple Alliance was directed solely against the Powers designated in the document or a coalition of Powers.

Yet even this favourable result failed to satisfy the French. Freycinet, then War Minister, one of the best brains of modern France, sought (November 1891) to determine at the outset the extent and direction of the forces with which, in the event of war, the allies should assist each other. Giers boggled at this. On different pretences he attempted to procrastinate. He mentioned to the German diplomats that the French were feverishly anxious to come to terms with him, but he assured them (so he said) that nothing would be done.

But the Russian went back on his word. And the French accomplished their object. Paris, the stateliest city in the world, which had for so many years influenced the trend of European politics—which had so often claimed to be the world metropolis—did not in vain adopt the cult of everything Russian. It was not for nothing that " *la grande nation* " confessed her affection for the rude Muscovite. Even the frigid, haughty Czar could not long remain insensible to such homage, which was of historic importance. As somewhat earlier the Autocrat had stood bareheaded as a mark of respect to the strains of the revolutionary "*Marseillaise*," so now he complacently signed the desired military convention with his adversary in home politics, the French Republic, against his imperial kinsman with whom his interests were common. Under the glamour of the French naval celebrations at Toulon, and influenced by the latest military law of the German Empire, the Russian Government at length (December 1893), after a delay of two years, signed the treaty.

However, the treaty did not give the French everything they craved. Just as we, in 1879, had been reluctant to promise Germany assistance in the event of French aggression, so France now hesitated to bind herself to support Russia if she got involved in war with Austria-Hungary. The French were well aware that the power of Francis Joseph's Dual Monarchy was not inimical to French interests, and was even desirable from the point of view of the balance of power in Europe. But the French diplomats were not so independent with regard to the Russians as Andrássy had been with Bismarck in 1879. Then Bismarck gave way ; now Ribot, who promised the same assistance to the Russians against us as against Germany, though he was aware that there were no conflicting interests and sentiments between the Republic and the Dual Monarchy. As a set-off to this concession France achieved the important result that whenever the Triple Alliance or even one member thereof should mobilise, Russia and France were likewise bound to mobilise. Another great *coup* for France was the specifying in the treaty of the precise number of troops to be called up and rushed to the German frontier, so that the German Empire should be simultaneously attacked from both east and west by an overwhelming majority of the forces of France and Russia.

It was an important feature of this military convention that it was aimed solely against the Triple Alliance, obliging no common action against either England or Japan. Thereby France avoided the risk of having to take sides on account of Russia's operations in Asia and having to draw the sword on her behalf there.

The obligation with regard to mobilisation is also important in that thereby the *revanche* could be connected with the policy of the treaties and draw Russia in with it. For if France, through an aggressive policy, should succeed in making Germany mobilise, the Czar also would be obliged to mobilise ; which would mean his participation in the war, since it would then be clear that general mobilisation of conscript forces could have no other significance than war.

This alliance and military convention caused a great change in the political situation. Though they did no more than give a form to what had already existed for years, yet it constituted a new factor for power by having converted a political probability into a legal *fait accompli*, thereby raising the courage of Paris to a remarkable degree. Giers was partly right in telling the French Ambassador that the alliance put an end to German supremacy and restored the balance of power. There was no doubt that it tended in that direction, though it is doubtful whether peace had become more firmly established thereby. The supremacy of Germany had hitherto preserved peace for the simple reason that no one had been bold enough to assail the Triple Alliance—neither France nor Russia, who could not safely rely on each other—while the leading members of the Triple Alliance, Germany and Austria-Hungary, and Great Britain had their hands so full that they could not think of provoking a breach. Much less could they think of doing so as

Bismarck considered the Franco-Russian friendship itself without the alliance so strong that he preferred to avoid falling foul of it if possible. He thought the risk too great to attempt, by warlike means, to consolidate German supremacy, as his military advisers so often urged him to do.

Now, however, that France and Russia knew that they could henceforth safely rely on each other, would not a war be more likely to break out ? Since both France and Russia had their great historic ambitions to be realised at the expense of the *status quo*—the former in Alsace-Lorraine, and the latter in the Dardanelles—what would happen should these two Powers feel themselves strong enough to try conclusions ?

Czar Alexander III observed to the French Ambassador that the French would not deserve the name of patriots if they failed to look forward to getting back their lost provinces ; he consoled himself, however, with the hope that the spirit of revenge was not in their minds and that they would be able to " wait with dignity." But would this be possible for long if they felt a reasonable hope of being able to deliver their suffering brethren ? The Czar, too, envisaged this danger, and trusted only that his great influence might outweigh the chauvinist longings of Paris.

Who could say whether he would not be disappointed in this laudable hope ? The only thing certain was that France would become bolder and more self-conscious with time. She would cease to be the defeated country with which no other cared to seek an alliance ; she would escape from the magic circle of Sedan. And being able to conclude alliances, she would adopt a more definite and bolder foreign policy than before. Her unremitting efforts at home, the gradual development of her army, her careful, assertive, in its main features consistent foreign policy, yielded their first fruits. The secret mistress became the openly acknowledged legal wife ; the denied liaison was superseded by marriage, a union confessed in the sight of God and man.

The French General Staff (February 1890) estimated the forces of the two allied Powers to be somewhat more numerous than those of the Triple Alliance, i.e. 3,150,000 as against 2,180,000. Notwithstanding this favourable disclosure, the French were not disposed to rashness. They took into consideration that the numerical disadvantage of the Central Powers was off-set and compensated for by their quicker mobilisation. Probably also they realised that the central situation of their opponents had other valuable advantages ; so they resolved that to begin a war would be inexpedient.

Even granting, however, that the new allies sincerely desired to avoid hostilities, would not the opposing policies of the apparently equal and self-assertive Powers and their constant collisions aggravated day by day, precipitate a conflict ? France could resume her overseas expansion without being, as in Jules Ferry's day, dependent on the good-will of Germany. She would not have to submit at any price if she fell out with her Teuton neighbour on the colonial question, as she could now depend on Russian support. What would become of the peace of Europe if the nations opposed on the Rhine were to come into antagonism overseas ?

For a long time our Governments refused to believe in the conclusion of the new alliance. The Russians denied the treaty (May 1893). Giers even told Kálnoky he would not listen to the French, nor undertake any obligations towards them, as they were dominated by the spirit of revenge. When our Governments could no longer ignore the fact, they pretended to be glad of the alliance and to see in it a safeguard of peace. But that attitude could not have been sincere.

Münster and Schweinitz reported from Paris and St. Petersburg respectively that although there was no reason to fear an immediate rupture, yet they were troubled about the future. Münster (October 1893) said that though the French were not anxious for war, they were preparing for that contingency by seeking to alienate Italy from Germany through economic pressure, and Austria-Hungary by strengthening the Slav influence.

The news of the alliance (October 1893) depressed Emperor William. He was apprehensive lest the mistrustful French should sooner or later display an intention to precipitate a war. He likened the existing peace to a person suffering from heart-disease ; though such an one may live for years, yet, on the other hand, he may drop dead at any moment.

The formation of the Dual Alliance was the first relapse from the position of power we had reached under Bismarck, a relapse to be followed in due time by a further fall.

CHAPTER III

RELATIONS WITH ENGLAND (HELIGOLAND, EGYPT, TUNIS, THE DARDANELLES)

THE Franco-Russian treaty necessitated more than ever the maintenance of Bismarck's bequest :—the friendship of the Triple Alliance. The division of power would have kept the Russian and French allies from hostile projects only if they had to reckon with England as a potential enemy. Unfortunately Caprivi was not so successful as Bismarck had been in influencing the British Government, although the chances were as good as ever.

Thanks to the Chancellor's wisdom, the Germanophil policy had gained ground in England. In the last years of Caprivi's chancellorship the young Emperor William was ostentatiously fêted in London. The Prince of Wales (afterwards King Edward VII), toasting the imperial guest, referred to the possibility of the British navy and the German army together maintaining peace. The Emperor, on the other hand, reminded his English host of their comradeship-in-arms at Malplaquet and Waterloo. At the time of Bismarck's fall Salisbury presided over the British Cabinet. This statesman was the greatest authority of his day on English foreign policy, who had till then striven to conduct a Germanophil policy, and he could now follow his convictions the more easily since his opponents in foreign policy—the Liberals—no longer attacked his foreign policy with such unity and consistency as in the past. In those days the parliamentary struggle was not dominated by foreign politics as it was before and after the Berlin Congress, when Beaconsfield was defeated at the polls by Gladstone's slogan of "No imperialism." The eternal Irish Question was forcing itself more and more into the foreground.

Gladstone himself was not the man he had once been. When he was last Premier, on account of his Egyptian venture he had been compelled to follow a Germanophil and anti-French policy. And Lord Rosebery, by far the best informed, with regard to foreign politics, in the Liberal Party, one of its most distinguished members and an ambitious statesman, preferred to follow the conservative policy of Salisbury rather than remain loyal to the Liberal tradition. He was as great an imperialist as the Tory leader himself. He went so far as to confess that he accepted the post of Foreign Under-Secretary in Gladstone's Cabinet solely in order to maintain the continuity of British policy and to keep England in the path trodden by Salisbury. On becoming Foreign Minister in the victorious Gladstone Government, he emphasised that, like his predecessor, he would have the Triple Alliance for his support, and that he would conduct foreign policy according to his own convictions, even if differences should on account thereof arise between him and his chief, the Grand Old Man—who, by the way, was ignorant of foreign affairs and did not deny it. Moreover, he had already become senile and unable to lead with that vigour and decision he had displayed so brilliantly in the past. The root idea of Salisbury—and after him of Rosebery —was free co-operation between England and the Triple Alliance, based on community of interests, mutual confidence, and good-will, but not fixed by treaty and involving no legal obligation. Such a policy would not provoke Britain's two rivals, France and Russia, while

13

it would be strong enough, in the event of hostilities, to be immediately transformed into a war alliance. It gave England a free hand; it did not compel her to take part in a war that might perhaps prove unpopular, dangerous, and difficult; it avoided the risk of isolation, and prepared the way for a powerful alliance at a critical time. It seemed to combine the advantages of both isolation and alliance while avoiding their drawbacks; and raised up a mighty bulwark in defence of peace and the *status quo*.

Caprivi was not satisfied with this English view. He wished to go further than Salisbury. He attached great importance to the friendship of England—greater than he did to that of Russia, with whom he regarded a war as sooner or later inevitable. He had, however, less confidence in England. He aimed, therefore, at bringing about a binding treaty—yet not between Great Britain and Germany, but between Great Britain and the continental allies of Germany, i.e. Austria-Hungary and Italy, with a provision regarding the Eastern Question. He was ambitious to follow the example of Bismarck, who had succeeded therein. Indeed he desired even to surpass Bismarck in the sense of giving the treaty more volume, to render it more stable and definite. This scheme would set England directly against Russia and indirectly against France, the latter's ally, without Germany losing her chance to intervene in the event of a conflict between her own allies on the one hand and Russia and France on the other, even of playing the rôle of umpire between them. In short, he was scheming to reserve to himself the opportunity to intervene in a potential resort to arms at the moment most auspicious for his country.

The new régime started well. William II saw the

fulfilment of his long-cherished wish. England (July 1890) exchanged Heligoland for certain German possessions in Africa. Some of the British Cabinet ministers objected to this transaction on the ground that "the contingency of war between England and Germany was not excluded for all time," and, in such an event, Heligoland would constitute an invaluable weapon in the hands of Germany for the defence of her coastline. When, notwithstanding these objections, England consented to the exchange, she proved thereby that such a war was far from her thoughts ; she considered it indeed quite out of the question that Britons and Teutons should ever meet as foes. For this very reason the exchange might well have paved the way for greater trust and led to the consolidation of an Anglo-German friendship.

Unfortunately German public opinion failed to realise the value of Heligoland, considering it a barren rock not worth Zanzibar and the other territory ceded for it. Thus the initial result of the new régime did not improve the situation between Britain and Germany. It even made it worse ; especially as Bismarck censured the exchange and attacked it with all the vehemence of opposition. It was the irony of fate that the ruthless critic of the deal was far more highly respected among the people than the man who spoke in the name of the Fatherland and whose duty it was to lead it. Bismarck's scathing condemnation of the transaction gave rise to the universal belief in Germany that they had been imposed upon by the wily English ; though the fact was that the military power of Germany was enormously strengthened thereby. What should have brought the two countries close together only served to estrange them from each other.

The Egyptian Question, too, might at this time

have favourably influenced Anglo-German relations. The salient features of the situation were as follows: France could not reconcile herself to the idea that the shopkeepers of *perfide Albion* should hold sway over that enchanted land of hoary antiquity that had been the scene of the glorious victories of the immortal Bonaparte. She aimed at the gradual ousting of Great Britain from the valley of the Nile. On the other hand, England sat tight on her new seat of power and refused to budge or surrender an inch of the soil of Tut-ankh-amen. She perceived in the Suez Canal the connecting-link with her overseas empire. Thus for the time being Egypt formed a dangerous bone of contention between the two neighbour Powers.

The best assistance against France could have been rendered to England by Germany, the Teutons having no interests worth mentioning in the Nile Valley, and so they might easily have adapted their Egyptian policy to the exigencies of British friendship. Bismarck availed himself to the full of the opportunity thus afforded. He consistently supported the English in Egypt. He won over Gladstone and fed the Anglo-French quarrel thereby. Nevertheless, whenever he could do so without risk, he never failed to exploit the Egyptian situation for the purpose of extorting colonial concessions from England.

William II and Caprivi equally desired to follow the same path. When informed that great lack of confidence existed between Paris and London on account of the Egyptian Question, the Emperor remarked that he " hoped it would last a long time." Also when he heard that the Sultan was being encouraged by Paris to demand the evacuation of Egypt, William ordered that London should be informed thereof without delay.

Caprivi did much to influence the Sultan in favour of England. He would have liked to bring about an agreement between the Sublime Porte and Great Britain by which the latter would recognise the Sultan's suzerainty over Egypt, and the Sultan, on his part, would withdraw his demand for the British evacuation. But as the German Government failed in this object, and Caprivi, following Bismarck's example, took several occasions to exploit rather inconsiderately England's difficulties in Egypt to extort concessions, it may justly be supposed that an Anglo-German friendship was not thereby promoted. Münster, the German Ambassador to Paris, though he trusted in the Egyptian situation preventing any co-operation between France and England, nevertheless proved very far-seeing when he hinted to his Government that the barrier formed by Egypt between Paris and London might after all collapse at a moment of some great crisis.

Anglo-German relations were at this time considerably affected also by the North African territory to the west of Egypt. These relations were especially important on account of the conviction prevailing in Rome, London, and Berlin that France was out to acquire Morocco and Tripoli, as well as to strengthen her position in Tunis, both by proclaiming her annexation of the territory and by constructing a naval harbour at Bizerta.

Such monopolisation of Northern Africa by France was viewed by England with suspicion and by Italy with grave anxiety. Would not this state of affairs then unite Italy and England for common action in the protection of mutual interests, thereby creating a link between the Triple Alliance and Great Britain which would in some measure bind Germany too and thus stabilise friendly relations between the two last-named countries ? It had a bad influence in Italy that the African provinces of the ancient Roman Empire were mostly in the hands of France, though she (Italy), the natural heir and successor to the great world-empire, had claimed them, and as she had inherited the great commercial and military interests which had actuated the Scipios and Cæsars and compelled them to expand into Africa.

Italy had joined the two Emperors and dissembled her antipathy to Austria in order that she might prevent the possessor of Carthage laying her hands on the other old Roman provinces as well and secure for herself a considerable portion of Northern Africa in the event of a collapse of the *status quo* in that region. Crispi was a vigorous exponent of this policy. Just as Bismarck had been haunted by the bugbear of coalitions, so Crispi passed many sleepless nights in his anxiety lest another Power, France—already too powerful, in his view— should seize the most natural and legitimate sphere of influence of his own country. Germany had to reckon with this instinct and anxiety of Italy. Bismarck had observed that being on good terms with Italy implied making concessions in her favour in either Africa or Albania, or in the direction of Trieste. With a vision no less acute Bülow (who had exchanged Bucarest for the Quirinal) remarked that " if Italy were allowed no opportunities for expansion in Africa she would be forced to ' exploit her irredentism ' at the expense of the tranquillity of Europe."

The probable alteration of the *status quo* in Africa brought Germany into somewhat of a dilemma. By ignoring Italy's aspirations and her resolute will, Germany risked the loss of Italian friendship. If, on the other hand, Germany identified herself with the Italian ambitions, she might get entangled in a way by no means approved by the German people, and thus fail to arouse that enthusiasm which, as the Chancellor had said, was the primary condition of success. To such a deplorable event Caprivi would have preferred even the dissolution of the Triple Alliance. A war on account of North Africa—especially without the aid of England—was not to be thought of. As Bismarck had once declared, amidst the applause of the nation, that " all Bulgaria was not worth the life of a single Prussian soldier," why should not the nation now say the same of an African oasis the name of which was unknown to many an educated German ? And would not such a policy on the part of Germany but tend to stir up the fire of French *revanche* ? Would not the combustible material be increased by the very fact that Germany had become the antagonist of France not only in Europe but in Africa also ?

Caprivi would have liked to escape from the difficulty of choosing by bringing England forward and enlisting her in the cause of Italy in Africa. For England, like Germany, would prefer the growth of Italian power in the Mediterranean to that of her Gallic neighbour, already powerful enough, who even then looked askance at British rule in Egypt, who had become allied with Russia, another great rival of England, who menaced her Indian empire. If Caprivi could succeed in persuading England to support the Italians against the French, then France and England would be once more at loggerheads ; England would be obliged to incline towards Germany, while Italy could adhere calmly to her former political orientation.

This was the Chancellor's motive when informed by Crispi (August 1890) that France intended to annex

Tuat, an oasis on the Moroccan border, and to make a naval station of Bizerta. Then Caprivi manœuvred to keep the Italian statesman inactive and make England nervous. He said that he thought the naval harbour at Bizerta would mean a greater danger to the power of England in the Mediterranean than to that of Italy. He emphasised the importance of England extending to the Mediterranean the treaty concluded in 1887 with Italy and Austria-Hungary relating to the Ægean and the Black Seas. He did his utmost to persuade the British Premier to promise Crispi that he would at least institute enquiries with reference to Bizerta, and if convinced that it was going to be transformed into a naval base, then he would seriously consider what steps he could take in the matter.

Caprivi sought also to egg on England when it appeared (January 1891) that France was contemplating " frontier rectification " at the expense of Tripoli. He then suggested to Salisbury that he should protest to the Sultan against any such proceedings.

The same desire actuated the Germans in the Morocco affair too. As soon as Germany got the impression that England coveted Morocco, and when Salisbury informed the German Ambassador that England had an appetite for that territory, Caprivi thought it a lucky chance. He much desired England to pursue a more vigorous policy in Northern Africa, and feared only lest his keenness in this respect should be perceived in London.

But while he fanned the flame of British cupidity, he to the same degree restrained Italy, lest Rome, without England, should fall out with the French. In the Morocco dispute he advised Rome and Madrid (October 1891) not to provoke the French without first assuring themselves of the certainty of British support.

He planned to drive England into a corner by advising the Spanish Government (November 1891) to ascertain direct from London what steps the British Government were disposed to take over Tuat, which was menaced by the French, but not to take any risks without a definite reassuring declaration from Albion. England must know, he said, that no nation would jeopardise herself for the sake of British interests, though if England would shoulder a part of the burden, supporters would be forthcoming.

England, however, saw through the trick and declined to be drawn. She replied that she objected to the over-vigorous expansion of France between Egypt and Gibraltar ; her sympathies lay rather with Italy than with France ; in the contingency of a world war she saw her place beside the Triple Alliance, and consequently she made a point of Italy continuing her orientation ; she was aware that a preliminary to this was that Italy should not have to suffer insults from France such as those she had endured when in a position of isolation ; nevertheless, England was unwilling to expose herself for the sake of those interests. Both Salisbury and Rosebery in turn stated quite frankly in Berlin that British public opinion would not tolerate such a war, and consequently they were unable to bind themselves to such a policy. They were willing to go the way desired by the Germans, but must stop short of pledging themselves to positive military assistance. They were likewise willing to support Italy, but not to the extent of entering into definite obligations. When therefore the Italians feared that the French were about to invade Tripoli and conceived the idea of stealing a march on them, Salisbury, in spite of his declaration that it would be against British interests to allow Tripoli to share the fate of Tunis and that it must be prevented, took no steps to that end ; he even cautioned Italy to refrain from everything calculated to worry the Sultan, the lawful sovereign of Tripoli.

A similar aim was followed by Ferguson, Under-Secretary for Foreign Affairs, in his answers to two interpellations. To one (August 1891) he said that the Italian statesmen were aware that the British Government agreed with them in regard to the need of maintaining the *status quo* in the Mediterranean, and that the sympathies of England would be with those who defended the situation so important for her ; but he gave no promise of assistance.

In the other case (July 1891) Ferguson stated that the good relations between England and France remained unimpaired, but England would sympathise with those who desired peace and respected international treaties (i.e. the Italians), though he was careful to promise no more than sympathy.

Again, the same aim was followed by Rosebery when he stated that if France were to attack Italy, it was his personal view that England would support the latter— prompted by her interests both in the Mediterranean and in India, as well as by the sympathy she felt for the cause of Italian freedom ; but at the same time he would not bind himself to this. He was, he said, only expressing his private opinion that, if and when danger arose, the defensive alliance so desired by the Italians would be brought about.

These cautious statements nevertheless accomplished their object in reassuring the Italians, who for that time sought no new means, but contented themselves with their reliance on England and the Triple Alliance.

The fate of Caprivi's policy towards England was

finally settled in the negotiations which took place on the Eastern Question in the strict sense of the term, on the one hand between the German Chancellor, England, and Turkey, and on the other between England, Germany, Austria-Hungary, and Italy, on the question of the agreement which Bismarck had concluded with them in 1887.

The first negotiations were opened by Salisbury, taking the standpoint of the *status quo* on condition that the assistance of Turkey should be secured for the contingency of having to defend the *status quo* by force of arms. He remarked to Hatzfeld that, in order to prevent Russia from producing a *fait accompli*, he always managed to keep the British fleet so near to the Dardanelles that it could always get there before Russia, and that all he feared was lest the Sultan should allow the Russian fleet to enter the Straits ere the British fleet could appear on the scene.

For the Cyprus Treaty bound England unilaterally to defend the integrity of Turkey, leaving the Sultan free as regards England. It would therefore have been important for the latter to remedy this serious defect in her armour, to off-set England's obligation to Turkey by obtaining Turkey's pledge to guard the Straits and to solicit England's aid to that end.

If Caprivi could prevail upon the Sultan to give such a pledge, he might thereby succeed in binding England to the policy which had brought Disraeli alongside Andrássy and Bismarck, Salisbury alongside Kálnoky and Crispi, and at the same time prepare the way for the extension and confirmation of the Mediterranean Treaty concluded by the three statesmen last named without Germany herself having to undertake any further obligation in the East. Consequently when Caprivi intervened between the Porte and England on the question of Egypt, he mentioned the matter of the Straits too. The undertaking of permanent obligations, however, did not fit in with the system of the hyper-cautious and wily Abdul Hamid; his fundamental conception of governing was by playing off the different European Powers one against another. His desire was always to be in a position to join whichever party proved the stronger. Had Germany attached herself to the political car of England, she (Germany) would probably have drawn the Sultan with her; but since Caprivi had failed in that, Abdul Hamid was chary of exposing himself, without German backing, to the risk of war with Russia.

Thus the German intervention was fruitless as regarded the Straits and did not tend to improve the relations between London and Berlin. The result was no better in the matter of the English-Italian-Austro-Hungarian Agreement of 1887.

In this matter Caprivi found a staunch supporter in Kálnoky. The *rapprochement* between France and England caused anxiety at the Ballplatz lest Russia, emboldened thereby, should thenceforth pursue her aims more vigorously; lest some fine day she should present Europe with the *fait accompli* of the Straits. Austria-Hungary and Italy did not feel themselves strong enough to cope with a united Russian and French pressure and to maintain the *status quo* of the tottering Ottoman Empire if they were deprived of the aid of England. The former situation afforded no sufficient guarantee; as England's obligation to stand by them, in accordance with the agreement concluded in Bismarck's time, was too elastic and indefinite for Vienna and Rome.

Kálnoky proposed to compensate for this by the conclusion of a more satisfactory agreement with England. Should this prove impracticable, and he could not say beforehand whether England might be relied upon at the moment of crisis, he thought it better to come to a timely agreement with the Muscovites; for that, according to his view, had become feasible since Russia did not attribute such a decisive importance as previously to the Bulgarian Question, in which the Dual Monarchy was more closely interested, and since the Russian aspirations in the Balkans were confined to the Straits, which interested England rather than Austria-Hungary.

Hatzfeld, German Ambassador to London—a clear-headed statesman whom Bismarck had styled " the best horse in the diplomatic stable of Germany "—felt the reasonableness of Kálnoky's ambitions and desired to promote them to the best of his ability. He argued that it would be detrimental if Austria-Hungary had to come to terms with St. Petersburg; for the consequence of that would be that Russia would rule in Constantinople, Austria-Hungary would forfeit her position as a Power in the East and fall to a secondary place in the world-order, while even England would have ultimately to abandon her present Oriental policy (December 1893). To avert this danger the German Ambassador explained to Rosebery that if Great Britain did not wish to see Italy and Austria-Hungary forced into the Muscovite camp she would have to declare her mind more plainly than she had done hitherto. Hatzfeld thought London saw the matter in this light and was disposed for a more energetic policy in the East. Nevertheless all efforts would be futile—reported the Ambassador—if England got the impression that she could not rely on the assistance of Germany, even though she on her part fulfilled all the desires of the German Government.

Unfortunately, however, Caprivi did not see the situation so clearly as did Hatzfeld, and accordingly acted in such a manner that, as the Ambassador justly points out, he rendered success impossible.

Rosebery (February 1894) informed Kálnoky that England could hold her own against Russia at sea, and therefore all she asked of the Triple Alliance was to keep France from meddling if she (England) got involved in war with the Czar on account of the Straits. It is to be regretted that Caprivi considered this proposal excessive. He hesitated to give the desired promise, suspecting that Rosebery and Kálnoky were in league to impose upon him, and that their scheme was to get the German Empire to endorse their political bills. He objected that, should he promise, England would be under no obligation to resist Russia and could make terms with her ; she might frustrate the design of Russia or not, as she chose, while Germany would be bound at any time to protect England against France. Moreover, Germany would incur the risk of a war on two fronts without affecting the *casus belli*, as that would depend entirely on England's will. Caprivi held tenaciously to his fundamental idea—he desired to avoid discouraging Austria-Hungary and Italy, but to keep his own hands free to intervene for peace as soon as the British ships had fired their first shots (March 1894). Much less did he desire to bind himself with regard to England, as the English parliamentary Government was unable to speak in the name of the country : it could only speak for itself as a Government, while the voice of the German imperial Government was the voice of all Germany.

In these circumstances Kálnoky had to withdraw. Without Germany he could not win England. Nothing short of the pressure of the whole Triple Alliance would be powerful enough to force the French sword back into the scabbard, or to break it. Without the entire Triple Alliance, England regarded it as too risky to undertake a war against France and Russia, with the possibility even of Turkey joining the coalition against her.

Thus Kálnoky was reluctantly compelled to close his negotiations started with such high promise, by simply stating that since it was, after all, scarcely probable that Russia would attempt a forcible solution of the Straits question, it would be sufficient if they could agree with regard to the steps to be taken in the event of peaceful action on the part of Russia.

These proceedings made the impression in England that she could not depend upon Germany and that therefore it would be unsafe for England to bind herself for the maintenance of the *status quo* in the East. The attempt to enlist England more closely in the anti-Russian policy ended in failure and a set-back.

Caprivi's policy was decidedly wrong. Kálnoky was right in insisting that England should be taken on her own terms, and if we could not conclude with her a formal agreement valid for a long period, we must do without it. The fact that the Liberal Government, including Gladstone himself, agreed with us, and further that England and ourselves had followed parallel policies for a number of years past, should have created a favourable atmosphere for us with the British public opinion, which is the sole arbiter of England's policy.

The fatal error of the German Government consisted in reasoning that, since it was impossible to conclude with England a legally binding long-term secret treaty, it was better to conclude no agreement at all. Such a view was wrong ; for it would have been easy to give the treaty a form which would not have legally bound Germany either, signifying merely a temporary moral obligation for both parties. There are many examples of similar covenants. The very treaty whose extension was now contemplated, concluded in 1887–8 at Bismarck's suggestion by Salisbury, Kálnoky, and Crispi, was such an one in its original form. Though such a treaty was not permanently binding on the States signatory thereto, yet the policy of all the parties had since then been directed by this document. Even after the fall of Salisbury his successor, Rosebery, desired to proceed in accordance with it, stating that he considered himself bound by it until it should be rescinded.

The Russians and French were less difficult and pedantic than Caprivi. The former, as above mentioned, had absolutely bound themselves to France, though the signature of the French Government imposed on them no obligation to declare war. Nevertheless this one-sided pact proved strong enough to stand the test even of the Great War. The sleep of the Russian diplomats was not disturbed by the theoretical possibility that the French Chamber might at the last moment not vote for the declaration of war. The Anglo-French and the Anglo-Russian Ententes had no written bases whatever, and there were no clauses binding the parties to support each other ; yet those Ententes played an important rôle in deciding world-history, uniting in one camp all the parties signatory thereto. These agreements, corresponding to the sentiments and interests of the nations concerned, caused them to recognise their common fate, brought their peoples closer to each other, made their Governments accustomed to following a common policy; so that the formally defective and legally objectionable treaties succeeded better in uniting the nations than did not a few perfectly valid and secret treaties, like, for instance, that between Rumania and Austria-Hungary, which, in spite of its secrecy and undoubted validity, proved to be of no effect whatever.

Caprivi was led astray by the teaching of Bismarck, who had often asserted that the pledge of a parliamentary Government was not of equal value with the pledge of the Emperor, and that consequently it would not be useful to conclude an alliance with a country like England. If, however, Caprivi had witnessed the deeds of Bismarck and could have risen to their height, the effect of the Iron Chancellor's example would have been quite different.

In 1887 and 1888 Bismarck was in a situation similar to that of Caprivi at this time. Before concluding with Austria-Hungary and Italy the treaty suggested by Bismarck, Salisbury had enquired of the latter the same thing as his successor now enquired of Caprivi, i.e. whether he could rely on German support if he should get involved in war over the treaty. And Bismarck succeeded in reassuring him. He proved with the clearest and soundest logic that Germany's interests were bound up with the maintenance of the position of England and of Austria-Hungary as Great Powers, and that no German Government could afford to neglect the defence of those interests. That was sufficient for Salisbury. He saw in Bismarck's letter and declarations such a moral obligation and guarantee that he forthwith concluded the agreement with Bismarck's allies. Hatzfeld, who had already been the Ambassador under

14

Bismarck's régime, reminded Caprivi of this precedent and of the fact that he then, at the request of the Chancellor, declared in London that should England on account of the alliance become entangled in war she could safely depend on the support of Germany.

But Caprivi lacked the courage to go even such a short distance as this. He coldly emphasised the statement that he could take no responsibilities towards England and was unable to sign any treaty binding him to render her assistance. It was not surprising, therefore, that he failed where Bismarck had succeeded, though the Iron Chancellor's situation was exceedingly more unfavourable than Caprivi's. Bismarck was obliged, by virtue of the secret treaty with Russia, to support the latter in the matter of the Straits, while Caprivi was perfectly free. He was not expected to do even as much as Bismarck had thought when asked the thing people were now trying to induce his successor to do. When persuading Salisbury to conclude the Oriental agreement, Bismarck entertained the idea of turning immediately against France and, after defeating her, of intervening in the Oriental war ; whereas now all that Rosebery asked of Caprivi was to keep France quiet.

Caprivi could have all the easier satisfied the desire of the British Premier as he would in any case have acted in accordance with its spirit. Whenever the time of peril arose, he would have as little thought of leaving in the lurch the Powers that Germany inclined towards and whose assistance she needed, as did the Iron Chancellor. Many declarations of the period go to prove this (March 1894).

At the very time when declaring his attitude on the Eastern Question, the Chancellor stated that he would always support Austria-Hungary, as it was a necessity for Germany that the Dual Monarchy should continue to be a Power.

The Emperor, however, expressed himself with even greater clearness. At Abbazia, in March, Kaiser William assured Francis Joseph that if, as was to be expected, England should fire the first shot in the Mediterranean and a single member of the Triple Alliance should participate in the war, the whole of the Alliance would do its duty. This statement was probably mere verbiage on the part of the young Emperor and prompted by friendship and admiration for his senior imperial colleague, but on that account it may be taken as a sincere expression of the German policy.

But however we may judge the attitude of the German Government, the fact remains that owing thereto no further or more intimate relations were established between Great Britain and the Triple Alliance. And even the experiments and futile interventions with the object of making intimate co-operation in the Eastern Question possible between Germany (or at least the other members of the Triple Alliance) and England made a decidedly adverse impression in London. The old Russophobe spirit notwithstanding, the idea became ever stronger and stronger that it would be well to open the doors towards Russia and render it possible for England to come to terms with the Czar also on the question of Turkey.

CHAPTER IV

ENGLAND AND THE CONGO DISPUTE

IN the closing years of Caprivi's chancellorship there was unfortunately a danger of England and Germany becoming enemies. In my opinion, this danger was the natural result of the British policy. While the forging of firmer links had become impossible chiefly through the defects of the German policy, the collision in question was, in the first place, the direct consequence of the imperialistic tendencies of the English. One of the most striking traits in the English character is the unshakable conviction that the sea is their special and peculiar possession—that Britannia alone has the right to rule the waves—and further that to England has been awarded " the white man's burden " of maintaining and spreading European civilisation to the remotest corners of the globe : a mental attitude which Rosebery vividly and with classical exactness set forth when he said in the course of a public speech : " They should acquire not only the colonies they needed just then, but also such as they might need in the future," and that " it was their duty to press the British stamp upon the world before some other nation anticipated them."

This conviction, amounting to an obsession, has done far more to develop the world-empire of the British race than the acts of all their Governments. The British Empire did not arise from the conception of any individual sovereign, dynasty, or statesman : like Prussia, who owed her origin to the Hohenzollerns and Bismarck ; like Russia, whose rise can be traced back to Peter the Great,

Catherine II, and Nicholas I ; like France, built up by the constant struggle of her kings against their vassals and provinces ; or like the Austrian Empire, created by the Habsburgs. The British Empire, on the contrary, owes practically everything to the all-pervading initiative and imperialistic talents of the British race. Their strong instinct of domination is demonstrated most vividly in their colonies, those busy hives of imperial development. Most colonies desire to conquer and to expand in their own interests. They all take jealous care that no foreign Power shall be allowed to thrive in their neighbourhood ; that they and no one else shall secure all the ports, economic markets, important strategic points, etc., which serve to promote—or in the hands of foreigners to prevent—their development. This trait in the British character has often proved highly advantageous and always promoted the cause of the Empire. But it is nevertheless a two-edged sword. It has sometimes brought the Empire to a serious pass : into conflict with nations with which she would prefer for general considerations to go hand in hand. It has rendered it difficult for her to make and keep friends, as the British instinct of domination might at some unlooked-for moment bring them into opposition with some Power or other. Individual initiative might imperil peace at a most critical time and place the Government in embarrassment : compelled either to make a stand against the public opinion of the colonies (sometimes even against that of the Mother-country), or else quarrel most inopportunely with a Power with whom she had intended to follow a common policy.

In the period now under review (the eighties and nineties) Britain's colonial interests and aspirations more than once ran counter to the paths of France, Italy,

Portugal, Germany, and America. In Caprivi's time occurred the first serious colonial dispute between England and France.

Just when the German Emperor was enjoying a good time in England (August 1895), Rosebery, with dramatic solemnity, sought immediate contact with the Germans. He impressed upon them that he was faced with a problem of tremendous gravity, in that the French demanded the immediate withdrawal of the British ships from the Siamese ports—a demand with which he simply could not comply.

In this situation a war between England and France loomed so palpably that Hatzfeld enquired of Berlin whether such a contest would be in the interests of Germany, since she would scarcely be able to keep out of it. Caprivi did not regard the contingency as unfavourable from the standpoint of his domestic policy, and thought that from the military point of view it would not matter much whether the struggle took place then or later on. In his opinion, it would be certainly the best for Germany that hostilities should be opened by shots from an English warship. By no means should England's suggestion be entertained, that Italy should intervene and get pushed into the foreground. No intervention should take place until after the anticipated Anglo-French war had actually broken out.

The other ministers likewise came to the conclusion that it would be inexpedient to assist Great Britain diplomatically, as in that case France would withdraw and vent her wrath on the Triple Alliance instead of on England. They could come forward only when England had fired the first shots, or concluded a binding treaty with the Triple Alliance regarding the war.

These highly important negotiations, however, soon

appeared to be futile. Rosebery neither ordered the firing of the first shots nor showed a disposition to come to an agreement with the Triple Alliance, but came to an agreement with France instead. In a few hours the French ultimatum was pronounced a " mistake " and the more important differences were amicably settled. Somewhat later Rosebery attributed this compromise to the fact that the Siamese Question was " not yet " ripe enough for a settlement with France owing to the state of British public opinion. In Berlin and Rome, however, Rosebery's proceedings had created a very bad impression : both considered it a rather undignified backing out. They were particularly disappointed at England's neglect, after so imminent a peril, even to endeavour to make clear her attitude towards the Triple Alliance and thus ensure to herself its assistance for a future similar contingency. Berlin conceived the impression that, as Marschall said, " London wanted Berlin merely as a lightning-conductor—not as an ally."

I must confess that I consider this suspicion and anger to have been without justification. Rosebery had not taken a single step which could justly lay him open to the charge of duplicity. Fearing the outbreak of war, he made overtures to Berlin, certainly with the object of enlisting her aid. But as soon as the immediate danger was past, desiring to avoid war, he returned to the policy of not continuing permanent treaties, and only desired to keep on sufficiently good terms with Germany so that an alliance might result therefrom if necessary. Germany had no right to reproach Rosebery for his unwillingness to declare war on account of the Siamese question ; the differences in that affair were really not worth the shedding of blood. The safety of India was in nowise menaced by the agreement concluded. The English Foreign Minister first thought of war only because his country would have been humbled and her prestige in Asia lowered by surrendering to the French ultimatum. On the other hand, it is intelligible and to be approved that he seized with pleasure the timely offer of a peaceful solution, that he declined to risk the position of Britain as a Great Power for comparatively minor considerations and to undertake the awful responsibility involved in a resort to arms.

Britain's jealousy at the colonial expansion of other nations endangered her good relations also with Italy. When the latter gained a footing in Abyssinia, the Italians found that the English regarded them as interlopers, and were afraid they might cast their eyes on the Sudan too, which was claimed by Egypt and which Britain was absolutely indisposed to cede to any other State. This jealousy, however, led to no grave complication, and the community of interests between the two rivals bridged over the gulf caused by the differences, so that eventually (5th May 1894) an agreement was concluded rendering it possible for England and Italy to co-operate.

Only a few days after this settlement Britain found herself in opposition simultaneously to both Germany and France, the first named having concluded with the Congo Free State (12th May 1894) a treaty which was considered by both the other Powers mentioned to be prejudicial to their interests. Hatzfeld soon got an estimate of the significance of the affair and with unerring judgment established that Germany could act firmly and boldly without serious risk. He based this confident conviction on the fact that Germany was then in a position to place a variety of obstacles in

Britain's way in Egypt by raising adroit objections to the latter's propositions before the international forums ; besides which France also was dissatisfied with the Congo Treaty and would be sure to try to upset it.

Emperor William concurred with his Ambassador. The latter spoke after William's own heart ; and on the margin of the report appeared the imperial auto-graph : " Vorzüglich ! " (Excellent !) The numerous petty pin-pricks with which England had annoyed Germany in several colonial questions and the final break-down of the negotiations with regard to the more important political questions seem to have affected the Emperor's nerves, and he entered the arena of the dispute with all the ardour and excessive zeal so char-acteristic of him.

The injury that Germany had sustained in this matter was particularly serious and profound. England's proceedings could not fail to produce the impression of her ignoring the German interests and desires. Such an impression was inevitable from the leasing by England of the Congo region surrounding German East Africa and cutting it off from the Congo Free State, and at the same time bringing British East Africa and British South Africa into immediate touch with each other ; this in spite of the fact that Great Britain had once before abandoned this deal in deference to the protests of Germany. Thus Berlin could only con-clude that England intended deliberately to cross the will of Germany.

The friction between the two Powers became acute. Both threatened to change the direction of their world-policy. Berlin and Paris aligned themselves against England. Kálnoky and Crispi took alarm and hastened to offer mediation. At length (18th June) the British

Government yielded to the combined pressure of France and Germany and agreed to the desired concessions, modifying the treaty in such a manner that German interests should remain intact.

This incident, however, had a deleterious aftermath. Mutual confidence became ever more shaken in both Germany and England. Each Government felt a sense of having been injured by the other. Rosebery denied that he had been actuated by ill-will; he stated that certain subordinate officials had blundered through an insufficient acquaintance with the antecedents of the question. Though freely confessing that " a stupid " error had been committed, he was wantonly angry with Germany for the failure. He was particularly aggrieved and unfavourably impressed by the Emperor's exhibition of himself with unwonted heat and impetuosity. On two occasions (1st and 14th May) William administered personal castigation to Sir Edward Malet, British Ambassador to Berlin. He alluded to the disloyalty of England; declared that Rosebery had not deceived him, as he had always been aware that he was no friend of Germany. His Imperial Majesty called attention to the irreparable consequences of the collision—and this in a somewhat threatening manner. William remarked afterwards that Sir Edward bit his lip and blushed scarlet; he appeared taken by surprise and made no answer to the imperial ebullition. That was quite comprehensible. Such a personal interference with diplomatic affairs on the part of a sovereign ruler was quite unprecedented. In London the Kaiser was labelled an Anglophobe. His bitter outburst had a momentary success, but it affected the future in a sinister way.

The Congo affair was the last of Caprivi's official

tasks. A few weeks later (29th October 1894) the Emperor dismissed him. The chief cause of his fall was his domestic policy. The Chancellor was an honest soldier, a man of sound common sense, but withal was not a genius, and unequal to supporting the heavy burden of the legacy bequeathed to him by the great Bismarck. After the departure of the diplomatic giant, he appeared a veritable pigmy.

Caprivi was succeeded by old Prince Hohenlohe, Bismarck's former henchman, who as Premier of Bavaria had played a prominent rôle in the foundation of the German Empire after the events of 1870–1. The Kaiser turned to him especially in the hope that he would restore cordial relations with Bismarck. The rage of the old lion had become intolerable. An imperial Government to which Bismarck was opposed had *ipso facto* no authority and was powerless to achieve anything useful. The consequences of the crushing blow Caprivi had inflicted on the Man of Iron by contriving that, on the occasion of Count Herbert's marriage in Vienna, Kaiser Francis Joseph should refuse to receive the famous statesman—who had concluded the Alliance between Austria-Hungary and Germany—were wellnigh irreparable. Therefore Kaiser William expected first of all that Hohenlohe would put an end, as speedily as might be, to that dangerous antagonism so ruinous to the prosperity of the Fatherland.

CHAPTER V

SUMMARY

THE final account of Caprivi's activities in the sphere of foreign politics was by no means pleasing. The successor was unable to maintain fully the prestige handed down from his predecessor. Though our group was still the stronger, our influence and prestige had begun to wane.

Formerly France was less isolated than in Bismarck's time. Once more an alliance had been concluded between France and Russia, who in 1807 at Tilsit had wanted to divide the world between themselves, and in 1830 had proposed to give the Bourbons the Rhine for a frontier and make the Muscovite lord of Turkey. Would not this third alliance foster dangerous ambitions both in the east and in the west of Europe ?

In these circumstances it was impossible to regard as important the fact that the relations between the Russian and German Governments were at this time more confidential than they had been in the last years of Bismarck's régime ; since this arose solely from the fact that just at this moment there existed no sharp antagonism between Austria-Hungary and Russia in the Balkans. But the future was darker and more uncertain than hitherto ; for the alliance with France placed Russia in the anti-German camp, rendering difficult any attempt at an intimate permanent agreement. Thenceforth German Governments would have to deal not only with St. Petersburg but also with

Paris when desiring to come to terms with the former. Moreover, we lost ground in England just when British friendship was becoming more valuable for us owing to the Russo-French Alliance, and Caprivi was on less good terms with England than Bismarck had been. Our chief aims continued the same; English and Germans had to apprehend the same dangers—the Russians and the French—but mutual confidence had been undermined. Berlin and London began to threaten each other with new hostile orientations; and in such cases words are often followed by acts. While diplomatic negotiations were in progress (though under the cloak of the customary secrecy) sharp passages-at-arms occurred which left an indelible impression on the memories in exalted circles, making subsequent cordial relations difficult. Each party of course re-criminated the other. England had to pocket the rudeness of Germany, but the unpleasantness left a lasting impression and prepared the way for the change of orientation. The Emperor became a victim of Anglophobia.

Perhaps he, in his regrettable outspokenness, was animated by the conviction he has since expressed in his *Memoirs*, that " the important thing when dealing with the English is to be quite frank." " The English are not usually offended at rudeness, being themselves rude. They are indignant only when they discover that someone has tried to deceive them." However, it is plain that the egotism and domineering spirit of Britain overseas were getting on William's nerves.

This slight though perceptible change in the balance of power at the expense of the Triple Alliance brought forth its fruits everywhere. Spain, who had been bound to the Triple Alliance by a treaty arranged by Bismarck, showed a disposition to gravitate towards France. England and Italy were powerless to counteract the French influence in Morocco, because Spain (without whom neither was willing to take any decisive step against France) seemed to desire to come to an agreement with her neighbour beyond the Pyrenees rather than with us. The Madrid representatives of the Triple Alliance complained that Spain was " sailing entirely in French waters." The Germans were very dissatisfied with the economic policy of Spain. In the Balkans also the shifting of power was observable. The mercurial, would-be autocrat of Bulgaria grew tired of the dictatorial Stambuloff, the main prop of the Central Powers, and dismissed him, appointing in his stead a Government of Russophil propensities, anxious to propitiate the Czar. In Serbia—which, as we have seen, had become entirely a dependency of Austria-Hungary—there was likewise a change of direction. Sultan Abdul Hamid manœuvred between the two groups of States even more cautiously than before.

With what changes would the chancellorship of Hohenlohe be fraught ? Would he be able to restore the position of power as of old ?

BOOK II

FROM BISMARCK TO BÜLOW

II. HOHENLOHE (1894–1897)

CHAPTER I

THE TRIPLE ALLIANCE OF ASIA

THE third Chancellor of the German Empire accepted the logical consequences of Caprivi's policy. As, in spite of the laudable intentions of his predecessor, it was impossible to cement more cordial relations with England, and since finally the relations between London and Berlin had become exceedingly strained, Hohenlohe decided to approach St. Petersburg.

This step was hastened by Berlin's impression that Rosebery was preparing for a change of front and himself wanted to gain over Russia. Berlin drew this inference from the British Premier's speech (November 1894), in which he stated that he had come to an understanding with the Russians regarding Central Asia and had reason to hope that the agreement would not be limited to remote parts of the globe; as well as from the satisfaction and approval with which the British public received this declaration. A similar effect was produced by Great Britain and Russia uniting to urge immediate reforms in Armenia on the occasion of the excesses and atrocities reported from that region. It is true that this co-operation (December 1894) was fully explained by England and Russia being the first to occupy themselves with this question. Russia herself had an Armenian population adjoining the Armenian territory of Turkey; while England, since the Cyprus Treaty of Beaconsfield, was protector of Asia Minor, and thus felt morally responsible for the state of affairs prevailing there. All the same, the united action of these two rivals seemed an event of the highest significance and the forerunner of an important change in the political outlook.

The German Government, however, had no faith in the genuineness of the Anglo-Russian *rapprochement*. It did not believe that England could acquire the confidence of the Czar, being well aware how she had always endeavoured to thwart the most modest colonial ambitions of Germany, and it scouted the idea that England would be so generous as to make such concessions to Russia as would induce her to become estranged from France ; or that England could satisfy France as well as Russia. It was apparent that there were many difficulties in the way of *rapprochement* between England and Russia.

That it was nevertheless realised some years later was simply in consequence of the blunders of Germany. Nothing but Germany's founding of a great navy, her increasing colonial appetite, and Britain's intelligible though mistaken anxiety lest Germany should destroy her world-empire could have made bed-fellows of such inveterate rivals as Britain and Russia.

Yet no matter how little value the German Government set upon the stability of the *rapprochement* between London and St. Petersburg, the increasing mistrust towards England, the failure of Caprivi's Anglophil policy, and the wounded susceptibilities of the Emperor, all induced the German Government to abandon the Anglophil for a Russophil policy.

The Emperor William was so irritated by the English that on being informed from Constantinople (November 1894) that the mere appearance of a British officer in Armenia would suffice to cause the Armenians to revolt, his Majesty testily remarked that " he wouldn't mind that in the least, if only England burnt her fingers in the fire of the rebellion."

In such a state of things it was but natural that Hohenlohe should eagerly seize the opportunity afforded by the Far East to make advances to Russia without, as in the past, having to sacrifice the interests of Austria-Hungary or Italy for the sake of them. True that he had to run the risk of still further alienating England, but Berlin, in its then frame of mind, did not care much about that.

To this an opportunity was presented by the Chino-Japanese War. In its initial stage (October 1894) Great Britain was inclined to mediate between the two foes, but Germany refused the request. Now that, after the final triumph of Japan, Russia resisted the demands of Tokio, Germany immediately identified herself with the Czar's action. This aroused such indignation in England as might easily have been foreseen. The Kaiser (April 1895) wrote on the Russian proposal a marginal note to the effect that it must be *erst recht* accepted if refused by England.

The *leitmotif* of this highly important decision was as follows: It was desired to divert the attention of Russia to the Far East ; to break up the Franco-Russian understanding before it could be consolidated by a successful joint enterprise ; and to compel the French to continue a common action with the Germans. The Kaiser also counted on winning, in Russia, the support of the most powerful factor in Asia, and thus on being able to spread German influence in China. Russia would not be so jealous as England, who had always exploited Germany and left her in the lurch at a critical moment (April 1895). His chief object, however, was to change the

15

political situation in Europe. He sought to put the Triple Alliance plus Russia in place of the Triple Entente plus England—as he said in a marginal note.

His scheme was only partially successful. Japan could not oppose the combined might of Russia, France, and Germany, and consequently she yielded. England stood aside and, for a time at least, seemed isolated. Germany, Russia, and France (the last against her will, as it were) continued the common action in Asia, and the Czar's attention was for a considerable time attracted to the Far East.

Nevertheless these pleasing results were discounted by serious drawbacks. A new controversy arose between England and Germany. The ill-humour for which the wretched Congo incident was responsible caused further bad blood and exercised a sinister influence upon the subsequent course of events.

The Germans had miscalculated the rival forces in Asia. In the long run Japan remained the stronger. Emperor William predicted that England's standing aloof would be resented by the Japanese—but it did not so turn out. She had put her money on the better horse. Her temporary isolation was rewarded by her subsequent alliance with Japan. The Germans had also committed the perfectly wanton blunder of having offended the Japanese during the war—and that the yellow men could not forgive or forget. The German Ambassador was the only one to use threatening terms in delivering the common *démarche* at Tokio. When later (April 1895) the Japanese Government reproached Germany for this, she shifted the entire blame of the affair on to the shoulders of the Ambassador. But this was palpably unjust, as the Ambassador only carried out the instructions of his Chief.

Nor was the hope realised that Russia would prove more reliable and generous than England. Hardly had they achieved their common success, when Berlin was surprised to discover that France and Russia, in spite of the claims of comradeship, had excluded her from contributing to the loan granted to China, and that the loan had been all arranged by these two Powers behind Germany's back. France being indisposed to Germany's participation in the loan negotiations, Russia left her comrade in the lurch and slyly excluded her from the advantages of a splendid bargain.

Henceforward the German policy was rather frigid towards the Muscovites. Berlin declined to support Russia in the fresh complication that arose. There was an acrimonious squabble between the German Ambassador and the Russian Foreign Minister. The Russians attributed the new difficulties to the lukewarm attitude of the Germans. Hatzfeld, Ambassador to London, accused the Czarist Government (18th July) of being willing to use Germany as a catspaw while they felt not the slightest gratitude if the Germans were unable to give way to them in everything. He had, by the way, previously said the same of the English.

Of Lobanoff, the successor of Giers, Hatzfeld wrote that he was neither reliable nor sincere. William had but little confidence in his friend and cousin " Nicky." He suspected that France, in collusion with Russia, was arming against Germany. At that time the Czar held a restraining hand upon his Gallic ally—he did not consider her strong enough—but as soon as the situation became ripe, he would no doubt give the word. The Czar, said William, had no idea of the real state of things. If the letter he had written should impress the Czar, either Lobanoff or Witte would next day put an end to

its influence. He was aware—he said—what to expect
from Russia.

It became evident that no relation resembling the
Three Emperors' Alliance could be restored since the
independent foreign policy of Russia had been superseded by the Russo-French foreign policy. Berlin was
attached to St. Petersburg by a long-standing friendship,
but not to St. Petersburg and Paris ; and at this period
the two capitals were inseparable, one body and one soul.

When Lobanoff visited France, attended the military manœuvres at Longchamps, and when in the
Chamber it was resolved to transfer the Algiers army
of occupation to Europe, the suspicions of leading circles
in Berlin were naturally confirmed. William addressed
a reproachful epistle to his imperial cousin. He reminded
him in impassioned terms of the awful responsibility
of starting a European conflagration. Berlin took it
for granted that Lobanoff—who prosecuted an astute,
independent, and ambitious policy, but who (as I see
it) desired for the time being to expand in Asia and
consequently preferred no European complications, but
to be on good terms with Austria-Hungary—had far-
reaching anti-German aims. Marschall, Under-Secretary of State, explained that Lobanoff sought to follow
an anti-German policy on the one hand with France
and on the other hand with Austria, i.e. the old Austria desirous of supremacy over Germany—not with
Hungary. By means of such an alliance he would
restore the Rhine-Main frontier of 1866, so that little
Prussia might be reduced to an obedient vassal of his
protégé (November 1895).

When, in the affair of the Armenian massacres,
William despatched a personal telegram to the Czar,
the latter returned such an evasive answer that, as the

Chancellor said, it showed little friendship or trust. The Czar had no desire to settle the Armenian Question in conjunction with Germany, as William wished, but with the whole Concert of Europe.

To sum up, the campaign in Asia failed to bring about the consummation desired by Kaiser William, i.e. the Triple Alliance *plus* Russia ; but rather strengthened the undesired Triple Alliance *minus* England and Russia, from which gradually developed the Triple Alliance *versus* England and Russia.

CHAPTER II

STRAINED RELATIONS BETWEEN ENGLAND AND GERMANY

WHILE our relations with Russia did not materially improve and her friendship for us remained an unknown quantity, the antagonism between England and Germany unfortunately became very bitter. The political situation in England underwent a change. Rosebery had to resign (June 1895) and Salisbury came to power once more. The latter was a man open to conviction ; and it was an auspicious sign that the new British Premier sought to discuss his foreign policy first of all with his old friend Hatzfeld. Unfortunately, however, their first conversation was censured most severely in Berlin. It engendered all sorts of unworthy suspicions.

Hatzfeld mentioned to Salisbury the desire of the Italians that England should alleviate the position of their compatriots in Abyssinia, where France and Russia were working against them simply because Italy was a member of the Triple Alliance and sympathised with England. Salisbury considered it important to do something for Italy, but was unwilling that England should pay for it, and therefore suggested making Italy a present of Albania.

This most unfortunate suggestion sent Berlin wild with rage. It could be explained only on the assumption that perfidious Albion sought to set Austria-Hungary and Italy at loggerheads, to slice up Turkey, and thus cause a general conflict. Holstein, the evil genius of the Minister for Foreign Affairs, was " profoundly convinced " of Salisbury's Machiavellism. This remarkable German did incalculable harm to the cause of his Fatherland. A man without vanity, devoid of ambition, despising rank and decorations so coveted by almost all his colleagues, he led practically a recluse life, never donned evening dress, morosely declined to appear before his Emperor, and saw an enemy in everybody : he was a man who could and did influence all his official superiors, usually for the worse. He condemned Salisbury equally with Lobanoff : neither of them (he said) considered anyone but himself ; neither of them recognised that any States had rights except his own. Salisbury was diabolically scheming to set the continental Powers at each other's throats. England was at her old game again. The British Premier wanted to enjoy, as from a box at the theatre, the spectacle of mutual throat-cutting, and when it was all over to make a bargain with the survivor. Thus this champion misanthrope! (August 1895).

All this was, of course, mere piffle ; Salisbury never dreamt of setting Austria-Hungary against Italy. Had he so intended, he would have whetted the Italian appetite for Albania and not have suggested in advance the idea to Hatzfeld. And why should he be regarded as perfidious, seeing that Bismarck had previously made Crispi a similar offer ? The Iron Chancellor was never suspected of inciting or desiring to play off his two friends against each other ; he was, on the contrary, labouring to bring them closer together. Salisbury, too, proved by his conduct that he had no ulterior motive—no *arrière pensée*—as he immediately took Hatzfeld's hint and allowed the matter to drop.

He invited the German Ambassador to draft a plan

suitable, in the event of the imminent collapse of the Ottoman Empire, to satisfy all the Powers concerned therein.

Holstein read the history of England through spectacles coloured by hate. It is true (he said) that England did not participate in all the local disturbances in Europe of which she had been directly or indirectly the cause (e.g. the Italo-Austrian War, 1859; the Danish War, 1864; the Russo-Turkish War, 1876); but she had never remained neutral in a world war; from the time of Louis XIV to Napoleon I she had entered them all with her entire strength. Thus their own experiences were by no means likely to encourage the English to set the four corners of Europe ablaze merely in order that they might warm their hands comfortably without the risk of getting burnt.

Salisbury well knew that in a great war he could no more avoid having to make momentous decisions and wage struggles of doubtful issue than could Chatham and Pitt; that it is comparatively easy to cause a war, but often difficult to keep out of it, however much one may desire to do so.

Hatzfeld also announced that Salisbury was aware that the defeat of the Triple Alliance in a general conflict would finally deliver England over to her enemies; that her rivals France and Russia would gain the precedence; and in a peace concluded without her, her interests would be ignored by the victors. Salisbury had no Machiavellian plans—he might rather be reproached for the lack of any definite object with regard to Oriental policy. On the whole, during his entire term of office he halted between two policies: one originating in the possibility and even the necessity of maintaining the *status quo* in the East—if necessary even by the sword, lest the Turkish capital and the Straits should fall into the hands of the Russians ; the other being founded on the conviction that the Ottoman Empire was doomed and therefore should be divided, and that it was essential for England to maintain at all costs the road to India via the Suez Canal. In the Beaconsfield Government at the period of the Russo-Turkish War he inclined to the latter solution. But his chief, Beaconsfield, bolder and more imaginative than himself, convinced him that it was in the highest interest of Great Britain—with regard to the Mussulman millions of India—to court the friendship of the Sultan, and above all to let the Sublime Porte see in England her faithful supporter. Beaconsfield converted Salisbury to the view that it would be a tremendous catastrophe for England if the Mohammedan world came under the " protection " of St. Petersburg ; for then the Czar's influence would extend to Suez and Bombay, troubling the internal peace of India, and menacing all the lines connecting England with her empire in Asia.

When Salisbury formed his first Government, he adhered to the fundamental principle of Beaconsfield. At that time this best suited his domestic political interests. Bulgaria especially was menaced by Russian encroachment, and it was an easier task for Salisbury to excite public opinion in England in behalf of this small Christian State than it had been some years before for Beaconsfield to champion the Turks who stood in the way of the liberation of the Christians. Besides this, he thought he could then support Turkey and oppose Russian ambitions at the same time without any great risk ; for Bismarck succeeded in convincing him that he could rely on the greatest military Power in Europe—the Triple Alliance—if compelled through Muscovite aggression to draw the sword. Now, however, on taking office a second time, the Prime Minister found the position altered.

The Armenian Question was in the forefront. Should he elect to support the Turks, a small Christian nation must be sacrificed to Moslem fanaticism. Besides this, he hardly had any choice. A *fait accompli* confronted him. Rosebery, his predecessor, had already enlisted England in the cause of the Armenians. Gladstone's fiery eloquence had converted every man, woman, and child in England into an enthusiastic pro-Armenian. Salisbury, if he attempted to follow a Turkophil policy, would most certainly be defeated.

Salisbury on more than one occasion told Hatzfeld that foreigners very frequently misunderstood the foreign political aims of British ministers ; they could not realise that the principal object of the latter was to remain in power as long as possible.

But, moreover, England was under the influence of her past. Since Beaconsfield's time she had become the protector of the Christians in Asia Minor, with the double object of strengthening the Turks and reassuring the Sultan's Christian subjects.

If Beaconsfield had remained longer in power after the Berlin Treaty he might have witnessed the fruits of his policy : Turkey, the " Sick Man," put on his legs again under the ægis of England, reconciled to the acceptance of her leadership, and, besides, the Christian population well looked after. But after his fall Gladstone's anti-Turk policy rendered all this impossible. The Beaconsfield traditions were dropped, England lost her influence at the Sublime Porte, and thus was powerless to induce the Turks to carry out any serious reforms.

But the burdens of the Beaconsfield policy remained : a heavy moral responsibility rested upon England in the view of the Christians of the East ; and the consciousness of this responsibility excited the public opinion of England and made it—much to its disadvantage—anti-Turkish. The torture of the ill-fated Armenians by the Bashi-Bazouks and Kurds was regarded both in the East and England as a foul blot on the fair name of the latter, and the British Government was looked for to help.

Salisbury, too, was exasperated by the Sultan, and turned against him. He saw that Abdul Hamid was perfectly untrustworthy. The Turkish unfitness for rule, the chaotic conditions prevailing throughout the Ottoman Empire, all reconverted him to his former faith that Turkey was past redemption. He no longer relied on the assistance of Germany in exposing himself for the sake of Turkey. Since the efforts of Rosebery and Kálnoky to enlist the help of Germany, at least to cover their line of retreat, had been entirely frustrated, since a bitter antagonism had sprung up on the Congo Question between England and Germany, and since in Asia Germany had gone over to the policy of Russia instead of that of England, Salisbury came to the conclusion that he could no longer count on the aid of the Germans against the Muscovites.

He therefore cast about for a solution which would preserve peace as well as defend British interests without having to draw the sword for the Sultan. This did not signify, however, that he desired to follow an Oriental policy directed against the Triple Alliance. He would prefer to attain this latest aim also, which pressure of circumstances had compelled him to choose, in co-operation with the Triple Alliance. For this reason he first of all turned to his old confidant, Hatzfeld ; listened to his advice, and on that advice abandoned the idea above-mentioned.

Probably he was himself by no means sure as to the best thing to do. He tried to formulate more clearly his definite opinion and to find the right way. The French Ambassador during the negotiations well described Salisbury in saying that he (the British Premier) liked to consider the problems of the future and to discuss them. He was vacillating, undecided. He was less conspicuous for lofty initiative than for patiently plodding, cautious progress. He possessed none of the inspired boldness of the Pitts and Cannings, nor of the imagination of Beaconsfield. He was circumspection and hesitancy personified.

The conversation with Hatzfeld had an interesting sequel. No sooner had the German Ambassador pointed out to his Foreign Minister that at any eventual carving up of Turkey Salisbury was disposed to satisfy Russia, than the German attitude to Salisbury's plan underwent a change. Even Holstein said (5th August) that this new information altered the position of things entirely, and since it appeared that Salisbury would really satisfy Russia in regard to the Straits, thereby disposing of the *raison d'être* of the Franco-Russian Alliance, he should be directly encouraged in his project.

Holstein's view was accepted not only by the Chancellor but also by the Emperor. The latter proposed to Szögyény-Marich, our Ambassador to Berlin, that Austria-Hungary should also accept Salisbury's scheme, and consent to Russia having the Straits and keeping Salonica for herself.

It was an interesting moment. There seemed a hope of England and Germany coming to an understanding on the basis of Bismarck's old idea of satisfying Russia, agreeing with Austria-Hungary, and solving the Eastern Question by peaceful means.

This delightful picture, was, however, only a mirage. Fate decreed otherwise. It so happened (5th August) that before the Emperor had become fully acquainted with the altered state of affairs, his Majesty had met Salisbury in England and categorically rejected the scheme which a few days later was discovered to be so attractive. This being so, it was difficult to reopen the matter now. And all the more difficult would have been co-operation with England as the meeting between the German Emperor and the British Premier had left behind it a certain bitterness. To this day not all the particulars of this fateful interview are known, but one fact at least is clear—that the English statesman took umbrage at the disdainful refusal of the Kaiser to consider and study his scheme for the dissolution of the Ottoman Empire. On the other hand, William was indignant with Salisbury either because that statesman failed to keep an appointment with his Majesty aboard the imperial yacht *Hohenzollern*, or else, as Holstein afterwards affirmed, on account of the sharp correspondence occasioned by the incident.

But this agreement as to the division of the spoil could hardly have been carried out without accident and in a peaceful manner. In all probability Salisbury had sounded St. Petersburg and Paris and convinced himself that the demands of those two Powers could not be satisfied. He doubtless discovered the truth— that it was sheerly utopian to contemplate a peaceful distribution of the effects of the (to be) late " Sick Man of Europe," and that an unseemly scramble for the tit-bits would be inevitable.

However, it would have been quite as difficult for Berlin to have made the division, since Austria-Hungary held tenaciously to the idea of the *status quo* and would not hear of the proposed change thereof.   Thus the whole scheme was shelved and remained a barren theory.

Salisbury returned to the beaten track.   When, owing to the Sultan's promised reforms in Armenia (October), the situation somewhat improved for the moment, Salisbury declared to Hatzfeld that he desired to maintain the *status quo*, and if Russia caused a crisis in the Eastern Question, he would try first to come to an agreement with Berlin and Vienna.

Such an announcement buried the scheme for distribution, but at the same time failed to restore cordial relations between London and Berlin.   After that, the Emperor could feel no confidence in the British Government.   He always associated it with risky plans.   He kept an eye on his mother, " The Englishwoman," and found in her utterances the key to the mysteries of British policy.   At one time he entertained the suspicion that Salisbury would have liked to entice the Russians to Constantinople in order that they might there come into opposition with Moslem fanaticism ; and that the collision might furnish England with pretext for the occupation of the Dardanelles.   At another time (November) he gathered from the words of the Empress-Dowager that Salisbury intended to divide up the Ottoman Empire ; and that he had no objection to the Russians getting the Dardanelles provided they agreed finally to let the English have Egypt in exchange.   Then (December) he thought he had discovered that the real aim of England was to foment a war between the continental Powers.   He used the simile of England shaking the Turkish apple-tree to set the continental nations squabbling for the possession of the fallen fruit. On another occasion the Emperor William, who could even " hear the grass grow," was convinced that Salisbury had a diabolical plot for playing off Austria-Hungary and Italy against Russia in order to withdraw when his friends had fallen out with each other.

At length, influenced by the gossip of the Russian Ambassador Osten-Sacken, he got the idea that Salisbury was planning a secret agreement with Lobanoff behind the backs of the Germans ; he even charged the British Military Attaché with " perfidy " (December). He informed that unfortunate officer that such a trick was *unqualifizierbar*. Gladstone was " a mean person." " If England was out to upset the *status quo*, she should not resort to back-stairs secrecy, but act openly and aboveboard, as was customary with the continental Powers. England's dubious and hypocritical attitude, her remarkable manœuvres, gave the impression that she wanted to spur on the Powers against each other—but she would not succeed. The Powers of the Continent remained loyally by each other, while England had so often backed out of her obligations that no one believed in her ability to make up her mind. If England had a new Oriental policy to introduce, let her trot it out and not insidiously attempt to induce her friends by diplomatic chicanery to join her, only to find themselves deceived in the end."

This was serious language, serious in anyone's mouth, and especially so in that of a monarch. If a minister thus speaks, the party attacked is free to reply ; but what can a simple military officer do against a foreign sovereign, to whose Government he is accredited, to say nothing of the fact that the august personage happens to be the grandson of his own Queen ? If a minister acts so indiscreetly there is always the hope that he may resign and thus leave the way clear for the restoration of friendly relations between the two Governments concerned. But one can only count on a state of perpetual enmity between nations one of whose sovereigns can speak with such contempt of the other. Moreover, the Emperor's amazing blunder was rendered all the more serious as he was unable to substantiate the charges he made. When the matter was investigated, all the evidence went against him and he was decidedly worsted. Salisbury denied having offered Lobanoff any agreement, and the Russian Minister for Foreign Affairs confirmed the denial.

The strained relations between England and Germany affected also the inner life of the Triple Alliance, starting Berlin, Vienna, and Rome on divergent paths—a state of things which boded no good for the authority of the Alliance.

At this time the historic mansion in the Ballplatz got a new tenant. Kálnoky came into conflict with Bánffy, the Hungarian Premier, and so was quietly dropped by Francis Joseph. He was succeeded by Goluchowsky, a man who, while neither highly educated nor so keen an observer as Kálnoky, certainly possessed more initiative and force of character than his predecessor, and therefore made a better leader of the foreign affairs of the Dual Monarchy. Kálnoky had hardly that audacity so indispensable to the successful prosecution of foreign policy. For none will trust, no one fear, no one befriend a man who is afraid to trust even himself, afraid of everyone else, and who is irresolute and vacillating.

The aims of Goluchowsky's policy were to some extent different from Kálnoky's. He rather inclined to those of Andrássy than to those of his immediate predecessor. Like the Hungarian statesman, he was ambitious to distinguish himself by his activities on the Ballplatz. He was anxious to counteract the Russian influence there, and to maintain the *status quo* in the Balkans. The division of the Ottoman Empire, or the idea of " spheres of influence," to which Kálnoky—under the pressure of Bismarck and later of William II—had at times almost become reconciled, his successor rejected, as Andrássy had done. He approximated to the personal views of Francis Joseph, who held it most important that Constantinople should not be allowed to fall into the hands of Russia and always adhered to the principles by which he had been guided in the Crimean War and at the Congress of Berlin. Goluchowsky saw more clearly than did his predecessor that the western Balkan region offered to us in the projected apportionment would be no real source of strength ; rather it would weaken us. We should acquire a barbarian population, difficult to govern, unwilling to live under the rule of the Dual Monarchy and gravitating outward. The new acquisition, as proposed, could never be shaped to fit the frame of dualism. On its account the Dual Monarchy would be compelled to look for quite new solutions in common law. But should we be able to find such ? Would not *federalism*—the only conceivable substitute for dualism—give rise to an international quarrel that might in the end destroy the position of the Dual Monarchy as a Great Power ?

While the entire Orthodox and Slav world would rally to the Czar, who would now have become master of Constantinople, the Dual Monarchy would be crushed under the Slav influence by means of internecine strife. Consequently Goluchowsky was prepared to draw the sword in the cause of the *status quo*. But for this, it would in the first place be necessary to enlist the aid of

16

England. And could there be any hope from that quarter, seeing that England and William II were not on speaking terms, that Berlin followed a Russophil policy, and, as was supposed in England, Austria-Hungary was led by Berlin ?

In Italy, on the whole, a similar view prevailed. Blanqui, Crispi's successor, remarked to Bülow that Constantinople was too near Trieste for him to look calmly on at Russian rule there. If the French and Russians joined hands across the Mediterranean, Italy, crushed between them, would soon lose her independence, and therefore she had no alternative but to adhere to the *status quo*. Consequently she too desired above all to win England and, side by side with her, proceed to a solution of the Eastern Question.

Owing to these considerations, Austria-Hungary and Italy, in the Armenian Question now to the fore, followed aims differing from those of Berlin. It is true that the warm heart and impulsive nature of the German Emperor had at first been sadly shocked at the massacre of the Armenians by the Turks, and he wrote that Sultan Abdul Hamid was a hideous monster into whose residence, Yildis Kiosk, a few bombs thrown would not be an ill act, and that merely to touch such a wretch would be a defilement for a Christian. Yet in spite of this, William showed a disinclination to back his sentiments by appropriate deeds and put pressure on the Sultan, because by so doing he would be rendering the task of England all the easier ! That he would not do at any price. He gloated over the scrape into which England had got. The English had encouraged the Armenians, and now they should see what would come of it. The Triple Alliance should if possible simply stand aside and look on, letting the English bear the whole burden of the affair, for, after all, they were the real culprits !

England would have succeeded only by coercing the Sultan ; and as she could not gain access by land to the territory inhabited by the Armenians, and the British fleet might fall into a trap on the Black Sea if the Dardanelles remained in the hands of the Turks, she could only accomplish her object by threatening the Sultan himself in Constantinople. But how was even this possible, seeing that the Dardanelles were closed by international treaty regulations ? Would her violation thereof lead to war ?—a war in which England might find herself opposed by the combined forces of Turkey and Russia. And yet, should she allow the Armenian horrors to continue, her prestige would suffer. These weighty decisions could only be avoided if all Europe supported her and, together with her, put pressure upon Abdul Hamid. This the Emperor William wished to frustrate if possible.

He did everything he could to keep the other Powers from exposing themselves on behalf of England. Let no one do England's work for her. Let her do it herself. Let her act first. One can never be sure of England unless she is cornered and sees that no one else is disposed to take the chestnuts out of the fire for her, and, instead of and without her, defy the Russians. Until she has been made to see that, England will always play the egger-on and try to saddle the backs of other people with her proper burdens.

Russia shared the Kaiser's view in this matter. She manifested no enthusiasm for the Armenian cause ; rather she attempted to defend the alarmed Sultan and to gain him to her side, as Nicholas I had done in the days of Mahomet Ali.

William's policy, however, did not coincide with the views of his most intimate ally, Austria-Hungary. Goluchowsky's policy was by no means anti-English; it was rather anti-Russian. He did not regard the Eastern crisis as an opportunity to embarrass England; he had personal interests in the Eastern Question. Contrary to his ally at Berlin, he considered that his only chance of winning England lay in acting in concert with her and assisting her in defence of their mutual interests.

The members of the Triple Alliance therefore went different ways. Goluchowsky proposed that the Powers should proceed side by side. He took the initiative instead of England, but in the interest of the latter. Up to that period England had co-operated with Russia and France only, two antagonists, jealous lookers-on; but now someone with interests common with their own had joined the movement, and that could not fail to improve the situation. Salisbury counted, moreover, on Russia being disposed more gladly to follow the advice of Austria-Hungary than that of England, and believed that the Sultan would after all tread the path of reform if all Europe united to put the screw upon him.

Italy concurred with Goluchowsky. She was resolved to play her part in all the Oriental and African questions, lest, when it came to the division of the spoil, she would remain empty handed.

The German Emperor strongly disapproved of Goluchowsky's initiative. He called Count Deym, Austro-Hungarian Ambassador to London, a "consummate ass," and devoutly hoped for Goluchowsky's failure. He said that the young Pole "ought to go to school again."

Goluchowsky began independent action also in London. The cooler the relations between Berlin and

London, the more important he thought it to get nearer to Salisbury and to bind him by a new treaty. Like his predecessor, Kálnoky, he wished to have the accord of 1887 with the Italian Government in detail and more clearly defined. He would like to fix a distinct *casus belli* for the contingency of a Russian attack, whereas the only obligation so far undertaken consisted of Austria-Hungary, Italy, and England discussing together the further steps to be taken in such case.

However, this step of Goluchowsky's was as futile as Kálnoky's had been. It was wrecked on the very same rock : England would not hear of undertaking obligations against Russia except in conjunction with Germany ; and Germany was equally chary of making any promises. Salisbury declared (February 1895) that in the then state of British public opinion he dare not undertake to defend the integrity of Turkey. If the Czar were willing to concede in favour of England all the rights in the Straits that she claimed therein, he would be able to come to an agreement with him. But, he added, this did not mean that England intended to be a passive spectator of the advance of Russia. She would determine her attitude according to the requirements of the situation. If Russia sought to obtain one-sided advantages for herself by means of aggression, Salisbury trusted that the British public would demand resistance. But he would not bind himself in advance.

This had been Salisbury's attitude once before, when he had rejected similar overtures from Kálnoky. He deviated from their chief proviso in 1887 solely because he trusted that, should necessity arise, the greatest European Powers—i.e. the Triple Alliance—would support him. Now, however, he had no ground for any such confidence. Germany's frigid attitude gave not the slightest hope of her assistance in any complication arising out of the Eastern Question ; as a few days before the decisive negotiations the relations between England and Germany had become even worse, and the former had to regard Germany in the light of a potential foe rather than as a friend.

CHAPTER III

THE BOERS

AT this period the British imperialists cast their covetous eyes on the country of the Boers, which was highly valuable on account of the rich gold- and diamond-mines with which nature had blessed —or cursed—it, besides its peculiarly advantageous geographical position. If only this favoured land were brought under British overlordship, the star of Great Britain in Africa would have reached its zenith. Her rule would then extend from Cape Town on the south to Alexandria on the north coast ; thus, by means of the iron road already partly constructed, joining the Indian Ocean with the Mediterranean and bringing the two great seaports within a few days' journey of each other. What splendid visions of economic development were thus conjured up before the ravished eyes of Britons of a certain sort ! It was a dream of empire worthy of a Julius Cæsar or an Alexander the Great.

Cecil Rhodes, the magnate of Cape Colony, was obsessed by such grandiose ideas, and set his fertile brain to work to encompass the overthrow of the Boer Government and to bring the Transvaal Republic under the British flag. The central Government in London could not openly identify itself with the adventurous schemes of Rhodes, though it was certain that in the event of their success it would not be averse to accepting and exploiting the *fait accompli*. It was certain that it would resist all counteractions and discountenance all attempts at intervention, since in its view the

Transvaal was already a quasi part of the British Empire, England being its suzerain.

The German policy and the British policy differed materially. The Germans aimed at bringing both Dutch and German East Africa into intimate relationship under German protection. They keenly resented British supremacy in South Africa and insisted on the independence of the Boers.

Either of these two conceptions excluded the other. Both were born of interests of immense importance; but while that of the British corresponded with the existing circumstances, as regards power, and was therefore in accordance with reason, that of the Germans was opposed to both fact and reason, and therefore constituted a dangerous *ignis fatuus*. For the time being, however, the German Government chased this will-o'-the-wisp and vigorously protested against the violence and rascality of the Jameson Raid. It loudly declared that if the British Government should seal its approval of such an act of lawlessness, the German Ambassador in London should ask for his passports. It further incited President Krüger to resistance against British tyranny. It assured him that any alteration in the *status quo* would never be tolerated by Germany. England was naturally much disturbed by these proceedings. Sir Edward Malet, at Berlin, bitterly criticised the German Foreign Minister on the occasion of the former's *visite de congé* prior to his departure from the German capital (November 1895). He informed the Foreign Minister that England could not countenance the coquetting of the Germans with the Boers; that such conduct might have grave consequences, as England was not in the mood to allow any foreign Power to meddle in the affairs of the British Empire.

The Emperor, on hearing of this, fumed with rage ; though the British Ambassador had merely used language similar to that he himself so often used in London. But to an Emperor was permissible what was forbidden to less exalted persons. And he administered a stinging castigation to Swain, the British Military Attaché, who had perforce to serve as whipping-boy for Malet's offence. The British Ambassador had had the astounding audacity (said the Emperor) to threaten *him*, the grandson of the Queen of England, with war ! But Germany would not brook such an outrage from England. He should be compelled to make overtures to Russia and France. If England wanted the support of Germany, she had better sue for an alliance with her.

The cautious Salisbury lost no time in disavowing Malet's utterances, declaring that he had given the Ambassador no authority to make such statements.

William II was delighted with the result of the dressing-down he had administered by proxy to Sir Edward Malet. He afterwards boasted of the success which had attended his bullying. He ordered the Government to make what capital they could out of the incident ; if it should have no other effect, it would at least be useful as propaganda for the German navy. What incredible infatuation ! What playing with fire—to promote the building of the German navy by means of Anglophobe propaganda ! This was the first step towards that fatal error which constituted one of the fundamental causes of the Great War.

But the South African crisis was precipitated after all. Jameson's filibusters wantonly violated the territory of the Boer Republic (January 1896), to be disgracefully routed by a handful of the intrepid burghers.

Kaiser William appeared to be favoured by fortune. His standpoint was maintained. The independence of the Transvaal Republic had been vindicated without the necessity of German intervention ; so that relations with England need not be permanently strained. Here, however, Germany added to her initial blunder by perpetrating another.

It was not on his own initiative (as was believed for a long time), but on the advice of his Government, that the Emperor wired his congratulations to Krüger, the imperial telegram being published in the press and thereby arousing the ire of the British public. The English were mortified by the Emperor's blatant celebration of the victory of another nation over themselves—and such an insignificant nation too !—by his meddling with a peculiarly British affair such as the question of Boer independence, which the British denied in principle ; by his reference to " the friends of the Boers," who would have helped them had they only applied. This, the English considered, should be a lesson to them for the future. It was not so much the telegram itself that the English resented, but the deep-laid conspiracy it revealed to establish German hegemony in East Africa and to frustrate the consolidation of British power in that region.

The British press discharged its batteries of vituperation against Germany, and the public opinion of the island kingdom became nervous with regard to the Emperor. This excitement was quite comprehensible. Germany's action did not emanate from African local interests exclusively, but rather from her growing distrust of the English and a greater political conception. This conception was averse to war with England, though it sought, by isolation, to compel the

British to a more modest policy. Its aim was to invite the whole Continent without England to join the Triple Alliance and Double Entente in a programme for the solution of certain important questions against England. According to this conception, the continental Powers ought to have agreed to the Transvaal's absolute independence of England; to France's acquisition of the Congo; Russia getting Corea; Italy, Abyssinia; and Germany a harbour in China: to all of which stipulations Britain of course objected. It meant further to satisfy Austria-Hungary by the maintenance of the *status quo* in the Balkans. An interesting and rare phenomenon. The Power destined within the next few years to be accused by the Entente of unwarrantable aggression, which was destined to be torn to pieces and sentenced to death by "unbiassed judges" in the cause of world-peace, was found so satisfied, so conservative and peaceable, by her best friend, who knew her most intimately, that she was not offered the chance of her least expansion, the least chance of conquest. She was not offered Salonica—out of her alleged longing for which her enemies' diplomats spun such veracious yarns. They well knew that Austria-Hungary never coveted Salonica; that the German Government since Bismarck's days has more than once tried in vain to stimulate in her a desire for the Western Balkans, and that the sole thing that Austria-Hungary ever cared for was, in fact, the maintenance of the *status quo* in the East.

The German politicians did not contemplate war with England, and therefore freely and openly declared that their plan did not affect British possessions; that they sought no changes which might jeopardise the vital interests of England, such as represented by India and the routes thereto. All they desired—said the Chancellor—was to check England's perpetual and boundless expansion and insatiable appetite for all the still unoccupied tracts of earth. The trend of German thoughts was even then towards friendly relations with Britain. According to the leading statesmen of Germany, England had up to that time omitted to conclude an agreement with the Triple Alliance because she imagined that the Franco-Russians would never manage to come to terms with the latter, consequently England would be always in a position to play off one group against the other in order to defend herself against attack and to have the final word in all important questions of world-policy. Should England fail to realise her expectations in this respect, she would be compelled to seek the assistance of one or other of the European groups—even to sacrifice something to gain it—and the group chosen would certainly be the Triple Alliance, since she was separated therefrom by lesser differences than those separating her from the Franco-Russian group.

This mentality of the Germans reminds one of the vulgar cynical English proverb:

> "A wife, a bitch, and a walnut-tree—
> The more they're beaten the better they be."

In their view England would not become amenable until after a good thrashing. When, however, they sought to bend England by constant pressure and menaces—to worry her into becoming friendly, as it were—they forgot that while such a method might answer for a time with a federated nation led by weak-kneed politicians, it would assuredly fail in the case of a proud, triumphant, imperialistic race like the British.

And so it proved : the result of the persistent nagging was that England, instead of becoming the friend, became the enemy of Germany.

Moreover, this policy was still-born. If one had not read it in official documents, it would be difficult to believe that such a fanciful offspring would have exacted the homage of serious-minded people. It was wrong from its starting-point, i.e. the assumption that two groups of European Powers could come to terms with each other more easily than with England. Wrong also was the view that all the continental Powers would be ready to unite against England because, forsooth, they all shared the German opinion that England was never useful, while she was sometimes harmful. It made no allowance for the possibility of an inimical Government arising which would decline to go against England because she regarded Germany as never useful and always harmful ! The French Ambassador to Berlin soon put the damper on Holstein, the father of this strange child.

Why should France, he demanded, come to terms with Germany on questions in which the Germans themselves are primarily interested, if she may not in questions which concern herself (France) most of all—such as, for instance, the Egyptian Question ? It was reported from Rome that the French Premier, Bourgeois, had remarked to an Italian friend that France would never forget Alsace-Lorraine, that in the course of events those provinces would have to be returned to France, and that all their energies would be directed to the realisation of that patriotic aim. By this he justified France's inability to range herself on the side of Italy, so long as the latter was the ally of Germany. How, then, could she participate with Germany in a common action against England ?

At first the French press sympathised with the Boers, but when the Anglo-German antagonism became so acute it took on a decided Germanophobe (and consequently a less pro-Boer) complexion. The semi-official publications warned the people against unnatural alliances.

Thus the Anglo-German controversy did not, after all, lead to a *rapprochement* between Germany and France, as Holstein had fondly hoped ; but rather to a *rapprochement* between France and England. Courcel, French Ambassador to London, said that France had only one enemy—Germany ; and that in the event of war between England and Germany, England could absolutely rely on the good-will, and probably also on the support, of France.

Actual developments proved the correctness of the English thesis—that England was nearer to either of the two groups than they were to each other, and hence a written alliance would have been much more advantageous for us than for England. But even within the Triple Alliance itself it would have been impossible to accept Holstein's proposition. Goluchowsky was averse to taking part in any anti-English coalition. As we have already seen, notwithstanding the Anglo-German dispute, he continued in London the negotiations for the alliance. For in the friendship of England he very rightly saw one of the fundamental conditions or bases of the stability of the Dual Monarchy. What a pity his successors did not follow the trail blazed by him and more successfully intervene between England and Germany ! That would have been the historic vocation of Austria-Hungary.

The new plans of Germany caused tremendous excitement also in Italy. Rome, while condemning

Salisbury, had not the temerity to oppose England. The Italians feared lest the *rapprochement* between France and Germany should lead to an increase of the power of the former and lest they should prove unable to defend their interests in the Mediterranean and North Africa against France.

The German Government, however, did not push its ideas too insistently. It soon woke up to the fact that they were untenable. It shortly found a new direction and laid down the principle that the Triple Alliance should seek no new ally, neither in England, France, nor Russia, but should go its own way alone, its members adhering the more closely to each other. Certainly a better plan than Holstein's, based on division. Even this, however, could be no more than provisional.

The only true object of German policy (especially since the Franco-Russian Alliance had made relations with the Czar impossible) was an alliance with England. Without British support it was difficult for the Triple Alliance itself to hold together. It was originally conceived with the idea of British support : would it not degenerate without it ?

Goluchowsky was pessimistic. He thought that harmony within the Alliance could be secured only by Germany identifying herself more closely with the interests of Austria-Hungary and Italy than she had been wont to do in the past. Welsersheimb, Foreign Under-Secretary (February 20th), strongly complained to Prince Lichnowsky, Councillor of Embassy. Austria-Hungary was in sad straits ; England and Germany had both withdrawn from Eastern affairs, and Italy was unreliable. Germany had always preached to Vienna that they should come to an understanding with the Russians regarding the division of the Balkans ;

but such a thing was impracticable : it would mean the hegemony of the Czar from the Black Sea to the Adriatic. The sole necessity for Austria-Hungary of the Triple Alliance was afforded by the Russian peril. If the Triple Alliance failed in that respect, it would thereby lose its *raison d'être* so far as the Dual Monarchy was concerned. For the latter it was not of the slightest consequence to whom Alsace-Lorraine belonged. Therefore, in his opinion, it was necessary for both Berlin and Vienna to review the situation, to discuss it frankly together, and to come to an agreement thereon. Emperor William was, needless to say, displeased with Welsersheimb's view. He said it seemed as though the Austro-Hungarian Foreign Minister aimed at becoming a second Bismarck ; the Polish Count was still a very young man ; he could be useful to the Monarchy ; only let him try not to be so foolish (*töricht*).

Goluchowsky's soundings, as may be supposed, failed of their object. Germany resolved to undertake no new obligations in the Eastern Question, and Austria-Hungary was not firm and influential enough to press Berlin to change her intention.

Hohenlohe had a queer idea for composing the differences. He gave us permission to offer England an alliance, if necessary even at the price of throwing overboard the Triple Alliance. He counted upon London's rejection of the proposal, which would show Goluchowsky that his (Goluchowsky's) efforts to win England had not been frustrated by any fault of Germany's, but because she was averse to binding herself to an anti-Russian policy. Hohenlohe, however, could hardly make Goluchowsky see this. The latter was quite well aware that an agreement between London and Vienna was not rendered difficult by the fact that we were an ally of Germany, but rather because our alliance with Germany was not far-reaching enough : it did not include the East, and therefore all agreements with us on the Balkan Question would fail to secure the support of the entire Triple Alliance, whereas England would bind herself to protect Constantinople and help against the Russians only if she could count absolutely on the bayonets of the entire Triple Alliance, as she had ground for hope in Bismarck's time. Goluchowsky might have been convinced of his error if the German Government had promised to guarantee the neutrality of France in the event of hostilities in the Near East, as Rosebery had asked and Salisbury expected of Bismarck ; and if England, in spite of this promise, had been unwilling to follow a common Oriental policy with Austria-Hungary and Italy. But I believe that Goluchowsky did not avail himself of Berlin's permission. He surely knew that such an extraordinary proceeding would not have had the least effect for good, while it would have done much harm to the prestige of the Triple Alliance.

17

CHAPTER IV

WEAKENING OF THE TRIPLE ALLIANCE

AT this time the Triple Alliance met with much adversity. Misfortune dogged it everywhere. The defeat by King Menelik of the Italian forces in Africa came as a bolt from the blue. This event led to the fall of Crispi, the staunchest adherent of the Triple Alliance, the representative of the anti-French policy. He was succeeded by Rudini, who, through the influence of Visconti Venosta, Minister for Foreign Affairs, desired to restore good relations with France. Nevertheless, the new Italian Government had no intention of breaking with the Triple Alliance: it even renewed the old bond (May 1896). He had, however, no longer any confidence in Italy. Bülow described the new departure as following Guicciardini, who had advised the nation to " endeavour to be always on the winning side."

In the negotiations for the prolongation of the Triple Alliance there was an interesting episode : a diplomatic success on our part which subsequently took its revenge to our discomfiture. The Italian Government, with a frankness and loyalty worthy of all respect, offered to renew the official declaration made at the original conclusion of the Triple Alliance to the effect that the *casus fœderis* was not to be applied to the event of war against England. That declaration was not renewed in 1887 simply because then—on the initiative and advice of Germany—was concluded the Anglo-Italian Mediterranean Agreement, which excluded the possibility of the allies demanding the aid of Italy against England.

Goluchowsky very properly wished to acknowledge the Italian declaration. But Hohenlohe entertained a contrary opinion. He managed that the two allies should reject the offer of Italy, on the ground that it was unnecessary, since the Triple Alliance, even without the declaration, was never likely to quarrel with England; moreover, the declaration was harmful, as such a reservation would give the Triple Alliance an anti-Russian complexion, which would only provoke the Czar. Thus the Italian Government had no alternative but to yield, and the matter could not be put into documentary form. Hence the weakness of the Triple Alliance was that it afforded no protection against England without the fact being publicly acknowledged —a fact with which all the Ministers of Foreign Affairs had to reckon and which was perfectly clear to the various nations concerned. In 1914 Italy acted as though her declaration, above referred to, had actually been put into documentary form. In my opinion, it would have been better had the treaty not seemed to mean more than life was able to afford. A policy of self-delusion, or refusal to face cold facts, is always most dangerous.

At this period the Triple Alliance was further weakened by the expiration, in May 1896, of our convention with Spain and the failure of our efforts to renew it. The Madrid Government most probably considered our position to be no longer as stable as in 1887, when it had first concluded the pact with us. It no longer desired to be a member of the anti-French group, and therefore coupled its willingness to renew the convention with the quite unacceptable condition that the Triple Alliance should guarantee to it Cuba, then menaced by the United States.

Not on the west alone, but also on the east, the Triple Alliance lost strength about this time. Ferdinand of Coburg, Prince of Bulgaria, after the dismissal of Stambuloff, prepared for a change of front, and sought (February 1896) to curry favour with the Czar by the conversion of his sons Boris and Alexander to the faith of the Orthodox Church.

The German Government attributed this important loss to the policy of Kálnoky. They contended that the Minister for Foreign Affairs of the Dual Monarchy had failed sufficiently to support his Balkan friends. King Milan was dropped by him just as Stambuloff had been —from personal antipathy—at the expense of the Triple Alliance. The German Government likewise found fault with Burian, at that period our Chargé d'Affaires in Sofia—who was later destined to become Foreign Minister—because he was against Stambuloff, and also because he had failed to see that, with Stambuloff's fall, the party leaning on us would also fall.

Goluchowsky himself admitted that the German Government was in the right and condemned the procedure of his predecessor. He stated that he had had a sharp dispute with Kálnoky with regard to Stambuloff. Thus we are compelled to the belief that the policy of both Kálnoky and Burian was unsound. Our acts were by no means bold and firm enough to inspire our friends with confidence and our foes with fear.

However, for the radical cause of our failure we must look to anterior events. Owing to Bismarck's pressure, Austria-Hungary was unable either to save Battenberg or to secure for Ferdinand the recognition of the Sublime Porte, and thus establish him in a safe international position. Had not Bismarck, in the eighties, scotched the freedom of action of the Dual Monarchy, we should by the end of the century have been much stronger in the Balkans than we were ; and as we thus might have been expected to be capable of doing more, we should have had more friends. It is comprehensible that Ferdinand, who failed by our intervention, even when we were stronger, to attain the consolidation he so badly needed, should now, when our power had to a certain extent fallen, endeavour to reach his goal by cementing a friendship with the Russians. His success justified his calculations.

Lobanoff, the Russian Foreign Minister, drew a veil over the past, took Ferdinand's case in hand, and procured his recognition. Fortunately, in spite of our great indignation, partly as the result of Berlin's sensible advice, we refrained from following the example set by Alexander III towards Battenberg and Coburg, but recognised Ferdinand ; so that the road between Sofia and Vienna remained open without any obstacles of an insurmountable nature.

CHAPTER V

ENGLAND, EGYPT, THE ARMENIAN QUESTION, CRETE

AMONG the many unfavourable events a pleasing incident occurred on the banks of the Thames. As already pointed out, relations with England since Bismarck's retirement had become gradually worse and worse, both when Caprivi thought winning her friendship was the all-important thing and also when under Hohenlohe the Russophil orientation prevailed. Fortunately, there were always hopes of improvement, as the two great Germanic Powers had no wish to become finally and completely estranged. In spite of her antipathy against London, Germany desired no actual breach in that quarter ; she really wanted to improve the relations between Berlin and London. The ultimate object even for her anti-British policy was to stimulate Great Britain into becoming more reliable and amenable towards Germany.

The English leader, Salisbury, with consummate adroitness avoided any acts or utterances likely to offend the susceptibilities of the Germans. At this time Salisbury's basic motive was the policy of the " free hand," of splendid isolation, of manœuvring between the two European groups, but with the conviction that he was nearer to the Triple Alliance than to its antagonist, and that in the event of a European conflagration it would most probably be found to Britain's interest to side with the Triple Alliance. Salisbury was inclined to this view, on the one hand because he knew that two members of the Triple Alliance (Austria-Hungary and Italy) were staunch friends who saw in England's power their own safeguard, and on the other hand he was equally aware that Russia and France were the two chief rivals that England had to fear. One of them had threatened India ever since Napoleon I had turned the thoughts of the Muscovites in that direction ; and the other would like to be able to force England to evacuate Egypt.

Thus the way to a *rapprochement* between Great Britain and ourselves remained open, and the possibility thereof was about to be transmuted into fact under the influence of the disaster suffered by the Italian army in Africa referred to in the previous chapter. Though at first England watched the advance of Italy towards the Nile with a certain amount of jealousy, she now became alarmed at the victory of Menelik, King of Abyssinia, behind whom she strongly suspected the machinations of France and Russia ; and nothing could have thwarted Britain's ambitious schemes in East Africa more effectively than the French and Russian rule in the vicinity of the Nile, supported by the Dervishes and the Abyssinians. This would have severed the Suez-India line, which, now that the British influence over the Turks had waned and she could no longer depend on the Triple Alliance for the guarding of the Straits, had become more important than ever. Therefore Salisbury intended to help Italy and at the same time strike a blow at the Mahdi, the lord of the Sudan, the conqueror of Gordon, by the occupation of Dongola.

For a long time before the German Government had vainly advised London to take the steps now contemplated. Now, immediately after the defeat of the Italians, Kaiser William called on the British Ambassador and depicted in a most vivid manner the peril that the new situation in Africa would have for England. He asserted that Menelik was being backed by both Russia and France, gravitating towards the Nile. He pointed out that England could place no reliance on France, since the Republic was entirely under Russian influence ; also that England and Austria-Hungary both were regarded by Russia as her enemies, whom she would crush even at the cost of a ten-years' war. The Muscovite aim was to destroy Austria-Hungary and Turkey and unite under the sceptre of the Czar all the Slavs of those regions. France would be appeased by the offer of Egypt ; an attempt would be made to neutralise Germany by diverting the French attention to Egypt and thus removing from the Teuton mind that nightmare fear of an invasion of Alsace-Lorraine. And besides all this, it was proposed to offer German Austria to Germany. The Czar himself —said the Kaiser—had been won over to the conspiracy.

This imperial hotch-potch of fact and fiction might well produce an effect on Salisbury. The amount of truth in the Emperor's statement was enough to render Salisbury cautious ; for it was unquestionable that the Russian Foreign Minister, Lobanoff, the sworn foe of England, wanted to bring forward the Egyptian Question. He loudly proclaimed that it would work serious damage to Russian interests if the Suez Canal, the shortest sea-route between Europe and Asia, should be permanently dominated by England. This alone was sufficient to cause Salisbury to ask himself whether it would not be better to make Italy stronger in Africa and to make friendly advances to Germany.

To the Emperor's intense delight, Salisbury decided on a military advance towards Dongola, thereby alleviating the situation of the Italians. Once more Egypt occupied the position she had in Bismarck's time, as a connecting-link between England and Germany. William II and his allies once more stood by Great Britain, and defended her freedom of action, while France and Russia again presented obstacles, and were again in the opposite camp. The Dongola expedition was bound to be disliked in Paris and St. Petersburg at any time, but especially now that, on account of the conversation with Salisbury and the differences between England and Germany, they were beginning to count on the possibility of England relinquishing her valuable spoils, while they interpreted the latest action as signifying her intention to strengthen her position in Egypt. When, therefore, England proposed that Egypt should pay the expenses of the expedition, Paris and St. Petersburg were against, while the Triple Alliance was for, the proposal. Again, when England intended to use Indian troops in Africa, the Double Alliance protested, while the Triple Alliance approved the idea. When Lobanoff suggested that the question of Egypt should be dealt with by an international conference, Emperor William objected in the interests of England and immediately reported the matter to Salisbury.

William II was quite satisfied with the course of events. He says (21st March 1896) that he had accomplished his purpose : England was suspect in the eyes of Paris and St. Petersburg ; an end had been put to Franco-Russian and English philandering. The Kaiser's joy can be understood ; but it is nevertheless regrettable that he should have considered his purpose attained when, as subsequent events proved, he was merely through the less difficult part of his task.

At this period William could always have stopped the coquetting of London by not giving England the impression that he bore her ill-will. The difficult stage of the task would have been reached when the good disposition had to be made permanent and the *rapproche-*

ment on the Egyptian Question fructified in the constant co-operation of the two Powers. But the Emperor seemed to have forgotten these things entirely. For the time being he was quite satisfied with the estrangement of England from France and Russia, and with the consequent impossibility of her turning against Germany. He need not now conclude an alliance with her.

It is often said that policies are dictated by self-interest and that nations always take the course that is best for themselves. Would that this were true! Unfortunately it is a mistake. Certainly nations generally act in accordance with their *seeming* interests—but their seeming interests are not always their real ones. Moral myopia, political passion, hatred, and prejudice, frequently start a nation on the downward track. Lucidity of judgment is the indispensable but, alas! not the peculiar attribute of the statesman. Many a nation has been ruined because she failed to perceive in which direction her true interests lay. Had the various nations been guided by their real interests, a cataclysm like the late World War would have been impossible. The genuine, important interests of the nation are often lost sight of, obscured by constant frictions, petty insults, ill-humours, mutual recriminations, suspicions and jealousies, cowardice, pessimism, hyper-caution, and personal ambitions.

The case of Germany and England is a deplorable example of this truth. Both Powers earnestly desired peace ; and both of them might easily have agreed with each other. Each played a leading rôle in a sphere in which the other could not justly lay claim to leadership, in which the supremacy of the one could by no means weaken that of the other. No real ground for antagonism existed between these two Empires, kindred to each other. Neither the true power of Germany on the European Continent nor her colonial ambitions did or could have done the least injury to Great Britain. Germany's political conviction that overseas possessions were essential to her progress rendered British friendship of paramount importance for her and strengthened England's influence over Germany. Side by side with the naval supremacy of England, Germany might have continued to enjoy the position of the first military Power of Europe and at the same time have achieved a reasonable maritime expansion. The Government of each country saw this truth ; but petty squabbles, rufflings of vanity, want of tact, and instances of trifling local antagonism all combined to render them ill-disposed towards each other and destroyed their confidence in each other, so that although they became once more united by the Egyptian Question, the further development of Anglo-German relations was not satisfactory. Small errors counted for more than great interests.

Notwithstanding the temporary and purely local *rapprochement* between these two great Powers, one of the chief motive forces of diplomatic life still consisted in the Anglo-German antagonism. This became remarkably evident during the new Oriental crisis, which without the collision of local interests arose from this antagonism.

The first of the later differences between England and Germany arose out of the Armenian Question. After a demonstration of Armenians in Constantinople occurred a wholesale massacre of Armenians throughout the Ottoman Empire. The Sultan, calculating on the impotence of Europe—the various nations being so divided against themselves—sought to solve the Armenian Question in the most drastic fashion, by a general slaughter of these troublesome subjects. Here, once again, was the imperative necessity of energetic measures of intervention on the part of Europe; and once again they proved to be impossible. Russia, the hereditary foe of the Turks, was afraid of a premature collapse of the Ottoman Empire. Since Lobanoff's day she saw her mission in the Far East, gravitating towards China and Corea. Until her object there was accomplished, she thought it expedient to spare the Sultan, the obedient doorkeeper of her house.

These events again disgusted the German Emperor. He wrote: " It is shameful for us Christians to look on idly at such wicked deeds! " And later (August 1896) he wrote: " The Sultan ought to be dethroned." This, however, was only a passing mood—empty phrases with no will to back them. He had not the slightest intention of coercing the Turks, or of appearing as the friend of England and the foe of Russia.

He would not lighten the burden of Salisbury or share his failure—which he foresaw. He preferred to stifle his sense of shame and let the massacres proceed. He turned a deaf ear even to his own Government when (8th–29th August) they recommended him to despatch warships to protect the Christians. He preferred not to advise the Sultan to be more moderate, lest he (William) should be held responsible for the latter's crimes. Though he denounced the Turkish Government, his endeavours to preserve it were becoming more and more apparent.

Nothing less than the most ruthless and energetic action could have stopped the massacres, but the timid Salisbury had not the nerve to run the risk of isolated intervention. He confined himself to bold words, which made not the slightest impression on Abdul Hamid, who was well acquainted with the situation and knew that these words would not be followed by corresponding actions.

Thus the horrible slaughter continued daily undisturbed. Events justified Emperor William in sarcastically dubbing the Powers " *les Impuissances.*"

Meanwhile another conflagration had broken out among the combustible material piled up in the East— the Oriental disease had made its appearance at a new point. The Turks and Greeks on the island of Crete found they could not live together without quarrelling. Here, again, the numerically stronger Turks massacred the weaker Christians. But in this case the situation was even more dangerous for peace and for the Turks than in the regions inhabited by the Armenians ; for the independent and kindred State of Greece was nearby, and her people made haste to succour their persecuted brethren, whose sufferings commanded the strong sympathy of all Europe. The Greeks aroused the interest of Europe more readily than did the Armenians. The heroic exploits of the ancient Hellenes, the thrilling story of the struggles of their more modern descendants in the days of Kanaris, the martyrdom of Byron in their cause, the intervention of Canning and the French to mitigate their fate, were moral forces and precedents pleading for the Greeks with which the European Governments, especially in the democratic States, were bound to reckon, even against their will.

Generally speaking, the Powers were actuated by the same interests and views as in the Armenian Question. The Czar, having his hands full in Asia, desired, for the time being, to prolong the life of " the Sick

Man of Europe " and to put off the settling-day until his hands were free, and when he could thus devote his whole attention and forces to the matter.

Salisbury was certainly a Philhellene and against the Sultan, whom he regarded as incapable of bringing about a lasting peace by proper measures of reform. And English public opinion was with him. In France also Philhellenism was very strong.

Germany, who had hitherto shown herself quite indifferent to the fate of Turkey and willing to sacrifice the Ottoman Empire to the Powers' appetite for expansion, and thereby haply ensure peace, now turned to a strongly Turkophil policy, and, of all the Powers, she manifested the most pronounced anti-Hellenic tendency. In doing so she, on the one hand, ranged herself on the side of Russia and estranged the latter from France, whose sympathies were for Greece ; on the other, she administered a rebuff to England which raised difficulties for the island empire.

Of all the European Powers, the most objective and sincere was perhaps Austria-Hungary. Goluchowsky's policy sought only to secure rest and peace and had no subsidiary aim. Unfortunately he was not strong enough to unite the other Powers.

After a brief interruption early in 1897, the Cretan Question once more loomed on the political horizon, and in a more dangerous form than before. Greece now became bolder, the Czar having declared (doubtless under the influence of his relations and in opposition to his Government) that he did not mind what happened with regard to Crete. On the strength of this declaration Greece despatched troops and ships to the aid of the insurgents. A conflict between Turkey and Greece could have been avoided only by prompt and successful action on the part of Europe. But that was again frustrated by the same old obstacles.

Salisbury refused to make the Greek forces evacuate the island until the Powers had agreed to guarantee its autonomy ; while English public opinion also refused to tolerate an action the aim of which was the bolstering up of Turkish misrule.

Germany adopted a vigorous anti-Hellenic policy. She declined to proceed against the Turks in conjunction with the other Powers unless they declared in advance that Crete should remain under the sovereignty of the Sultan. William II took part personally in the negotiations and proposed that the Powers should blockade not only Crete but also Greece. He was so proud of his idea of intervention that he became very angry when Marschall, Under-Secretary for Foreign Affairs, announced in the Reichsrath that the Chancellor Hohenlohe would in due time render account with regard to recent events, and he (the Kaiser) emphatically protested that since he personally had evolved the idea for the preservation of world-peace, so he himself would furnish the necessary information and would summon the Reichsrath before him for that purpose. He was dissuaded from this purpose only by the calm and determined, yet perfectly correct declaration of Hohenlohe that, since the foreign policy of the Fatherland must be subject to free criticism, and since it was not permissible to criticise the utterances of the Emperor, he, as the responsible Chancellor, intended, after due notice being given to him, to submit the foreign policy to the Reichsrath.

In the whole Cretan affair and throughout its duration William favoured the most ruthless action. At the very outset he proposed to blow the Greek warships out of the water; he suggested the capture of Prince George of Greece while *en route* for Crete and holding him a prisoner until the Greeks had evacuated the island.

Russia could not follow the impetuous Kaiser, and intervened in company with Austria-Hungary. Lobanoff at length (March 1897) succeeded in bringing about an agreement between the Powers on the basis of Turkey's being asked to grant autonomy to Crete in a manner satisfactory to the English, and Greece to withdraw her troops according to the demand of Germany.

Various difficulties, however, remained unsettled. As Turkey accepted the autonomy proposal and Greece proclaimed her annexation of the island, the Powers had to settle the new question of how to compel the Greeks to obedience, how to unite the discordant Powers in such concentrated action as would bring the Greeks to unconditional compliance.

England was willing to carry out a naval blockade of Greece and to demand a strict evacuation of the Greek troops occupying Crete, provided that internal order could be preserved after their withdrawal. So long as the island was the scene of massacres by the Turks, which the presence of Greek troops alone could stop, England would, however, decline to acquiesce in their withdrawal. How could order be restored and maintained without them?

The first plan was for the Powers to furnish their own troops in equal quotas for the purpose. But this was rendered nugatory by a number of obstacles. Germany and Austria-Hungary were unwilling to offer more than 600 men each—a quite inadequate number —and even these they stipulated must be used only for policing the ports and not employed in the interior.

The other Powers could not see why they should undertake the greater part of the risk and expense, getting no glory, but playing a purely altruistic rôle !

The idea was then mooted that one or two Powers should be charged by the rest with the restoration of order. This, too, was found impracticable ; as, on the one hand, no one was eager to take up the task, and, on the other, each Power objected to any one of the others occupying the island !

At one time it seemed as though the deadlock might be removed by Salisbury's accepting the mandate of Europe ; but Russia would not have that at any price. She suspected that England would make herself at home in Crete, just as she had done in Egypt and Cyprus ; when once British troops got a footing anywhere, that place usually became a British possession in the end !

So of course Europe had to sustain a fiasco, and had to try a solution by force, since diplomacy was unable to reach the goal.

The Greco-Turkish War broke out in April 1897. The Turks obtained a decisive victory, and Europe had again to face a new situation. The Powers had to intervene for peace before Greece should entirely collapse, lest the Philhellenic disposition of almost all Europe should make an anti-Turkish intervention inevitable.

England then—probably in the hope of neutralising the Grecophobe influence of Germany—proposed that those Powers only who had guaranteed the existence of Greece when the Hellenic State was formed should join England, Russia, and France in arranging the peace. This proposal had no success. St. Petersburg immediately rejected it. It was made at an inopportune

18

moment, at the very time when Francis Joseph was in St. Petersburg and the Russians and Austro-Hungarians were hoping for an agreement.

There was a united intervention of all the Powers. But Germany, in conformity with her previous policy, joined the others only when, prior to the armistice, Greece abandoned her intention to annex Crete and recognised its autonomy. This formed the basis of the armistice concluded in May 1897.

All the Powers were agreed in principle upon the peace terms, which expressly stipulated that the Christians *de facto* liberated from the Turkish yoke should never again be allowed to be brought under it.

Emperor William was enthusiastic in his congratulations to Francis Joseph and the Czar, which he wired from Hungarian soil—the beautiful deer-park of Archduke Frederick. He boasted, in an Anglophobe vein, that the peace was due to the efforts of the continental *bloc*. The Czar, in reply, referred to the unity among the continental Powers. Francis Joseph, however, with characteristic tactfulness, replied expressing the hope that all the Powers would stand together in the cause of peace and international amity. This epilogue was in complete harmony with the political nature of the whole campaign. The entire affair was a diplomatic competition arising out of the alienation of England and Germany—of Salisbury and William II. The latter did his utmost in order that England, whom he considered the enemy of peace, and whom he charged with dangerous intrigues, should be isolated and kept as far as possible away from Russia.

The Emperor William's Anglophobe mind was clearly manifested by his groundless mistrust of London when (October 1896) he suddenly began to express his fear that England had designs on the German colonies. He demanded the opening of negotiations with Paris and St. Petersburg with regard to the common defence of their colonial possessions. The German Government was fortunately able to dissuade him from this glaring indiscretion, of which England would have become immediately cognisant, and which would have constituted another grievance on the part of English diplomats against the Emperor.

Later he and his Government came to the conclusion that England was bent on war in the East so that Russia might thereby become opposed to the Triple Alliance, and thus would be crippled from carrying out those of her plans in Asia which ran counter to the schemes of Great Britain. The Germans reminded Italy that England was no friend of hers and that she was working to thwart her African aspirations by opposing her to Russia and France.

Marschall, Foreign Under-Secretary, wrote (March 1897) that England was scheming to bring about a war between continental States in order by that means to regain the predominance she had enjoyed in the age of Napoleon. Kaiser William held the same view, and thought that Salisbury wished to set Austria-Hungary and Russia at variance in the hope that the entire Triple Alliance would intervene in the affair. And in that event, said the Emperor, then " *Adieu, Africa !* " (January 1897). " Salisbury worked against the Sultan only because he thought Prussia would make the fall of the latter a pretext for occupying Constantinople, which would bring Francis Joseph into action." William further accused England of financing the Armenian insurrection. The Chancellor took a somewhat more reasonable view. He recognised that

England was useful, her mere existence serving to maintain the balance of power in Europe, as she was a sort of lighting-conductor, though her policy was without character—it caused her to be hated and forced Germany to a defensive against her.

At this period, as in the past, Holstein was actuated by his fantastic and unnatural suspicions. He averred that Salisbury had spread a report to the effect that he wanted Crete for England, for the purpose of provoking the other Powers into demanding slices of Turkish territory, in order that a great war might result. Holstein never could see anything but trouble in store for us! Even in the things he had formerly regarded with favour, he now saw potential disaster. He gloomily predicted the alienation of Russia and France—formerly devoutly desired by Germany, and now feared by him. According to him France would come to an understanding with England regarding Egypt ; Italy and Austria-Hungary would join the Western Powers, and Germany would be left alone with the treacherous Muscovites. He justified this view by pointing out that the real aim of Goluchowsky was to restore the former Crimean Coalition—England, France, and Austria-Hungary— in one camp, against Russia, and not the Triple Alliance. And that was in effect true—that Goluchowsky as a Pole had naturally a sympathy towards France and would have liked to see all Europe, including Germany, united in an anti-Russian policy. On one occasion Goluchowsky even hinted to Eulenburg the idea of Germany restoring Alsace-Lorraine to France as a preliminary to concluding an alliance with her against Russia. But Goluchowsky did not contemplate for a moment following a Francophil and anti-Russian policy without or against Germany.

It was as clear as the noonday sun that the prime condition of any anti-German policy would be friendship with Russia, whereas his policy was mainly anti-Russian in tendency. Goluchowsky well knew that should Germany and Russia unite, we were lost!

Russo-German co-operation would have swept the Balkans into the orbit of those two Great Powers, so that we should have been surrounded and crushed from three sides ere either France or England could have come to our rescue.

The German premisses were all wrong. Salisbury was entirely innocent of the charge of fomenting a continental war. The British Premier was aware how impossible it would be for England to stand aloof from a war once begun, and the odds were that she would lose too much and win too little for him to find pleasure in starting a conflagration for the pleasure of assisting to put it out. Britannia ruled the waves; she could defend her colonial empire, even extend it if necessary —why, then, should she want a world war?

Salisbury's Greek policy was just as easy to understand as his Armenian, without the necessity for adventurous explanation. With regard to domestic policy, it would have been too costly and risky to co-operate with the blood-stained Sultan Abdul Hamid, who was so detested in England by the nickname of "*Abdul the Damned.*" Salisbury would most certainly have fallen if he had had the temerity to propose to maintain Turkish domination over Christian peoples. Apart from this, it was to the real interest of England to strengthen Greece. The latter lived entirely from maritime commerce; and England, commanding the seas, could always depend on her assistance, since, if at any time she should turn refractory, England could strangle her.

Seeing that the Turkish rule in Crete could not be restored at the cost of defeating and massacring the insurgents, the best solution of the problem was the cession of the island to Greece. The British policy at this period was therefore perfectly comprehensible, without the least Germanophobe mental reservation or Machiavellian hope in a general clash of arms. Why, then, fall back on suspicions of plots and schemes which would have been contrary to the real interests of the British, and to the character, habits, well-known caution and circumspection of Salisbury? Why apply improbable explanations when there was an explanation that was simple, clear, logical, and to the point?

CHAPTER VI

WILLIAM II AND NICHOLAS II

AT this period (February 1894) Emperor William's cherished ambition was personally to win the friendship of the new Czar and keep him under his influence. He had no thought of an alliance with Russia—that had been rendered impossible by the Franco-Russian Entente—though he contemplated Russia and Germany following a united policy on various questions of world-import; and he even entertained the idea that he—a stronger-willed personality—might contrive to guide and hypnotise his imperial cousin Nicholas through the medium of regular correspondence, to prevent him, in conjunction with France, from prosecuting an anti-German policy. The cooler the relations between Downing Street and the Wilhelmstrasse, the more important it was that the Kaiser should keep the Czar under his influence. Knowing that confidence begets confidence, he wrote in the most frank and unrestrained manner to " Nicky," freely criticising his own people and foreigners alike. William treated his cousin with the frankness and sincerity of a beloved brother. A thorough autocrat himself, he knew how to play with consummate skill on the delicate chords of sentiment of his fellow-autocrat. For example, he confided to " Nicky " (February 1895) that Bismarck was " quite a common person "; and that " the Ultramontanes and Jew-ridden Socialists were ripe for the gallows " ! Referring to the French, he expressed the hope that if Nicholas must make friends with those " damned rascals," he would at least endeavour to make them behave themselves. On another occasion, also referring to the French, he expressed the conviction that they were " cursed for their sin in shedding the blood of their divinely appointed monarch." How—asked Kaiser of Czar—can the latter have Russian revolutionaries and republicans hanged when he is at the same time consorting in Paris with other revolutionaries and republicans ? Moreover, William was constantly reminding " Nicky " of his (the latter's) aspirations in Asia and encouraging him to prosecute them. He painted in vivid colours the glorious destiny of Russia to conquer the yellow race. He (William) would be her shield in the West, while she in the East distinguished herself as the redoubtable champion of European culture. What effect might all this be expected to have on the impressionable mind of the degenerate Czar ? The fact is that for a long time it rather alarmed than attracted him : " Nicky " became afraid of his more vigorous kinsman and fellow-autocrat. Witte, in his *Memoirs*, says : " The physically and mentally weak Czar entertained an insensate jealousy of his cousin William." A photograph representing the tall, strong, imperious, soldierly figure of " Willy " side by side with the emaciated, weary, listless " Nicky " made such a sensation as soon as it was seen that it was forbidden to take copies of it. Such a striking contrast between strength and weakness would have wrought irreparable mischief to the authority of the Czar. He was for years obsessed by the feeling that the Kaiser desired to exploit him and lead him astray.

The German official policy was entirely in harmony with the personal efforts of the Emperor. Under Hohenlohe's Chancellorship the guiding motive of

German foreign policy was the cultivation of friendly relations with Russia. This was what actuated Germany when she, together with France and Russia, took up an anti-Japanese attitude in the Far East; just as it had been with regard to the Armenian and Greek Questions some time earlier. But this attempt at *rapprochement* also failed to set Russo-German relations on a firmer basis than that represented by the personal efforts of the Kaiser. As we have seen, the after-effect of the Asiatic Triple Alliance was not fortunate; the combined action left a certain mistrust behind it. The permanent weakness of the Russian orientation constituted a kind of Damocles' sword hanging over it.

The possibility of a conflict between the aims of Austria-Hungary and Russia in the Balkans was not to be ignored; Russia could not depend on Germany, as she felt in the event of a war with Austria-Hungary, Germany would be found in the opposite camp, even if —as in the time of Bismarck—the Balkan policy of Russia were nearer to Germany than to Austria-Hungary. True it was that, since the Bulgarian Question was settled, there had been no acute antagonism between the two rivals in the Balkans, but it might break out at any time, the ultimate aims of Austria-Hungary and Russia—especially in the matters of the Straits and Constantinople—being still diametrically opposed. This contingency Emperor William was anxious to eliminate, to promote friendship with Russia, and safeguard the peace of Europe, by solving this dangerous problem peacefully by way of compromise. With this object he enquired confidentially of England whether it were not possible to have all the forts guarding the Dardanelles dismantled and to have the Straits thrown open to the vessels of all nations.

But this suggestion led to nothing. It was largely based on a misconception, as the idea suited the interests of the English alone, whereas the Emperor wished to follow a Russophil and not an Anglophil policy. It was against the interest of Russia, for whom the *Mare Clausum* was more profitable than the opening of the Straits, which would have extended the power of the British navy to the Black Sea. The proposal was even less welcome to Turkey, who could not preserve her independence without the means of defending herself at sea. If the Russian or the British fleet could at any moment sail up to the very gates of Dolma Bagtsche, defence would be impossible. Neither was the proposal compatible with the interests of the Dual Monarchy, who desired the preservation of the integrity of the Ottoman Empire. Furthermore, the proposal was inopportune. England, who could the most easily have accepted it, lacked confidence in Germany, whose ruler had mooted the idea ; and she preferred not to raise needlessly the question of the Straits. The Czar likewise was reluctant to put the question on the agenda. It is true that on one occasion Lobanoff (August 1896) made a statement to Eulenburg, from which he might draw the inference that he was occupied with the Straits problem, but it was only a passing impression, that was never confirmed by any single act on the part of Russia. And at the unexpected death of Lobanoff, which occurred a few days after the conversation alluded to, Russia decided to let the matter drop.

Nelidoff, Russian Ambassador to Constantinople, recommended that they should occupy the Straits ; the majority in the Russian Government, however, voted against the proposal (December 1896). Lobanoff's successor was that very Muravieff who, as Minister of

Justice, together with Witte, Finance Minister, had most resolutely opposed the Ambassador's recommendation. The policy of Russia stood entirely for expansion in the Far East, and therefore sought in the first place to maintain the *status quo* in the Near East ; so that it was not a matter for surprise that the Emperor's idea was barren of result.

Then, however—no thanks to the diplomatic skill of either William or his Government, but entirely to the credit of Goluchowsky—a *rapprochement* was achieved between Austria-Hungary and Russia. As Russia at this period took care to avoid European complications and the Dual Monarchy defended the *status quo*, following a strictly conservative policy, it was possible for both these Powers to come to an agreement, which was reached through the assistance, intelligence, and influence of Capnist, Russian Ambassador to Vienna. When Francis Joseph, in the company of his Foreign Minister, visited St. Petersburg (April 1897), the main provisions of the agreement were as follows : the question of Constantinople and the Straits, being a purely European affair, should not be brought up ; the *status quo* in the Balkans should be maintained by the two Powers, or, should this be found impossible, they undertook not only not to acquire territory themselves in that region, but also to prevent any third party from doing so.

It seems there was some misunderstanding with regard to details between St. Petersburg and Vienna. Goluchowsky summed up the gist of the verbal resolutions as that they had agreed that in the event of a change of the *status quo*, Austria-Hungary should annex Bosnia-Herzegovina and the Sandjak of Novi Bazar, Albania to be created an independent State, and no one of the Christian States of the Balkans to have the preference over the others. According to Muravieff, however, no agreement was reached on the two last-named points. They constituted matters for future consideration on which it was impossible then to occupy any definite standpoint. Separate negotiations and agreements would be necessary in their case, as with regard to the annexation of Bosnia-Herzegovina and the delimitation of the boundaries of the Sandjak.

Though the German Government rejoiced to see these differences between Russia and the Dual Monarchy happily composed, it was far from content with the transaction as a whole. It could not regard the future as sufficiently safe. Holstein, the eternal croaker, gave his opinion that the after-effect might be dangerous, as Russia would not be really satisfied because the agreement failed to secure for her a favourable solution of the Dardanelles Question ; while Italy would be equally disappointed when she learnt that the agreement put a stop to her aspirations in the Balkans ; consequently it might turn out that Russia and Italy would both come to the conviction that their Oriental schemes could be realised only through opposition to Austria-Hungary. However, this adverse criticism notwithstanding, it cannot be denied that the diplomacy of Goluchowsky for a long time warded off the infection of the Balkan antagonism between Russia and Austria-Hungary, thereby rendering valuable service to Germany also.

BOOK III
WELTPOLITIK

CHAPTER I

WILLIAM II AND BÜLOW

IN October 1897 William II appointed Prince Bülow, erstwhile Ambassador to Rome, as his Minister for Foreign Affairs. This was an event of far-reaching importance, as it inaugurated the period of German policy in which the extra-European world-interests caused the interests of the Continent to be relegated to the background. Hitherto the Emperor had chosen his advisers from the senior ranks, from men who adhered more or less to the fundamental principles of the Iron Chancellor and followed a strictly continental policy, with the main object of preserving the continental supremacy of Germany that had been won at the cost of so much blood and treasure.

Now, in the person of Bülow, who took charge of the Foreign Office under the Chancellorship of the old Hohenlohe, there came into its own for the first time in modern history the generation which, reared in a victorious Germany, instinctively followed the star of newer and higher ambitions. William II and Bülow complemented each other. The Emperor's political conceptions took definite shape in Bülow's time alone, for prior to his taking office the sovereign had been unable to find a suitable instrument for their execution.

Here, then, is the proper place to say a few words with regard to the personality and political importance of William II.

The Emperor was unquestionably a man of no mean talents. A patriot of the first order, Bismarck could not have loved his country more sincerely than his imperial master. A chauvinist to the backbone, William held the Germans to be the finest and first race on God's earth—while he was, of course, the first German! Whosoever injured Germany, wounded him. He even despised his illustrious mother, the Dowager-Empress Frederick, for the sole reason that he thought her more English in sentiment than German. He came very near hating her for her ' perversity,' as he viewed it, in remaining in her heart and soul English after having become the wife of a German Emperor—the supreme representative of the German nation. It was a monstrous thing! The whole English people had become hateful in his eyes.

I once had an opportunity personally to observe the Emperor William in his quality as a German chauvinist. In the spring preceding the outbreak of the memorable World War I happened to be at Corfu with certain members of his Imperial Majesty's suite. Excavations were in progress, and it was inspecting these that the Kaiser called my attention to the fact that the ground-plan of the ancient Greek houses was exactly identical with that of the primitive German dwellings, which (he said) was a clear proof that the Hellenic people had received their culture from the creations of the original Germanic genius!

Emperor William had by no means the " single-track mind " of a certain prominent statesman recently deceased. He was exceedingly versatile, many-sided, and broad-minded. He could grasp the importance and the preliminaries of the economic development and cultural progress of his country better than most others. He extended his attention to the politics of the whole world. He rose to the height of studying the united interests of entire continents and of the races *en masse*. At one time he represented the Pan-Europe view-point, to rally all Europe against America. Later he identified himself with the white races and saw the enemy in " the Yellow Peril." Of course he invariably envisaged himself as the head, centre, and representative of these great truths and grand moral forces. He possessed literary talent of the first order, good rhetorical ability, an excellent acquaintance with the classics, and a profound knowledge of the best scientific works. In Corfu he astonished us all by speaking for hours at a time, without preparation, on the subject of the excavations. His speech, teeming with brilliant remarks, enlivened by flashes of wit, and delivered in a lucid, easy style, manifested an exceedingly fine scholarship. When I expressed to His Majesty's entourage my admiration of the Kaiser's oratorical gift, I was assured that he could speak with similar fluency and erudition on almost every branch of art and science ; the catholicity of his learning had often surprised savants of world-repute with whom he had come into contact.

It was really remarkable that, in spite of the tremendous amount of work he accomplished and of his multifarious duties, he could yet devote so much time to the most widely different branches of culture. What quick perception, excellent memory, and great staying power were necessary for all this ! The Emperor's letters were always entertaining, often beautiful literary examples, and bore the impress of a virile character. He was a real *charmeur*. His moral character, moreover, was elevated ; his nature at bottom reliable, honest ; he was ever actuated by the loftiest motives. He considered that he fulfilled a Divine vocation in leading the most gifted and upright nation on earth (i.e. the Germans) to that position of precedence and leadership to which de-

19

stiny intended them and from which all humanity would profit. In this sacred mission he believed he was upheld and blessed by the Almighty Himself. When during the Russo-Japanese War he contemplated an alliance with Russia, after much anxious pondering (as he wrote to the Chancellor Bülow), he prayed to God for His guidance, and the Lord vouchsafed to answer his prayer. " He would bring together them that should be brought together."

The miracle came to pass in the subsequent meeting of the Kaiser and the Czar! The Czar had never been so friendly and confidential towards him before. And on his return home after the first day's conversation, William opened his Bible at random and read : "*He shall reward every man according to his works.*"* From that he drew renewed strength and confidence in the Lord's guidance. And behold! next morning his cherished desire was fulfilled—the Czar and he signed the treaty of alliance. His heart overflowing with joy, William wrote : " How near to us must have been the spirits of our common ancestors at that solemn moment so fraught with importance for the future! " How little, however, did William know then that the Czar's signature was utterly worthless, that the treaty would remain a dead letter, a mere " scrap of paper," that that event of " far-reaching historic importance " would prove nothing but a farce!

Emperor William's intentions were always eminently pacific. It was his laudable ambition to raise his country to the highest pinnacle of culture that she was capable of attaining and thus to enrich her. But at the same time he was a soldier from the crown of his head to the sole of his foot. He placed unbounded faith in his army, which he petted in every possible way and delighted in leading, though he never yearned for martial glory,

* St. Matt. xvi. 27.

even in his youth. With his high sense of duty, life to him was not mere ostentation and pleasure, pomp and circumstance, but strenuous work and constant study to keep abreast of the times.

In spite, however, of his good intentions and excellent qualities, William lacked the essentials of a great statesman and soldier. He was an artist rather than a politician. He was not by any means as bold and resolute as he liked to believe himself, and as it was absolutely necessary that he should be, in order to accomplish his sublime aims and reach the goal he had set himself. Behind the awe-inspiring Imperator Rex was hidden a vacillating, undecided, irresolute spirit more akin to Hamlet than to Cæsar. The ruthless proclamations he at times issued were probably only intended to cover his real state of indecision. His uncle King Edward VII once gave him the testimonial that he was *" the most brilliant failure on record "! * He was undoubtedly a dilettante to a certain extent: he meddled too much, made speeches too often, and insisted on leading in matters in which he was incompetent. Louis XIV of France on one occasion said that " Kings should take heed to their words, for it is impossible to speak overmuch without making mistakes, and kings should endeavour to avoid making mistakes." More than once the late Kaiser Francis Joseph said to me, with a shake of his venerable head: *" Wenn nur der deutsche Kaiser schweigen könnte ! Er spricht zu viel, zu oft. Es ist besser, dass wir schweigen und lassen unsere Minister reden "* ("What a pity the German Emperor cannot hold his tongue ! He talks too much and too often. It is better for us to be silent and let our ministers make the speeches.")

Both these exalted rulers were unquestionably right.

Though opposed in many respects, they resembled each other in the one thing, of thoroughly understanding their profession of governing nations.

William II was impetuous, easily influenced, and sometimes weak. There were occasions, not seldom, when he yielded to the advice of others against his own better judgment and knowledge. Too impressionable, a passing whim, a mood, a symptom, a mere sign, were sometimes sufficient to captivate him and cause him to regard what was merely possible as a certainty.

Such impulsiveness made him appear fickle. What to-day he said was proper would to-morrow be quite inadmissible—he would declare for the very opposite. He would erect complete systems on the flimsiest premisses. From the most trivial exterior symptoms he would pretend to read the inmost secrets of the hearts of others. He had a too vivid imagination, which sometimes ran riot and caused his policy to be inconsistent, reckless, improvised, and based on merely superficial observations.

Imagination is a very necessary quality in a statesman; without it no really successful statesman can be conceived. In political life one cannot always work with positively known factors, figures, and data which can be tested by any scientific process. Unlike the scientist, the politician cannot make experiments; he must often, from the known facts, deduce conclusions with regard to the unknown. The void between the known and the unknown must be filled in solely from his imagination, his intuition. The wings of imagination often help the statesman to mount above the mists of uncertainty to the serene regions of light and truth. Yet the most valuable quality of the armour of every statesman is pure common sense, in order to form sound judgment. Wherever there exists no just balance between cold reason and imagination, and the visionary world of the latter disturbs and obstructs clarity of vision, it is only too easy to make mistakes and arrive at false conclusions on grave questions for which nations may have to pay the price in their blood and perhaps even the loss of their liberty.

That gifted statesman Disraeli, in one of his novels, puts into the mouth of one of his characters the following: "Cyprus is necessary to England." Beaconsfield, as Prime Minister, brought this seemingly venturous idea into line with the requirements of practical politics and carried it out. In this case we have imagination and hard-headed thinking supplementing and balancing each other so evenly that neither quality prevented the healthy exercise of the other.

In Hungary Stephen Széchényi was perhaps the statesman *par excellence* who was endowed with the most useful imagination, and whose imagination, inspired by his heart which beat so passionately for his country, felt and appreciated the dangers which it was scarcely possible by scientific means alone to foresee and combat. Just as a loving mother's intuition warns her of peril menacing her children, so Széchényi perceived the ailments of his country earlier than anyone else. The Emperor William had unfortunately not the mental equipment necessary to his difficult task, and his imagination sometimes led him astray. Thus, when he conceived the idea of arraying Europe against America, he forgot that the former, as a moral unity, simply had no existence—that England, e.g., was nearer in sympathy to America than to any European country; and Emperor William himself would have been only too happy to gain the support of the Transatlantic

Republic in his fulminations against the Yellow men.
He forgot further that Japan was nearer in sympathy
to England than to Russia, the representative of the
white race ; that Japanese officers were studying in
German colleges, and that the assistance of Dai Nippon
might some day be invaluable also to Germany. Many
interesting and useful books might have been written
on these theoretical generalisations of the Emperor, as
they could throw light upon and prepare the way for
the realisation of existing forces ; they were, however,
most unsuitable as the utterances of a practical statesman—more especially of a sovereign—being profoundly
offensive and calculated to create a permanent antipathy where previously had been merely a temporary
conflict of interests, for they presented the problems of
the future as though they were those of the present
day.

William II's inordinate vanity and fondness for the
limelight unnecessarily exposed him to not a few failures,
rebuffs, and aspersions. He could not suppress the
theatrical in him ; he liked to strut about as on a stage.
Quick of temper, in his anger he was apt to lose sight
of the high importance of his words, and utterances
escaped him which ought never to have been spoken,
and for which he had to pay the penalty in misunderstanding and loss of respect.

I have often had occasion to refer to the sharp personal attacks he made, so unworthy of and degrading
to his exalted rank and station, and which increased
the number of Germany's enemies.

Sometimes his inconsiderate outbursts caused the
imperial policy to appear in a wrong light. As an
example of this *gaucherie*, once, in conversation with
the Boer Envoy, the Emperor remarked that Delagoa

Bay, connecting the Transvaal Republic with the sea, should be either Boer or German. This was merely a thoughtless personal utterance of the Kaiser's; the German Government did not dream of acquiring the Bay by conquest or otherwise. Yet it caused the seeds of suspicion to be sown among Boers, British, and French, all three being interested in the question. So little did Germany think of the acquisition of Delagoa Bay that Holstein said " she was not so stupid as to wish to be bothered with it."

William's impulsiveness frequently led to his discomfiture: as when he made statements and brought accusations that he found himself unable to substantiate. Such indiscretions naturally had the effect of weakening his authority. It had a deleterious effect on the development of his character that he had been on bad terms with his parents; he had come to the throne too young, he was surrounded by flatterers, and by so very few who had the courage to tell him the plain truth. Nevertheless, take him altogether, William II was a man of parts, from whom much good might have been expected; born in any sphere, he would undoubtedly have made his mark and left a name behind him.

His importance was not due to his rank alone, but to his innate personal qualities. He was a splendid representative of his then rising Fatherland before the forum of the world. His versatility, genuine patriotism, and fine natural talents, had in not a few directions a beneficent influence on the welfare of his nation. It was due to him in a great measure that Germany up to the outbreak of the war was able to show such wonderful progress in most branches of her cultural and economic life; that her production had risen by leaps and bounds; that her army was the first and best-equipped in the world, unequalled for moral, discipline, and intelligence ; that her latest offspring—the German navy—was healthy and growing rapidly ; and finally, that the age of William II had achieved a worthy place in the spheres of art and science. The Kaiser's personal merits had exalted the German self-consciousness and awakened confidence in the future of the Teutonic race. The verdict of posterity on his reign would undoubtedly have been favourable if only he could have confined his ambitions within proper bounds ; if only he could have averted the crowning disaster and preserved the peace of the world, he would in spite of his foibles have been acclaimed as one of the best of rulers and awarded an illustrious niche in the temple of fame.

However, the time has not yet arrived to deliver a correct judgment on the character of William II. We lack all the evidence and are too close to the events to be free from the bias of personal experiences and a too vivid tradition. Future ages will certainly judge William more leniently than the present, which is unjust to him, losing sight of his unexampled tragedy and awful penance under the effect of the universal suffering and distress associated with his name, but for which he was only partly responsible. The Germans will never forget that he was a sincere lover of the Father-land, devoted heart and soul to the welfare of his people, and therefore they will not withhold their meed of sympathy for their fallen monarch sitting disconsolate within the shadow of adversity. When the scales of prejudice no longer obstruct our eyes, we shall see that William was a man of peace who sought his true glory in enriching and elevating his people, and that the abomi-nable World War was not his doing (though the cataclysm may perhaps have been contributed to by his errors and fallacious calculations—like those of so many other statesmen and patriots), and that his moral reprobation, the desire to take revenge upon him, is, or was, the intelgible but insensate exasperation of his enemies : a mental aberration, which history will certainly correct and of which many are already beginning to feel ashamed.

It was the fate of William II and the world that he should be moved to strike out new paths for his people, that he should be ambitious to be numbered among the great Hohenzollerns and to mark an epoch in the history of the German race. Not content with keeping what his ancestors had acquired and to go steadily forward along the well-beaten track, he would play the part of pioneer in uncharted regions of political activity and add his own contribution to the lustre of his imperial House. But he was lacking in the strength of character and statesmanship necessary to achieve a task so stupendous.

In removing Bismarck, his erstwhile mentor, his political model until then, the genius who had founded the German Empire, the man to whom the Hohenzollerns and all Germany owed a debt of gratitude they could never repay, young William was actuated by the motive, comprehensible in princes, of ruling alone, of sharing his power and prestige with no other man. It was no more than Matthias Corvinus, King of Hungary, had done when he dismissed his uncle, Michael Szilágyi, to whom he owed his crown ; than King Louis XIV in getting rid of Cardinal Mazarin, the victor of the Fronde campaign—the last serious rebellion of the powerful vassals—the man who had made him (Louis) the mightiest among the rulers of the world. In William's case, however, the act avenged itself upon its author by swelling his self-conceit and obsessing him with the idea that he was predestined to accomplish infinitely more glorious deeds than could be expected of a Chancellor ; he had to justify his harsh and arbitrary act by splendid achievements in the field of statesmanship—a task, alas ! too great for his limited powers.

The great Elector, by his wise policy and firm administration, founded Prussia and made her one of the strongest of the German States. Frederick II, the most renowned political and military genius born to the throne in the last centuries, raised the Kingdom of Prussia to a European Power capable of holding its own in a seven years' struggle against three Powers and which eventually became one of the leading factors in European politics. William I—aided by his faithful lieutenants, Moltke and Bismarck—welded together the loose components of the German race under Prussian hegemony into the mightiest State of continental Europe.

William II wished to go a step—or a series of steps—further. Of this first continental Power he would make a great World-Power. He announced that the "future of Germany is on the sea." Germans scattered all over the globe were to be gathered into a higher moral unity. Not in Europe alone, but in every part of the world, German culture, German power, German prestige, should be accorded their just due. His ambition was perfectly comprehensible and, though so grandiose, was not without justification. The German nation could not properly develop all her powers and resources, increase in wealth to the limit attainable, manifest her qualities of statesmanship, make her influence felt upon the future of humanity to the extent to which her cultural and moral standard entitled her, and make her voice heard on questions of world-import, except by possessing a powerful navy and considerable colonies—by representing on and over the seas a World-Power with which even mighty Britain would not care to try conclusions, which (given a suitable ally) might even defeat Britain, and to look askance at which might entail serious consequences.

Remarkable as it may seem to English readers, it was William's English blood that impelled him along this road towards collision with England ; the subconscious effect of English traditions. His own experience, however, also taught him the high importance of naval power. It was his poverty in warships that had obliged him to play second fiddle in the Eastern Question, the German naval strength being inadequate to sustain an independent rôle before Greece, Crete, and Constantinople. William realised that England was master of the situation in Africa simply because of her predominant position at sea. In the Boer Question she adopted a solution repugnant to everybody and against the interests of Germany, without anyone being in a position to gainsay her. Germany was of no account in most questions affecting the fate of mankind at large. In vain were the Emperor's great qualities and power ; he must remain in the second rank unless he could become important at sea. The real Lord of the World was not he, nor yet Germany, but his odious uncle King Edward VII and the proud British nation over whom he reigned. Until he had a strong navy he would have to bear much from England. He was not even master of his own fate. Therefore he must have a navy as soon as possible. Then he could command the attention of other nations. Then he would be accorded precedence. Then the German people would become what God destined them to be—the leaders of the world.

William's was a grand and beautiful ideal. What historic importance it lent to his own person ! Its success would relegate his scurvy treatment of Bismarck to oblivion. It was, however, incompatible with the actual conditions and situation of world-politics. The trial would be too great for his country to sustain, it being, apart from that, already sufficiently handicapped by its geographical position. Catastrophe might overtake his scheme ere it had time to fructify. It would create new enemies, arouse new clashings of interests, when even the existing ones taxed a considerable part of the strength of Germany. She would be no longer able to give attention to her vital interests in Europe alone—the preservation of peace and the maintenance of the balance of power —but she would have to give ear to her distant interests in Asia, Africa, and America, which might often come into conflict with her interests in Europe.

Hitherto the overseas ambitions of all the other Powers had worked for the good of Germany. Bismarck used the British plans in Egypt and those of the French in Tunis for the purpose of winning England and isolating France, if only temporarily. The Iron Chancellor would have similarly exploited the French appetite for Morocco ; but in that age of *Weltpolitik* the ambitions of France in that quarter had become a source of bitter struggle, pernicious rivalry, and dark suspicion. Germany lost the ascendancy derived from her interests and prestige not being everywhere affected. In Central Europe, with many enemies east and west, with few to understand and sympathise with her, her upward path was almost as thorny as it had been in Bismarck's time, when the union of the German people was in question. Notwithstanding this, William II was anxious to accomplish his object by pacific means, though it was hardly probable that he would succeed. Such a position of power as he contemplated was difficult to attain and retain short of fire and sword and the smile of fortune—the latter a factor on which no one ought absolutely to rely. Bismarck was persuaded that war alone could place him in possession of the object of his desires, and he therefore directed all his efforts to bringing about the—as he believed—indispensable conflict. In the earlier part of his career he had schemed to prosecute such campaigns as were most profitable for his country at the moment that promised the best chances of success, and at the same time to shift the odium for the bloodshed on to his foes. William would have preferred to reach the necessary position of power without war ; and for that very reason he had to face the risk of his enemies choosing the moment most auspicious for themselves to attack him ; or else owing to the universal rivalry, loss of confidence, and anxiety caused by the *Weltpolitik,* the overstrained cord might snap at an inopportune moment.

In determining his aim the Emperor omitted also to reckon with the impossibility of securing the desired result by the single-handed efforts of his own country, even though she were willing to sacrifice everything for it. There was the contingency—even the probability— that other States would make up their minds to efforts similar to his ; especially England, the island kingdom, which for so many centuries had never been burdened with the maintenance of immense standing armies. Rich as she was, she was capable of enlarging her navy to an extent that Germany could not dream of ; and the final result of the wild competition thus initiated would be no change in the proportion of power, but the overburdening of all the nations, without Germany being one whit nearer the naval standard of the historic Mistress of the Seas. Britain's naval supremacy was the chief guarantee of her safety, of her very existence, and it might well be believed that she would sacrifice her last farthing in its behalf.

William's new conception brought the development of Europe under a new constellation, multiplying the contingencies of war and *casus belli*. It meant a long step downwards towards the abyss. After the triumphs of Bismarck the only aim of the new Empire should have been to maintain peace, without prejudicing of course the authority and honour of the nation. Two of the Iron Chancellor's successors—Caprivi and Hohenlohe—had followed in the footsteps of the great empire-builder. But now things had changed. Though William II equally wanted peace, not satisfied with that alone, he had advanced a new pretension : the acquisition of power in world-politics. He aimed at founding a new world-empire, thereby changing and jeopardising the whole European situation.

This *Weltpolitik* was not the result of inevitable necessity. The colonies acquired in Bismarck's time and subsequently, as well as the spoils already marked out for future acquisition, were trifling matters compared to the great economic markets which German productions needed, and which could only be found within the bounds of Germany and under alien sway, and not on the newly acquired, newly conquered, thinly populated, uncivilised territory. Germany's economic future depended not on her colonising achievements, but on a proper customs and commercial policy, and especially on her avoiding a foreign political competition which might have disastrous consequences for her. Her economic development was not and could not be based on the number, size, and wealth of her colonies, but on the work done in Germany herself, on the learning of the German race, on her ability to organise her industry, and on her commerce, maintained not only by the home market but also by the immense consuming areas of the cultured nations abroad. The almost incredible economic development upon which the colonisers based their arguments for expansion proved just to the contrary, that *Weltpolitik* was unnecessary, since it was possible, without extensive colonies, to grow rich at a rate and to a degree seldom experienced in history.

The *Weltpolitik* piled up plenty of explosive material, nervousness, and suspicion, and added to the risks of collision, which were especially facilitated by the Emperor's obtrusiveness, waywardness, swollen head, and sabre-rattling, the elusiveness of his entire personality, and his imperious barrack-room manner—all apparently belying his pacific proclivities.

Unfortunately Bülow was powerless to do anything to tone down these blemishes. Since Bismarck, he was the most talented minister of William II, the most talented of German diplomats, resourceful and sagacious, with the knack of presenting his aims and actions in the light rendered necessary by the situation of the moment or for the composing of conflicting interests. He was never at a loss for a bridge over any difficulty that might arise, if necessary to beat a retreat and cover up his tracks. Quick-witted, highly educated, he was one of the most brilliant *causeurs* I have ever met. His conversation was enlivened by the scintillation of intellectual pyrotechnics, with which none of his audience could dare to compete. He had an elegantly polished literary style ; his official reports were models of clear, interesting, and brilliant diction. He had diplomatic history at his finger-tips. An excellent orator, his speeches were always full of colourful, illuminating similes, quick repartee, sharp, clear epigram. Not a few of his *bons mots* found their way to the general public and became household words. With all these rare gifts, he possessed consummate skill in handling the press and in disarming political opponents. He desired popularity, and he certainly knew how to get it. A disciple of Bismarck and one of the confidants of that great statesman, yet he did not fall with him. A proof of his skill is furnished by the fact that he could keep in the good graces of the Emperor without being cut by the ex-Chancellor ; and when he became minister it was this very friendship with Bismarck which added to his importance and facilitated his task.

Unfortunately, however, Bülow was a diplomat, a parliamentary tactician rather than a far-sighted statesman, who must stand high above the changing moods of the people, and be able to recognise, analyse, and assert the true interests of the nation in accordance with their value and importance, even if necessary in defiance of the popular opinion. Bülow could gauge to a nicety the odds on diplomatic contests ; he could skilfully choose suitable instruments for the jobs on hand, and possessed strong nerves capable of sustaining perilous responsibility. And if he could act with resolution, he knew also how to climb down gracefully and put a smiling face on a lost game. He had a fund of native astuteness ; but though his cunning sometimes succeeded, it was too transparent, too obvious ; it created mistrust —which was to be regretted, since the new ambitions would remain in a peaceful groove only if the new policy of the Fatherland avoided causing general anxiety and mistrust. Bülow was rather an alarming, disturbing element in the rivalry of the Cabinets ; he created fear and uncertainty rather than calm reassurance ; for though he was known to be a strong man, yet he was at the same time not regarded as a safe man. The chief trouble, however, lay in his failure to understand the highest interests, the real situation and strength of his country. He pointed the Germans to ambitions involving too great risks. He lost sight of the fundamental truth of the policy of his Fatherland that so long as the French problem remained unsolved, so long as France must be faced as a potential enemy in all wars in which Germany might be engaged, it was not permissible for the latter to pursue a policy calculated to estrange England, particularly if she were not convinced of her ability to alienate Russia from France and attach the Muscovites to herself against England.

The *Weltpolitik*, by adding new antagonism and hatred to the old, to an extent which the sentiment of solidarity of the civilised world was powerless adequately to counterbalance, had rendered inevitable the final division of continental Europe into two opposing hosts. It added to the Franco-German and German-Slav antagonism the Anglo-German, which as a recently developed force gave the old antagonisms (which were beginning to subside) a new impetus and thus rendered the situation far worse than before. Whereas up to this time we had, since the Peace of Frankfort; witnessed no more than duels between single nations and diplomatic squabbles which did not necessarily involve all Europe in them, now, since the great progress of *Weltpolitik*, diplomatic disputes frequently arose in which all the Great Powers were concerned and in which not merely separate States were opposed, but mighty groups of States, alliances, and coalitions. This was just what prepared the way for the World War. And more, this piling of Pelion upon Ossa—in antagonisms and hatreds —was responsible for that other crying shame of modern history—the tyrannical Peace : a perpetration so monstrously unjust that it could never have been possible

20

had there been any neutral Powers whose impartiality could have been relied on—as had been the case since 1815 up to that time.　Only after the defeat of Napoleon I could conquerors have behaved in a fashion so disgracefully ruthless, callous, and savage as now.　For in deciding the further fate of the Corsican, nearly all the States of any consequence took part.　But then the Bourbons succeeded in saving France, by putting their country under the protection of the sentiment of solidarity animating the sovereigns.　Now, however, the defeated States sought in democratic and republican sentiments that protection afforded in the past by legitimism.　In vain !　The feeling of antagonism and hatred was more rabid in the democracies than in the former monarchies ; and the calculations of those who expected to be pardoned and saved if only they would place themselves beneath the protecting folds of the banner of Democracy proved a childish dream.

Only by such machinations could have arisen the impossible situation in which we exist to-day : nations with full rights, nations with half rights ; nations officially innocent, nations officially guilty ; nations armed to the teeth, and nations stripped to the skin,— a situation that was fondly expected to usher in an era of righteousness and peace, on frontiers and economic conditions bound up together with the most unjust punitive measures !

CHAPTER II

OPENING OF ALLIANCES. ITALY, AUSTRIA-HUNGARY, RUMANIA

GERMANY could have achieved a more conspicuous success with the new world-policy on and overseas and accomplished her object only by preserving her European supremacy and her predominant continental situation. Consequently it was Bülow's chief care to strengthen the Triple Alliance. This was a difficult task, however, as by this time the old structure had not a few defects and was becoming decrepit.

The policy of Italy was not what it had been in the past. The régime of Crispi—the age when Italy was the most ferocious member of the Triple Alliance, when it was difficult to restrain her from attacking France— was now over. The failure of Crispi's policy had weakened in Rome the adherence to the Triple Alliance. The defeat of the Italian troops in Abyssinia ; the failure to realise the expansion expected from the assistance of the Triple Alliance ; the fact that England (regarded as an external member of the Triple Alliance) appraised the interests of Italy at a lower rate than did the Italians ; the economic losses resulting from the tariff war against France ; the tremendous burden of armaments, which, though having nothing whatever to do with the Alliance, was demanded in its interests and therefore put to its account,—were all things which deterred Crispi's successors from following his example.

They, however, had no wish to desert the Triple Alliance, or to change their direction. The old Alliance had maintained the balance of power in Europe, and with that the peace which Italy so badly needed, especially after the *débâcle* in Africa. Would not Italy risk forfeiting valuable advantages by turning her back on these tried friends and accepting the leadership of the French ? The domestic policy of France might change at any moment ; Catholicism might triumph over Liberalism once more, and align itself with the Pope, thereby jeopardising Italian unity achieved at the expense of the Pope and by exploiting the political disabilities of France.

Though the Governments succeeding Crispi would certainly not have concluded the Triple Alliance, nevertheless they dared not take the responsibility of changing their direction and seeking new allies. Their aim was to make overtures to France, to restore friendly relations with that country, and thus facilitate an eventual change of direction without disputing the Triple Alliance and thus losing the protection it afforded.

They sought, in the first place, to improve their economic relations with France, to open for Italy the rich French money market, to create the opportunity for Italy to have the choice of two directions, to keep two irons in the fire—either to improve her position within the Triple Alliance by exploiting the possibility of an alliance with France, or to increase her own importance in French eyes by virtue of her membership of the Triple Alliance. Italy elected to occupy a middle place in order that both groups might be obliged to court her favours.

This political direction or theory was considerably enhanced by the skill and zeal of Barrère, the French Ambassador to Rome, who in his youth had taken part in the Paris Commune. Later in life he had been entrusted with several missions, in which he had proved himself a born diplomat. Thoroughly acquainted with the psychology of the masses, he not only observed and reported thereon, but acted. Besides negotiating with the Italian Government, he influenced the press and the general public. Not content with observing and taking advantage of changes in public opinion, he even created them. Diplomats are frequently the means whereby foreign ministers win glory and renown. Barrère has written his name on the scroll of French history. During his long term of office he exerted an immense influence on Italian foreign policy and became a powerful factor in the transformation of the political views of the Italians.

His work was advanced by the assassination (June 1900) of King Humbert—a staunch adherent of the Triple Alliance, whom we too trusted—by an anarchist, and this monarch's successor, Victor Emmanuel II, favouring a more active and ambitious foreign policy. His wife, Princess Helen of Montenegro, enlisted his interest in the Balkan Question, and excited his sympathies for the Slav aspirations, which were inimical to us. The King became envious of our successes in the Balkans and our intimacy with Russia. He was anxious lest Austria-Hungary should manifest a disposition to expand towards Albania or Salonica and thereby disturb the position of power on the Adriatic at Italy's expense. Thus he was without difficulty won for a policy diametrically opposed to that of King Humbert. He was troubled more about Balkan affairs than his father had been. For the time being, however, his objective was North Africa, where he hoped to achieve greater things than the preceding régime had done. The first tangible result of the new policy—good relations with the French—was a secret agreement between Italy and France with regard to Tripoli and Morocco, concluded behind the backs of the two other members of the Triple Alliance ; a treaty followed, as regards Tripoli, by another with England, setting forth that there was no conflict of interest between the two contracting parties in the Tripoli Question.

This double agreement meant a great step towards the attainment of the old aims, the *sacro egoismo* of the Italians. Crispi had designed the Triple Alliance with a view to preventing the spread of France in North Africa without any equivalent expansion on the part of Italy ; and to procure for the latter eventually suitable compensation in respect of Tunis. But this result was not completely realised, and instead of positive assistance, Italy had to be content with a promise to defend the unfavourable *status quo*. She could not even bind the Triple Alliance as a whole to so much. As to North Africa, she could gain the support of Germany, but that only in the event of France violating the *status quo*.

Italy made an excellent beginning with her new policy. She was able to agree with France in positive aims. She was at liberty to take to herself Turkish Tripoli on condition that she gave France a free hand in Morocco, where the latter asserted priority of claim.

By this means Italy acquired and accorded to others the right, contrary to obligations as a member of the Triple Alliance, to defend the *status quo* in North Africa ; and got nearer to the realisation of her old true ambition— expansion in Africa.

She approached with circumspection the victim selected for her repast. Her most redoubtable rival, her Gallic neighbour, had given her a free hand in Tripoli. And if the latter should ever repent of her bargain and quarrel with Italy, Germany would be obliged to support the Italians and defend them against an attack from the

French. Holstein, in his customary piquant style, wrote : " Italy is setting out in company with France on a burgling expedition ; and she wants to put the swag, for safety against everybody (even her accomplice, France), under the protection of the Triple Alliance " (December 1901).

The terms of this agreement were secret. Subsequently, however, the Italians informed Bülow about it. He, of course, disliked the whole affair, but put a good face on a bad job, and made use of a simile, which afterwards became famous : " Though a husband," he said, " should not object to his wife's favouring an admirer with a dance, he should endeavour to make her find her happiness in his own [i.e. her husband's] company." Truly sententious ! Bülow, however, resembled somewhat that type of husband who euphemistically terms his wife's deliberate unfaithfulness as " merely a dance," either because he is unwilling to notice it lest the affair should end in the divorce court, or because he is foolishly blind to what everybody else can see with their eyes shut. For by this time the innocent " dance " has been followed by clandestine assignations. Bülow was not told the real truth. Prinetti, the Italian Foreign Minister, protested that in his view it would be disloyal to make any far-reaching treaty with France without informing his allies of the fact. Nevertheless he committed this disloyalty ! He concluded with Barrère (November 1902) a treaty providing that Italy should remain neutral if France were to be attacked by one or more Powers, or even if France were provoked into attacking Germany in defence of her honour or interests. A few years afterwards (1906) Foreign Minister San Giuliano acknowledged to the German Ambassador that he would never have concluded such a treaty.

And I can believe him ; for indeed it was not in keeping with the spirit of the Triple Alliance, and therefore not a sincere policy.

In spite of the transformation of the Italian soul and her political aspirations, the Triple Alliance remained externally the same ; and Bülow and Goluchowsky even succeeded in renewing the Alliance by dint of skilful and deliberate tactics and without undertaking any further burdens.

This time, too, Italy advanced a number of pretensions. She demanded the renewal of the expiring economic agreement simultaneously with the conclusion of the new political treaty ; for only thus could she hope to carry the important wine duty clause in the teeth of the clamour of the wine-producers of the Dual Monarchy, and of Hungary in particular. Further, the Italians wanted an agreement with regard to the Balkans, in which they wished it expressly set forth that the *status quo* could only be changed in granting autonomy—especially to Albania, in which direction they feared the expansion of Austria-Hungary. Italian diplomacy also sought to give the Triple Alliance an anti-Russian complexion, though there was at that time a rather close co-operation between Austria-Hungary and the Czar in the Balkan Question. The Italians, e.g., tried to compel the Triple Alliance to defend the *status quo* also in the question of the Dardanelles. They sought to have a clause inserted in the treaty to the effect that Germany was absolutely disinterested in Tripoli. They also stipulated that the term of denunciation of the treaty should be shortened.

In the end, however, the Italian Government yielded all along the line. The treaty was simply prolonged. With regard to Tripoli and the Balkans the Italians were reassured by the identity of aims among the different contracting parties as demonstrated during the course of the negotiations. They dropped the economic agreement, and the commercial treaty was concluded only after a tremendous disputation by way of a compromise.

Italy yielded because, though she did not want to break with the Triple Alliance, she did want to preserve the opportunity of choosing from the two combinations. By picking a quarrel with her old allies she would be left entirely at the mercy of France. Therefore she must be careful to retain the confidence of the French. Consequently Barrère was given such a version of the alliance as would reassure Delcassé, the French Foreign Minister. The latter was able to state in the Chamber that, according to the Italian Government, the policy of Italy was not directed against France ; that there was nothing menacing in the Triple Alliance, neither in the military measures nor in the diplomatic protocols thereof ; that Italy would never lend herself or be a party to an attack upon France,—all of which, though not quite true, was consonant with the views and aims of the Italians and would allay the misgivings of the French.

Italy's new mentality was further manifested in her emancipation from her allies in the contingency of a crisis. According to the military convention in force up to that time, the Italian Third Army was immediately on a declaration of war to be despatched via Austria to the French front, to join in the offensive against the French. From the view-point of strategy this measure was quite correct ; for the struggle would have to be decided on the French front ; and unless the Italian troops wanted to shed their blood to no purpose on the Alpine heights, fortified by the French, or to play the inglorious rôle of passive spectators, they had no alternative but to proceed to the Rhine.   Such eminently wise and justifiable action would have created common cause between Italy and her allies from the moment of mobilisation, and on that account it would have been very objectionable to the changed soul of the Italians.

The new Government regarded this old obligation as rather disturbing.   When the German General Staff became aware of this, they relinquished their claim to the fulfilment thereof by the Italians, well knowing that to enforce the pledge would reduce it to a mere " scrap of paper " which would be even dangerous in creating illusions and leading astray.   In this manner the King of Italy received a free hand in the event of war to dispose of his troops as seemed to him best.   He was bound by no pledge any longer, and he could decide according to circumstances where his military forces should be sent.   They might—said the Italian Government—make an effort in the Alps ; or they might either invade Switzerland (violating neutrality) or reach France by way of Austria.

From this period the German General Staff were convinced that no positive assistance from Italy could be relied on.   The only value of the Alliance in their eyes was the fact—an important fact, however,—that it at least would prevent Italy from turning against us, so that the entire Austro-Hungarian military strength could be devoted to the common cause.

Italy managed her diplomatic action with admirable skill.   She succeeded in retaining the protection of the Triple Alliance, while at the same time leaving a loophole by which she could, if it suited her interests, join its enemies.   Legally and formally she was bound ; politically she retained her freedom to choose between the two groups of States. Thus her vote had acquired an enhanced value.

It omened ill for us that public sentiment between Austria-Hungary and Italy became cooler from day to day. Rome, as may be understood, could not forget that Francis Joseph (owing to Vatican relations) had never returned King Humbert's visit to Vienna. The absolutely unfounded suspicion that Austria-Hungary had designs on Albania gained more and more credence ; and as, on the other hand, Rome certainly wanted Albania in the Italian sphere of influence, this meant a collision with the aim of the Dual Monarchy to play the leading part in that region. On the ground of an ancient right as protectors of the Catholics in Turkey, we exerted a certain influence over the Albanian schools. Without any such treaty right, but solely in virtue of her proximity, Italy commenced a competition with us to serve her own political interests ; and this had a bad effect on the cordiality of the relations between the two countries. The maintenance of true friendship was rendered exceedingly difficult by the anti-Italian temper of the Austrian Slav population and the irredentist tendencies of the Italian Youth movement, manifested in a number of demonstrations in both Italy and Austria.

Once, on the occasion of the annual military manœuvres, the Italian King himself became involved in the irredentist demonstrations—an incident which gave great offence to Goluchowsky, the Foreign Minister at Vienna, and caused him to consider whether the " free-handed " policy would not be preferable to the one-sided obligation towards Italy into which the Triple Alliance had now fallen.

The alliance between Austria-Hungary and Germany was at this time without difficulty prolonged—automatically, as it were—though a few difficulties still existed between the two States. Of late the home policy of Austria had assumed a Slav tendency, and that circumstance might endanger the future of the Alliance. The rising Czech and Polish influence was viewed with mistrust at Berlin, and there was a sharp dispute in connection with the Polish exiles between the Austrian and Prussian Governments in their respective Parliaments, a dispute which decidedly exacerbated the prevailing sentiments. The Sovereigns and Foreign Ministers, however, adhered firmly to the old direction and German supremacy was gradually re-established in Austria. The Alliance was durable, though Germany looked with coolness on the development of Austria, the Polish influence, the struggle between the two halves of the Dual Monarchy culminating in the *Ausgleich* (compromise) and the military problem agitating the Hungarian parties and the Austrian Germans. Ambassador Wedell (September 1903) gave vent to his anxiety on the matter. Everywhere were misgivings felt with regard to the future of the Dual Monarchy.

Goluchowsky was a man of greater independence than Kálnoky had been, and the good relations cemented by the former with St. Petersburg to no small extent disturbed the German Ambassador and even the Emperor himself. William feared lest the friendship of Austria-Hungary and Russia should reduce Germany to second rank and create in Vienna the mistaken idea that German friendship was less valuable than heretofore.

This was but a passing mood, however. The real permanent conviction was, as the Emperor wrote in a marginal note (February 1902), that Austria would always obey him and the Czar, for the two made history and directed fate.

This tone, as may be supposed, dissatisfied Vienna and strengthened the hands of those in the Imperial City who desired another orientation, who complained of the *præpotentia* of the Germans and of the fact that even in the Balkans Germany was scheming for economic and political connections behind the back of Austria-Hungary.

Rumania, moreover, desired to alter the old relations, though at this time she appeared thoroughly reliable. So far she had concluded a treaty of defence only with Austria-Hungary, which was accepted separately by Italy and Germany. But now Stourdza, the Rumanian Premier, would have liked his country to join the Triple Alliance as a fourth. This would have flattered the vanity of King Carol far more than the hitherto secret rôle. Most probably the Rumanian public, too, would have been gratified, and they would have helped to root more firmly the idea of international friendship. But Germany was unwilling, especially as such an enlargement and alteration of the Triple Alliance might create a bad impression in Russia, causing the latter to take more pains than hitherto to win Rumania and exert in Bucarest a livelier activity. Goluchowsky was willing to yield, for the sake of the King of Rumania, but he too finally adopted the German standpoint and the Rumanians withdrew their application.

Another demand of Rumania was more important. Owing to the ambitions of the Bulgarians in Macedonia, Rumania desired the *casus fœderis* to be extended to the contingency of Rumania attacking Bulgaria on account of the latter's schemes for the conquest of Macedonia. Bülow, however, very rightly objected to the Triple Alliance being given an offensive character. Thus Rumania failed also again, and could do no more than renew the Alliance in the old form (April 1902).

CHAPTER III

GERMANY'S FAVOURABLE SITUATION

AT first the general situation was favourable for Germany's programme of a new world-policy. The Powers who might stand in the way of German expansion, on whose jealousy it was necessary to reckon, became on bad terms with each other. Their extra-European interests and antagonisms came uppermost, disturbing the Powers' connections with each other. A return to the situation of the early eighties was expected, when Gladstone's Egyptian and Ferry's Tunis adventures rendered the good-will of Germany a valuable asset for them both.

The one fact of prime importance emerging therefrom was that, since Lobanoff's day, Russia had gravitated towards Eastern Asia, thereby arousing the jealousy of England and Japan and giving to Russian sentiment an anti-British and anti-Japanese turn. This necessitated that St. Petersburg should court the friendship of Berlin and Vienna.

The perennial sources of Oriental trouble were still active, but the entente between Russia and Austria-Hungary stood the difficult test. In the Balkans was an external cause of unrest : Bulgaria, who was ambitious to become " Great Bulgaria " and who was counting on a Macedonian rising accompanied with atrocities which would result in Russian or British intervention. But there were also internal causes for the return of the former anarchy. The Turkish administration was utterly corrupt. Its treasury was empty, so that it could not pay the salaries of its officials. Neither could it carry out reforms for the benefit of the community. The control of the administration, the final decision in all matters, rested with the cowardly, cunning, and cruel Assassin of Stamboul, or with his scarcely less contemptible ministers, wretches devoid of character or convictions, whom Marschall, the German Ambassador, correctly described when he wrote that (under Ottoman rule) " the ministerial office and convictions were incompatible, an independent-minded man with convictions being the most unsuitable person for a minister."

The problem of administration was wellnigh impossible of solution. Even a good bureaucracy would scarcely have been equal to the task, to say nothing of the rotten Turkish tyranny misnamed *government*. For peace had to be preserved and justice meted out among savage races imbued with hatred against each other— not striving for right and liberty, law and order, but each for himself, those lofty and noble watchwords being used only to throw dust in the eyes of Europe. The Turks dare not openly resort to military measures to suppress the rebellion, since that was forbidden by the public opinion of Russia and England. The European Powers, in their jealousy of each other, had been constantly meddling with the domestic affairs of the Ottoman Empire, and thus had weakened the authority and power of the central government just when its authority and power were essentially necessary for the suppression of anarchy. The advice offered to Turkey by the various Powers was mostly contradictory, countering each other, being not the result of the objective deliberations of experts but of selfishness, mutual jealousy, and rivalry.

At this time the Macedonian disturbances were agitating the public mind. The situation was particularly complicated, as the region in question was populated by a conglomeration of the most heterogeneous peoples of the Balkans. Goluchowsky and Lobanoff were fortunately able to avoid a conflagration by agreeing (December 1902) on a moderate programme by which it was possible to save the Sultan's authority and give him a free hand to act with that vigour and promptness the case demanded. But when, notwithstanding, the potentate of Yildiz failed to restore order, and Bulgarian intervention still seemed likely, Russia and Austria-Hungary made new demands upon him. These too, however, were reasonable and, after some bluster, the Sultan accepted them (November 1903).

This likewise, alas! led to no rest and tranquillity. The Macedonian problem had still to experience many trials, and for a long time kept on tenterhooks all the diplomats of Europe. Nevertheless, the peace of Europe was not seriously disturbed : for Austria-Hungary and Russia held together, Germany backed them up, and England—though she insisted upon radical reforms, in order to maintain her prestige and embarrass the Russians, whose policy she detested—refrained from any particular action. Now also the Germans affected to see veiled malice in every step that England took. Their pessimism, however, had no serious consequences; the Balkan imbroglio was unable to disturb the rather favourable European situation, proving that it was not the controversies on the Balkan Question that were the real reasons for the great complications, but, on the contrary, the Balkan situation became critical as the relations of the European Powers became unpropitious.

The accomplishment of Bülow's great plans was not favoured by the good relations between Russia and Austria-Hungary alone, but also by the sharp antagonism subsisting between France and England.

In 1897 a small force of Frenchmen from the East African coast turned up, after an adventurous march lasting several years, in the neighbourhood of the Nile Valley, with the avowed intention of proclaiming the sovereignty of the French Republic over that tract. This, of course, was in opposition to the English point of view that England alone was entitled to occupy the riparian region so vitally important for the British Empire. In the following summer (1898), Major Marchand, of the French army, hoisted the *tricolor* at Fashoda. The British commander, General Kitchener, hurried to the scene and protested against the act (19th September). A serious diplomatic collision ensued, and hostilities came within a hair-breadth. But France at length yielded. Indeed she could not do otherwise, for British power exceeded that of the French. Kitchener was on the spot with the victorious troops with which he had smashed the Mahdi, reconquered the whole Sudan, and thereby extended the military might of Britain in Egypt held since Gladstone's time.

Against such a Great Power, France could not depend on any serious support from any quarter. She could not transport her troops to the scene of action, since Britain held the seas. France realised that ever since Napoleon I the Island Kingdom had been able to inflict upon her far greater wounds than she could hope to return. This explains why, in spite of the hate of the French for the English since the defeat of the former at Waterloo, their Gallic neighbours have never dared seriously to oppose them. And how could they hope to do so now, when they were in permanently hostile relations with their big continental neighbour ? After Sedan, they could not risk another Trafalgar. The credit for England's swift and stern action was due chiefly to

Chamberlain, who possessed greater will-power and higher perspicacity than Salisbury, though he had less diplomatic skill and experience. He was rather a type of the modern, egoistic, bluff, but straight and practical business-man than a suave diplomatist of the Metternich or Talleyrand school.

The antagonism of England, which became so critical, lay heavily on the French idea of *revanche* for 1870–1. Now was the time—if ever—when France must beware of offending Germany. If she must bend before England on account of Germany, she must be equally cautious towards Germany on account of England.

For the time being neither France nor England could continue an anti-German policy. The Fashoda incident eased the situation of Germany also by loosening the ties binding France to Russia. When the French, in their hour of humiliation, needed the support of their ally, they had to make the bitter discovery that she was a broken reed. Though the Muscovites were ready to identify themselves in principle with the cause of France, yet they declared that, owing to affairs in Asia requiring their present attention and in view also of the approach of winter, they would be unable to assist France for some time at least. This discounted the practical value of the friendship and dissipated the blind confidence of the French in their Russian Ally.

The fact that England, besides having incurred the wrath and animosity of the French, also had her hands full with the South African problem was exceedingly opportune for Germany at that time. The differences between the Boer Republic and England were becoming daily more acute. The indefatigable Chamberlain, the most energetic member of the Salisbury Cabinet, had made up his mind to annex the peasants' commonwealth.

He might have been content with consolidating the British power there, instead of the Dutch, by constitutional means, through the enfranchising of the English fortune-hunters, employers and employés, who dwelt in considerable numbers in the Transvaal. But President Krüger seeing that in the long run the granting of the franchise was the surrendering of the independence of the Boers, and that to comply with the demands of the British Government would mean British supremacy over the Republic, there was but little prospect of arriving at an agreement. A war followed (October 1899), which was not without danger for England, in view of the valour, excellent military training, and (at the beginning) numerical superiority of the burghers.

CHAPTER IV

THE " FREE HAND " POLICY. FIRST OVERTURES FROM ENGLAND

IN this situation Bülow deemed himself strong enough to make a bold bid for colonies ; openly to declare his ultimate aim : the building of a powerful navy, without seeking new allies, without limiting his freedom of action by new trammels, without fear of any war against a Great Power. In his opinion, the best plan was to choose the middle path between England and Russia and wait. The good-will of Germany was important for everybody, and therefore she could afford to wait and demand for herself a " place in the sun." She risked little by acting boldly.

Bülow, unlike Bismarck, was not perturbed by the nightmare of coalitions. He thought it out of the question for the time being that England, France, and Russia should come to any understanding ; and so long as the difference existed between France and England, he just as little feared that France and Russia would follow any active policy against Germany.

Emperor William and Bülow made their début on the political stage when Germany had already become a Great Power. Both men were reared in an atmosphere of German supremacy, and thought that much more was in their reach than did Bismarck, to whom German supremacy on the Continent was a sort of miracle ; for he well remembered the time when Prussia had to defer to the Habsburgs in regard to the domestic affairs of Germany. Bismarck's aspirations and ambitions were within more modest limits than those of his successors, who had obtained from his very successes the opportunity and the impetus for greater and bolder pretensions.

William and Bülow thought that, without undue risk, Germany could by increasing her navy rise to be the first military Power in the world—just as she was already the first in Europe. This was an achievement that Bismarck had never dreamt of. When in the eighties the other Powers were seized with the itch for acquiring possessions overseas, Bismarck took advantage of their preoccupation by enhancing Germany's political importance on the Continent, to arrange alliances, and to play off the Powers against each other by constantly suggesting new enterprises in which they should engage.

In the question of colonies Bülow acted quite differently. He did not seek to strengthen still further his continental position, as the Greatest German would have done ; he was ambitious to take part in the race for possessions overseas, as well as on the Continent. Consequently he followed the policy of the " free hand," and declined new alliances. The conclusion of a new alliance was the equivalent of forging new fetters ; and Bülow preferred freedom to act. A new alliance was tantamount to new *casus belli* and new restrictions—all of which Bülow feared and avoided as much as possible, even if the *casus belli* were, properly speaking, theoretical, if peace was secured by the defensive character of the aim and the impressiveness of the forces arrayed in defence of it. Yet Germany could never have made her continental position so strong as at this period, never at any other time could she have concluded such advantageous alliances as now when the three Powers outside the Triple Alliance so badly needed the good-will of Germany on account of their extra-European interests. At this period even France was contemplating coming to an agreement with her. Münster, German Ambassador to Paris (November 1898), reported that the conviction was spreading in the French capital (owing to England's inflexible attitude on the Fashoda incident and Russia's coolness) that a *rapprochement* with Germany was desirable. To encourage this idea, the Ambassador advised that the compulsory use of passports for Alsace-Lorraine, which was a source of much friction, should be abolished. It is to be regretted that, though the Emperor himself favoured this step, the corps commanders of the districts concerned all vetoed it. Nevertheless the arguments for *rapprochement* with Germany were so cogent that, in spite of the courtesy advised by Münster being refused, Paris manifested a certain tendency to make overtures to Berlin. Even Delcassé, the newly appointed Foreign Minister, who later initiated the bitterest anti-German policy, made secret enquiries as to whether it were possible to get nearer to Germany. Only a short time previously the enquiry addressed by Germany to his predecessor as to the possibility of co-operation with France in the question of the Portuguese colonies had been left by Delcassé in the drawer of his writing-table—his answer being rude silence. Now, however (December 1898), he explained to a German journalist that as England wanted to pick a quarrel with France as a pretext for destroying her fleet, there was only one remedy for that—a French *rapprochement* with Germany.

Many persons abroad also believed in the feasibility of a Franco-German Entente. A Spanish minister (April 1899) expounded his view that the continental Powers could be combined against England; and was convinced only after exhaustive investigation that the time for a Franco-German Alliance was not yet ripe. The Queen-Regent of Spain—a Habsburg archduchess with excellent political insight—(August 1899) thought the *rapprochement* not impracticable. She suggested for this purpose that Alsace-Lorraine should be made an independent principality. That would flatter Gallic vanity and pave the way for further steps.

But the Emperor unfortunately declined to entertain the idea. He dismissed the recommendation with the abrupt marginal note : " Stupidity ! " Alsace-Lorraine, he said, was German : he should do as he liked there ; it was no business of the French.

In Russia also the idea took root that the continental Powers, including France and Germany, should unite against England. As early as September 1897 Obrutseff, Russian Chief-of-Staff, recommended to Bülow the conclusion of a Russo-Franco-German Alliance with an anti-English point. The German diplomat, however, declined to take the recommendation seriously.

Witte, the Russian Finance Minister, the most prominent figure in the political life of Czardom, perhaps its only real statesman at that time, also deemed it worth while to consider the question of a continental alliance, which in his view was not only possible but necessary, as without such protection England would become dictator of all Europe. By competition, in the constant increase of their land-forces, the continental States were doing immense harm to each other. Instead of that, their navies should be increased, and efforts made to put an end to England's dominion over the seas (December 1898 and April 1899).

Germany, however, had her doubts on the matter. She mistrusted the advances of France. Radolin, the new German Ambassador to Paris, expressed the views of Berlin in stating that " Germany was not so simple as to suppose that France would not avail herself of the first opportunity to turn on Germany. Though Germany wished to live at peace with everybody, she must look to her own power for safety."

The same superior sense of certainty was manifested some years later (1903) by Kaiser William, when Radolin reported that French sentiment was improving and that the Alsace-Lorraine question might be amicably solved by the exchange of that province for Madagascar. The Kaiser ironically remarked that " he would rather be elected Emperor of the French by plebiscite. In which event he would undertake to spend six months of every year in Paris and the other six months in Berlin. The Empire of Charlemagne would thus be restored, and France as a part thereof would recover Alsace-Lorraine."

Though this remark was probably only intended as a witticism, it was characteristic satire, revealing the spirit which constituted a permanent obstacle in the way of good relations between Germany and France.

But Russia attempted to gain Germany over to herself, without France. Osten-Sacken, the Russian Ambassador (April 1899), asked Bülow whether it would not be wise to come to an agreement in the Turkish Question by means of a written treaty. If Germany would undertake to back the Russian claims in the matter of the Straits and Constantinople, Russia, on the other part, would promote Germany's economic expansion in Asia Minor. But, for a complete agreement, Bülow's personal promise to continue the Bismarckian policy and not to thwart the expansion of Russia was not sufficient —a written document was absolutely necessary. Muravieff explained that though he would not upset the Sultan's throne, he should nevertheless object to Turkey's rehabilitation and reconstruction, and therefore asked to be enlightened as to the Oriental policy of Germany.

" If the influence of Germany in the East should continue to increase without her coming to an understanding with Russia," continued Muravieff, " the Czar would be compelled to make overtures to England, to make the best bargain he can."

Russia, however, failed to attain her object, either by promises or threats. Emperor William was disgusted at Muravieff's cynicism, which was indeed shocking. Germany would conclude an alliance with Russia only on the condition that France also would join it, and mutually guarantee each other's territorial integrity. Failing that, Russia could offer nothing but economic advantages while Germany would be undertaking political obligations. So long as he had to apprehend a French attack, Bülow declined to discuss a Russophil policy which appeared Anglophobe, for such might lead to an *entente cordiale* between France and England. Even if the treaty were secret, the danger would still be there ; enough might leak out to bring Germany into opposition with those two Powers. Hatzfeld, Ambassador to London, pointed out that there was no need for new alliances, as the actual friction between Great Britain and Russia created an exceedingly favourable situation for Germany, and Berlin could afford to wait. The time would come when she would be able to come to an agreement with either Power under much more favourable conditions—that is to say, if she should want to come to any agreement at all.

He was quite right. The only trouble was that Berlin desired no agreement with either of them ; she objected to binding herself either then or in the near future. The Germans intended to make no new promises to anyone ; above all, they preferred not to expose themselves to the enmity of one Power by making overtures to another.

Emperor William, moreover, was influenced by the profound dislike he felt for Muravieff, the Russian Minister for Foreign Affairs. In his marginal notes he frequently stigmatised the Muscovite diplomat as a " liar " ; sometimes as a " mendacious rascal." The Emperor always read hidden menaces between the lines of Muravieff's statements, and this added to his anger. " Let him," wrote William (July 1899), " stand at the salute when he addresses the German Emperor. The time is long past since the Czar Nicholas I could issue orders to the King of Prussia."

On the Russian Foreign Minister complaining of two German officers attending a review of Turkish troops near the Russian frontier, the Emperor wrote : " This is an impertinence. No one has any right to attribute to my officers intentions which are far from their thoughts. I protest against the base insinuation, and Muravieff should be told of my protest. What right has the Russian Government to object to what takes place on Turkish territory ? " This was equivalent to telling Muravieff to mind his own business.

So no Russo-German Treaty was concluded. There was not the remotest prospect of France assenting to Germany's demands—of France guaranteeing Germany's possession of Alsace-Lorraine. Bülow subsequently informed certain English statesmen that he had made this stipulation only as a polite way of declining advances which did not suit him, knowing that the French would never consent to such a condition. This was so, in fact. Bülow knew the French too well to expect them seriously to guarantee to another Power the provinces the annexation of which they had always denounced as an act of lawless brigandage. It remained for our day to witness such political depravity as, after the World War, the conquered nations being solemnly required in the Covenant of the League of Nations to assist in the defence of a *status quo* made against their own interests ; and, moreover, to do so after being rendered incapable even of defending themselves while their enemies are armed to the very teeth.

Had Bülow avoided concluding a treaty with Russia because he wanted an agreement with England, he would have acted wisely. But unfortunately he was just as averse to the latter as to the former. At this time the latter was possible ; he could have really concluded an agreement with England. Even before the Fashoda crisis (March 1898) Chamberlain proposed an alliance to Hatzfeld. It must be stated that this was done unofficially, in Chamberlain's private capacity only. England, he said, would be willing to join the Triple Alliance on condition that Germany undertook to defend England.

Chamberlain justified his proposal as follows : Russia menaced the interests of the British Empire in the Far East ; France gravitated towards the Nile ; the Boer Question had become critical ; thus England needed a friend. Her former isolation no longer corresponded to the present situation.

Germany was averse to an agreement with Russia, being afraid lest she might thereby provoke England and cause her to support France. Neither did Germany favour an alliance with England, lest she might provoke Russia ; for Great Britain, with all her warships, was powerless to defend the smallest village of Posen against an inroad of Cossacks. This view was only partially correct, and by no means relevant ; as the chief object of German policy was not to save Posen villages from the Cossacks, but to effect an alliance powerful enough to ensure peace, or, if war must come, to secure the victory.

This double aim was attainable by British help. Though British warships might be unable to defend Posen villages, yet the naval prestige and power of England would probably compel Russia to desist, while Germany's military superiority on land combined with a naval blockade would, in the event of war, be practically irresistible.

Though Bülow desired to be on good terms with both Powers, he preferred not to be under obligation to either of them ; choice was invidious, since by choosing either he would be certain to make an enemy of the other.

Against Chamberlain he defended himself by skilful arguments. He demonstrated that the proposed alliance with England failed to afford adequate guarantee ; it signified less for Germany than for England ; for whereas the signature of the German Emperor would bind Germany for all time, that of the British Government would bind England temporarily only—merely for the lifetime of the particular Government contracting. Instead of concluding the alliance as proposed, the German Chancellor would have liked to use Chamberlain's declarations as means to induce England to follow a policy calculated to alienate France and Russia from each other. He advised Chamberlain to try to satisfy Russia in Asia without considering France, because then Great Britain could easily settle her account with France. In such a conflict Germany would remain neutral—which alone would be sufficient to provide occupation for the land forces of the Gallic Republic. In the event of England's position becoming precarious, Germany would hasten to her aid. So much would be due to her own interests— and interests are stronger than treaties. To wait would not be good for England. If Russia could only finish the Trans-Siberian strategic and commercial railway-line and France build her navy, England would be in a far more serious plight.

In vain Chamberlain protested that England was unable to satisfy Russia in Asia, as the latter was constantly putting forward new demands, which in the long run were bound to damage British interests. He denied that he had any aggressive designs against Russia ; he was perfectly willing to recognise her acquisitions in Asia, all he desired being to save the so far still intact and independent China. He emphasised his willingness to conclude with Germany an open treaty, ratified by Parliament, which would bind England equally with Germany. Bülow refused to budge ; he was fertile with counter-arguments. According to him, the publication of the proposed treaty and its passage through the British Parliament would provoke Russia, and if afterwards—as might easily happen—Parliament were to decline to ratify the treaty, the result would be that Germany had made an enemy of Russia without securing England's obligation to assist her. The publication of the treaty might cause hostilities between Germany and Russia before the obligation of England had been declared. However, this was the situation at the moment only ; with a change in the public opinion of England, the situation also would be changed. At some time or other a favourable change of public opinion might occur, influencing the British Parliament, and thereby securing the sanctioning of the treaty. Then it would be possible to conclude it. Apart from that consideration, England must know that she had no truer friends than the Germans and that the interests of the latter would suffice to deter them from allowing England to be defeated. All that Germany now desired of England was that she would be reasonable with regard to the solution of concrete colonial questions. This would prove the safest means of preparing the way for subsequent co-operation and alliance.

German diplomacy applied in London the identical tactics that it had used towards Russia : polite words, friendly speech, but no undertaking of new obligations, no new alliances ; final decisions to be delayed as long as possible. The Emperor observed (June 1898) that " he would not make an agreement with England until she begged for it on her knees ! "

Besides Chamberlain, Balfour, another member of the Cabinet, also negotiated at this time with Hatzfeld. He acted more cautiously, however, without positively proposing an alliance. Nevertheless Hatzfeld, in spite of the more cautious tactics of Balfour, was of opinion that Chamberlain's move was made with the full knowledge and approval of the entire British Government ; and the Ambassador went so far as to add that some of the leading members of the opposition also declared that they would have no objection to an alliance with Germany. Even the hyper-cautious Premier, Salisbury, was not averse to such an alliance.

Bülow's attitude and the rejection of the proposed alliance were not justified by the arguments he advanced. Had he genuinely desired a closer connection with England, he could easily have found a means of eliminating the obstacles in the way. For instance, a temporary agreement might have been concluded, valid for the duration of the two Governments only, and at the same time a declaration made that they would settle the colonial questions in a friendly manner, the projected alliance not being laid before Parliament until a favourable juncture should have been secured by the removal of all colonial differences and by practical co-operation.

The real cause of the rejection was that for the time being Bülow was indisposed to the conclusion of any new alliances, even with England ; that both William II and Bülow agreed (10th April) in their desire to remain in a position to decide the balance of power. The object of the negotiations with the English statesmen was, instead of seeking at the conclusion of the treaty to obtain better conditions than those offered by the English, to postpone it, but to do so in such a manner as to lead the English to hope for its conclusion at some future time, and to renew their efforts for such an alliance.

Hatzfeld would have to employ in England the tactics described by Madame de Maintenon, who said that " she never fully satisfied Louis XIV, but always gave him hope ! " Thus Hatzfeld must keep England in a state of discontent with regard to a prospective alliance, but be careful not to extinguish the bright flame of hope. However, the task of the diplomat was far more difficult than that of the courtesan. The infatuated lover, led by the nose, has no eyes for anyone except his goddess, and becomes more and more compliant and lavish of his presents as the ardour of his passion increases ; whereas the cold-shouldered, mistrusted statesman is by no means so limited or prejudiced in his diplomatic love affairs, but will soon seek and find consolation elsewhere.

Chamberlain quite frankly remarked to Eckhardtstein, an official of the German Embassy in London, that if he were thrown over by Germany he should have to make overtures to the enemies of Germany, for he had no intention of remaining in isolation. Berlin, however, did not take this hint seriously. Bülow considered it improbable that England would find an ally elsewhere. Overtures to France would simply prepare the way for friendship with Germany, as the negotiations would soon

show England that she could not choose one of the allies
and leave the other out, and she could not come to an
agreement with France and Russia. What a delusion !
And how different the lesson taught by facts !

For a while, however, Chamberlain made no move
towards putting his threat into execution, but still
adhered to the idea of an alliance with Germany.   In a
public speech (13th May) he suggested the advisability,
in view of the Chinese menace, of coming to an agreement
with those Powers who concurred with England in the
matter (i.e. the Triple Alliance).

In spite of this plain invitation, the decision of the
Germans remained unaltered. No alliance was concluded.
So little value was set by Berlin on the desired alliance
that the Emperor informed the Czar of the English offer
—most probably in order to prevent England finding
consolation for his rejection by turning to Russia.

The Czar, replying, referred to the fact that three
months previously England had proposed an agreement
with him—a piece of information which caused William
to suspect English good faith more than ever.

Yet even then the English would not abandon their
cherished idea—the German Alliance. Before the
threatening Boer War it seemed advantageous and
became even urgent during the war, conducted with
immense sacrifice and attended with grave perils. When,
in the course of the struggle, William evinced a somewhat
sympathetic attitude towards England, and paid a visit
to the country, where he had not been seen for several
years (i.e. since 1891), Chamberlain seized the opportunity
to repeat the offer to his Imperial Majesty in person
(November 1899). He observed that he was convinced
a triple alliance comprising America, Britain, and Germany the wisest combination. He predicted that ere

long Europe would have to reckon with the Russians enlisting the millions of Chinese and Tartars under their flag—a prophecy that seems destined to be fulfilled even in our own day.

For at the present time the Soviet Republic is near to realising what the Czars had hoped for and Chamberlain had feared—the subjection of Asia to Russia ; and then with revolutionary catch-words the hurling of their millions against the old-established order of Europe. Perhaps this most ominous turn of the wheel of history was perceived by the clairvoyant mind of the squire of Highbury—the peril which, by the irony of fate, has now to be faced by his son Austen, the present Foreign Minister of England !

Chamberlain then offered the Germans an agreement with regard to Morocco, where shortly afterwards the bitterest antagonism burst out between Germans and English. What a different course history might have taken if only Berlin had accepted the offer ! It is regrettable that the words of the English statesman once again fell upon deaf ears in the Fatherland. Bülow said that though England needed Germany, Germany had no need of England. And when Chamberlain again (November 1899) proclaimed his idea, in spite of so much discouragement, and advocated an alliance of the three Germanic Powers, the German Foreign Minister returned a most unfriendly answer in the Reichsrat. He would not even use the term " alliance," but merely referred to good relations, and urged that Germany must have a navy powerful enough to resist all attacks—a thrust directed of course against England and tantamount to a threat. The effect of Bülow's speech in London was the more painful as Chamberlain had interpreted the German statesman's previous utterances as a distinct encouragement to put his views before the public. Bülow, in his Reichsrat speech, had yielded to the pressure of the Anglophobe public opinion then prevailing in Germany on account of the Boer War. He caused Chamberlain to be informed of this, adding that he was still an advocate of an Anglo-German *rapprochement*. We cannot, however, be surprised that this message obtained but little credence, and at Chamberlain closing the correspondence with the remark that "After what had happened it would be a long time before he reopened the subject of an alliance with Germany. At the end of the war the situation might be different."

Bülow took full responsibility for the failure of these negotiations. Germany was strong, and England was at the time in danger ; she had a bitter struggle before her in South Africa. Germany was on good terms with Russia, and France did not manifest a hostile spirit ; consequently Bülow had no need of London and was not inclined to undertake new obligations on her behalf. He exemplified his own witty saying that " the relations between man and horse are good—for the man ; and he preferred to play the rôle of the man." He feared an alliance with England, because in that case the preferred rôle might not be secured for Germany. Further, it was certain that the scale of the German fleet would have to be modified to please England. Why should Germany submit to that, when there was no burning necessity for England's support, which Germany would almost certainly get when she wanted it, without an alliance ? Though the Fatherland did not intend to abuse her freedom of action, she considered herself and her actual allies strong enough to justify her in maintaining it.

But might she not have been deceiving herself ? Is it not better to conclude an alliance while the other party is in the humour for it, even though one has no absolute need of it at present ? Is it not good to take time by the forelock—to act in the living present in order to avoid future danger ? For a State to postpone an alliance until trouble has overtaken it is to risk being left in the lurch, without a friend.

CHAPTER V

WELTPOLITIK SUCCESSES. THE GERMAN NAVY

IN order to reach his aim and enhance his importance in world-politics without new obligations, Bülow wished to exploit the differences existing between the Powers, and not, as Bismarck in a similar situation had done, by concluding new alliances. And Bülow's first idea as a means to his end was to get a footing in China.

Japan's victory over the Celestials had upset the internal balance and order of the most populous empire in the world ; and an immense commercial market might now be opened up for the European Powers. The prospect was an alluring one. Germany must not miss her part in the inevitable division. A short time before Germany had helped to save China from Japan ; now China must pay the bill for the service rendered on that occasion.

Bülow accomplished this object with masterly skill ; his unerring estimate of the situation, quick decision, and diplomacy—not over-scrupulous as to means, astute, formidable—revealed him as a perfect master of his craft. The Emperor shared the merit with his minister. Perhaps it was William who first thought of the spoils to be gathered in the Flowery Land. When Russia turned upon Japan, and Germany, in co-operation with the Muscovites, stopped Japanese action in China, Kaiser William already counted on substantial reward and took steps to prepare the Czar for his demands. During a visit to the Czar, the Emperor astonished his cousin " Nicky," taken unawares and in the absence of his advisers, by bluntly asking whether he had any objection to the port of Kiao-Chau being occupied by the Germans. The courteous host could not be so impolite as to return an unfavourable answer ; but according to Witte's *Memoirs* the Czar afterwards (August 1897) bitterly complained of the sharp practice of which William had made him the victim.   In moments of crisis the Emperor stimulated his Government to resolute and courageous action without rashness.   Though inflexible in essentials, he was sufficiently complaisant in minor details ; though firm, he was neither impatient nor inconsiderate.   As a lawless aggression without the basis of previous provocation would damage his prestige far more than the conquest would be worth, he waited patiently for the Chinese to afford him a pretext for the presentation of his bill.   And he had not long to wait.   Several German missionaries were murdered.   The pretence of desiring to punish the murderers served to cover the annexation decided on long before and so eagerly awaited.   The Emperor (November 1897) applied directly to the Czar, and, reminding him of their recent conversation and the latter's promise, demanded permission to land marines at Kiao-Chau from German warships, in order that from thence he might obtain satisfaction for the outrage.

The Czar was embarrassed.   His answer to the request was neither assent nor refusal, but was to the effect that " he believed that he had some years before lost his right to the seaport in question."   Muravieff, the Russian Foreign Minister, was, however, of a different opinion, and ordered the Russian fleet to follow the German ships and lie at anchor in the bay, as Russia had a prior claim there.   Moreover, he aimed at Russian intervention to induce China to offer Germany suitable amends without delay, and thus upset the Kaiser's apple-cart, depriving him of both pretext and opportunity at one stroke.

It was a moment to hold one's breath ; the slightest hesitation spelt failure—perhaps even war with the hosts of Muscovy.

But there was no hesitation about Emperor William : he acted with the speed of a lightning-flash. Not for a moment did the Russian menaces make the slightest impression upon him. He held unswervingly on his course. The German fleet entered the harbour of Kiao-Chau and the German troops were promptly landed. Neither William nor Bülow feared war. Russia could not do without Germany and she would therefore bow to the *fait accompli*.

And so it came to pass. Russia sulked, but yielded. Nor was England by any means delighted at Germany's claim to certain economic advantages in the hinterland after grabbing the port. Both Japan and China were furious at this latest example of European expansion by illegal annexation. In the end, however, Germany succeeded in pacifying them all.

Russia, instead of challenging Germany's acquisition, consoled herself by occupying Port Arthur ; while Great Britain followed suit by taking Wei-hai-wei. Bülow (January 1898) concluded with the Chinese Government a lease of the occupied territory for one hundred years, thus technically acknowledging the Chinese sovereignty over it. He attempted to appease Japan by giving her a written promise to change his policy towards her, and by declaring that he would no longer place obstacles in the way of her expansion in the interior of China as in the past. England he stuffed with the announcement that he intended to make Kiao-Chau a free port, so that British commerce too might use it. Out of regard for England, he said, he had refrained from taking a more southerly port, near to the British sphere of influence. At the same time, with similar plausibility, Bülow proved to the Russians that in establishing himself near the Russian sphere of influence he had decided on a Russophil policy and identified himself with the interests of Russia. He admitted the claims of Russia in Manchuria when, at the request of the Russians (January 1898), he had forbidden German officers to undertake the instruction of the native troops there.

These manœuvres resulted in a splendid success : Bülow had avoided making a single declaration involving positive obligations ; and Germany owed it all to him, to his energy and determination, and to no one else. His Chinese policy was the same as the European at that time—the policy of the " free hand." He balanced himself very skilfully between England on the one side and Russia on the other, without offending or allying himself with either. However, his brilliant achievement had its drawbacks, like all other successes of importance in the sphere of *Weltpolitik*. The German initiative and the land-grabbing resulting therefrom created envy and ill-will all round. It was a particularly disturbing proceeding to hoist the German flag where it might prove necessary to use force to defend it ; where Germany might become involved in a world war without a navy strong enough to protect her new acquisitions.

For a while, however, the situation presented no great dangers, for the simple reason that the after-effects of the German action brought England and Japan into more acute antagonism with Russia than that existing between Germany and those Powers. Witte, the Russian Finance

Minister, best forecast the future when he said that the acquisition of Kiao-Chau by the Germans would compel Russia to commit the blunder of occupying Port Arthur, which would certainly entangle her with Japan. As everyone knows, this prophecy was fulfilled to the very letter.

The occupation first of Kiao-Chau and then of Port Arthur started the avalanche which led to the despoiling of China, as a reaction to the Boxer Rebellion and the Russo-Japanese War; during the world war to the intervention of Japan, the new Japanese conquests in China ; and in our own day to the Washington Conference (1921), at which America endeavoured to undo the effects of this policy of encroachment.

Rooted in these encroachments is the hatred prevailing to-day on the part of Asia against Europe. And it must be confessed that the conduct of Europe at the period referred to was far from praiseworthy, presenting indeed a sorry spectacle rather evocative of shame and regret.

This ignoble scramble for economic advantages and veritable highway robbery makes an ugly chapter in contemporary history. The Powers were as beasts of prey snarling and snapping at each other in their mad greed to devour the most appetising morsels of the carcase of China. An empire boasting one of the most ancient civilisations in the world was, in the name of civilisation, torn to pieces by nations who happened to have superior brute force at their disposal. Their loud protestations of unselfishness, of lofty and righteous motives, were but so much camouflage, behind which was consummated the sacrifice to the golden calf.

A further result of Bülow's policy was the abolition of the Anglo-American condominium over the Samoa

Islands, a disadvantage for Germany dating back to Bismarck's time.   Germany first succeeded with England, offering her an exchange as an inducement to withdraw ; then she shared with America. This by no means important result had, however, to be extorted by dint of much threatening and pressure. Hatzfeld, the Ambassador, conducting the negotiations in London, said that the threats failed of their effect owing to constant repetition.   Finally, this had a bad influence upon the relations between England and Germany.

The most interesting and typical incident in these negotiations was the correspondence of Emperor William with his grandmother, Queen Victoria of England.   In a private letter he roundly abused Salisbury.   " He had better treat the Germans with more respect," he wrote ; " he (Salisbury) simply ignored Germany in the matter of the Samoa Islands."   His grandmother replied that he (William) " seemed to be carried away by his feelings in his outburst against her Prime Minister.   She, on her part, might make many complaints against Bismarck, yet she refrained from doing so."

The old Queen was right.   Such a virulent attack on the Prime Minister of another sovereign—especially of his venerable grandmother—exceeded the bounds of all propriety.   It tended to destroy good relations between Germany and England ; it was without precedent ; it caused the Emperor to be cordially disliked by persons of decisive influence and prepared the way for that Germanophobe temper which subsequently came to prevail in English political life.

But, as I have said, the Samoa affair was settled in spite of all.   When the Boer War broke out, England became less exacting in certain respects, and even if the Samoa Agreement was not of much value to Germany, at any rate it meant political success and eliminated the potentialities of a future quarrel.

Besides this, England and Germany came to an arrangement in regard to the Portuguese colonies in Africa. The essence of this agreement was that the two Powers named should grant a loan to Portugal, as security for which the latter should mortgage her colonies equally between her two creditors. When (June 1898) England seemed likely to move in the matter by herself alone, Bülow thought to ascertain the views of Paris and if possible prevent the English action. As soon, however, as he found that Salisbury was disposed to treat with him, Bülow quickly made up his mind. There was the usual dispute over the details. Salisbury charged Germany with constantly threatening and hardly ever uttering a friendly word for England ; Bülow retorted that though the failure of the present negotiations might not necessarily destroy the friendly political relations between the two countries, he felt that they had reached a critical stage. Their relations would either improve or deteriorate.

The Emperor, too, must appear upon the stage in his customary flamboyant manner. He imparted to the British Ambassador " some unpleasant truths. He did not wish to humiliate England—England had indeed humiliated herself by her policy in China, where Russia had obtained all the best concessions. If England did not show a more considerate attitude towards him, his Ambassador in London would soon have nothing to do there ! He (the Emperor) would be compelled to look towards other Powers." One may well imagine the rage of this self-conceited Imperator Rex had the position been reversed !

In August 1898 the treaty was concluded. Though

it never became anything more than a " scrap of paper," for Portugal backed out of the loan in question, yet it was nevertheless highly important and useful. It did away with the Anglo-German antagonism in Africa, and accordingly altered the German attitude towards the Boer War. From that time on she ceased to support and encourage the Boers, which she must have done if she had had to fear that England would not only abolish and suppress the independence of the Boers but also acquire the Portuguese colonies, Germany getting nothing to counterbalance the enormous accession to power on the part of England. It was only the prospect of Germany getting her share of the Portuguese colonies which put an end to the perilous tendency that, on the occasion of the famous " Krüger telegram," nearly plunged the two Great Powers into war, and which sooner or later would certainly have caused war.

Another diplomatic stroke of Bülow was his acquisition of the Caroline Islands. Before the Spanish-American War the Emperor William wished a vigorous anti-American policy on the part of Europe in general. He would have liked to keep America from declaring war on Spain (September 1898) ; but Bülow did quite right in dissuading him from interference. The Foreign Minister manœuvred to push others into the foreground instead of Germany, lest she might draw down upon her the ill-will of America. In this, however, he failed, the result being the mistrust of Germany by the most powerful republic in the world—a mistrust which was only aggravated by his action during the war in despatching a powerful fleet to the Philippines, thereby arousing the suspicion that Germany, eluding the contending parties, wished to be offered the protectorate over the revolting natives.

The object of Germany's naval expedition was, in fact, to enable the German admiral to study the situation on the spot and to take such action as might be necessary to secure Germany's interests in the eventual division of the territory. Her hunger for colonies might here again have brought her into trouble. Not only America, but also England, France, and Russia might have turned against Germany. Should Germany be too pushful in her claims, an anti-German coalition might be the result. Instead of Europe *versus* America, as the Kaiser had intended, it might have been America *plus* Europe *versus* Germany! A truly pitiable plight for the Fatherland.

The Emperor considered that the Philippines group of islands ought not to be ceded to any other Power—at any rate not without Germany obtaining a suitable *quid pro quo*. This agreed with the views of the new régime, which was anxious to seize every single opportunity of getting an island or a port or a strip of territory, however small, anywhere; and which held that whenever any other Power expanded in the least, Germany had a right to compensation. German policy at this time was completely pervaded with the idea of colonial imperialism: the Empire was ready to draw the sword in the cause of the balance of world-power, finally breaking away from the Bismarckian traditions, according to which German blood should be shed only in defence of hearth and home—that is to say, for continental safety.

With regard to the islands coveted by Germany, the first stage of her policy was to temporise, to postpone the decision until the German navy had become stronger; till then the Germans would prefer the islands neutralised. This also, however, was not without its dangers. It disposed England and America alike to be antagonistic to Germany. England, influenced by the rejection of

Chamberlain's offers by Berlin, desired to secure herself against the potential dangers from that quarter and, by intimacy with America, even to compel Germany to make overtures to England.

In order to counteract this tendency, Bülow suggested to America that the friendship of Germany would be much more valuable for her than that of England ; as the pretensions of the former would always be more modest, having to keep her forces on the Continent. If Washington should conclude an alliance with London, the European Continent would be obliged to combine against it, immense activity in enlarging and reinforcing the respective navies would result, and thus America would be involved in international strife. On the other hand, by satisfying the reasonable claims of Germany, German neutrality would render any European action against America *a priori* impossible, thereby enabling America to remain in her hitherto comfortable situation. The neutrality of Germany would check Anglo-Russian and Anglo-French rivalry and thereby make for the peace of the world.

But all Bülow's arguments fell flat before the not easily explicable presence of the German fleet in the vicinity of America's military and naval operations. The admirals of the two fleets came to high words, and it was by sheer luck only that their verbal battle was not followed by the *ultima ratio*.

In the end all the German combinations were broken up by America claiming the centre group of islands and, moreover, getting them from defeated Spain by virtue of the peace treaty. Germany now applied to Spain with a proposal regarding the Carolines (February 1898), and finally succeeded in acquiring the islands by purchase.

However, among all these colonising endeavours and

efforts at expansion, the most significant as regarded the future was the Kaiser's inauguration of a vigorous policy in the Near East, i.e. in Turkey-in-Asia. The *Drang nach Osten* began. The sentimental, lively spirit of the Emperor was smitten with the glamour of the Orient. Who that loved the beautiful, that was interested in human history, could resist the lure? Who could be deaf to the appeal of the marvellous, gorgeous East, with its splendour, its picturesque population, its slender minarets and crescent-crowned mosques? Who could fail to be captivated by the cradle of religion—as well as the primeval home of every form of superstition—the resplendent, the incomputably ancient yet withal ever-youthful and unsophisticated world of the *Arabian Nights*? The great Napoleon saw in Europe nothing but a molehill; in the home of Alexander and Mahomet he saw a land of limitless possibilities. How could William II remain unmoved and cold at the prospect of impressing his name upon the land associated with such paladins as the immortal conqueror of Persia and the Indies, the illustrious prophet of Mecca, and, in more modern days, with the soldier-genius Napoleon I?

Apart from such idealistic motives, the Emperor was also attracted to the Ottoman Empire by its immense economic and military advantages. He perceived that enormous profits would accrue to the man who could put this naturally wealthy country on its feet—profits not only for himself but for the whole world; to the man who could win the good-will of the Mussulmans; to the man able to reorganise the military forces of the empire of the Padishah! Why should this rôle not be played by the Germans, and the profits reaped by them? Why should not the Germans, whom fate had barred from valuable colonies, enjoy these advantages? Who had the necessary organising ability like the honest, efficient, reliable Germans, his own people ?

William proceeded (1898) to put his new idea into practice with his usual self-assertiveness. He made a tour of Constantinople and Palestine ; visited Jerusalem ; bumptiously declared in Damascus that " three hundred millions of Mohammedans could count on his friendship." It was certainly a far-reaching announcement, of interest to other Powers, in view of the fact that the three hundred million followers of Islam are scattered over, not only Turkey, but Asia, India, Africa, Egypt, and under British, French, and Russian rule. What would be the consequence if they all decided to pin their faith to the German Kaiser, expecting his support in their various, often conflicting, troubles ?

The Emperor promoted the Sultan (of whom he had not long before expressed his abhorrence) to the rank of his friend. The good-will he had up to this time manifested towards Abdul Hamid, in spite of the latter's cruel persecution of his non-Moslem subjects, became general, and Germany appeared as the champion of the *status quo* in the Near East.

William's pilgrimage to the burial-place of the Saviour was not merely an act of piety or even of policy—it was also a good business stroke : it won over the Turks to the idea that they could safely accept the aid of Germany since she had no interest in the dismemberment of their country. It made Germany popular in the East, obtained her a front seat, as it were, procured her a number of valuable concessions from the Porte—particularly the concession for the Berlin-to-Bagdad railway line, destined to be one of the greatest traffic enterprises in the world.

Germany's plans in Asia Minor were lofty, justifiable,

and no more aggressive than Germany's original scheme of expansion, though the political consequences might be far-reaching and dangerous, especially if unaccompanied by a foreign policy calculated to reassure the world as to Germany's real intentions.

Foreseeing this, the Emperor attempted to win the Czar for his Oriental policy. As we have seen, Russia at this time was not at all willing to bring the Near East Question to a head. She was on bad terms with England and might perhaps live to see that her best card to play against England would be the sympathy of the Mohammedan world. England by her new policy had lost the authority she previously had at the Sublime Porte. The Czar could now exploit this situation and open up new opportunities for himself by co-operation with the German Emperor.

From Constantinople William wrote to the Czar a letter containing a glowing description of the advantages to be derived from Turkish friendship. If, said the Emperor, the Czar should allow England to follow in the Cretan Question the same policy as before, the Sultan would be assassinated and his blood would be on the Czar's head. If, however, the Czar would defend the Turks, the Moslems would prove incredibly useful to him, especially in the event of a quarrel with England.

Bülow supported his master by announcing in St. Petersburg his intention to continue the old Russophil Oriental policy in the question of the Straits and would throw no obstacles in the way of the Czar.

But those efforts were doomed to failure. They could hardly have succeeded. St. Petersburg could not help feeling that, as Germany intended to develop the Turkish resources by persistent labour, all her promises were but windy words. For even though Germany herself might not stand in the way of Russia's progress, she was working to put the Turks in a position to do so. The German Emperor (December 1899) wrote : " We want to put the brave Turk in a position to defend himself in the future." How could St. Petersburg misunderstand such a clear statement ? Would not the Czar's Government realise that an extensive use of European capital for the enhancement of the economic and military situation of Turkey would cause all Europe to be interested in the maintenance of the integrity of the Turkish Empire ?

Moreover, Russia was opposed to Germany's economic schemes for the simple reason that she had no share in them. She had no capital to spare for the purpose of putting foreign nations on the road to prosperity ; and thus she had to be a passive spectator of others getting a firm footing where she had hoped sooner or later to be master. Russian friendship for the Turks had been temporary only, depending on certain circumstances. Though at one time she would not have the Sultan's throne upset, she could not stomach the idea of his becoming more powerful. She desired to remain in a position to subject the Balkans and Asia Minor to her domination when the questions of the Far East had ceased to interest her. She had never relinquished this ambition, and for that very reason she viewed with anxiety and dissatisfaction the movement to restore and reinvigorate " the Sick Man " and make him a power to be reckoned with between Russia and the Mediterranean.

I have previously shown that under the influence of these considerations Muravieff wanted to come to an understanding with Bülow, that the latter was averse thereto, and that consequently Russia viewed with antipathy the Oriental plans of the German Emperor. Germany might more easily have won England, for the

23

latter could have shared the profits, apart from which consideration it would have been useful for England to be on good terms with the Sultan, who was not only the head of the Ottoman Empire but also the supreme Caliph of the Moslem world. It is true that the friendly feelings of England for Turkey had cooled down, and that at one time Salisbury had even thought seriously of dismembering Turkey ; but in those circles where more attention was devoted to foreign politics the old traditions were still in vogue, and those of the Turkophil Beaconsfield might easily, with the assistance of Germany, have been revived.

Let us bear in mind that the Turkophobe policy prevailed in London only when a Turkophil one seemed dangerous, because England would have found no support sufficiently strong if it had caused complications. This would not be so if Germany undertook the task of reconstructing Turkey and were prepared to co-operate with England.

When, in spite of all this, Germany sought the support of Russia, and not that of England, she ran the risk of turning both Powers against her, and of the *Drang nach Osten* creating an agreement between England and Russia, notwithstanding it ought to have promoted friendship between England and Germany, and prevented *rapprochement* between St. Petersburg and London.

We have reviewed the colonial acquisitions and successes of the first years of Bülow's régime. Very valuable as they all undoubtedly were, yet I think they were not worth losing British friendship for. They failed to increase the power and prestige of Germany to such a degree as an alliance with Great Britain would have done ; and it is even conceivable that if Germany had only concluded an alliance with Britannia she might have acquired more or bigger colonies by that means. I think Bülow could have made a better use of his first auspicious years if, instead of devoting his energies to acquiring colonies and overseas possessions, he had striven with similar zeal to come to an agreement with London.

To be precise, however, Bülow's chief activities were not directed to colonising, but to navy-building. He did not shut his eyes to the important fact that until Germany had a first-class fleet, it was foolish to think of playing the rôle of a World-Power. The indispensable condition of gaining—and keeping—colonies was a powerful navy. Without that, every new colony acquired would be simply another Achilles' heel, another vulnerable part of the German policy, which could scarcely be healed by the most consummate skill and diplomacy, obsequiousness, bluff, and—finally—good luck to turn the scales in her favour. Until this *sine qua non* were a concrete fact, it was absolutely futile to contemplate a colonial empire ; for such would only involve the Fatherland in a constant struggle for which she was so inadequately equipped—a veritable unarmed gladiator in the arena.

With this truth staring him in the face, William had some time before (1897) said that it would be a stupid blunder to acquire overseas possessions without a fleet to protect them. Such a proceeding would only make Germany dependent upon England and engage her in a life-and-death struggle with British industries. The German press, said the anxious Emperor, was constantly boasting of German achievements without reflecting that their mercantile marine, growing day by day, was utterly defenceless. Against one hundred and thirty British warships Germany could put *four* ! As soon as ever England realised the superiority of German industry, she would stick at nothing to destroy it unless they created an adequate naval force in the meantime!

The Emperor had not the remotest idea of hostile operations against England ; though he wanted to be able to put up a successful defence (perhaps an alliance with another Power) even against the " Mistress of the Seas " should the occasion unfortunately arise, and to continue his colonising policy in spite of her ill-will.

The long-cherished hope crystallised into the will as soon as the Emperor found a suitable man whom he could entrust with the execution of his plan. About the time that he chose Bülow to carry out his foreign policy, seeing in him a man capable of understanding and making his own the ideas of the Kaiser, Bülow also discovered in Admiral Tirpitz the right man to be his able lieutenant in building the navy.

Tirpitz was an expert in his profession. He was animated with the sacred flame of an enthusiast in all matters pertaining to seamanship. A man of brains, of resource, and of firm convictions, he was able to instil his own faith into the minds of others, and carry the entire nation with him. He could raise to an all-conquering national sentiment the desire of the Kaiser's heart for a mighty navy that should be second to none on the ocean. The German navy would be the source and emblem of German wealth and power, of the security and glory of the Fatherland. Unless the Germans could liberate themselves at sea, they must be for ever under British bondage, and enjoy the fruit of their industrial and commercial labours only so much and so long as proud England chose to allow them. England—mean, avaricious, perfidious—would afford to Germany no more than a bare pittance ; she would exclude Germany from all the blessings of colonial empire so long as she (Germany) was not strong enough to break her chains asunder and stand forth free and unfettered, to guard her birthright!

Thus, to Germany's ultimate undoing, the movement for the navy was inaugurated in an anti-British spirit —not with the object of breaking England, but of being able to do so if necessary. They failed, however, to consider whether England would look calmly on, waiting until their preparations were all complete, though the leading men of England could correctly count on Germany's ambition for overseas empire culminating in conflict. They knew that the Emperor mistrusted England ; and that *Prussianism* was but another name for hereditary rudeness and ruthlessness. Would not England be placed in an impossible situation if ever she were faced by the armed chauvinist Kaiser, hankering after precedence, who might again be overcome by the spirit he manifested on the occasion of the Krüger telegram and more than once since evinced in his impatient sallies and ill-mannered reproaches levelled at English statesmen and diplomats ? Would not England be tempted to act upon William's own suggestion—to take him at his word—as he had once said, before the realisation of his naval programme, that she (England) could with one gesture as it were wipe the German colonies off the map, and with a single grasp strangle the life out of German commerce and industry, and annihilate the German navy which might in time challenge her supremacy on the waves ? And even though England might not contemplate war, would she not make an alliance likely to offset the dangerous preponderance of Germany ? How could Germany expand abroad if the seas were ruled by an apprehensive England ?

Neither Bülow nor Tirpitz feared these dangers; at any rate, they deemed them avoidable by a skilful and proper policy. Under the guidance and with the blessing of William they set about their great task of acquiring colonies, of enriching the Fatherland, developing export, bringing Asia Minor under German influence, and at the same time constructing their proud bulwark—the Imperial German Navy. Their minds entertained no thought of evil; they had no greedy designs on the property of others; they never dreamt of achieving their object by " blood and iron," as Bismarck had done in the foundation of German unity. At this period each of the Powers was following an imperialistic policy and trying to increase its power at sea—why should not Germany do likewise? Why should Germany be the only one to resign the chances that Providence would certainly put in her way if only she had colonies? Why should it be accounted to the Germans as a crime what when practised by others was " a noble work in the cause of humanity and civilisation " ?

Tirpitz accordingly laid himself out to reorganise the German navy. He must have a powerful fighting fleet instead of merely swift cruisers for use in distant waters. He must have a navy that could efficiently play its part in the balance of naval power between the Thames and the Elbe.

The first step in this direction was taken in 1898, and the next step followed hard on its heels in 1900. The second Navy Bill was especially remarkable for the proud aims expressed therein. While it was unnecessary, it stated, to reach the standard of the greatest navy in the world (the British), yet a fleet should be built on the near seas that " the most formidable navy " (namely, the British navy) " could not hope to attack with impunity."

This was a great step forward. It opened out quite a new political prospect. It was an official announcement that Germany intended to become a World-Power, instead of remaining the continental Power she had been hitherto ; that besides being a great military, she would also be a great naval Power. Germany, said Bülow, must occupy such a strong position that she need not have to pocket insults from any quarter—not even from England. The Fatherland ought not to remain so weak as to seem contemptible in the eyes of any Power. In the words of the old Chancellor Hohenlohe : " We must rid ourselves of this bugbear of England and learn to stand on our own feet."

The Boer War, with the keen Anglophobia aroused thereby, was fully exploited at this time by the German Government, who used it as a text for a homily on the beauty of sacrifice in the sacred cause of one's country. The Anglophobia of the Germans, Bülow himself confessed, far exceeded in virulence the antipathy of the English for the Germans.

But was it not to be expected that such hatred would provoke animosity in England and lead in time to a more serious counteraction ?

CHAPTER VI

THE BOER WAR AND THE CHINESE QUESTION

DURING the Boer War the policy of Germany followed the lines indicated. Now also it did not favour an alliance with England, though at the same time it had no thought of exploiting the troubles of the Island Kingdom for the purpose of attacking and breaking her. Its consistent aim was to maintain cordial relations with her while building the navy and extending the colonial empire of the Fatherland. These cordial relations served as a shield while the Anglophobe public opinion in Germany was used as a lever, both promoting the schemes of the Big Navyites.

Their task was not easy, however. Could official cordiality exist side by side with the popular animosity necessary to bring the work of navy-building to a successful conclusion ? When Bülow came to an agreement with England regarding the Portuguese colonies and abandoned his former pro-Boer policy, when (August 1901) he counselled Krüger to submit as he was surrounded and his cause was hopeless, he found himself at issue with German popular sentiment. Bülow swam against the stream ; he tried to influence the national press and save it from committing a similar error to that perpetrated in the Spanish-American War—the mistake of being on the losing side. But all his efforts were weakened by the fact that the Emperor himself was at the bottom of his heart in sympathy with the Boers, as was clearly shown when, e.g., the British protested against German pro-Boerism and the Kaiser warmly retorted : " Thank Heaven the sense of justice of the German people cannot be stifled by an order ! "

The official Anglophil policy also was rendered difficult by the efforts of many to play Germany off against England. At the very inception of the war (October 1899) the Russian Ambassador observed to the Emperor at the theatre, that the time had perhaps arrived to unite against England. William rejoined that "in that case the British navy would make short work of German commerce. He might act differently when his fleet was ready ; now, however, he could only say what his father had once said to the Grand Duke of Hesse, when the latter was on the point of following him into the toilet-room. He slammed the door in his face with the words : ' *Pas encore fertig !* ' " A witty sally, though not quite innocuous, as it clearly revealed the Anglophobe destination of his naval activities, notwithstanding his ostensible Anglophil policy. He was useful for England certainly, but if the British Government came to hear of the incident above recorded their confidence in him would be considerably diminished.

The Czar's Government attempted also to incite Berlin with a report of England's alleged intention to occupy the Portuguese colonies, to which Germany was by treaty entitled, in order to cut off the Boers from the sea, and enquired whether Bülow would not frustrate this. Fortunately Bülow was at that very time in receipt of reassuring information from London ; and so, as a counterstroke, he asked the Russians whether France could not be induced to join them in the protest. He explained that, Germany turning against England without adequate cause would be an exceedingly grave matter, since the former was not strong enough to protect her commerce.

Later (March 1900) the Russian Government addressed to Germany the official enquiry whether the latter would not exert friendly pressure on England in the interests of peace ; to which the Emperor himself replied that he would do so only on condition that France should conclude with him a pact to defend the actual German integrity. Here again, as we see, Russia got the customary retort courteous. This was of great service for England, enabling her to continue the fight to a finish without foreign intervention.

When Muravieff sought to justify his action by stating that, according to his knowledge, the Emperor had declared his intention to intervene, William wrote : " The foul-mouthed rascal ! He lies."

Replying to a request of the German Government, the Russian Foreign Minister said that the idea of a French Government becoming a party to a pact guaranteeing Alsace-Lorraine to the Germans was not for a moment to be entertained. And this was of course the case. The Germans were ever sensitive with regard to *their* honour and should now understand *others* being so.

The Prince of Wales (later King Edward) at the period of these diplomatic passages, spoke in warm terms of his nephew the German Emperor, and stated that it was to him mainly that the credit was due that no intervention had taken place. " *Donnerwetter !* " exclaimed William, always as appreciative of a kind word as he was resentful of an offence, " that is the first time the English Prince has ever done me justice ; and I am much obliged to him ! "

The Prince of Wales, in correspondence, on various occasions emphasised his friendly sentiments. " We all," he wrote, " consider Germany as our best friend so long as William rules there."

How far away was his mind then from the policy of *Einkreisung*—which yet was even near in regard to time !

On the Czar observing to the Dutch Minister that he considered the German Emperor the most fitting personage to lead intervention, William commented : " If that rogue Muravieff wants peace, let him seek it, either alone or with France." On Krüger appealing direct to the Emperor, the latter informed England that he should not interfere unless agreeable to both sides.

At this time the Queen of Holland, actuated by her sympathy for the sufferings of the Boers, also applied to William in their behalf. The Emperor, in an interesting reply, wrote : " If he were to intervene he would be cold-shouldered, as in 1896 after the Krüger telegram, when he had to face the contingency of a war with Great Britain. Injustice had often to be endured, but God would surely sooner or later punish the oppressor, and it was the statesman's duty to be prepared to act, if called upon, as the instrument of Divine Providence to this end. Therefore the German navy was a paramount necessity. If only that were ready, the German and Dutch flags might fly proudly side by side. Till then, however, they must be content to wait and work in silence."

These words furnish a deeper insight into the future than diplomatic notes do as a rule. They show us the Emperor's firm resolve assiduously to avoid any and every difference with England so long as she was so much stronger at sea ; but some day the situation would change —the boot would be on the other leg—and then Germany could follow an independent policy, even though it might lead to war.

But would England wait Germany's convenience ?

Would she not attempt to forestall her either by some powerful defensive alliance or by a preventive attack ?

The favourable mood created by Bülow's unpopular yet loyal attitude was, we regret to say, soon dissipated by the incidents arising from the want of forbearance displayed by the English naval authorities and aggravated by the brusque manners of the Germans. The British had (January 1900) on insufficient ground seized three German merchant-ships, and their release could not be obtained for a considerable time. Germany considered her honour impugned by the affair, and threatened a change of direction, or even a short-time ultimatum. The British Government pointed out that differences occasionally arose with other States too, yet they could always be settled in a courteous manner and without that friction which invariably accompanied dealings with the Germans. The publication by the English Government of the diplomatic notes exchanged in connection with this affair only added fuel to the fire and caused the British people to consider their honour at stake. Thus the final outcome of the German policy with regard to the Boers was not particularly profitable ; though it did the British cause a service, it reached nothing, gained nothing, accomplished nothing ; it failed even to secure the gratitude, confidence, and good-will of the English.

During the course of the long Boer War (October 1899 —May 1902) the Chinese problem once more cropped up, affecting the Powers in their relations to each other. A general systematic movement against the Europeans arose and quickly spread throughout the Celestial Empire ; murder, robbery, and arson became so rife that the outrages could no longer be tolerated. The Legations of the European States were besieged, and the German Minister to Pekin was assassinated. The sanguinary

Boxer Rising was the awful climax to more than a century of wrong, cruelty, and tyranny of Europeans over Asiatics. The bloody protest of the Chinese was not without provocation : they had only too many just causes for complaint against the " foreign devils." In Palmerston's time England—to her eternal shame, as thousands of her best people hold to this day—forced a war upon China for the nefarious purpose of compelling her to take that fatal poison, opium, so largely cultivated in British India, and from which of course such a handsome revenue is derived. The anarchy following the Japanese victory was wantonly exploited by the European Powers to carve up the body of China in their own interests, in the name of the balance of power. The most flagrant example of the doctrine that Might is Right was the Czar's action, who, immediately after pledging himself to defend the integrity of China from the rapacity of Japan, himself invested Port Arthur and grabbed Manchuria ! The Emperor of China esteemed so highly the Czar's autograph, attaching such exalted value to the Autocrat's written word, that he kept the letter constantly before his eyes in his sleeping-apartment instead of depositing it in the State archives according to custom. Alas ! what the simple Manchu had venerated as the most sacred palladium became the proof of the basest perfidy.

The Emperor William waxed wrathful over the Boxer outrages. In the heat of his rage he proposed to have Pekin levelled with the ground. Addressing his departing troops, he advised them to " take no prisoners, but slaughter all who crossed their path." This, however, was only a passing fit of frenzy and not to be taken too seriously. The revolt of the Chinese people imperilled the honour and dignity of Germany, the commerce founded on German prestige, and lastly (though, we trust, not least) the labours of the German missionaries—therefore the Kaiser demanded heavy amends, stern retribution, reprisals. He was inexorable in his resolve to humble and terrify the Chinese, " so that for ages to come no Chinaman should dare to look askance at a German " !

He, however, was bent only on punishing, not dismembering, China. He stood for the *status quo ante* (June 1900). He intended military action to last only until the Chinese had yielded, apologised, and executed condign punishment on the actual criminals. He was not out for material profit or conquest—as said Holstein —but to maintain the honour of the Fatherland.

But that policy presented certain serious drawbacks. Though keenly ambitious to win Russia, he must now oppose her, her views being entirely different, her commercial interests hardly worth mentioning, while she sought to exploit the Boxer Rebellion to acquire Manchuria and Corea and extend her political sway over the whole of China. The Russian Government cared little for the prestige of Germany, or of any other part of Europe, or for the safety of European commercial interests ; they aimed solely at preserving for themselves the possibilities of expansion and the local interests of influence and power Russia possessed as China's neighbour.

The Russians took part in the punitive expedition merely for the sake of appearance ; it was all the same to them whether it succeeded or not. Though the Czar, out of compliment to the Emperor, proposed Count Waldersee as Commander-in-Chief of the international force, Russia's aims were different from those of Germany and consequently lent a different orientation to her policy.

While Waldersee was *en route* to China, the Czar executed a lightning move and occupied Pekin (August 1900), and with that act proposed to terminate the military operations and turn the settlement of affairs over to the diplomats. The cunning scheme of the Autocrat was to save China from the loss and suffering entailed in the international punitive expedition, and to get Manchuria in return for the valuable service thus rendered.

The Emperor William was furious at this Russian trick. The Czar, he said, was " an ignorant person, and the Muscovites were hypocrites and considered none but their greedy selves. They had availed themselves of European intervention to annex Manchuria, and would now fling Europe away like a squeezed lemon ! "

Subsequently, when the Russians again displayed a desire to divide up the Celestial Empire, William exploded with rage and disgust ; " the idea was barbarous, impertinent, unmitigated blackguardism, a monstrous outrage, which only the cunning brain of a Muscovite could conceive ! "

After all these agitations and ebullitions it may well be supposed that, though an agreement was eventually reached with China (January 1901) by which the German objects were accomplished, the friendly relations hitherto existing between the Russians and the Germans were shattered beyond hope of repair.

On the other hand, however, the Chinese affair did just as little to promote amity with England. Generally speaking, the British interests were nearer to those of the Germans. The Prince of Wales (to William's intense delight) strongly advocated the arrest of Li-Hung-Chang (" that dirty dog "—" that arch-rascal ") who had treated with the Russians. But there was no real harmony between Germany and England. Already at the very outset the Emperor took umbrage at the reluctance of the English to accept Waldersee's leadership of the expedition. Berlin feared that England intended to annex the Yang-tse Valley, the richest and most densely populated region in the Flowery Land ; and it was for this very reason that the Germans objected to independent action on the part of Britain, and urged the desirability of a treaty providing for equal rights to all the European Powers. They succeeded in coming to an understanding with England (October 1900) on the basic principle of the " open door " in China.

But, alas ! this agreement abounded with the germs of new dangers. England and Germany each started from a different point of view. Bülow wanted to pin England down to a policy of self-abnegation in China— to abstain from acquiring privileges and making conquests, while he would not be bound to an anti-Russian policy. On the other hand, England wanted to use Germany as a foil to the intrigues of Russia in China. Bülow scored the better at the negotiations. In the first article of the treaty England engaged nowhere to endeavour to obtain a monopoly and to allow no monopolies. Thus Germany obtained all she sought without having to give any undertaking to act counter to the Russian policy in Manchuria. There an exception was made in Russia's favour in restricting the principle of the " open door " to that part of China where England and Germany could exert their influence.

So far, however, as the observance of territorial integrity was concerned, England seemed to achieve more, as the contracting parties set forth the principle of Chinese integrity without exception of any kind in favour of Russia. Nevertheless England failed really to reach her aim in this matter also, the obligation undertaken therein not being enforced by sanctions. The treaty stated no *casus belli*; it merely provided that the parties should direct their respective policies in such wise that the integrity of China might be preserved, and that in the event of a third party violating this principle and acquiring Chinese territory by any means whatever, "both Powers should agree together upon the best course of action to protect their interests." An elastic text, full of loopholes, rendering the principle of compensations just as valid as those of active resistance or intervention. This very vagueness caused the Anglo-German Treaty to be, in the long run, harmful, a fruitful cause of misunderstandings and misconstructions.

The contrary views of London and Berlin came to light when Japan and China complained that the Czar had exerted improper pressure on the latter State in order to compel her to accept an agreement placing Manchuria under Russian suzerainty. England declined to allow this and expected Germany's support therein, in accordance with their agreement. It would seem that the Emperor himself was disposed to accept England's view, but he was restrained by Bülow. William was certainly disappointed with the Czar; though he felt and also said (February 1901) that if the shilly-shallying continued much longer between England and Russia, Germany would fall between two stools with a serious bump. Finally, however, the advice of the Foreign Minister was followed, and Germany went on her vacillating course, manœuvring between the two Powers.

Bülow declared that Germany could not go to war for the sake of Manchuria, and that she must remain neutral in an eventual Russo-Japanese War, whether

24

England supported the Japanese or not. He explained that he thought he could in that way be more useful to England. He wanted to go no further than to let China know that she would do better by not negotiating with any of the Powers individually before coming to terms with them all collectively.

Bülow's policy really strengthened England's case and correspondingly weakened that of Russia against England and Japan, yet failed to satisfy England, who demanded more and expected Germany to render positive assistance in accordance with the treaty provisions. Salisbury regarded the German attitude as a flagrant breach of treaty obligations. And if Bülow was correct in stating that he was not bound to declare war on account of an annexation of Manchuria (for the treaty fixed no such obligation) and also that he had not identified himself with the policy of the " open door " in Manchuria, yet he was nevertheless wrong in his contention that the entire treaty referred only to the territory circumscribed by the Great Chinese Wall. By demanding and carrying the insertion in one section of the treaty of a special saving clause guaranteeing Manchuria against the " open door " policy, he himself recognised that where this limitation was not expressed, the treaty referred to the Chinese Empire as a whole, including Manchuria. And it was certainly not in conformity with the spirit of the treaty that Bülow informed the Russians that he had nothing to do with Manchuria, and would by no means stand in their way there.

This over-smartness did Germany no good, for it created discontent in St. Petersburg and London alike. The Russian Ambassador to Berlin (March 1901) gave expression to his anxiety lest Russia should be seriously offended at Germany's attitude ; while Salisbury and

Bülow interpreted the treaty differently before their respective Parliaments.

England would no longer trust Bülow; his policy was considered hypocritical. He had in fact deceived Salisbury in binding him to the policy that Germany desired to follow in China and giving nothing in return therefor. The Anglo-German friendship was damaged further by the circumstance that, at the conclusion of peace in China, those two Powers took opposing standpoints in certain matters of detail.

Thus Germany ultimately succeeded by the expedition to China in securing her " free hand " policy there, though Bülow had to pay dearly for it. He failed to become really intimate with either of the Powers ; both were dissatisfied, and consequently there was the danger of their turning against him. He had his " free hand " certainly, but the other Powers also had it. In both simultaneously the desire might arise to exploit against Germany the possibilities of their freedom of action in China.

CHAPTER VII

ENGLAND'S LAST OVERTURES TO GERMANY

AT this time the differences between England and Germany might have yet been amicably composed. England had not yet finally turned her back on Germany. No decision had as yet been taken, though it was impending. The relations between the two countries could not remain long as they were ; as Bülow had said, they would have to be " either mended or ended."

England likewise felt this, and wanted the situation cleared up. Her great interests demanded that she should emerge from her splendid isolation and be able to rely on one of the two factions into which Europe was divided. The British were beginning to be alarmed lest their isolation should cease to be " splendid " and become mere ostracism. During the Boer War the British public had had some unpleasant experiences. The position of absolute superiority that England had for so many generations enjoyed on the sea and in colonial questions ; the constant jealousy with which the Island Realm regarded the successes of other nations at sea or oversea ; her continual growth in size, power, and prestige ; her imperialism, which had become so pronounced during the last few decades ; her skilful manœuvring between the two opposing groups of alliances (sometimes with disagreeable results for both), aroused envy and enmity against her everywhere : in the language of the poet, she was verily " the dread and envy of them all." No sooner did trouble overtake her than the curs of ill-will began yelping at her from every side. Europe was practically unanimous for the Boers. Not merely because the heroic struggle of the small farmer-nation to preserve their hard-won liberty struck the chord of universal sympathy—not merely because brute force exercised by others than ourselves can never be justified ; but really because people almost everywhere rejoiced to see that proud England was at last in distress, and they all charitably hoped that she was about to get her deserts. Except the Scandinavian States, the Liberals of Italy and Hungary (in which countries Anglophil sentiments were traditional), all the nations wished the Boers to be victorious. Navy-founding and augmenting having become so general in Europe, it was by no means excluded that some continental Power or Powers, burning with jealousy and hate against England, might seize the occasion to assemble a naval force capable of striking a serious blow at " that God-blessed isle amidst the cerulean sea."

Therefore isolation could not be the last word of English policy. It was tenable only so long as other Powers had no fleets worth boasting of. The time had now come to throw it overboard. As I have already pointed out, English statesmen clearly realised this—especially Chamberlain, who with his broad outlook and common sense seldom failed to hit the nail on the head. Besides him, also Balfour, Lansdowne, Rosebery, Devon-shire, in short nearly all the British leaders, realised it ; and even the aged and weary Salisbury saw that his former political watchword, isolation, had had its day and that England must cast about for friends. Others also, having pondered the gigantic interests of the Empire, saw that the best thing would be the aid of Germany and the Triple Alliance, to both of whom England was indebted for her success in Egypt. There she was constantly opposed by Russia and France, whose malignity could only be outweighed by the benevolence of the Triple Alliance.

The Sudan triumph, which consolidated and confirmed British rule in Egypt, was also contributed to by William II. The campaign was even recommended by the Emperor. Further, it was with German support that the British were enabled to arrest the progress of the French on the Upper Nile. The happy issue of the Fashoda affair was due to the anti-French policy of the Germans. Again, it would have been impossible for England to have concentrated her undisturbed attention on subjecting the Boers had she not come to an agreement with Germany in the matter of the Portuguese colonies, and had William continued his policy in conformity with the Krüger telegram.

The minor clashes of interest between Germany and England in the Samoa Islands were settled in the meantime. In the chief colonial problem of the present and the future, i.e. the Chinese Question, the attitudes of England and Germany were strikingly similar and easiest to bring into line. Both were advocates of the policy of the " open door," and both apprehended the expansion of Russia. In Asia Minor the English and the Germans might easily have understood and complemented each other.

True it is that the commercial and industrial rivalry prevailing between Britain and Germany became far more intense and undoubtedly caused bad blood between the two kindred peoples ; but in the case of thinking nations endowed with the gift of common sense, commercial competition ought never to give rise to political antagonism, to say nothing of causing war ; for a State anxious to develop its trade, a State whose business interests are of decisive importance, cannot afford to contemplate a devastating European war, to suffer the annihilation of one of its best customers. Such a State knows full well that peace is the prime condition of industrial and commercial progress, that the producer abroad is at the same time a consumer, that the material destruction of one State exercises a paralysing effect on the economic life of the world at large.

World-policy, which was of paramount importance for England, the first commercial State, would have been secured by the Triple Alliance better than by an agreement with the Franco-Russian Entente, since the Triple Alliance *plus* England could have preserved the power in the hands of those nations least likely to want war.

It may be said that at that period neither group of States seriously wanted war and that both treaties of alliance were, in essence, of a defensive character. That is true ; but France and Russia would certainly profit more by a victorious war than would their antagonists ; and might indeed have positive war aims—a thing utterly unthinkable in our case, as the maintenance of the *status quo* was most favourable for both England and Germany, the naval *status quo* being based on the superiority of Great Britain and the continental *status quo* on that of Germany, and they meant the maintenance of these in the future too.

These were probably the reasons guiding the English statesmen during the Boer War, inducing them, in spite of numerous petty insults, animosity, and general unfriendly atmosphere, to return to the idea of an Anglo-German *rapprochement*. Unfortunately the English statesmen failed, in my opinion, to choose the proper moment for their overtures. There were no psychological conditions present to render an unreserved and sincere *rapprochement* possible. But their mistake is sufficiently excusable considering their actual situation. The British Government had pressing and highly important interests urging them, by the aid of Germany and Japan, to check the steady advance of the Russians in China ; while 200,000 British soldiers were engaged in the struggle against the heroic Boers. Moreover, England could see the approach of a crisis in Morocco, which she would be best able to exploit with German support. Chamberlain explained his reasons privately to Eckhardtstein, the Anglophil Secretary of the German Embassy. He said that it would be a good thing to conclude an agreement with Germany, and perhaps this could be managed most appropriately by means of a pact regarding Morocco (January 1901). Chamberlain, however, never received any reply to this proposal— though silence was also a reply of a kind. Chamberlain informed Eckhardtstein that if Germany were unwilling to go hand-in-hand with England, he would have no alternative but to enter into negotiations with the Dual Alliance.

The English overtures, however, made no impression upon the German leaders. They were still for gaining time. A few days before Chamberlain took the initiative, Bülow informed the Emperor (10th January 1901) that the paths of England and Russia crossed everywhere, and therefore his best policy was to keep his hands free towards them both, to remain on good terms with each Power. By that means German prestige would be enhanced everywhere. " We must not take the chestnuts out of the fire for England," said he ; and the Emperor cordially assented.

When (January 1901), after Chamberlain's initial

steps, William hastened to England to the bedside of his dying grandmother, the Chancellor wired him advising that he should not throw cold water on the English overtures, but at the same time guard against committing himself. The same old tactics! Always the same astute manœuvring to get the better of the opponent! According to Bülow, England had now become weaker in Africa, Russia was acting perfidiously towards her, America was alienated from her, Japan was an unknown quantity and unreliable, France hated her—the public opinion of the whole world was against her. Ergo, England could not do without Germany. By waiting, Germany would eventually get far more advantageous offers from England. England could not even come to an understanding with the Dual Alliance; that would mean too great sacrifices. And even by dint of sacrifices she would be unable to avoid the conflict, which the concessions would merely postpone and which would be bound to ensue after the concessions had weakened England and rendered her less capable of sustaining a struggle. It would be an excellent stroke of diplomacy, said Bülow, if the Kaiser succeeded in keeping alive in the English (without undertaking any obligations) the fond belief that Germany would in the end come to an agreement with them.

Holstein likewise had no faith in the English. His most prominent characteristic, his utter mistrust of everything and everybody, once more exercised a decisive effect on his judgment. He stigmatised Chamberlain's declaration, that "if unable to come to terms with Germany, he must apply to Paris and St. Petersburg," as downright humbug. In his (Holstein's) opinion, such a thing was impossible: it would only lead to the humiliation and weakening of England.

Germany must bide her time till England saw that she had no choice in the matter. Time was on the side of Germany. An alliance with England would involve the risk of war with Russia and therefore could not be entertained until England had become more modest and compliant. Germany could not be sure of the good faith of London unless she came forward with distinct advantageous offers. Bülow, on his part, said that England must pay for her alliance not only in Asia but also in Africa.

The Emperor, during his sojourn in England, made and received the best impressions. Unfortunately, however, ever loyal to the policy of his Government, he declined to give the decisive turn to the negotiations. To Lord Lansdowne—an upright, strictly honourable nobleman of the old school, a statesman of sound common sense, in whom even the most suspicious of German diplomats were constrained to trust, in spite of their prejudices—the Emperor attempted to demonstrate the impossibility of England winning Russia, however tempting the bait offered to her ; the greater the concessions on the part of England, the more impertinent would be the insatiable demands of the Muscovite. Neither, argued William, could England hope to go with America. The Transatlantic Republic was forging ahead with youthful vigour and would not hamper her course for the sake of England. If England, in spite of warning, were to become so unequally yoked together with Russia and America, those two Powers would sooner or later bring her to ruin. In China, Russia and America had already come to an understanding : their united aim was to oust Europe from Asia. There was only one remedy against that danger : Europe must rally and close her ranks, presenting a solid phalanx to the common foe ; and this advice applied equally to England and France as to the rest of the continental States. The Emperor was convinced that this recommendaton was practicable. The French were beginning to see that they gained nothing by their Russian alliance. The only use of the alliance was to enable Russia to exploit France. England under King Edward, whose tact had so magnificently stood the test, could do great things.

These more or less wise observations led to nothing tangible. They were not the kind of thing to impress English common sense, accustomed to definite and practical propositions. The allusion to the French Question and the contingency of reconciliation between France and Germany was scarcely likely to convey the impression that the Emperor was in any hurry to conclude an agreement with the British Empire. And simple consternation was created by his announcement that the balance of power in Europe, for which the English had striven so much, was now at an end. Henceforth the former balance of power would be represented by his sword ! A modern amplification of Louis XIV's boast— " *L'état c'est moi !* "

This futile conversation was thoroughly consistent with the aim of the German policy, which was shy of new obligations and was of opinion that any partial agreement would result in Russia and France provoking a fight in which England would not be bound to assist. The German Government were quite willing to negotiate with London, but carefully avoided all definite conclusions. Hatzfeld and Eckhardtstein were enjoined to beware of proposing conversations with that object. " The long and the short of it is," said Holstein, " that, although the time for an agreement may come, it has certainly not yet arrived."

In spite of this frigid, negative attitude, Lansdowne in March resumed the conversations. The Foreign Minister now enquired of Eckhardtstein whether a common Anglo-German action against France would not be possible in the event of the latter attacking Japan in a war with Russia. The answer was that Germany could not think of such a one-sided obligation. On this the Foreign Minister suggested a defensive alliance of a general character. But of this, too, Bülow had nothing but doubts. He was constantly manufacturing difficulties. Against whom should the proposed defensive alliance be directed ? he asked. Germany was not in danger. Why should she undertake to defend, say, the British colonies ? The public opinion of Germany would never be reconciled to such an idea.

The Chancellor's instructions, however, did not seem quite such flat rejection as his peculiar convictions might have warranted. He emphasised that, though one should not show any eagerness to seize the offer, yet one should also not refuse it. He stipulated that, seeing the effect such a treaty would have on the Triple Alliance, Goluchowsky's approval should be obtained before concluding it. If Lansdowne put forward more detailed plans and made his offer more definitive, he should be referred to Vienna. He launched the query whether it would not be right to include Japan, Turkey, and Rumania as well. Bülow's scheme was for an alliance between England and the Triple Alliance solely directed against a coalition of two adversaries only, the aim of which would be, not the defence of the territorial integrity of the contracting parties, but merely the maintenance of the balance of power disturbed by the action of a coalition. Such a treaty, he contended, ought to be laid before Parliament. But this caution was not sufficient for Berlin. The Chancellor instructed Eckhardt-stein not to renew the negotiations on his own responsibility, but to wait for England to take further steps. For a time, however, the " further steps " were awaited in vain. The English diplomat's experiences regarding his proposals were not agreeable, and so for the present he felt in no mood to resume the negotiations.

Besides this, there was also a difference between the British and German Governments with regard to the conditions of peace with China. This too tended to put the question of the alliance into the shade for the time being.

Meanwhile Cambon, the experienced and able French Ambassador in London, started a vigorous counter-move. The situation, as he described it, was that William had definitely cast in his lot with the Russians, to counter-balance which the Emperor reprimanded the British Ambassador to Berlin and (according to Eckhardtstein's *Memoirs*) wrote a splenetic epistle to King Edward. These outbursts, however, did not avail much.

When the negotiations began again in London in May the English Government had no sanguine hopes of success. Hatzfeld reported that Salisbury seemed willing to conclude an agreement with Germany, but boggled at the inclusion of the whole Triple Alliance. It increased too much the number of potential *casus belli* and created many difficulties. The English Premier asked, as an example of the problems raised, what would have to be done if, on the death of Francis Joseph, Austria were to fall asunder ; if Russia and Turkey were simultaneously to attack the Dual Monarchy ; if Italy and Spain were to combine against France ? It would be far easier to get the English Parliament to accept an alliance with their Germanic sister than with Austria-Hungary, owing to the latter's enormous Slav population.

Unfortunately, Bülow made it a *conditio sine qua non* that England should enter into an agreement with Austria-Hungary and the whole Triple Alliance. In the Dual Monarchy at this time the Slav influence predominated. There was considerable misunderstanding and friction between the Prussian and Austrian Governments on the question of citizenship and cases of expulsion, which might have led to a rupture of the Alliance. If Berlin in such a situation were to conclude a new alliance without Vienna, the effect would be bad. If the Triple Alliance were to find itself outside the new German-English Agreement, its enemies might elude the protective intentions of the new alliance by attacking Austria-Hungary or Italy instead of Germany, and in that case Germany would be compelled to intervene, but not so England, who might declare Germany's compulsory intervention to be an attack. On the other hand, Germany would always be obliged to stand up for England and her colonies. Such an alliance would be worse than useless—no alliance at all.

These, however, were mere sophisms and pretexts. The German Government could hardly be deterred by anxiety lest an astute enemy might circumvent the provisions of the alliance and stultify the whole work ; for in every international treaty it is not the letter but the spirit which is of real importance. If an alliance conforms to the traditions and interests of the parties, it usually creates a much deeper community of interests than the mere words of the treaty warrant. There was but little ground for fear that any Power would attack a member or members of the Triple Alliance allied with England simply because England in that case would not be bound by the letter of the treaty to participate therein. Once England had undertaken to share our fate, our defeat would mean danger for England also, and her own interests would prompt her in the hour of peril to stand by her friends.

Less ground still for anxiety lest an agreement with Germany and England might jeopardise the intimacy of the Austro-Hungarian-German Alliance. The contrary was the case : nothing but this alliance could strengthen it, for Austria-Hungary had always desired good relations with England. Nothing would have given Goluchowsky greater pleasure than the news that London and Berlin had at last come to terms and become fellow-members of one and the same group of States. It was perfectly right and proper that the Germans should endeavour to include us in the agreement ; but it was a serious blunder and oversight to imperil the alliance just because England was at first averse to coming to an agreement with the Triple Alliance as a whole.

Bülow would never have been deterred by such doubts and fears if he had considered urgent and really desired the alliance with England. His conduct is explicable only on the assumption that he considered the policy of the " free hand " at that time more advantageous and thought he could later conclude the alliance on more favourable terms. For shortly afterwards (1904) the Emperor concluded at Björkö a defensive pact with the Czar without informing Austria-Hungary of the transaction, though it might well have come into collision with the aspirations and interests of the Dual Monarchy far more than the Anglo-German alliance could possibly have done.

If Bülow had asked Goluchowsky which he would prefer: an agreement with England without him (Goluchowsky), or the dropping of the whole idea of the alliance, Goluchowsky would doubtless have chosen the former alternative and made a point of Germany at least clearing up the situation with regard to England.

The German Government, however, was by no means disposed to discuss the matter further without Austria-Hungary. It would not even consent to Hatzfeld's suggestion that, if Salisbury wished to go into details, they should open negotiations and show Vienna the finished draft of the Anglo-German agreement.

Bülow insisted on Goluchowsky leading the negotiations and Vienna being the scene of the affair—a solution not consistent with the relations of power, or with German traditions and customs, confirming the impression that Berlin set exceedingly little value on an agreement with England.

Moreover, the German Foreign Office was morbidly afraid of indiscretions. In vain Hatzfeld insisted that Lansdowne was absolutely trustworthy ; Berlin had a nervous dread of treachery. They would not countenance the Ambassador giving a written document with regard to the negotiations. Before signing the treaty of 1879 Bismarck explained his attitude to Andrássy, and when he later wanted to come to an agreement with England, he expounded his entire policy to Salisbury without the least reserve. He was not afraid of treachery, and his confidence was rewarded by the desired agreement in both cases being reached. The mistrust now manifested by Berlin simply showed their lack of serious intention to conclude the treaty ; they could hardly want a treaty with a State with which they had not sufficient courage to negotiate, afraid lest the discussions should leak out ! Count Metternich (acting for Hatzfeld during his sickness and succeeding him on his decease) wrote in vain for an alliance with England ; in vain he pointed out that they could not win Russia ; that collision between the Germanic and Slavic races was sooner or later inevitable ; that it was not for them a matter of choice between England and Russia—they must either make the alliance with England or give up altogether the idea of any new alliance. In vain he explained that if Germany failed to bind England now the latter would turn to Russia and France, in which case the situation of the Triple Alliance would become most precarious, since, with England as an enemy, it was obvious they could not rely on Italy. In vain Metternich insisted that the proposed alliance with England would not increase the danger of war, since it was of a defensive character and so powerful that no one would have the temerity to challenge it. In vain he attempted to fascinate them with the brightest hopes of Germany, by virtue of the alliance, becoming a powerful factor in China, that most populous of world-markets.

Against Metternich's arguments Holstein committed his views to paper : a simple circumlocution which might well have been whittled down to the two words, " perfidious Albion." Now, as so often in the past, Holstein suspected Salisbury of wanting a continental war in order himself to play the rôle of arbitrator between the two belligerents. Again he was afraid lest Germany should be placed in the invidious position of having to get the chestnuts out of the fire for England. This hot-chestnut business became a veritable nightmare with Holstein. He warned his Fatherland persistently, in season and out of season, of the danger of burning their fingers, until by and by someone came along, valiantly seized the chestnuts, finding the embers not so hot after all, and ate the fruits with considerable relish.

This timid diplomat, afraid even of his own shadow, constantly argued that any agreement without the Triple

25

Alliance would exasperate the foes of Germany and cause them to attack, while it would enable England to escape her obligations and remain outside the arena.

With such appalling lack of confidence it was clearly impossible to think of concluding an agreement. The failure of the negotiations, however, is best explained by the important statement that if it were now impossible to conclude an alliance, Germany need not apply elsewhere, for the logic of history would sooner or later certainly bring England and Germany together. Unfortunately this prophecy was falsified by events. The very opposite came to pass.

The conversation between Emperor William and King Edward at Homburg failed to promote the success of the negotiations. The Emperor did little else than lecture his uncle and indulge in unpleasantnesses generally. He bluntly suggested to the King of England that the Japanese were dissatisfied with the British because the latter had promised to finance the cost of Japan arming against Russia and then left her in the lurch to foot the bill herself. " You must not be surprised," said the garrulous and tactless nephew, " if you continue to be regarded as ' perfidious Albion ' as in the past." The bonds of kinship and knowledge of the Emperor's impulsive nature doubtless tempered the ill-effect of this and similar outbursts, yet such an affront could not fail to do harm, shattering King Edward's confidence in the German Emperor, who had dared to tell him to his face that England was perfidious ! The sole mention of the projected alliance was when William told Edward that he would have to make his choice—either America or Europe—and that he (William) was prepared to conclude nothing but an alliance of full legal force and extending to the entire Triple Alliance.

After this meeting it would seem that the idea of an alliance was dropped. Metternich reported that it was no longer spoken of in London, and that he hoped Germany would succeed with her overtures to Russia ; for the colder her relations with England, the more essential it was to be on good terms with the Czar. The Germans could not continue for long—observed the Ambassador, with good reason—to oscillate between the two Powers.

In his reply to Metternich (September) Bülow no longer talked of an alliance with England, but of good relations only, and merely directed him to try to clear certain claims on the part of German subjects originating from the Boer War. And Holstein, speaking with Chirol, correspondent of *The Times*, said that it was impossible to come to an agreement with Salisbury, that Germany needed no support at that time, because the Russo-French alliance—which might signify danger—had become weaker, and the Czar was on excellent terms with the Emperor. Certainly the ways of England and Germany would converge in the future. All the same he, in the meantime, abused the country of the journalist.

Both Bülow and Holstein regarded a German-English alliance as the music of the future. It must not be hurried ; they could afford to wait. In due time it would come about spontaneously, from their interests. For the time being it was sufficient to avoid depressing and alienating England, or arousing her enmity. For the present it was more important to be on good terms with Russia too, and to prepare a *rapprochement* with France, than to come to an agreement with England.

Thus the conclusion of the alliance was frustrated by Germany regarding it as inopportune, her unwillingness to undertake any obligations, her obliviousness of danger from the East, and consequently by her considering the policy of the " free hand " as the best.

The King of England naturally perceived this and put an end to the negotiations. The British Ambassador informed the German Foreign Office of a letter from his sovereign (December 1901) in which his Majesty had written that he had intended friendly relations with Germany, but his Parliament would scarcely accept a formal alliance.

At the end of the year the German Emperor despatched an interesting telegram to his uncle Edward, in which he stated that his late grandmother Queen Victoria had bequeathed to him (King Edward) a splendid heritage. " Since the great days of ancient Rome there has been no such proud world-empire as that to which you have succeeded. God grant that you may ever be found on the side of peace and righteousness. Our two peoples, like ourselves their rulers, are one in blood and faith. By the Divine ordinance they are appointed to make the world happier and better. To lead the work of civilisation is the high privilege of the Germanic race —which alone is qualified for the task imposed upon it by God's will. Let them therefore stand firmly by each other and march side by side in the van of progress ! The press is evil, but I am the master of the German policy ; my nation must follow me, consequently England ought not to compel me to a policy which might prove disastrous for both peoples."

Such chauvinism and self-conceit cloaking a threat were really ill-calculated to captivate the English and win the favour of their King.

The Berliners, however, were pleased. They thought they had attained their object. They had left the door open for the future, and for the present they could move freely.   Good relations between England and Germany had been preserved without new obligations, burdens, *casus belli*, or dangers of war.

But this was only an outward and deceptive appearance.   The real result was something quite different. Chamberlain, the most influential and resolute of English statesmen, who had insisted so much on the alliance, in the course of the negotiations entirely changed his direction —a circumstance which was in itself a disquieting symptom.   It became deeply rooted in the minds of the English leaders that to come to an agreement with Germany was impossible and that the only way out of the isolation was through France.   Without an agreement with France the situation would be dangerous.   Constant differences with France and Russia, their dependence on the Germans, who really bore them no good-will, the suspicion and anxiety that the Germans were arming against them with the object of destroying their naval supremacy sooner or later, all tended to create an intolerable situation.   Relations with Paris must be cleared up, if necessary even at the price of sacrifices.   England and Germany had started to move in opposite directions. The probability was great that every day would see them further apart.   For the first step is always the most difficult ; the others follow naturally and spontaneously, as consequences of the first.

Ere long a violent controversy was raging between London and Berlin.   The German press roundly denounced the conduct of the British soldiers towards the Boers.   Chamberlain answered the accusations in a caustic speech in which he stated that different Continental armies had behaved far more cruelly and improperly than the British in South Africa, and he quoted German atrocities in the war of 1870–1.

Bülow riposted with exceeding hauteur in the Reichstag, though the ministers of the other Governments observed silence, not deeming it worth while to make a fuss about Chamberlain's wrathful explosion, which to them was quite comprehensible.

With a view to calming down the excited Anglophobe public opinion of Germany, the Chancellor declared (October) that whoever had the temerity to defame the German army, to call in question the morality and heroism displayed by the soldiers of the Fatherland in the stupendous struggle for German unity, would find that he was trying to bite through solid rock.

This acrimonious debate added fuel to the fire, exacerbating mutual antipathy on both sides. Count Mensdorff, a member of the Austro-Hungarian Embassy in London, who knew England thoroughly and was a warm Anglophil—being a relation of the English Royal Family—called the attention of Prince Lichnowsky, who subsequently became his colleague in London, to the fact that the conviction was spreading in England that it would be easier to conclude an alliance with Russia than with Germany ; and although, fortunately, Russia would not just then hear of England, a *rapprochement* between these two Powers in time was conceivable. Chamberlain freely confessed that he had been wrong in his previous policy—that the German hatred of England was invincible and was beginning to be reciprocated. The slightest untoward incident might lead to war. On the occasion of William's next visit to England (about the end of 1902) he himself perceived the change. He plainly saw that Chamberlain was offended and sore at being, as he considered, deceived. William further realised that such a disposition meant danger. He therefore issued a strict and definite order that everything tending to foster further controversy with England must be strenuously avoided. " Let the press be silent," he wrote, " or they may imperil the safety of the Fatherland ; as Germany has only eight ironclads against England's thirty-five." The position in 1905 was forty-five German ironclads against 196 English. I am convinced that on the whole William was at this time more willing to conclude an alliance with England than was his Government, and that Bülow intentionally neglected to inform him of all the particulars of the negotiations lest a *fait accompli* should be created by the intervention of the supreme authority. Eckhardtstein in his *Memoirs* wrote that he had subsequently called the Kaiser's attention to what had taken place, which caused the latter to be very angry with Bülow and to administer to him a scathing rebuke. Nothing but the consummate skill of Bülow could have succeeded in reassuring the Emperor.

The relations between England and Germany were rendered even more strained by the visit of the defeated Boer generals to Berlin and the erroneous idea prevalent in England that the Emperor would receive them. The tension was only allayed by the Kaiser announcing that he could not receive them except as British subjects and presented by the British Ambassador. No audience was sought by the generals, and none took place. Nevertheless, the affair left an unpleasant flavour behind it and had a sinister influence upon public opinion in London.

The Times lent its great journalistic prestige to a regular anti-German agitation, which was applauded by the majority of the British public. Asquith, a leader of the Liberal Opposition, who subsequently became Premier, admitted in a conversation with the German Ambassador (March 1903) that the attitude of *The Times* spelt international trouble and created an atmosphere liable to lead to exceedingly grave consequences in the future. Cromer, for another, pointed out that the English were beginning to prepare for hostilities with Germany. Not the Unionists only, but even the Liberal Opposition leaders—Rosebery, Asquith, and Grey—began to favour the idea of overtures to the Dual Alliance.

When two nations mistrust and fear each other, when the press stirs up the cauldron of suspicion and fans the flame of hatred, even events which otherwise might have made for close co-operation may have the effect of separating them. This was the experience of England and Germany in the Venezuela Question. This small South American State having in one of its frequently recurring civil wars subjected certain British and German citizens to loss and damage, the British and German Governments decided to proceed jointly in the claim for compensation. The German action was quite in the spirit of loyalty. They never dreamt of conquests ; but under the influence of their augmented self-consciousness they, like the English, regarded it as their simple duty to protect the interests of their fellow-countrymen with the utmost firmness. They consequently concerted together and issued a joint declaration of war against Venezuela (November 1902). But British public opinion being completely saturated with Germanophobe sentiments, the English were roused to indignation at the co-operation of their Government with the Germans. And the British dissatisfaction was aggravated as soon as the United States began to get uneasy about the matter. This naturally revived unpleasant memories among the Germans and destroyed the last remnants of their sympathy for the English.

These are sad recollections. We witnessed the sowing

of the seed of the calamitous harvest we are reaping to-day. Had England and Germany only understood each other better, there would have been no World War, and certainly not a war resulting, as this last has resulted, in overthrowing the balance of all Europe and bringing us to the brink of ruin. A sorry retrospect ; and an equally deplorable outlook : the causeless estrangement of two great nations, merely through errors and tactlessness.

CHAPTER VIII

THE ANGLO-FRENCH ENTENTE

THIS recrudescence of Anglo-German relations induced England to prosecute a more vigorous diplomatic activity. She had wanted to get nearer to Germany in order to avoid isolation ; but when it became patent to her that there was nothing doing in that quarter, she began to cast about for friends elsewhere. As soon as she was convinced of the impossibility of coming to an agreement with Germany, her first efforts were directed to counteracting the advance of the Russians in China with the aid of Japan. England's chief use for Germany was to check the Muscovites in the Celestial Empire ; but now that the impracticability of the idea was realised, she applied to Nippon. Eckhardtstein, the German diplomat, was the first to propose to the English statesmen the idea of enlisting Japan in the Far Eastern Question as well as Germany. Now, however, Downing Street entered into relations with Japan alone, without Germany.

This step was facilitated by the failure of the Japanese minister Ito to clear up matters satisfactorily with St. Petersburg. After her futile proposals to the Russians for a division, offering Manchuria against Corea, Japan evinced a disposition to align herself with England (January 1902). The ostensible object of the Anglo-Japanese Treaty that resulted was the maintenance of the integrity of Corea and China. Its real purport, however, was that the two contracting Powers should thenceforth be united in defence of their mutual interests, and that should either party become involved in war with any other two Powers on account of China, the other should lend her aid. In case of a collision with one Power only, the other party might remain neutral.

This alliance was a bold but eminently useful step. When a considerable part of the British forces were still engaged against the Boers in South Africa, England enlisted in defence of her Asiatic interests that Power which was paramount there.

Having regard to the course of subsequent events it is even more important to note that England made definitive overtures to France. At the time of Fashoda and the Dreyfus affair the cold-blooded English had severely censured the hysterical outbursts of their neighbours—outbursts which I can now only regard as symptomatic of a lack of conscience and of that cynicism peculiar to counter-revolutionary times, but which at that time I considered to be a peculiar characteristic of French chauvinism. Equally marked was the manifestation of French public opinion in favour of the Boers, Krüger's visit to Paris having stirred up once more the smouldering embers of the French hatred of England. Sir Thomas Barclay, the Francophil, who took a prominent part in preparing the Entente Cordiale between the two nations, says in his book on the subject that a proposal to make him a member of a Paris club was withdrawn lest he should be rejected on account of his being an Englishman ; that obscene caricatures of Queen Victoria were published which aroused great indignation in London ; that on an occasion of an Englishman at a French railway-station asking for a first-class ticket he was given a third with the remark that " that was good enough for a *sale Anglais*." On the other hand, no Frenchman could get accommodation in England simply because he was a Frenchman, and some French people appearing at a public meeting of Englishmen to protest in favour of Dreyfus were insulted and thrown out.

These things constituted serious disturbing elements, especially in the case of nations swayed by their public opinion. They tended naturally to cause grave anxiety in England at a time when Germany and Russia were both inimical.

England did not, however, acquiesce in the situation. The English, with their instinct of self-preservation, took the affair in hand, and, as so frequently happened in the past, prepared the action of the Government independently of the official direction by the enthusiastic and resolute efforts of private individuals. One of the most important advantages of England is individual initiative supported by the system of self-government ; that personal activity which neither waits for nor obeys orders, but if necessary acts even in defiance of the Government in what it considers the national interest. On the Continent one often hears the view expressed that the ways of the official foreign policy must not be crossed, and it is akin to high treason for a private person to make propaganda abroad in the cause of any other alliances than those actually existing—not to speak of fraternising with people who in given circumstances are diametrically opposed to our country's policy. Irresponsible individuals must not act so as to weaken the bond of an alliance which in given circumstances means the power of our country. In England we may frequently experience the very opposite of this. Individual action often crosses the official policy, and has not seldom carried public opinion with it and proved itself stronger than the will of the Government.

At this period also something like the above happened. Certain elements of the British public conceived, even at

the most unpropitious moment, the idea of friendship with
the French, and set energetically to work to prepare the
way for an agreement between the two nations. This
agitation had practically matured by the time Edward
VII ascended the throne. Though that monarch had
hitherto stood for a German orientation, yet he had
always entertained a sympathetic regard for the French
people, and was above all very fond of Paris. Seeing that
he could do nothing with his imperial nephew, Edward
began to devote his energies to the creation of friendly
relations with France.

After the resignation of Salisbury, the veteran
representative of " splendid isolation," and the appointment of his colleague Balfour as Premier, the new Foreign
Minister Lansdowne adopted a foreign policy coincident
with the views of King Edward and, together with the
sovereign, sought to promote a *rapprochement* with their
Gallic neighbour—a step which had become necessary
owing to the mistrust of Germany, which was constantly
growing.

William II and Edward VII could never understand
each other. The more morally disposed nephew despised
and scorned his uncle, whose earlier years had been less
edifying, and condemned him with all the severity of the
old Puritans. When on a certain occasion Edward,
then Prince of Wales, appeared as a witness in a card-
sharping case, the Emperor spoke of the affair to the
officers of his guard, saying that " the Prince had ceased
to be a gentleman and it would be impossible ever again
to shake hands with him." The danger of this spirit was
enhanced by William's too blunt outspokenness and
sincerity, which prevented him from keeping his views to
himself and constrained him to make his kinsman feel
their effect. William's bosom friend, Eulenburg, wrote

that " the Emperor showed his contempt for the Prince of Wales in an unmistakable manner. On his next visit to England [i.e. after the card-sharping case], the German Emperor hardly deigned to look at the most important Crown Prince in the World." These two exalted relatives were not born for mutual intercourse. The smart soldier-Emperor cordially despised the civilian-King who had no particular love for military display, nor indulged in blatant praises of the army ; who seldom appeared in uniform and knew not how to command a regiment ; who could listen to the babble of parliamentary debate, which William once likened to a " *troupe of monkeys chattering.*"

Edward, on the other hand, had not much love for William. With an incomparably superior knowledge of mankind, this experienced arbiter of fashion and refinement and elegant manners, this darling of the *beau monde*, looked down from his Olympian height upon the rude Emperor with his not always immaculate attire. Edward's *grand-seigneur* simplicity and thoroughbred air was a gulf fixed between him and the theatrical, flamboyant deportment of the German Emperor. The recognised leader of the international *dévots* of pleasure, the " First Gentleman " not of Europe only but of the world, was as far as the poles asunder from the (notwithstanding his wonderful linguistic accomplishments) typical Prussian soldier.

The Emperor quite spoilt the Cowes regattas for King Edward. The latter complained to his intimate friends that " William, with his eternal hurrahing, commanding, and military swagger, had poisoned the atmosphere of this fine old English sport." These two greatest rulers and spoilt children of the world, whose every expressed wish was a command, accustomed to deference and obedience from all, fairly detested each other. Being blood-relations, they met too frequently and were too much in each other's secrets to make it possible for the usual ceremonial and obligatory formalities inseparable from the meeting of two sovereigns to hide their opposite personalities, tastes, habits, views, and philosophies. Unrestrained intimate relations between kinsmen generally lead to mutual antipathy. And in this case the mutual antipathy was intensified by the family quarrel between William and his English mother ; which became so tragic during the illness and death of the Emperor Frederick owing to the bitterness between the German and the English physicians in attendance on the illustrious patient.

However, this personal antagonism and antipathy between the two Princes did not affect their policies to any material extent. Both sovereigns were worthy examples of a princely sense of duty. Neither desired to be influenced by sympathies and antipathies. Each was ready to live on friendly terms with the other, and I think they both even considered it desirable to do so. Either of them would no doubt have been willing to offer his hand to Beelzebub himself, had the interest of their respective realms rendered it expedient. Yet their personal animosity exercised a tremendous influence upon the course of events. It stood in the way of mutual understanding between the two sovereigns, of discovering the *via media* between the conflicting interests and aims, of discussing delicate questions calmly and objectively without danger of rupture. Their mutual antipathy affected their opinion of each other, and consequently of each other's policy. Emperor William was only too glad and too willing to believe that King Edward intrigued against him, was plotting to isolate and break his empire ; and that the entire policy of his uncle was founded on envy and jealousy of Germany as a new rising

World-Power. Edward likewise was prone to believe that the German policy was aggressive, jingoistic, and Anglophobe, because he hated the Emperor and considered him capable of any evil. If only he could have had confidence in William, if he had had any affection for him, if he had not believed him to be inordinately ambitious, vain, and brutal, he would have regarded German policy too with different eyes. It was not because they disliked each other and wished each other ill that the two sovereigns followed opposite policies ; but they considered each other's policy dangerous and directed against themselves because each regarded the other as his jealous foe. Each conceived it his duty to protect his country from the machinations of the other.

Both desired only what was useful for their respective countries ; but the views they entertained of each other reciprocally influenced their views of the policy to be expected from the other State.

King Edward knew and dreaded the impetuous, wayward nature, the bold aspirations and rash nautical propensities of his nephew. He regarded the future with uncertainty and misgiving because of the overweening ambition of his kinsman, and therefore he desired to safeguard Britain's command of the sea, the palladium of her freedom. For this reason he wished to eliminate the differences separating him from France, and to win the good-will of the French people. All the same, he was not disposed to any anti-German policy. He came near thereto only through his mistrust of the Kaiser, and his new friends, the French, being the irreconcilable foes of Germany. He had no mind to an anti-German policy, but he rendered possible a movement against the Germans by securing for himself a free hand in his relations with France. He wanted no war with Germany ; but he feared it might come to that, and therefore he looked for a friend to support him in that emergency. The majority of his people were with him in his efforts. The all-powerful public opinion of England assumed a decided Germanophobe tendency, for Germany was feared on account of her maritime ambitions, and the English were aware that in order to frustrate them heavy financial burdens were inevitable.

King Edward's first public act of importance in this connection was his visit to President Loubet at the Élysée in May 1903, a visit which was subsequently returned by Loubet in London. This auspicious double event put an end to the strained relations between the two neighbouring nations and led to the commencement of political negotiations between them.

Eckhardtstein hastened from London to Paris in order to be able to watch personally this highly interesting event. He afterwards reported that the visit to the King of England might be the starting-point of a new orientation in world-policies. One should be prepared to see not only the realisation of Anglo-French friendship, but also the success of the joint efforts of France and England to win Russia, as well as, at least in time, the conclusion of the Triple Entente. He had little faith in the durability of the combination, in view of the con-flicting interests of the parties, but reckoned with it temporarily as calculated to do much mischief in the course of its brief existence.

Bülow held a different opinion. He did not think that France and England would arrive at an agreement on the Morocco Question. Neither did he apprehend the possibility of England and Russia understanding each other, for the former aimed at excluding the latter from the warm seas and Russia could not relinquish the sea.

26

She could not desire much co-operation with England, for within the Triple Entente England and France would always work their own will against Russia. In the Oriental Question England and France would constantly want something different from the Czar and would not suffer the Russian policy to assert itself. Bülow's conclusion therefore was that for the time being one could not be too calm in regarding the coquetting of England and France. Holstein took the same view. England and France could only come to an agreement after the idea of *revanche* had abated in the Gallic mind.

Yet Bülow attached such importance to Eckhardtstein's pessimism that he informed certain important diplomats of his report. The German Chargé d'Affaires in London considered Eckhardtstein's view quite wrong. Though true that England had turned away from Germany, she would never be able to come to an agreement with Russia. He referred to the speech of the British Foreign Minister, in which the latter declared (May 1903) that England would strive her utmost to prevent any foreign Power from getting a footing in the Persian Gulf—the natural perpetual aim of Russia. According to him, Cambon, the French Ambassador in London, did not even attempt to include Russia, and desired only to bring about a friendship between England and France ; and the sole aspiration of the Russian Ambassador was to keep Germany and England far apart and to negotiate in Lombard Street a Russian loan—in which, however, he would hardly succeed. He advised that efforts should be made to induce the English to abandon the idea that Germany was dangerously or improperly ambitious, and that she would expand at all costs. Care should be taken to stop the German press stating that the navy was a matter of necessity against the designs of England. He thought that nothing more—no particular diplomatic action—was required.

From St. Petersburg the German Ambassador sent the same opinion. According to Alvensleben, Russia had no desire to come to terms with England. She was step by step advancing in Asia, steadily creeping onward, and it would not be to her interest there to make sacrifices for England. Chamberlain was probably only bluffing them when talking of a Russian *rapprochement*.

A similar view was also expressed by the Ambassador to Paris. According to Radolin, Delcassé might perhaps be dreaming of a Triple Entente, but the time for its fulfilment was yet very far distant. France and England must first of all come to terms regarding Morocco, which would prove a difficult task. It was quite as difficult to let France have the territory opposite Gibraltar as for France to surrender the same after having acquired the rest of the land of the Kabyles. France's aim was slowly to encircle Morocco from the south, Algiers serving as a base of operations, thence proceeding northwards. Opposing interests separated Russia and England in Asia. Germany was equally disliked in St. Petersburg, London, and Paris, but notwithstanding this antipathy they could not afford to sacrifice those great interests that parted them in the meantime.

Metternich, who had now been placed in charge of the London Embassy, also reported to the same effect. The English were never over-fond of Continental alliances, and that was precisely the case now. They had approached France simply to be able to deliver and defend themselves, if need arose, from Germany ; but they were not contemplating an anti-German offensive.

For the present there was no reason to fear their making up to Russia : they were at loggerheads about Asia. England intended to remain absolute master of the shores, while Russia wanted to reach the sea. He recommended patience and calm.

As may be supposed, these views, so coincident with each other, were eminently satisfactory to Bülow. He was right after all. There was no need to change his direction—no need to shoulder new and heavy burdens ; it was sufficient to moderate the Anglophobia of the German press.

But events moved faster and took a more decisive turn than the German diplomats had anticipated. Though at present the Anglo-French *rapprochement* only was on the tapis—without Russia—yet the agreement could boast of results surprisingly early. After King Edward's visit and President Loubet's return visit, diplomatic negotiations were immediately opened. The initial result of the deliberations was an international arbitration pact. All legal difficulties, especially such as were connected with the interpretations of treaties, should henceforth be submitted by the two Powers to the Peace Court at The Hague, always excepted cases involving the vital interests or the honour of either contracting Power. This was in itself an important and valuable achievement ; though the most important and valuable feature of the pact was the mutual good-will that it signified—the resolve to try as far as possible to avoid quarrels between themselves. This spirit of good-will bore further excellent fruit. After a few months of negotiations (April 1904) they succeeded in eliminating their definite colonial differences. They accomplished a work that Berlin had deemed an impossibility. The successful result was promoted by the outbreak in the meantime of the Russo-Japanese War. Russia became weaker, and thus France felt the need of fresh support—the King of England instead of (or in addition to) the Czar. The *rapprochement* at this time between Germany, Austria-Hungary, and Russia on the Balkans Question was another factor inducing France to come to terms with England, in order to avoid the risk of becoming isolated as in Bismarck's day.

France took an important step. She accepted finally and without mental reservation the *status quo* in Egypt, the British overlordship there, and consented to a modification of the international control of the finances which ameliorated and simplified England's situation in the land of the Pharaohs. Therewith they closed a chapter in history they had begun to write with such sanguine ambitions and great illusions, which had caused extreme bitterness, anger, and humiliation, and which now was terminated with complete renunciation on the one side. It is true that in return for their complaisance the French got from the English a promise regarding Morocco. Only a promise, however, which was quite a different thing from realisation. Yet the pact proved a good bargain for France, for the real price received for Egypt was the invaluable *rapprochement* with England.

The Anglo-French Agreement redounded to the credit of both signatories. What was usually obtained only as the result of a costly war or of protracted diplomatic altercations and controversies, had been attained by peaceful means. In a certain sense England and Germany had changed places. Under the effect of her new fear of Germany, England had been actuated chiefly by concern for the safety of Europe, which had been Bismarck's guiding star. And Germany, conscious of her power, now attached greater importance to manifold petty overseas interests than to the task of strengthening her already safe Continental situation—just as Salisbury had done before. Therefore it was that France and England could understand each other, and Germany had to remain in a certain state of opposition to each of her rivals.

Paris and London had followed a more far-sighted policy than Berlin thought, and than Berlin herself was following. The two first-named capitals were enabled to break with the past, to forget certain things over which it was best to draw the veil of oblivion, to make a uniform picture with regard to the thousands of interests great and small, to sacrifice the lesser for the sake of the greater ; while in Berlin the policy of particularisation, of the magnifying-glass, was asserted—small interests were allowed to usurp the rule of the great ones. In Berlin they never suspected their adversaries to be capable of taking the important decision that they had in fact taken. Therefore it was that their counter-attractions came too late ; therefore they lost ground ; and therefore, finally, the long quarrel between the two Western Powers—which hitherto had ensured the superiority of Germany—came to an end.

The further course of events depended to a considerable extent on Russia. Would she abide by the new Anglo-French Entente or the Triple Alliance ? Would the alliance with Russia take the place of the English for us ? or would France succeed in reconciling her old friend to the new, thereby finally securing the superiority for herself ?

CHAPTER IX

RUSSIAN FRIENDSHIP

AFTER the conclusion of peace following the rebellion in China (September 1901), the most important point of contact between Russia and Germany was Asia Minor—i.e. the Constantinople-Bagdad Railway, the question of which reached a new stage in January 1902, when Germany at last acquired the necessary licence to build the line.

The German Government remained loyal to its fundamental principle of avoiding the spoiling of good relations with any of the interested parties, without at the same time sacrificing any important interests. The statement of the Foreign Minister on Germany's tactics at that time was to the effect that she wanted to exploit the rivalry between England and France and, by bowing here to the Russian bear and there to the British lion, to get round to the Persian Gulf, to the harbour of Koweit.

Her obeisances to the Russian bear were, however, futile. St. Petersburg could not be induced to relish the German plan. The Czar always regarded the activities of other European Powers on Turkish soil as poaching on his preserves. He was the Sultan's heir-at-law, he was the successor of the Byzantine emperors. What had the West, otherwise Germany, to do in his empire of the future? The Czar's Government did its utmost to hinder and thwart the progress of Germany. First it sought to exclude German influence from the shores of the Black Sea. By dint of pressure on Constantinople a promise was exacted that the railway-line as far as the Black Sea should be built by Turkish and Russian capital alone—a promise not only prejudicial to the Germans, but arrestive to the development of Turkey, since it rendered useful investments the privilege of people whose pockets were empty! Later on the Russians sought to defeat the Bagdad Railway by demanding a concession for a parallel line on their own behalf, by which trick they would deprive the Germans of the traffic.

But the Sultan was alive to this secret intention and refused the request of the Russians. The Russian diplomatic intrigues in England were more dangerous. Germany looked for French and British capital in the carrying out of her scheme : firstly in order to settle the technical problem the more easily, and secondly, in order to allay the universal jealousy, and that the enterprise, though under German leadership, should nevertheless be thoroughly international. The English Government was disposed to assist in view of the economic and financial advantages promised by the undertaking ; but a press campaign under Russian inspiration was started (April 1903) before which the English Government had eventually to bow, and to decline the participation of British capital in the project. This example was followed by France (October 1903) too, owing to the Russophil sentiments of Delcassé. Germany stood alone, and was compelled to start the enterprise without foreign assistance, which caused loss of time and increase of the universal jealousy. This failure was, alas, a sign of her isolation in world-politics.

England too, however, had cause to view with misgiving the building of the Bagdad Railway. She regarded suspiciously the design to make Koweit the sea-end of this immense transverse, where England had plans of her own. Lord Curzon, Viceroy of India, one of the leading geniuses of the British Empire, particularly considered the Persian Gulf to be within the British sphere of influence and emphasised the prime importance of the Sheik of Koweit (an Arab prince nominally under Ottoman suzerainty but virtually independent) being retained under British influence. This statesman urged the high political doctrine that the road from England to India via Suez, Egypt, the Sudan, and the territories of the Arab tribes should be defended by British power throughout the whole way. Balfour, the Premier, entirely concurred with this view, and on the basis thereof desired to come to terms with Russia. He suggested that a straight line should be drawn from Port Alexandretta on the Mediterranean as far as the Yang-tse Valley in China, the territory north of which should be considered as in the Russian sphere of influence, and that on the south as in the British sphere. This grand scheme, however, would be disturbed by the railway connecting Koweit with Constantinople and furnishing the Sultan with a pretext for withdrawing the Sheik from British influence and subjecting him (by force if necessary) to himself. For this very reason the Sultan was pleased with the German Bagdad Railway enterprise. It would open up distant tracts of territory to the Padishah and his army. It was, moreover, important for the Germans to satisfy the Turks, and therefore the former spoke loudly against England when she appeared to be going to suborn the Sheik of Koweit to serve her purposes (summer and autumn 1903).

The cunning, cowardly Sultan Abdul Hamid made such a poor, weak defence that Lansdowne might well say (September) that the Germans were more Turkish than the Turks. But when at the close of the year Russia intervened and the impression was made that Russia and England would quarrel over Koweit, Germany became calmer. The Emperor William said that the English and Russians should settle the affair between themselves. And since England raised no protest against Koweit being made the terminus of the railway and desired only to secure the *status quo*, the hitherto independence of the Sheik, the question did not become critical. However, the *Drang nach Osten*, the most substantial feature of the German *Weltpolitik*, was beginning to make itself felt, and this constituted one of the chief obstacles to co-operation between Russia and Germany, since it made the Oriental policy of Berlin more and more pro-Turk, and which—if Russia should once more begin to turn her attention to the Dardanelles—would give it an anti-Russian tendency. It was becoming clearer day by day that the Kaiser was right when he said (1905) that " they must not play their last trump-card "—the friendship of the Moslems—" against a hostile coalition of the entire world "; as also was Marschall, German Ambassador to Constantinople, who said that Bismarck's famous reference to the bones of a Pomeranian grenadier was no longer applicable to Constantinople and the Straits, since the Germans had important interests at stake in that neighbourhood for which it might prove necessary to draw the sword.

A deleterious influence on the further development of Russo-German relations was produced by the after-effect of the Anglo-Japanese Alliance—the conclusion of which I have already alluded to. This after-effect was due to the fact that Lamsdorff—appointed Russian

Foreign Minister after the death of Muravieff (February 1902)—desired to minimise the moral effect of the Anglo-Japanese Agreement in the Far East by coming to terms with Germany, but the German politicians were indisposed to this. In order to restore the balance of power in the Far East, Lamsdorff proposed that Germany and Russia, and later France, should enter into a pact similar to the Anglo-Japanese. The formation of this group alone would keep China from yielding to Japan and England ; but for the sake of greater safety it was proposed to admonish China to beware of submitting herself to those two island empires. The treaty took the classic form of division, unctuously referring to the independence and integrity of the doomed victim, and providing for division only when the *status quo* could no longer be maintained, but preparing the collapse by *a priori* counting upon it. According to this old, tried method, the treaty defended the integrity of China, with the additional proviso that " should China or any other Power do prejudice to the interests of one of the contracting parties, they would deliberate upon the measures necessary, etc."—which might also be interpreted to mean that lest anyone else should injure their protégé, they would tear her to pieces and devour her themselves !

But broad and ambiguous as this treaty was, it involved too many obligations for Bülow's liking. Not long before he had refused to connect his fate to England lest he should have to face Russia. Now he was quite as anxious to avoid the opposite peril—of falling out with England for the sake of Russia. He wanted to follow the policy of the " free hand " in the Far East, and just as little relished the idea of dispute with the Island Kingdom as with his Continental neighbour.

Unfortunately, however, the final result of his Asiatic policy was simply to offend, in turn, England and Russia. At her first appearance in China, as intervener in the Chino-Japanese peace, Germany alienated Britain and Japan ; by independently hoisting her flag over Kiao-Chau she offended England, Japan, and Russia ; when concluding an agreement with the first-named in defence of Chinese integrity she offended Russia ; again, when interpreting a clause so that it might have no anti-Russian point, she offended England ; and now, by refusing to come to terms with Russia and France, she alienated Russia, who was the more sensitive as the offer had been made at the express command of the Czar. For there could be no denying that when the German flag was hoisted in China, the scene of the rivalry of the European Powers, interests sometimes arose which were quite opposed to the requirements of continental policy, rendering it difficult for Germany to act in accordance with those requirements and at the same time to remain on good terms with either England or Russia.

Lamsdorff was in dudgeon. He declared that henceforth Russia would go her own way in Asia ; and (March 1902) he came to an agreement with France on the basis of that offered to Germany. The Russian press took very ill the attitude of Germany. The refusal by Germany of their request, as well as the sympathetic policy of that Power towards the Poles, spoilt the temper of St. Petersburg. The *Novoje Vremja*, the most influential of Russian newspapers, assumed an anti-German rôle similar to that played by *The Times* in England. Hostile forces now began to take up those positions whence we were destined to suffer such devastating onslaughts during the World War.

For the time being, however, it was fortunate for us that the Czar and official circles declined to countenance an anti-German policy. Their Anglophobia was still stronger than their Germanophobia. At this period Russia was still ambitious to reach the warm seas, and in the direction of Persia, China, and India this met with the resistance not of Germany but of Britain. On this account the Czar desired to cultivate the friendship of Germany in so far as the limits of the alliance with France permitted, and subordinate to the idea of this alliance. I think the Czar was sincere when (June 1901) he told Bülow that his final object was to bring Germany and France together and form an alliance of the three continental Powers. In spite of the inimical public opinion prevailing in Russia, the two Courts often met and sedulously fostered good relations between them.

They met at Danzig (June 1901) and at Reval (August 1902). The latter meeting was preceded by an interesting event worth recording here, though it had no influence upon the course of history, as it throws light on the relations subsisting between William and Bülow. The irrepressible Emperor was now as angry with Lamsdorff as he had formerly been with Muravieff, his predecessor, for it had been whispered to William that since he had refused the alliance with Russia, Lamsdorff was working against him. Consequently the Kaiser objected to the Russian Foreign Minister being invited to the meeting. Bülow, on the other hand, emphasised the importance of the presence of his Russian colleague, as, in his view, that would enhance the value of the meeting. He even suggested that a decoration should be conferred upon the Muscovite statesman. The Kaiser, with his usual sharp tongue, said " Lamsdorff is an intriguing, sneaking, stinking bureaucrat—a mere ink-slinger—whom I would scorn to meet or to distinguish." After this explosion, however, the Emperor cooled down ; the Russian Minister was invited and in the end decorated !

These meetings and friendly greetings, whether with or without the Foreign Minister, led to no lasting results ; had no effect on the political grouping of the Powers— which was natural, since neither party cared for concluding an alliance with the other, but confined himself to the preservation of good relations. Thus the Russo-German relations were tolerable, but not secure. At the outbreak of the Russo-Japanese War the mainstay of Russia was still the alliance with France, which was firmly rooted in the numerous French loans to Russia, and in the circumstances the Russians could hardly expect adequate financial assistance from any quarter other than the Paris market with its abundant capital. But would not the war against Japan influence the policy of Russia, compelling her to strike out into new paths and seek an alliance with Germany, her neighbour ?

CHAPTER X

THE RUSSO-JAPANESE WAR. THE BJÖRKÖ ALLIANCE

WARS are frequently, perhaps generally, the result of miscalculations and weak government. Conflicting interests divert certain States to ways dangerous and harmful to other States ; and these lead to acrimonious diplomatic controversies, though neither of the disputants desires the final settlement through the direful arbitrament of the sword. Both hope and persuade themselves that the other party will yield, and each is himself prepared if necessary to give way at the last moment. But as the dispute proceeds they become embittered, their tempers suffer, public opinion steps in, to the embarrassment of the diplomats, evil passions are aroused and grow on both sides, until retreat is impossible and war becomes the sole and inevitable solution. It happens more often that countries get entangled in war against their will than that they deliberately prepare for and provoke it. There are, of course, cases where the appeal to arms is the result of deliberate intention, and where the object of diplomatic action is to encompass the defeat of the antagonist by force, one of the parties regarding the sword as the swiftest and most advantageous implement for cutting the Gordian knot.

Nearly all the wars since the Peace of Frankfort belong to the first category. Such was the Russo-Turkish War, which Czar Alexander II certainly did not want. The Pan-Slav idea carried Russia to the length of making demands upon the Sultan which the latter rejected, contrary to what Russia had reason to expect.

When this became manifest, the Czar had already gone too far to retreat without grave risk. The pressure of public opinion swept him away towards the dread wager of battle. Such too was the Spanish-American War, which neither of the Governments desired, into which the two nations were driven by the force of opposing interests and views. And, moreover, to this same category, so far as we can at present judge from the available data, belongs the late terrible World War. It was futile for the Peace Treaties solemnly to declare that we, the vanquished, were the guilty and therefore justly punished so severely. This savage indictment was not the result of unbiassed investigation by impartial judges, but a mere one-sided political act. The formal assent of the defeated side is no free and unfettered confession of guilt, but simply the expression of their will for peace —the consequence of their inability to continue the struggle against the overwhelming military and economic forces of the adversary. The more data come to light, the clearer it becomes that not one of the Powers engaged wanted the World War ; that the cataclysm was the result of chronic hatred and mistrust, of the fear of sinister intentions on the part of neighbours. If ever there was a horrible *débâcle* caused simply by fear and artificially manufactured suspicion, and not through ill-will, the recent universal disaster was such a case.

The Russo-Japanese War was one of those brought about by cold, calculating deliberation. There was such a magnitude of differing interests between the largest European Power and the largest island of Asia that both parties resolved to put their fate to the test of armed force. Neither would relinquish nor abate one jot of their high political aspirations. Russia was determined to become master of Manchuria and Corea, to reach the warm sea, to acquire an ice-free port, and finally to annex and strongly hold all the territory adjacent to that port and Russia. Japan, on the other hand, was equally determined not to allow this. The teeming population and great commercial activity of the Empire of Nippon were in absolute need of the neighbouring coastlands coveted by Russia. She aspired to reform the Chinese, put them on their feet, exploit them, and turn to account for herself the splendid economic opportunities there. If Japan should succeed in driving a wedge between Vladivostok and Port Arthur (occupied by the Muscovites), the Yellow Race would constitute a perpetual menace to those two naval stations; while if Russia ultimately gained the upper hand on the littoral opposite Japan, the Manchus would naturally come under Russian influence. Therefore both contending parties envisaged a trial of strength to settle the matter.

But whereas Russia would have preferred to postpone the final contest until a more convenient season, Japan was in a tremendous hurry to decide it. Each was naturally prompted by her actual interests. Russia was by no means ready and had much to do in concentrating her forces on the scene of the coming struggle. Japan had already about reached in the given circumstances what she was capable of. Russia's chances were likely to improve, while Japan's would get correspondingly less favourable with every day that passed. Time was on the side of the Russians. Delay would assuredly have meant victory for the Muscovites. Russia therefore committed an egregious blunder in hastening the decision before she was quite prepared. She counted upon the little Japanese David lacking the pluck to stand up against the terribly immense Russian Goliath. How little she knew the resolute determination and foresight

27

of the yellow islanders ! She underestimated her foe—
an error which took an awful revenge upon her. For
it afforded the Japanese an opportunity to attack Russia
without seeming the aggressors.

Hayashi had long before confided to Eckhardtstein
that Japan would have to bring about a war somehow.
And early in January 1904 he had stated that the whole
Japanese Government were aching to settle accounts
with their gigantic rival. They realised that it was
" now or never " for their hope of success.

Up to the last moment the Czar could not be induced
to believe that war would break out before he wanted it.
How could he be the almighty Czar if he must draw the
sword against his will ! The Emperor William shuddered
at his cousin's blindness and fatuity. " *Ein ahnungs-
loser Engel !* " (" A simple Simon ! ") he petulantly dubbed
him (January 1904). He attributed the war solely to
the Czar's arrant cowardice. As soon as the Czar
realised the danger and saw the intrepidity of the little
yellow men, he would have liked to withdraw, but it was
then too late. Had Britain and France intervened, he
would have had a pretext for accepting the Japanese
demands. But England declined to intervene. She
was even glad that the matter had come to a head. So
the Czar could put off the evil day no longer (February
1904). A craven withdrawal would have meant revolution at home, which would have had a worse effect than
defeat abroad.

The outbreak of the war exercised a great influence on
Russian policy. The quarrel with Japan alone did much
to induce the Czar to maintain good relations with the
German Emperor, in spite of the public opinion of Russia.
Would not the war and its disastrous consequences force
Russia to a new direction, compelling her into the arms of

the neighbouring Powers ? France called attention to the fact that she was not bound to help in Asia, and remained neutral. Would this not cool the friendship for the French on the banks of the Neva ?

Emperor William devoutly hoped it would. Bülow constantly manœuvred between Russia and England, though the Emperor shrewdly felt that sooner or later they would fall between the two stools. At first, when England made overtures, the Kaiser was disposed to accept them. Now, however, when an agreement with England had become impossible and the Emperor regarded his uncle the King of England with the greatest suspicion—one might even say hate—he would willingly have won Russia. The Emperor hoped to reach his aim by guaranteeing the neutrality of the Baltic with Russia, Sweden, and Denmark, thereby precluding the contingency of England menacing St. Petersburg and the North-Russian ports. He proposed this idea to Osten-Sacken, the Russian Ambassador (March 1903). The latter admitted that such an agreement would be a good thing, but it would be difficult owing to France. The Gallic Republic was a fickle friend, gravitating towards England and acting as if she were going to revive the policy she had followed prior to the Crimean War.

However, the Emperor's idea was not shared by his Government, which even then adhered to the policy of the " free hand." Bülow represented that it would provoke animosity and lead to reprisals from England.

The Emperor's idea came up again notwithstanding (November), in a conversation between him and the Czar. The two monarchs desired to ask for the authorisation of the King of Denmark (who alone was not strong enough for the task) to occupy with their combined forces and, if necessary, close the Sound.

The Emperor put the question to the Danish sovereign, who seemed willing to comply in principle, and to accept the guarantee of the two neighbour Powers in the interests of neutrality. This delighted the Czar, but on the other hand it alarmed the German Government. Holstein feared lest Germany, now in a safe position, should draw down upon herself the perils and animosities suffered by Russia. This would probably take the form of an alliance between England and Japan, and the opening of the Sound by force, which would embroil Germany in a war, or, more probably, of England retreating before Russia, taking up the cause of French *revanche* and attempting to square accounts with Germany, and to evade the Russian *casus fœderis*. To avert this danger the resourceful bureaucrat concocted (December) a cunning scheme : The King of Denmark should be cajoled into prominence and asked himself to suggest the plan of operations for blockading the Sound. Anxious for his independence and in order to avoid the responsibility for such a step, he would probably decline ; in which case Germany would thereby be able to escape the danger without offending Russia and coming into conflict with her previous declarations. The reports of the German Ambassadors to Washington and London were confirmatory of Holstein's view. They set forth that both England and America would take very ill the blockading of the Sound and that such a step would give an anti-German direction to the policy of both the Powers named.

Bülow shared Holstein's opinion. The Emperor yielded, though with a bad grace, for, according to him, the assistance of Denmark was urgently needed. It was perfectly obvious that England was trying to isolate Germany, and an alliance with Denmark was the only means of cutting the knot. The Emperor, however, deferred to his responsible adviser. Holstein's trick did what was expected of it. The King of Denmark dropped the affair and the Emperor's independent move had no serious consequences.

Yet the Kaiser continued entirely Russophil and wanted an alliance with Russia. He identified himself completely with the Czar's standpoint, when conversing with him (3rd January), that Russia had an inalienable right to an ice-free harbour in Corea, and that it rested entirely with him to make the necessary annexation at his pleasure ; everybody in Germany recognised that right. The Emperor, moreover, addressed Bülow to the same effect. He pointed out that since the occupation of Kiao-Chau he had on several occasions promised the Czar to guard his back-door if any complications arose in the Far East. He impressed on the Chancellor that he need not be afraid that standing by Russia would lead to any harm, since that had indeed already happened and everybody—Japan included—was aware that Germany was Russophil. When, notwithstanding this, the Chancellor desired to modify a letter of the Emperor, the imperial author vigorously expostulated : " his letter was not a diplomatic note but a private interchange of ideas, and if the Chancellor insisted on its modification to any considerable extent, the Emperor would in future decline to show his private correspondence to his responsible adviser."

Just before the outbreak of hostilities (middle of January) the Emperor invited Bülow's candid opinion with regard to their further attitude. He desired to settle the question of what Germany should do if Russia should solicit her aid against England. Bülow and Holstein, ever loyal to their convictions, wanted to make upon Russia the impression that Germany was her faithful friend but to pledge no assistance. The latter should be given only after Russia had on her part undertaken satisfactory and complete obligations towards Germany.

Holstein was for delay. Russia was isolated, and France neutral, while Japan inclined towards England and America, who, together with Japan, were "free-traders." If, as well as the Russo-Japanese War, the Balkan Question should once more crop up, France, the friend of the Russians (besides Italy, Austria-Hungary, and Rumania) would stand by the English. Russia would be able to find succour in Germany alone, and thus the latter had no reason to be in a hurry. She had better remain with her hands untied—in her present position, midway between the contending parties. She should not espouse the cause of Russia, but remain free to go with Japan if her interests pointed in that direction. This advice was scarcely palatable to the Kaiser. He, however, as luck had it, was never placed in a situation imperatively demanding a decision, since the expected question on the part of the Russians never arose.

Russia had no need of the positive assistance of Germany against Japan. Germany was not such a power-factor in the Far East as to have a decisive influence there on the questions of war and peace. Such assistance would really have been detrimental, for it would have compelled Great Britain, the greater Power in the Far East, to intervene, as she had declared she would punctiliously observe her treaty obligations to Japan, and hasten to the latter's assistance as soon as Russia secured an ally. England would be kept outside the conflict far more effectually by her new-found friend France, than by the sword of the Germans. The then relations with *Das Reich* perfectly suited the interests of Russia. The friendship of the Emperor and of Austria-Hungary (who had concluded with Russia a treaty of neutrality, November 1904) rendered it absolutely certain that no danger threatened her from the west or continental side, that the Balkan Question would not be brought up ; an open alliance with Germany might result in a change of French orientation. The Crimean coalition could be renewed and its superiority at sea and on land (in Asia) enhanced by America joining it. A positive alliance with Germany could be of use only when England had actually joined the belligerents against Russia. For the time being Russia's object was to prevent the intervention of England and not to seek means of defending herself against the Mistress of the Seas.

Consequently William's personal efforts to get hold of the Czar, instead of France, and to hinder him from approaching England were not appreciated in St. Petersburg. Their success was probably rendered difficult by the too ostentatious declaration of the Emperor of his partisanship for Russia, and by his showing himself a bigger Japophobe than even the Czar. Before the outbreak of the war (February) William was astonished at the Czar's display of weakness and gave him to understand that, if he were now to humble himself to Japan, the Yellow Peril would in twenty years' time be pounding at the gates of Moscow and menacing Posen. By cravenly kowtowing before the pigmy Japs the Czar would set in motion a wave of revolution throughout Russia. His wisest course was to mobilise his entire forces, and fire the enthusiasm of his people, as his ancestors had done in the great struggles of the past, from the holy city of Moscow.

Bülow had tremendous difficulty in dissuading the Emperor from despatching such an epistle to the Autocrat. As the Chancellor endeavoured to point out, no one—least of all a sovereign ruler—likes to have such lessons forced upon him from without, and the Emperor's harangue would be interpreted as an indication that he particularly wished the Czar not to seek a peaceful solution, but that the Emperor wanted war for some sinister design of his own.

Later on, during the struggle, the Emperor had his way and wrote his views ; which, as might be expected, were unwelcome, consisting as they did of gratuitous censure and futile *post-factum* criticism. When in August his Ambassador reported that Germany was suspect in Japanese eyes, the Emperor replied that the diplomats must not mind that ; the mistrust was natural and would increase as time went on. The champion of the Yellow Race instinctively feared the champion of the White Race. It was felt that sooner or later there would be a struggle for mastery between the Yellow men under Japanese leadership and the White Race organised by Germany. The Czar could be really quite satisfied with the state of things. Why should he pay for the active assistance of Germany when he would be able to get her services as vanguard without giving anything in return for them ?

The pro-Russian proclivities of the Emperor were palpably manifested by the fact that the Russian fleet received its coal supplies mostly from German vessels, thus facilitating the mobilisation of the Czar's navy— a proceeding which might have resulted in a protest on the part of Japan followed by an attack upon Germany. It might even have precipitated the intervention of England—for the British Government had warned the

Germans that they could not reject the *casus fœderis* if England's assistance were solicited by Japan owing to the violation of neutrality by Germany.

The danger of British intervention was brought very nigh by a mere accident. The Russian fleet under Admiral Rozhdestvensky, bound for Japanese waters, on the night of 21-22 October 1904, fired upon a group of English fishing-smacks, lying on the Dogger Bank, off Hull, in the panic belief that the innocent trawlers were Japanese torpedo-boats. When this news was flashed across the wires, the indignation of the English people mounted almost to delirium. Throughout the country mass-meetings were held and fiery denunciations delivered, furious outbursts of rage and hatred against the Russian " mad dogs," the Czar, and everything he stood for. An apology for the outrage was demanded, together with handsome pecuniary indemnities for the widows and orphans of the men killed and for the living victims, as well as compensation for the loss of the craft. The popular frenzy rose to fever-heat as the days passed by and no reply was received from St. Petersburg. Contempt for the Muscovites in general was visited upon the luckless heads of their compatriots in London— even in the City clubs—much to William's secret satisfaction. At length, when the " man in the street " was vociferating for war upon Russia and crying aloud for the bombardment of her capital, the official reply of the Czar's Government came. Every demand was granted in full, without question or quibble ! And the Russian Ambassador proceeded to Hull to represent his august master at the funeral of the unfortunate fishermen. Throughout this trying time the British Government behaved with the most exemplary calmness, relying on the good offices of the French

Government to put the grave incident in a just light before their ally.

The Dogger Bank outrage, moreover, tended to influence the public opinion of the English against the Germans, whom they blamed for the catastrophe, in the belief that, contrary to their neutrality obligation, the Germans had warned the Russian Admiral to expect the presence of enemy vessels in English waters. This, however, was false. The German Government refrained from passing on the news received from the Ambassador in London ; but the British public were as much excited by the lying scares as if they had been verified facts. In real life both lies and truths have frequently the same effect. If only there are a sufficient number of people to lie furiously, strenuously, and zealously, sham truths can be formed which may serve the desired purpose, for good or evil, just as well as genuine truths.

The nervous dread of the Germans became more acute than ever. The English were obsessed with the fixed idea that William's sole object in building his navy was that he might sooner or later use it against England. Scarcely anyone could be found to admit any other explanation. Time and again the question was raised, whether they (the English) ought not to steal a march on the Germans and go now and smash up their fleet while it was still in its infancy, and therefore to do so an easy game, rather than to wait until it had grown to maturity, when great sacrifices would be necessary to accomplish its destruction.

The German Naval Attaché had considered it his duty to report that a certain lady had told him in all seriousness that England was going to attack Germany now, while there could be no doubt about the result of the venture, in order to forestall Germany's projected attack on England later. Some of the periodicals incited to war ; *Vanity Fair* suggested that by destroying the German fleet now they would secure the peace of Europe for two generations at least. The *Sun* advised a surprise attack on the German navy. Members of Parliament openly stated that if an Anglo-Russian War should become inevitable, Germany too must be reckoned with ; she was the real enemy, and must be destroyed.

The melancholy Holstein seriously credited the rumours that the English were preparing to attack Germany. He averred that the Emperor had arrived at the stage of seriously contemplating a declaration of war against England as soon as the latter ordered her Mediterranean squadron to the vicinity of German ports, for such a step he regarded as the prelude to sudden hostilities. On being plainly asked, all the members of the German Embassy stated that there was not a shadow of doubt about it : England was absolutely anti-German, and it was King Edward's chief aim to win Russia for the new Anglo-French Entente. And although they admitted that the King was averse to war, they envisaged its possibility, for the hyper-excited British public would never be able to bear another " incident " like Fashoda or the Dogger Bank. In their view, even the construction of the German navy—which was part and parcel of an Anglophobe policy—was liable to provoke a war without any such " incidents." In Berlin, however, people went even further in scaremongering. The suspicion prevalent in England that Germany dreamt of attacking them was so ridiculous, they argued, that it could be nothing more than a pretext invented by the English for covering their own diabolical designs against the Fatherland.

It was impossible for the English to believe, said both the Kaiser and Bülow, that they (the Germans) wished to attack, when they had not the remotest chance against the naval might of Britain, when they would be ignominiously defeated in such an unequal contest.

Yet England did seriously fear invasion. A nervous public is always and everywhere ready to swallow the most preposterous tales. Frequently the errors of statesmen are due to their neglect to consider the peoples capable of certain excesses and faults, notwithstanding on occasions of great popular excitement even the cool English have not infrequently displayed the most astounding simplicity. How often had they suffered the nightmare of a sudden landing and lightning attack of the enemy when the idea existed in no one's imagination except their own ? And when, even though it had been thought of, it was a sheer impossibility. Is it not to-day also the symptom of a similar mental aberration on the part of the Little Entente to conclude alliances and pile up armaments and generally to profess mortal fear, all on account of a disarmed, truncated, and isolated country like Hungary—a considerably smaller State than any of her neighbours ? We have the farcical spectacle of the strong concluding alliances against the weak !

However, it was not unnatural that the Germans should get excited when Lord Lee, the Secretary of the Navy, suggested in a public speech that " in the event of war the German fleet should be suddenly and without warning attacked and sent to the bottom, without any declaration of war."

After that, it is surely not difficult to understand that, in such circumstances, the Germans could scarcely be lulled into tranquillity by the most pacific enunciations of King Edward, who stated (January 1905)—what however

was nothing less than the truth—that " there was plenty
of room on the ocean for both the German and the British
navies."

With such sinister influences at work, no wonder the
Emperor's intentions permeated the German Government and, it would seem, Berlin saw that the " free hand "
policy was not sufficient for salvation, that the disposition
of London had become so unfavourable that they must
conclude a treaty with St. Petersburg. The Emperor
wrote openly (October 1904) to the Czar proposing an
alliance with France, Germany, and Russia against England. Nicholas II agreed. " Such a coalition only,"
said he, " could put a stop to the impertinence of the
English and Japanese." He went so far as to invite
William to commit to paper his project of alliance.

But the negotiations started under such favourable
auspices were abruptly stopped, without result (November), as the German Emperor desired to finish the conclusion of the treaty before France got wind of it, while
Nicholas insisted on his Gallic ally being included in the
negotiations. William protested that " to do so would
be simply catastrophic, as in that case Paris would be
bound to inform London and then England would
attack before the treaty could be concluded."

It is my impression that German policy at that period
had not sufficient backbone and nerve to carry out its
ambitions. The Germans aimed high, but they had not
the courage to come to terms with the English on account
of the Russians, or with the Russians on account of the
English, and thus they failed to win either. Alarmed at
imaginary dangers, they created real ones.

The course desired by the Czar could hardly have led
to an English attack, as no serious politician or responsible leader in England dreamt of such a step. At the

utmost it might have resulted in an increased ship-building activity on the part of the English, which would doubtless have been unpleasant but insufficient to justify the breaking-off of the experiment. English public opinion was pacific. England was fully occupied with business, industry, trade ; she had no liking for sacrifices in a war that was not absolutely necessary.

There was, moreover, nothing of the warrior about King Edward ; he was no fighting man with an appetite for conquest or military glory. A refined, courteous, brainy diplomat, he simply wished to circumvent the designs of Germany, being firmly convinced that it would mean danger for England and for peace if Germany should succeed in acquiring predominance by means of her navy supplemented by auspicious policy.

The German Government wanted, above all, to secure the assistance of Russia for the contingency of hostilities on the part of England over the Germans having supplied the Russian fleet with coal. The Czar had promised so much. But the Germans afterwards got an attack of cold feet. Holstein, the prophet of gloom, took up his indispensable magnifying-glass, through which he saw that, should Japan come to hear of a projected German-Russian alliance, she would not bother about the coal question but simply capture the port of Kiao-Chau without deigning to make an excuse, and thus avoid the Russian *casus fœderis*—as if it were conceivable that Japan would entangle herself in a war with Germany without Russia helping the latter against her own enemy.

Holstein reminds one of the Lord Halifax who flourished in the seventeenth century, of whom Macaulay with playful irony wrote that " his mind was so clear that he could perceive every drawback, actual and potential, of every situation, which always prevented his taking any decisive step : like a man with eyes so sharp that he cannot drink the purest water on account of the infusoria being visible to him ! "

Under the effect of these *post-factum* worries the German Government noted the Czar's decision, but issued a counter-declaration to the effect that they would also in the future display good-will subject to the interests and the safety of the Fatherland.

This irresolution could hardly conduce to increased respect for the Germans, nor foster in the Russians the conviction that they ought to make an ally of Germany.

But towards the close of the war (July 1905) the Emperor harked back to his favourite idea, and at a personal meeting with the Czar at Björkö he at length succeeded in concluding the desired defensive alliance without France being informed in advance thereof. Not until afterwards, it was agreed, should the Czar invite his friends in Paris to join them. The Emperor was now a proud and happy man. He affected to see in his success the finger of God. In his eager delight he wanted to flash the good news to Roosevelt, President of the United States ; and Bülow had a strenuous time of it to dissuade him from committing such an indiscretion. It is easy to understand the Emperor's self-satisfaction. The success was entirely due to his personal superiority. The stronger mind dominated the weaker. For a long time the Czar had been carefully on his guard against the Emperor. But his attitude towards him had undergone a change during the war. He was probably expressing his true conviction when he observed that " William was the only real friend he had." Thus by his personal magnetism the Kaiser was able to win over the Czar to his views. A wonderful vista was opened before the Emperor. Russia would disarm France, who would thus be compelled to abandon her schemes of *revanche*, since a war against Germany could not be successfully waged without a powerful Continental ally's assistance, owing to the constantly growing numerical and financial superiority of her adversary. Henceforth Edward would be left alone in the diplomatic arena. Edward would not isolate William, but William would isolate Edward !

What a glorious victory ! " It marked the beginning of a new epoch in history," wrote the blissful Emperor. In this exalted frame of mind it is easy to comprehend his anger when Bülow, of whose intellect he had a very high opinion, and in whom he placed great confidence, treated the Kaiser's great achievement with little short of disdain. The Chancellor was displeased and threatened to resign his post because the Emperor had altered the text of the treaty without his consent and interpolated that " *Russia and Germany were bound to help each other only in Europe* "—which, according to Bülow, rendered the alliance entirely valueless. In the Chancellor's view, Great Britain's vulnerable part was India—that was the sole possession she had any anxiety about. Unless Russia menaced her there, the new combination lost its point ; it could not frighten her nor hope to keep her in the way of peace.

Bülow, however, was aggravating the whole thing. Unquestionably the fixing in advance of the precise scene of the assistance to be given by virtue of a long-term treaty is as superfluous as disadvantageous. But the stipulation that the assistance would be obligatory on European battlefields only can by no means be regarded as a fatal blunder. Even were it quite true that England's sole source of solicitude was her Indian Empire, it was a fallacious conclusion that the Russian alliance would keep England from attacking Germany only if Asia were included in the sphere of validity of the treaty. For when Russia had become Germany's ally, when once hostilities had begun between England and Russia, England would have no means of knowing whether her foe would not alter his plan of action and strike at India too. The menacing and alarming factor for Great Britain would not be that the scene of the stipulated assistance was described in the treaty—that was subject to change at any time as events dictated—but the war itself, with all its incalculable and unforeseeable consequences.

This was all so clear that Bülow's real motive could not have been anxiety on his part, but the sound and comprehensible reasoning that he could not bear the responsibility of the policy if the Emperor (with such an ineradicable propensity to rhapsodising and whose brilliance failed to compensate for his lack of judgment) were to be free to make such changes in official documents of paramount importance. He earnestly desired to make such vagaries on the part of the Emperor impossible for the future, and in this respect one cannot but admire the Chancellor's conscientiousness, firmness, and courage.

The Emperor was deeply wounded by his Chancellor's attitude. To receive lectures and caustic criticisms where he had expected enthusiastic encomiums! His disappointment affected his nerves. His subsequent utterances bore traces of a disturbed mental balance. "*God*," wrote the Emperor to the Chancellor (11th August), "*willed them to work together; he valued Bülow more than a hundred thousand treaties; and he would never be able to survive the resignation of his Chancellor! The day of Bülow's resignation would be the day of the*

28

Emperor's death.   He implored Bülow to think of his (the Emperor's) poor wife and children ! "

William, however, excited himself to no purpose, for the treaty remained a dead letter. The pusillanimous Czar threw his own work overboard, his advisers having succeeded in showing him that it was tantamount to a betrayal of France.

There was in fact a far more important difference between this Russo-German and the Franco-Russian treaty than between the Triple Alliance and Bismarck's famous pact of guarantee ; for the Iron Chancellor never promised armed assistance against Austria-Hungary, whereas Czar Nicholas would have been obliged to draw the sword for Germany against France if the latter attacked the Fatherland. The Autocrat would have been compelled to fight his so frequently fêted friend and ally in defence of Germany. The Czar was very sensitive about his good name. He desired to be honest, and doubtless he really was honest, so far as a weak, easily influenced, and capricious man can be. And now he had been induced to commit an act of shameful treachery ! Therefore he desired to alter the already concluded treaty. He besought the Emperor that it should not come into force from the date of signature of the Russo-Japanese Peace, but from the date of its approval by France ; and that should France refuse her approval, then the treaty should *expressis verbis* make an exception for the contingency of war with France.

William was inflexible : " *What is signed, is signed,*" said he pompously. But he was probably wrong there. I think it would have been far better to have been generous and have reopened the negotiations on a new basis ; to have limited them to common defence against England, and to have been content with neutrality in other cases, for it was futile to think of adhering to the treaty against the will of the other signatory. The Russo-French alliance, which had so deeply impressed the peoples concerned and which even the Czar had considered a necessity, could not be ousted by a secret treaty which one of the sovereign contracting parties considered dishonouring to himself, and impossible of execution because it involved his honour. Good-will and confidences between the two rulers would have been worth more than the treaty, which had not a single adherent in Russia, no party to defend it, and which the Czar himself could afterwards remember only with shame and regret.

This was the end of the *rapprochement* with Russia. For a long time the German Government had been afraid of it while it was perhaps easier to achieve. Then at one bound the Emperor went too far. And since he could not be induced to yield an inch of the ground gained, the success he had won was worse than failure. For it caused the Czar to take the impression that William was dangerous, that he bore him no good-will, that he was a false friend, that his real aim had been to set Russia at variance with her tried friend France and to compromise him in the eyes of Europe. The favourable disposition which would have rendered difficult an Anglo-Russian agreement and attached Russia more closely to Germany, the secret tie which would have bound St. Petersburg to Berlin, was transformed to an unpleasant memory separating the two rulers and the leaders of both great nations.

William had unintentionally done the work of his uncle Edward, and added a pile to the bridge to be built by the latter connecting London with St. Petersburg.

Somewhat previous to this time (March–April 1905)

another interesting exchange of views took place between St. Petersburg and Berlin. The internal troubles of the Austro-Hungarian Monarchy, the anticipated demise of the aged ruler and the uncertain character of the heir-presumptive, seemed to oppress Bülow with anxiety lest the Dual Monarchy should break up. This led to his enquiring of Lamsdorff whether it would not be advisable to put into treaty form that, in the event of the dissolution of Austria-Hungary, neither Germany nor Russia contemplated the acquisition of any territory therein. This idea was quickly killed, almost at birth, by Holstein, who, on the Russians suggesting a definite proposal from Germany, declared that " he suspected the Muscovites of baiting a trap to catch the Germans, and that, so sure as the Germans drafted a scheme, St. Petersburg would simply use it against them." By disseminating such pessimistic notions, Holstein succeeded in inducing the Chancellor to drop the matter.

Besides the dissatisfaction arising from the Björkö Conference fiasco and the French influence over the two countries, there were two other circumstances preparing the way to Anglo-Russian *rapprochement*. One was that Great Britain had made her position in Asia even stronger than before by extending the scope of her treaty with Japan. According to the terms of the amended treaty, Britain undertook to defend Japan not only against a coalition but even against a single Power ; while, on the other hand, Japan pledged herself to aid Great Britain not only in China but also in India. This was sufficient to convince Russia that the policy which had brought her into antagonism with England—expansion towards Asia, the inheritance of Lobanoff—would be quite impracticable, since it would meet with overwhelming resistance everywhere.

The other circumstance was that Japan had concluded peace with Russia (5th September 1905), a peace as wise and moderate as were the wisdom and foresight with which the statesmen of Dai Nippon had prepared the war and as the stern resolution and high intelligence with which she prosecuted it. This facilitated the conclusion of an agreement between the Czar on the one part and Great Britain and Japan on the other. By her praiseworthy moderation in the hour of victory Japan rose to the same height as Bismarck in 1866, when by his generous treatment of vanquished Austria he prepared the way to friendship with her ; to the same height as England, who, soon after the sound of the cannon had died away in South Africa, granted the Boers the fullest autonomy, so that they were constrained by gratitude to identify themselves with the cause of their late enemies during the Great War.

At the end of the Russo-Japanese War Germany's position was strengthened by her following a policy parallel with that of America. There were certain traits in common in the character of the Emperor William and President Roosevelt. Witte, in his *Memoirs*, wrote that both were chivalrous, original, energetic, choleric—both danced about with hot feet, though they managed to keep cool heads. Roosevelt was aware of the traits they shared in common, and was wont to say that " there was only one statesman in Europe capable of understanding him—the German Emperor." Bülow also noticed the similarity, and once said that Roosevelt regarded himself as the American counterpart of the Emperor William and would have liked to go halves with him in governing the world. Not only their personalities but also their interests brought these two eminent men together. Both feared the consequences of the break-up of China, both were adherents to the doctrine of free trade in the Far East, and both objected to the granting of new monopolies. Therefore the American President could appreciate William's anxiety lest the Anglo-Japanese Alliance should seek to conclude peace by dismembering China still further, and lest the Anglo-Japanese group and Russia (who had become dangerously alienated from each other owing to difference over China) might now be brought together again through the intervention of France by the dismemberment of the Flowery Land. Neither America nor Germany could afford to allow this. The alliance of these countries would not only be able to keep all the others out of China, but would constitute an overwhelming force that could impose its will at all times and everywhere.

At the Emperor's suggestion the President was immediately ready for a counter-move. He desired to forestall the danger imagined by them both, by requesting and procuring from the neutral States a declaration engaging not to annex Chinese territory. Roosevelt and William also exerted themselves to prevent the peace being concluded at an international conference, as was the Russo-Turkish Peace, but by immediate negotiations between the belligerent parties presided over by America. This aim was reached and the credit for it is due to William and Roosevelt in common.

Their co-operation was, however, of brief duration. America was too remote from Europe, and adhered too closely to the Monroe doctrine, to be a safe support for Germany. The dominating influence of the Anglo-Saxon race in the United States, the bond of sympathy with the mother-country England, and, on the other hand, the remembrance that only a few years before the Emperor had delivered speeches on the necessity of

European solidarity and advocated an anti-American co-operation—these factors militated against any firm friendship being cemented between America and Germany, to counterbalance the effect of the alienation of England.

CHAPTER XI

IN the preceding chapters we have sketched the diplomatic history of the fifteen years following the death of Bismarck. We have endeavoured to show how France obtained allies, and how Europe was divided into two camps. Now, before going further, we would offer a brief résumé of the whole.

It must in the first place be remarked that the dropping of the pilot, Bismarck, was visited by Nemesis. The Duc de Broglie, the last Premier to make any serious attempt to restore the monarchy in France, a few years before the fall of the Iron Chancellor accused the Republic of having followed a foreign policy which was disastrous for the country, in isolating her and surrounding her everywhere by foes. Broglie was perfectly right. Under the leadership of the great Chancellor the alliances of Germany were constantly extended, and increased in health and vigour, while France was unable to find suitors and pouted in her undesired solitude. Even the Czar, the avowed friend of France, would undertake no obligations on her behalf, being indeed secretly in relations with Germany. Since Bismarck's time, however, these things had changed. Under the new régime the number of Germany's allies had diminished, whereas France had made new alliances. Under Bismarck the diplomatic career of Germany showed an upward tendency; it was now the turn of France. She was no longer a forlorn figure with all Europe under the leadership of Bismarck against her. But Europe was rent in twain and in 1905 the French group of allies seemed in the ascendant.

The Franco-Russian Alliance was concluded, which became eventually one of the strongest factors in Europe. The connection between St. Petersburg and Berlin existed no longer ; the bonds of the Triple Alliance became very slack, and a secret cord attached Italy to France. Spain, Serbia, and Bulgaria—in Bismarck's time friends of the Triple Alliance—now made overtures to the Gallic Republic.

Of the States outside the Triple Alliance, Rumania alone was bound to the latter by treaty, and only Turkey seemed inclined towards her. But the Sultan was a most unreliable factor and any assistance from that quarter was doubtful.

The most important event, the greatest achievement of French diplomacy, was England identifying herself with France. This was a matter of the utmost import-ance, not only because Great Britain was without controversy the mightiest Power the world had ever seen—mightier than the empires of Alexander the Great, of Julius Cæsar, of Attila, or of Genghis Khan—but also because, with her magnificent culture, her unexampled genius for governing, her immense commerce, world-wide connections, and numerous colonies and posses-sions scattered all over the globe, her universal influence had made her a cult, as it were. As the nation *par excellence* in the enjoyment of the freest constitution ever known, she was ever the ideal of all liberty-loving States. The innumerable host of vulgar pretenders everywhere felt her influence. Paris and London, united under one banner, could form, direct, and control the public opinion of the world.

Since the secession of America in the eighteenth

century, England had never lost a war; she was surrounded with a halo of invincibility. Her friendship was a thing to be highly prized; and an actual alliance with her was of the most inestimable value, for she seemed to confer victory on her partner as a wedding-gift.

The chief weakness of the new system was that the two friends of France—i.e. England and Russia—had not yet come to an agreement. There were, however, already hopeful signs of London and St. Petersburg finding the way to *rapprochement*. The will to understand each other was already apparent, and making itself felt both in the court of Nicholas II and in the camp of Edward VII; while there was a living link between the two great Powers and former adversaries constituted by the French nation with their immense suggestive force.

The deterioration of Germany's position was the more striking, the more difficult to understand, as at this time the young Empire had become internally stronger; so that her natural superiority to France was greater than ever, and, as history shows, the strong can always and easily find friends. Blunders alone could cause Germany to lose ground, while France expanded in spite of Germany's superiority over her rival increasing day by day. The population of Germany was increasing far more rapidly than that of France; the development of the commerce and industry of the Fatherland and the growth of her wealth had already roused the envy of England and America; emigration was no longer a necessity, for all Germans could find employment and opportunities of preferment at home; she had acquired colonies; her navy was progressing, and her army was still unsurpassed for *moral* and intelligence, as exemplified under Moltke on the battlefields of Austria and France ; the self-respect and patriotism of the German masses had also increased. Though Byzantinism and opportunism—those twin satellites of autocracy—were beginning to be felt, yet the enormous strength of Germany fitted her to accomplish successes in the sphere of foreign politics. Why did she fail ? Why were her efforts in this respect barren of result ? What defects of her system were there at that time ? I will not enumerate them, but confine myself to pointing out the worst error committed by Germany at that period. This consisted in her neglect to come to terms with England, when the latter offered her friendship. An alliance with England would have been of incalculable value, for it would have been unassailable. It would have united in one mighty host the biggest navy and the biggest army. This alliance would at the same time have been the most natural, since it would have been not incongruous with the past of both countries, their most stable interests, and the practical considerations of the moment which usually guided all foreign policy.

England and Germany should have been allies from the consideration that they both were likely to be menaced most imminently from the same quarters—France and Russia. England could be attacked, with the most probability of success, from the French coast, owing to its proximity. It was on that very account that England had in the past experienced many anxious days when France ruled over the western parts of the European Continent, when Paris commanded the French and Belgian seaports, as in the periods of Louis XIV and Napoleon I. The geographical situation explains the fact that—except the Crimean War against the

Russians—all the great wars of England since the seventeenth century have been fought against France. This explains the principle enunciated by the elder Pitt, the most illustrious statesman of the eighteenth century, that " England could not afford to let France have a strong navy " ; and that his gifted son and namesake (William Pitt the younger) devoted most of his official life to fighting the French ; that Canning too wrote his name so brightly on the scroll of history in the struggle against the French.

The immutable geographical situation explains likewise that, while the island of Britain can be most easily approached from the French coast, the British Empire was exposed to the most crushing blows from Russia. From the country of the Muscovite went the shortest cut to India across Asia, and thence the connections could be most easily severed. This was the bugbear of Palmerston at the time of the Crimean War. Against this double peril Beaconsfield, Salisbury, and Rosebery fought with their anti-Russian policy. This was why Gladstone, in spite of his Russophilism, found himself on the verge of war with Russia.

After what we have said, it is clear how dangerous it might have become for England if France and Russia had combined against her. Such a coalition would have simultaneously imperilled the Island Kingdom, the Indian Empire, the Mediterranean supremacy, and the connections between England and India. England's historic luck ordained that this worst experience should fall to her but once : when Napoleon Bonaparte, inspired by his unerring military genius during his mortal struggle with British power, came to an agreement with the Czar at Tilsit. Napoleon would probably have accomplished his purpose of forcing his haughty foe Albion to her knees if the sanguinary guerilla war in Spain and the Austrian campaign of 1809 had not formed insuperable obstacles to his fully exploiting the advantages of his alliance with Russia.

The Franco-Russian Alliance concluded in the nineties of last century brought this Damocles' sword once more over the head of England, and compelled her to cast about for an agreement with Germany. Later realising her failure there, she turned with more success to France and Russia.

By her policy of the Entente, England seemed to have eliminated the double danger. The appearance, however, was deceptive; for if Czarist Russia had reached her aims and together with her ally had been victorious in the World War, the peril would have become more menacing than ever in the past. Without the Central Powers to hold them in check, France and Russia, by virtue of their alliance, would have been masters of Europe, and England's victory would have been of the Pyrrhic kind, an irreparable calamity.

A German-English alliance was natural by the circumstance that Germany was exposed to danger from the very same foes that menaced England. The most crushing blow could be delivered by enemies who could fall back on Verdun and Warsaw. Prussia had already been made acquainted with danger signified by the Franco-Russian Alliance. The Tilsit Treaty, which reconciled Napoleon I and Alexander I and menaced England, became the bane of Prussia. It sapped the vitality of the achievements of the Hohenzollerns. Prussia regained her independence in the Concert of Europe only when France and Russia had fallen out with each other and Prussia could turn against Paris with the support of the Muscovites. The signal successes of Bismarck were due to his clever handling of the Polish question so as to separate Napoleon III and Nicholas I.

Until the outbreak of the World War the policies of both England and Germany were dominated by the danger emanating from the Franco-Russian combination. It menaced England in Egypt, Persia, Afghanistan, and China. The chief employment of the German General Staff in Berlin was the maintenance of the military machine in constant working order for operations on the double front of Verdun–Warsaw. The most important task of the Austro-Hungarian and Triple Alliance was to protect Germany from the double pressure of the combination which equally menaced British rule. The political and military bureaus were occupied day by day with the solution of the same problem which was destined to be inscribed on the most thrilling pages of history, and the memory of which was most vivid in the nervous system of the English and German peoples—the consequences to be expected from the Russo-French friendship. The safest protection against them for both England and Germany would have been the alliance of both those countries with each other. The safest for the former, since the Triple Alliance could best secure London against a Franco-Russian attack, as it could engage the forces of both Powers and thus prevent them from jeopardising England ; while, on the other hand, the strategic situation of Central Europe could be fortified by nothing so well as the support of England, which would completely separate the two excentric enemies and render their co-operation impossible The superior military forces of the Central Powers supported by a naval blockade could not fail to attain the desired result. At that time this alliance would have been the only means by which Germany could have secured the loyalty of Italy.

A moderate *Weltpolitik* did nothing to alter this situation. On the very contrary, it made co-operation more urgent than ever for both parties. Germany with a navy was more likely to be either a blessing or a bane for England than she would be as merely a continental Power. Moreover, Germany could get more from England, as well as have more reason to fear her, if her (Germany's) ambitions turned to maritime endeavour ; and this agreement was rendered far more urgent and important for both parties in the times of *Weltpolitik*, than when the paths of the two Powers could not run counter to each other, since the risk of conflict was then greater. Germany's aspirations having become greater, a fair agreement was the sole means to harmonious relations with England—a fair agreement alone could guarantee Germany's ability to build her navy commensurate with her needs without England feeling her safety imperilled thereby.

All these considerations were understood equally in England and Germany. Berlin's fatal mistake was not that she was unwilling to follow a common policy with England, but that she sought to do this in a wrong way, and failed to recognise the importance of seizing the psychological moment when England extended to her the hand of friendship. The authorities in Berlin thought they risked nothing by refusing to conclude the agreement offered by England. England would wait, they believed. Berlin was aware that England disliked, as a rule, Continental alliances, so they imagined she would be in no hurry to undertake obligations to another Power. Since Beaconsfield's day England had —without any treaty or alliance and in spite of many differences and errors, in spite of the aversion of her most popular statesman Gladstone—generally followed a policy identical with that of the Triple Alliance. Why should she do otherwise now, when she seemed to attach greater importance to Germany's friendship than before ?

Berlin failed to appreciate the new situation of England, and the changed state of mind it involved. The Germans could not understand how the rapid building of their navy, their *Weltpolitik*, the development of their ambitions, had tended to transform England's entire feeling towards them. They lost sight of the fact that the two nations had never been connected by any real bonds of sympathy, that the Prussian and the English political systems had always been diametrically opposed, that their Prussian militarism was hated all the world over, that the ruthlessness and bloody deeds of Frederick II and of Bismarck had left a legacy of mistrust, and that this nervous frame of mind was of necessity aggravated by the danger that henceforth the inexorable Prussian would claim his part in all overseas questions too ; and that the imponderable, capricious Emperor would command not only the most powerful army but also a great navy, built with characteristic German thoroughness, expert knowledge, and care generally. The Germans could not understand that the blatant English attitude, which the former sought to make an excuse for a raid on the purse of the taxpayer, was as harmful as it was alarming. They were blind to the fact that, for the reasons set forth, England could no longer remain isolated ; she could not continue to suffer the old dangers, menaced by France and Russia, while Germany was daily becoming an object of dread ; but to escape the risk of getting between two fires, she would have to come to terms with both the French and the Russians, however enormous the cost.

And when at length Germany woke up to her mistake, and saw that London could come to an agreement with Paris, Germany still refused to believe that the cause of the step was fear and hatred towards herself. The Germans, conscious that they had no hostile intentions towards England, could not understand why the English could not see this also, or why they should fear and suspect them. They regarded this alleged mistrust and anxiety as a mere pretext to cloak the nefarious design of attacking Germany—a screen behind which to hide a real enmity.

It is difficult to judge as to which of the German leaders was most responsible for the blunders committed—not formally and legally, but morally responsible. The vivacious Emperor, with his frequent and unexpected and quite personal interference, with his antipathy for everybody he suspected of anti-German ideas, with his sometimes quick changes of mind, certainly on more than one occasion seriously embarrassed his Foreign Office and committed many glaring errors. Nevertheless, in his chief political aims, great decisions and general orientation, his instinct was often more correct than that of his advisers. He felt strongly that the " free hand " policy was dangerous and might lead to his downfall. He saw perhaps most clearly of all that they ought to agree with England, and when this had become no longer possible, when even he had turned against England, he wanted at least to secure good relations with Russia. It would seem that Holstein was in an especial degree to be blamed for the blunders perpetrated. Right up to the time of the Algeciras Conference he exercised a decisive influence over foreign

29

affairs ; and his suspicious, petty, narrow-minded—if in details clear—vision wrought great mischief and misled German policy.

The policy of Austria-Hungary was at this time more correct than that of Germany. Its aims were in a juster proportion to its powers, and more conformable with the interests of the Dual Monarchy. Her policy was perfectly defensive. She might be said to be the most pacific and conservative of all the European States, the only State without ambitions for expansion. Apart from the maintenance of peace, her sole aim was self-defence—defence against Pan-Slavism, the triumph of which in the Balkans would shake the foundations of Austria-Hungary and jeopardise her very existence. To this end she defended the integrity of the Ottoman Empire and the independence of the Christian States then newly founded in the Balkans.

Both Kálnoky and Goluchowsky felt that the friendship of England would be the most valuable complement of the Triple Alliance. As staunch friends of Germany and partners in British interests, they desired to act as a living link between those two Germanic Powers and at the same time to smooth the path of reconciliation between France and Germany.

Therefore the idea of Vienna was at bottom perfectly right. Unfortunately she had not sufficient weight, she was not listened to, had no influence over the counsels of Berlin, and consequently no satisfactory result could be achieved.

Goluchowsky could boast of greater success with regard to Russia than with regard to Germany. Whenever the Czar had displayed an aggressive attitude in the Balkans, the Dual Monarchy had always done its best to defend the independence of those States against the forces of Czarism. Now, however, that Russia had ceased to terrorise the Balkans and for the time being was employing her eternal proclivity for expansion towards the Far East, Austria-Hungary made overtures to her—a step which had a good effect in allaying the antagonism.

The affairs of Macedonia were directed by Vienna and St. Petersburg in common, and Balkan antagonisms were so far allayed that when King Alexander of Serbia was assassinated (June 1903), St. Petersburg (according to private information) would willingly have consented to our intervention. Also when, at the time of the Macedonian riots, a rumour was spread that we intended to send troops to the Sandjak to restore order, Kapnist, the Russian Ambassador, observed (November 1904) to his German colleague that " it would be wiser to occupy Serbia, as the occupation of the Sandjak might lead to dangerous complications in Albania."

That was an interesting and highly important statement. It not only signified the success of the Dual Monarchy at St. Petersburg at that time, but also proved how little ground there was for the accusation of tyranny on our part—which was used as a justification of the World War. The weakness of the Austro-Hungarian policy was in its treatment of Italy and the Balkan States.

On the Italians especially a bad impression was produced by the Slavophil domestic policy of Austria. To this must be added the anti-Italian spirit of the Austrians, their contempt for the Italians, for which, after Andrássy's time, the sympathy of the Hungarians could no longer compensate ; the fortifying of our Italian frontier, which, without increasing our strength, provoked the animosity of the Italians and presented the unedifying spectacle of allies arming against each other. It is true that the fault was not on one side only. The vulgar clamour of the irredentists, the implacable hate of the Italians towards the Austrians, the aspirations of Italy in Albania, all tended to render Austria's confidence in her ally a difficult matter ; while it must be noted that the aim of the Austro-Italian Alliance was to avoid war against each other rather than to make war on a third Power. It is to be regretted that we failed to use sufficient energy in the Balkans to protect the Christians there, partly, it must be admitted, on account of the German policy not adequately supporting our own in that region, out of regard for Russian friendship ; and when we might have won the Balkan States, the Vienna Government short-sightedly sought to enhance its prestige by inaugurating a system of schooling and pedantry which, instead of making friends, created nothing but enemies.

Wedel, the German Ambassador to Vienna, benevolently disposed to the Dual Monarchy, a man of common sense and an impartial observer, reported (August 1904) that " it was the custom of the Ballplatz to speak with everyone as from the heights of Olympus." He pointed out that King Peter of Serbia, who, shortly after his ascent of the throne, was specially anxious to obtain the good-will of Austria-Hungary, met with a frigid reception from Goluchowsky, who treated him most censoriously ; also that King Ferdinand of Bulgaria met with a similar reception. Goluchowsky's superciliousness offended the Sultan too. It cannot be denied that our Foreign Minister put on airs not warranted by our position in the political hierarchy.

If only Vienna had known how to use its inherently good policy more skilfully, if only Bülow had devoted his superior diplomacy and personal ability, coupled with the loftier prestige of Germany, to the cause of a better basal idea, the position of the Central Powers might have been far more favourable.

Unfortunately, we can only conclude that the successors of Bismarck and Andrássy, notwithstanding the increasing inner strength of their States, came into a less favourable situation as the result of the error they committed. But in admitting and emphasising this, I must strenuously deny the charge that the policy of the Central Powers was immoral and aggressive, and that the World War was precipitated because the other States, peaceful and law-abiding, could no longer tolerate those arch-conspirators against world-peace.

Germany was at that time quite as much in need of peace as any other of the Powers. Had she desired by force of arms to secure political superiority, to break her foes, she would have attacked England during the Boer War, and Russia after the disastrous Japanese campaign ; or she might have availed herself of the Russo-Japanese War to settle accounts with her hereditary enemy France. Schlieffen, Chief-of-Staff, demonstrated that the situation was eminently favourable for the defeat of France, as the Russian forces had been completely demoralised by the Japanese. During the course of the World War a High Court dignitary of Germany asserted that Bülow's most egregious error was his neglect to exploit the auspicious moment for putting France out of action, thereby securing the unchallengeable predominance of Germany on the Continent. Assuming that Germany really had an aim which she was convinced could not be attained without war, it certainly was a stupid oversight not to seize the opportunity when the strength of Russia was at its lowest ebb.

It was precisely the peaceful intentions of Germany and her fear of new *casus belli* which formed the chief guiding motives of her policy in declining new alliances which would have raised up new enemies—such as, e.g., the proposed alliance with England. In the twenty-five volumes of the Transactions of the German Foreign Office that I have so far been able to examine, there is not a single expression to lend colour to the allegation of belligerent aims on the part of any German statesman—not a single remark which even an unfriendly reader could interpret as bellicose.

But did not the *Weltpolitik* itself signify the will to war ? Was there not concealed in it, as one may sometimes hear it said, an ambition contrary to the political morals of the twentieth century ? Did it not mean retrogression to the mentality of the Middle Ages ? Did it not contain the idea of retaliation, as coveting the property of others ?—or of seriously endangering the position of others ? No ; that cannot justly be asserted. In that respect Germany can at the utmost be reproached with having adopted similar ambitions to those of the other Powers, to a lesser degree but with greater ostentation—that she went the same way as the others, but with drums beating and trumpets blaring. England, France, and Italy at this period made far more important conquests than Germany ; and even America was not behind in the race for annexations ; but they all sang to a pianissimo accompaniment, not unsoothing to the ears of their audience.

Regarded from the standpoint of high morality, Germany's policy cannot be awarded unqualified approval. She too had had a hand in the breaking up of China. She practised the doctrine that it was lawful to barter, buy, sell, and annex extra-European peoples like chattels or dumb driven cattle without rights of any kind. But she cannot justly be reproached for these things by the very Powers who set the bad example and took more by violence than she did, and more than German policy ever contemplated taking. What if Germany were willing to draw her sword for Morocco and the prestige involved in the question, ought she to be blamed for it by the other Powers who at that time actually waged sanguinary wars for similar colonial aims, and who were equally willing among other things to risk a war for Morocco ?

England fought the Boers for political and economic objects which from her egoistic standpoint were right, but which from the moral standpoint were highly reprehensible and justly condemned by the greater part of the public opinion of Europe. For many decades England and France contended for the hegemony over Egypt, to the immense detriment of their relations to each other, though neither of them had a right to a square inch of territory there ; unless we accept the plea put forward by the British that Egypt has profited by their occupation —an assertion which it is difficult to credit, since it is the custom of all conquerors to pretend that they confer a blessing on others by subjecting them to their rule, though it is seldom that the conquered are of that opinion. Rosebery was resolved to risk war with France over the Siam Question ; Salisbury despatched an ultimatum to Delcassé over Fashoda. The Spanish-American and Russo-Japanese Wars, the Italian campaign in Abyssinia, the French in Tunis, the coveting by France of Morocco, the colonial adventures of Jules Ferry, all overshadowed the taking of Kiao-Chau, the Samoan Islands, and the Carolines, and the deal in connection with the Portuguese colonies. Germany's colonial aspirations aroused more universal distrust and alarm than the similar efforts of

other States because they were more open and undis-
guised, giving the appearance that Germany was a new
and formidable rival. While each of the other States
declared itself content and ascribed all its further expansion to compelling local circumstances, to exceptional
interests, Germany frankly confessed, without subterfuge, that she wanted her " place in the sun "—that she
intended to found a colonial empire, to expand overseas ;
and all this at the very time when she loudly announced
the building of a powerful navy. This naturally created
nervousness and unrest everywhere. Everyone feared
this ostentatious rival newly appeared upon the scene ;
everyone regarded her as an interloper, and her successes
as new departures. These ugly features, however, make
no difference to the moral aspect of the case. What is
permissible for one is also permissible for another. If
it is right to develop, enlarge, and improve existing
overseas possessions, it cannot be wrong to found new
ones.

The German policy was no more and no less immoral
or egoistic than that of the other Powers. The German
people were no more bellicose than the other peoples.
In this respect it might be said that the policy of all the
nations at the head of European culture was on the same
level. In the traditional and historical individualities
of nations there are always certain propensities, susceptibilities, and traits observable. Thus, for instance,
to the Gaul the most successful appeal is always to *gloire*.
He is fired to enthusiasm by lofty ideals, to serve noble
causes, to discover or vindicate truth, to liberate enslaved
nations, to relieve the oppressed and downtrodden—
provided always that these lofty aims serve at the same
time some practical purpose. Thus Louis XVI drew
the sword in the cause of American freedom. Thus the

first French Revolution waged the struggle for democracy. Thus Napoleon III made war upon Austria for the cause of Italian liberty. Yet never once did France lose sight of her own interests or allow them to be obscured by the loftiest altruistic motives. Whenever her own interests were at stake, France could strike ruthlessly and crush other nations with that pitiless cruelty and barbarity exemplified so often in the campaigns of Louis XIV and Napoleon I.

The English are, above all things, a practical people, and never follow a policy that is not considered profitable in some way or other. Yet, secure in the protection afforded by their insular position, they are only too prone to meddle in the affairs of other nations. They raise their voices in all humanitarian causes, identify themselves with the sufferings and injustices of others ; and no tale of misfortune with them ever falls upon deaf or unsympathetic ears. Thus in 1848 the English gave valuable support to the cause of constitutional liberty in various lands. Thus English public opinion was solid for the oppressed Bulgarians, Greeks, and Armenians. The English name is said to stand for " fair play " all the world over—as that of the American for the " square deal "—yet their altruistic conception is ofttimes not unmixed with a generous dose of self. For example, Palmerston, who in 1848 championed the cause of popular freedom against Metternich's *ancien régime*, was the same man who forced the abominable opium upon China. At a time of profound peace between the two countries a British fleet under Nelson and Parker was sent to bombard Copenhagen and sink or take the entire Danish navy—in order to prevent Napoleon capturing the vessels !

The Prussians regard their rough honesty as a precious attribute of their character, a thing to be proud of ; yet it frequently leads them to cynicism. The Italians prefer skill and guile to violence. Cavour avowed that " he had done many things in the interests of his country that he would have shrunk in shame from doing for himself." During the Great War it was an Italian statesman who popularised the expression " *sacro egoismo.*" When all is said and done, however, not only the Italians but all other peoples follow a policy of national egoism. At all times and in all places the aim and object of the policy is or should be to promote the national welfare. It cannot very well be otherwise. If to-day, when there is no impartial supra-national court of justice, the Governments should act otherwise, they would betray the interests of the millions who have confided their destinies to their hands, to serve whom is their first and sworn duty. Unstinted praise and admiration be to the man who defies the flames or the billows to save the life of a fellow-creature. But that statesman would be a criminal indeed who, for alien interests and rights, should jeopardise the existence of his State, that marvellous living entity which has wrought, struggled, and suffered for generations or centuries to become stronger and nobler and more perfect, and which is to-day, for his people, the chief worker in the cause of human progress. No statesman is free to gamble with the future opportunities and vital interests of his nation. And I cannot recall a single instance in history of a Government willingly and wittingly sacrificing their own country for the sake of justice or to the rights of another country. Should there be a certain difference between the moral character of the actions of the most highly civilised States, this is due rather to the characters and conceptions of their leaders, the situation and the compelling circumstances, than to the difference in the permanent moral value of the nations in question. In this twentieth century war is feared far more than it was in the past because it involves far greater loss. Far more pacifist activity is manifested nowadays, far more energy has been put forth of late years to ensure the settlement of international quarrels, disputes, and differences by means of suitable institutions. So far, however, this change, this progress, has had no particularly decisive results. All the States are agreed that war becomes a greater misfortune every day—but not the greatest! Each of them, while willing to arbitrate on secondary matters, is inflexibly determined to draw the sword for its own *honour* and *vital interests*!

It is regrettable that the German Government, with its rude and cynical demeanour, was always more averse than that of any other nation to all movements for the preservation of peace. Following in the footsteps of Bismarck, they declared with brutal frankness that " the interests of the Fatherland were their sole concern." To the Germans it was a point of honour to emphasise the egoism which every other State also practised. But in this they gravely miscalculated. For they came into conflict with those lofty sentiments and ideals which should animate every human breast and lead us all to do our parts in the steadily growing movement towards the preparation of a better future for mankind. The Germans incurred intense odium, which engendered a bitter anti-German public opinion, without their sincerity profiting them in the least. The impression was produced that German power made improvement impossible and only prolonged the reign of brute force.

It was—perhaps is also to-day—the fashion to charge Austria-Hungary with following an aggressive policy, by aiming at expansion towards Salonica ; and it was said

that the Dual Monarchy ought to be dismembered in the
cause of peace. Such a statement was not only untrue,
it was ridiculous. Any expansion on our part was so
entirely out of the question that when at one time Germany wanted us to get some advantage, and invited us
to suggest something, we could suggest nothing except
the maintenance of the *status quo* in the Balkans and the
prevention of the Dardanelles getting into the hands of
Russia. It is a queer sort of *aggressive* State that can be
satisfied with the maintenance of the *status quo* in the
very region where it is alleged to have designs. None of
our Foreign Ministers ever thought of occupying Salonica.
The Dual Monarchy, however, never made pretensions to
being actuated by any purer or nobler ideals than the
others. The secret of her absolutely pacific and conservative policy was that all her leading elements were pacific
and conservative. Our revered sovereign, from sheer
weariness and caution, after several disastrous campaigns,
desired nothing more than to keep what he had, and he
abhorred war with his whole heart. The Austro-Germans had long before lost the precedence they had once
enjoyed in the time of Joseph II and Schwartzenberg.
They had such a bitter struggle with their Slavs at home
in Austria, they would have been risking their future
by adding to the number of their foreign nationalities.
The other half of the Dual Monarchy, Hungary, also was
absolutely conservative and afraid of expansion in any
direction. She had no extraneous chauvinism. As
there was no Hungarian foreign policy or diplomacy, and
as externally the Monarchy retained its Austrian character, Hungarian public opinion was quite indifferent to
most important questions of prestige. She craved no
political victories. The national self-consciousness and
ambition were directed towards questions of common

law and the nationality problems instead of towards foreign politics, the Hungarian interest in which was small to a fault. Foreign politics was excluded from the parliamentary life, and consequently did nothing to stir public opinion. The Hungarian soul was not alive to remembrance of any popular national war. The wars of the Dynasty, whether on the Rhine or the Po, in which the Hungarians acquitted themselves with honour and displayed their wonted valour, had no power to fire the imagination of the Magyars. Even the Turkish wars, by which the integrity of Hungary was restored, were unpopular, owing to the generally German character of the leaders; and their victories made but an indifferent impression on the minds of the masses, as the same troops which had won back our territorial integrity afterwards menaced our national liberties! When in the eighties of last century Bismarck accused Hungary of plotting a war against Russia, that was simply because the Man of Iron suspected everyone whose ways ran counter to his own. It was not because the Hungarians wanted war that they defended the independence of the Balkan States, but because they were convinced a war must break out the sooner if, by their supineness, they encouraged the Russians to make claims that they (the Hungarians) could not endorse, than if the Czar knew beforehand that insistence on his demands would lead to a struggle which he too would prefer to avoid. The Magyars were ill-disposed towards all conquests, as the burden imposed by the acquisition of alien subject-races would constitute a serious menace to their position in the Dual Monarchy as well as in their own land.

The sole ambition which had arisen in Vienna since the Berlin Congress was to transform the occupation and administration of Bosnia-Herzegovina into an annexation;

though this idea was neither general nor popular. It left the public in both Austria and Hungary perfectly cold, and at the time the wisdom of the step was questioned by responsible ministers. Goluchowsky, for one, was against it. The Hungarian Government looked askance at it. Very few cared about touching or altering the mandate given with the universal consent of Europe and accepted by the Turks. And even the exponents of this idea were guided by their conservative sentiment alone, and not by any desire for conquest. For the annexation did not give the Dual Monarchy a single village, a single soldier, or a single penny.

Italy, the most ambitious member of the Triple Alliance, was compelled, by her enormous growth of population, to attempt expansion in Northern Africa. The Italian ambitions, however, were not translated into acts, and the Entente could the less refer to them when attributing the World War to the aggressive spirit of the Central Powers, since Italy did not take our side, but theirs against us, in the stupendous struggle. The very fact that Italy, the member of the Triple Alliance whose land-hunger was the most insatiable of the three, was considered by the Entente as good enough to be their ally, should be sufficient to prove that they had not to defend themselves against our offensive spirit.

It is comprehensible that amidst the perils and suffering occasioned by the World War, enthusiastic patriots on either side should condemn in the most extravagant terms the actions of the " enemy," exaggerating his faults and painting him in the most lurid colours, in order to incite hatred and thus provoke and maintain the fighting spirit of their own side against the other. In their jaundiced state of mind it was futile to expect an unbiassed judgment.

To-day, however, the case is otherwise, and we may now appeal from Philip drunk to Philip sober. The time has arrived for calm sifting of the available evidence and the delivery of the verdict. If we would banish the spirit of hate engendered by the old war-time quarrel, if we would have lasting harmony and neighbourly relations, let us cease from the mutual dissemination of slanders, abuse, recrimination, let us investigate the past with an objective mind, with a sincere desire to arrive at the truth. In that spirit alone can self-respecting nations co-operate with each other. By constantly impugning each other's veracity and good faith, all co-operation is impossible.

A correct understanding of and attitude towards the past is the *sine qua non* of any attempt to remedy the present and re-establish the future on the firm foundation of justice and peace.

www.ingramcontent.com/pod-product-compliance
Lightning Source LLC
Chambersburg PA
CBHW032138050726
47591CB00001B/18